Central Banking, Monetary Policies, and the Implications for Transition Economies

Central Banking, Monetary Policies, and the Implications for Transition Economies

Mario I. Blejer
Marko Škreb

Kluwer Academic Publishers
Boston/Dordrecht/London

Distributors for North, Central and South America:
Kluwer Academic Publishers
101 Philip Drive
Assinippi Park
Norwell, Massachusetts 02061 USA
Telephone (781) 871-6600
Fax (781) 871-6528
E-Mail <kluwer@wkap.com>

Distributors for all other countries:
Kluwer Academic Publishers Group
Distribution Centre
Post Office Box 322
3300 AH Dordrecht, THE NETHERLANDS
Telephone 31 78 6392 392
Fax 31 78 6546 474
E-Mail <services@wkap.nl>

 Electronic Services <http://www.wkap.nl>

Library of Congress Cataloging-in-Publication Data

Blejer, Mario I.
Central banking, monetary policies, and the implications for
transition economies / by Mario I. Blejer and Marko Škreb.
     p. c.m.
  Includes bibliographical references and index.
  ISBN 0-7923-8441-5
  1. Banks and banking, Central. 2. Monetary policy. 3. Banks
and banking, Central - - Europe, Eastern. I. Škreb, Marko, 1957
II. Title
HG1811.B54 1999
332.1'1 - - dc21   99 – 11865
                                                               CIP

Printed on acid-free paper.

Printed in the United States of America

Contents

About the Editors

Mario I. Blejer is senior advisor at the Monetary and Exchange Affairs Department of the International Monetary Fund and currently holds the Walter Rathenau Chair in Economics at the Hebrew University of Jerusalem. He began his career at the IMF in 1980, and during his tenure he has been involved in a wide range of issues, including work on the assessment of the effectiveness of Fund stabilization programs, financial policies, and economic reforms. He was chief of the Fund's Fiscal Studies Division and also worked as head of the Macroeconomic Division of the World Bank in the early 1990s. He was in charge of the preparation of the monetary and financial section of the Joint Study of the Soviet Economy, produced by the IMF together with the World Bank, the OECD, and the EBRD in 1990.

Mario I. Blejer took a B.A. and a M.A. from the Hebrew University of Jerusalem and received a Ph.D. in economics from the University of Chicago. He worked at the Center for Monetary Studies in Latin America (Mexico) and has taught at Boston University, New York University, and the Graduate Institute for International Studies in Geneva. He has Served as a consultant with the Inter-American Development Bank and currently maintains recurrent visiting professorial appointments at the Central European University in Budapest and at the Universidad de San Andres in Buenos Aires. He is currently a member of board of editors of the *European Journal of Political Economy*.

His numerous articles have appeared in international journals including the *American Economic Review*, the *Journal of Political Economy*, the *Review of Economics and Statistics*, and others and have dealt with fiscal issues, trade and balance-of-payment problems, monetary economics, and economic stabilization and liberalization in Latin America and in economies in transition. He is the author of several books and has also coedited a large number books on fiscal policies, international macroeconomic issues, and economic and financial reforms. His most recent publications include The Making of Economic Reforms in Eastern Europe: Conversations with Leading Reformers in Poland, Hungary, and the Czech Republic (with F. Coricelli); Financial Factors in Economic Stabilization and Growth (with L. Leiderman et al.); The Macroeconomic Dimensions of Public Finance (with T. Ter-Minassian); Macroeconomic Stabilization in Transition Economies (with M. Skreb); and Financial Sector Transformation: Lessons from Transition Economies (with M. Skreb).

Marko Škreb received a B.A. (1980), an M.A. (1984), and a Ph.D. (1990) in economics from the Faculty of Economics at the University of Zagreb (Croatia).

He received a certificate from the Salzburg Seminar in American Studies (Austria) in August 1984 and a certificate from the Economics Institute (Boulder, Colonado) in August 1987 as a Fulbright fellow. Also as a Fulbright fellow, he spent academic year 1987 to 1988 at the Department of Economics at the University of Pittsburgh.

He started his professional work as planner at the Bureau of Planning of Croatia and continued it as assistant and then senior assistant at the Faculty of Economics, the Department of National Economy. From September 1991 to November 1992, he was assistant professor at the Department for Macroeconomics and Economic Policy.

He became director of the Croatian National Bank Research and Analysis Department in 1992, which has since expanded into the Research and Statistics Area.

He was appointed economic adviser to the President of the Republic of Croatia in 1995 and was appointed for a six-year term as governor of the Croatian National Bank in 1996, the youngest governor of the central monetary authority ever to be appointed in the new Croatian state. Since 1997, he also has been associate professor at the University of Zagreb.

In 1997, he was awarded Central European Annual Award for Excellence—Best Central Bank Governor and was proclaimed the Best Eastern European Banker by Euromoney Publications. He received the Order of Prince Branimir with Collar for his outstanding contributions to promoting the international position and reputation of the Republic of Croatia and the Order of the Croatian Morning Star with the Figure of Blaz Lorkovic for exceptional achievements in economy.

He is also the author of innumerable articles, books, and other publications and has been an active participant in a number of conferences, seminars, and workshops. His publications include "Croatia: An Insider's View of Transition," *Sais Review* 18(2) (Summer) (Summer-Fall, 1988); *Macroeconomic Stabilization in Transition Economies* (coedited with Mario I. Blejer, 1997); "A Paradox of Transition to a Market Economy: How Will the Role of the State Change?" (with Ivo Bicanic), in F. Targetti (ed.), *Privatization in Europe: West and East European Experiences* (1992); "Service Policy and Development," in S. Sharma (ed.), *Development Policy* (1992); "The Service Sector in East European Economies: What Role Can It Play in Future Development?" (with Ivo Bicanic), *Communist Economies and Economic Transformation* 3(2) (1991).

I INTRODUCTION

1 CENTRAL BANKING AND MONETARY POLICY
Major Issues and Implications for Transition Economies

Mario I. Blejer

International Monetary Fund and Hebrew University of Jerusalem

Marko Škreb

Croatian National Bank and University of Zagreb

The polemic about the proper role of monetary policies and the appropriate functions of central banks, which is not a new debate by any means, has received renewed and vigorous stimulus from a number of current events. In Europe, the once utopian project of creating a supranational central bank has become a reality: the European Central Bank was launched in mid-1998, and the introduction of the European single currency, the euro, is on schedule. In the United States and in other industrial as well as emerging markets, the debate continues about the location and the attributes of the supervisory authority, and its relations with the monetary authorities. Professional interest has also been centered again on the issue of the proper targeting for monetary policy and the matter of central-bank independence.

The significant and very rapid changes in the nature of and operations in the financial markets have altered in more than one way the transmission mechanism of monetary policies and have imposed on all economic agents, and particularly central banks, the need for adapt. Such need to adapt has been more acute in the former socialist states. In these countries, the adaptation of the institutional settings of monetary policy to deal with an emerging market economy had to be carried out in the midst of an unprecedented stabilization effort and, therefore, was particularly urgent and complicated. In many of the transition countries, the transformation effort implied not just changes in procedures but the establishment of a central bank from scratch, a process that involved an important effort, precisely at a time when the whole system was in serious turmoil. While the process of reforms is not yet completed in all the transition countries, an immense amount of progress has been achieved, and many of the transition countries face today monetary and central banking conditions that are close to those of Western economies.

In this volume, we collect a number of important contributions that discuss the most burning aspects of the current debates on central banking and monetary policy and draw implications for the postsocialist transition economies. The various papers included in the volume deal with a broad set of related issues, which are highly relevant not just for transition economies but for other emerging markets and for advanced economies as well. The subjects covered in the book are divided into seven major categories (Sections II to VIII), some of which overlap.

Section II includes four chapters that concentrate on the definition, meaning, and consequences of central-bank independence. Chapter 1, by Jacob A. Frenkel, sets up the framework for analyzing the concept of central-bank independence and its connections to monetary policy. While recognizing that the concept of central-bank independence needs some refining and, particularly, should be used in the context of very specific issues, Frenkel discusses the practical matters related to the policy implications of independence and concludes that probably the best guide to analyzing the degree of independence of a central bank is to gauge whether, after tasks are assigned to it, it is free to pursue these tasks without interference.

However, while it is generally recognized that granting independence and minimizing interferences tend to improve overall economic performance, it is also evident that it cannot operate unconstrained and that limitations to the roles and to the standing of the monetary authorities should be in place (and, in practice, limitations materialize through the political process). The main sources of limitations to central-bank powers emerge from various sources and are discussed in Chapters 3, 4, and 5: Frederick S. Mishkin considers in detail the issue raised by accountability requirements, Allan Drazen discusses the high likelihood that central banks would voluntarily tend (for opportunistic reasons or to defend the overall independence of the institution) to accommodate political demands, particularly before elections, and Arye L. Hillman concentrates on the fact that, in most cases, politicians in power would tend to find ways to coerce central banks, even if constrained legally, to perform (or not perform) certain actions if they are deemed to be an essential imperative of political reality. In addition, there are economic constrains to central-bank policies imposed by the presence of announced commitments. For example, adopting a fixed exchange-rate regime would limit the ability of the central bank to implement monetary policies. Therefore, a central bank may be independent but could have little power to fine-tune the economy. The stricter the policy rules adopted or the nominal commitments to be upheld, the lower the ability of the central bank to affect the system. The degree of independence of a currency board—the degree to which the monetary authority is in fact put on automatic pilot—may simply be nonconsequential. These latter issues are discussed in detail in Section VII in the chapters by Stephen H. Hanke and Warren Coats.

Section III discusses the issue of defining the functions of central banks. In Chapter 6, Maxwell T. Fry poses a fundamental question that arises if, regardless of the magnitude of the interferences of the government in the decisions of the central bank, monetary policy is not the most relevant determinant of economic outcomes, particularly in the context of transition and emerging economies. There is some support for the view that, in fact, it is fiscal performance that determines the outcomes (and even conditions the quality of monetary policies). In this context, it is important for central banks to concentrate on some of the function in which it has a technical advantage, such as strengthening the payment system.

While the achievement and maintenance of price stability have been accepted as the central and sometimes unique role that is played by central banks today, it is also widely accepted that price stability cannot be reached or sustained without monetary stability, which, in turn, depends largely on the health of the financial sector. Central banks have, therefore, assumed— implicitly or explicitly—the role of ensuring the proper functioning and the soundness of the financial and, particularly, of the banking sector. Most central banks, including even formal currency boards as in Estonia, do fulfill a function as lenders of last resort and provide some type of guarantee to depositors in the domestic banking sector. These functions could create moral-hazard and other systemic problems, and it is crucial to be able to design the most appropriate mechanisms within the specific conditions of each country.

Problems in the financial sector have continuously affected the perfor- mance of mature as well as developing economies and play a determining role in the attainment of stability and growth in transition economies. But it is important to realize that only part of the banking problems can be directly addressed by the central bank. Many of the banking difficulties may have clear roots in the real side of the economy and may be caused by lack of proper governance in the financial institutions. Pouring central bank resources into unrestructured or bankrupted banks is not likely to ease the problems and, in fact, is bound to worsen the macroeconomic situation. These problems are the subject discussed in detail in Section IV by George G. Kaufman (Chapter 7) and in the context of Slovenia by Velimir Bole (Chapter 8).

The question of the role and mandate of central banks has been closely tied to the discussions regarding its independence. As mentioned above, the usual or conventional wisdom that has emerged from most modern elucidation of the subject is that the main—if not the sole—goal of the central bank is to maintain price stability and to avoid trying to affect directly the performance of the real sector (through employment, growth, or distributional objectives). But viewed in a more realistic fashion, it is becoming evident that this well-defined, clear-cut, and single-minded objective cannot be pursued in isolation and that other roles, because of emergencies, specific needs, or just by default, would fall well within the responsibility of the central bank.

Among such contingencies, it is possible that central banks must pursue the objective of restoring external competitiveness when a country is facing serious balance-of-payments difficulties. In these cases, it is likely that the objective of absolute price stability could be replaced by the maintenance of a relative (traded or nontraded goods) price objective. This could be sought through the setting of an exchange-rate target. At times, however, the addition of targets and objectives could simply result in conflicts that are difficult to solve with a limited number of instruments. If, in addition to exchange-rate targets, the central bank should also attempt to reach an inflationary target, the monetary authorities are faced with policy dilemmas that may affect its credibility and long-run ability to attain its goals. Gil Bufman and Leonardo Leiderman (Chapter 9) analyze these issues in Section V, looking at the recent experience of Israel as an example of these type of quandaries.

Many analysts following closely the monetary of developments in emerging and transition countries are faced with a simple dilemma: while capital flows are indeed an important source of foreign savings, and they tend to play a constructive and effective role in promoting growth and integration within the world markets, they also seem to magnify the risks of financial crises. This is so because capital flows tend to be volatile and therefore cause exchange-rate variability and increase overall uncertainty. The question is, then, how to solve this dilemma. Clearly, the adoption of very strict exchange-rate rules—such as the setting of a currency board—may prevent exchange-rate volatilities and reduce the perception of risks. However, the fact that currency crises have coincided with periods of increased capital flows—and particularly short-term capital flows—has led to the view that it is both imperative and effective to impose some type of controls over the free movement of capital and, in particular, over short-term, speculative flows. These questions and the overall implication of capital flows are discussed in Section VI by Charles Wyplosz (Chapter 10) and, based on the Croatian experience, by Velimir Šonje (Chapter 12). The issue, however, remains controversial. It is not only difficult to differentiate between short-term and longer-term flows and to enforce restrictions, with evasion mechanisms and derivative markets developing all the time to offset the regulations, but it is also possible to question the desirability of curtailing short-term capital movements. In Chapter 11, Marcelo Selowski and Ricardo Martin claim that if short- and long-term capital flows are correlated (since, for example, short-term flows perform a learning function for international investors), the imposition of restrictions not only would be inefficient but also could negatively affect long-term direct investment.

Finally Part VIII is devoted to a discussion of the implications of European Monetary Unification for transition economies and contains essays by Robert A. Mundell (Chapter 15) and Paul A. Masson (Chapter 16). The introduction of the euro can be seen as one of the most important developments in monetary history, and it possesses challenges and opportunities for the transition economies. The most important decision for these countries concerns their exchange rate, and consequently, their monetary policies. There is a complete spectrum of possible arrangements, but, whatever is the decision made, it should be kept in mind that there will be in Europe a major international currency that would be a suitable anchor for neighboring countries.

II CENTRAL-BANK INDEPENDENCE

2 CENTRAL-BANK INDEPENDENCE AND MONETARY POLICY

Jacob A. Frenkel

Bank of Israel

Introduction

This chapter addresses the issue of central-bank independence and its implication for monetary policy. If this chapter had been written twenty years ago, the presentation would have been very different. But the world of today is very different from that of the past. There is a new understanding about the role that governments should play in the economic system, about the role that central banks should play in the economic policy-making process, about the importance of price stability, about the limitations of exploiting the alleged tradeoff between inflation and unemployment for the generation of sustainable growth, and about the domestic and international transmission mechanisms of economic policies. In the new world there is a growing recognition that central-bank independence is a key ingredient in the design of the institutional structure necessary for the successful attainment of the goals of economic policy in general and price stability in particular.

We live in a changing world that is becoming a global marketplace. Today, because of the globalization of markets, because of the universality of economic laws, because of the globalization of ideas, because of the professional consensus that has emerged about what it means to pursue good economic policies, each country can benefit from the lessons and experience gained by others. I believe that the economic principles I discuss here are universal and therefore are applicable to a large variety of countries that may be very different in their economic structures and history.

In this chapter I argue that in order to achieve and maintain price stability it is very important to have an independent central bank. In what follows, I examine the reasons for the growing interest in the subject of central-bank independence and address the notion of the inflation bias that needs to be corrected. Alternative forms of independence are defined, and special attention is given to the role that credibility, accountability, and transparency play in promoting the independence. The question of whether the function of bank supervision should be part of the responsibilities of the independent central bank is also explored. The useful role that inflation targets can play in facilitating the disinflation efforts of the central bank and in achieving and maintaining price stability is highlighted. I conclude the discussion with an examination of the ways that policy coordination and cooperation can be incorporated into the activities of the independent central bank. It is useful to begin by discussing some recent world developments that provide the background for recent thinking about, and practices of, central-bank independence.

Recent Economic Developments

The world today is very different from what it used to be even a decade ago. Growth in the major industrial countries (except for Japan) is expected to be very similar. A decade ago the average growth rate was very similar, but the diversity among the different countries was much larger. In terms of growth rates, there is much greater convergence today than was seen a decade ago.

Inflation in the industrial world in 1998 was expected to be less than 2 percent. A decade ago, in the same countries, average inflation was three to four times higher—about 7.5 percent. A decade ago there were debates about the Uruguay Round that aimed at reducing barriers to international trade and about the completion of the (GATT) negotiations. By now this process has been completed, the World Trade Organization (WTO) is in place, and the world trading system is much more open.

These developments mean that the industrial world today is much more harmonious than it was in the past. There is no more sharp division between fast-growing and slow-growing countries; the fast-growing countries aren't telling the other countries, "Expand your budget in order to get our country out of recession and to improve the current account of our balance of payments." We don't have the controversies that marred relations among the G-7 countries in the late 1980s.

The world today is a much more harmonious than it used to be, it is more open to trade, and it is characterized by much lower inflation. The reduction in inflation was achieved as a result of an explicit decision by policy makers who recognized that to create conditions for sustainable economic growth one needs to create an environment of price stability and that to create such an environment one needs to have an independent central bank.

Growing Interest in the Topic of Central-Bank Independence

What institutions and legislations need to be designed and put in place to bring about this objective of lower inflation? There is a growing consensus that the systematic reduction in inflation depends on monetary policy that is conducted by an independent central bank. Analyses of the key issues relating to central-bank independence are ample (see, for example, Cukierman, 1992, 1996; Fischer, 1995a, 1995b; Goodhart, 1994; Volcker, 1990, 1993).

Interest in the topic of central-bank independence has grown significantly over the past few years. From 1989 to the present, almost thirty central bank laws were revised and rewritten—and all in the direction of strengthening the independence of the central bank. This is true for industrial countries, such as the United Kingdom, France, Belgium, and Italy; for Latin American countries, such as Argentina, Chile, Mexico, and Venezuela; for the republics that belonged to the former Soviet Union, such as Russia, Lithuania, Ukraine, and Belarus; and for countries in Eastern Europe, such as the Czech Republic, Hungary, and Poland. It is noteworthy that interest in the topic and legislative processes aimed at strengthening the independence of the Bank of Japan are also underway (see Fukui, 1993; Central Bank Study Group, 1996).

Several reasons underlie the movement toward strengthening central-bank independence. First, countries that were successful in maintaining low inflation have typically enjoyed better economic performance than countries that were unable to control inflation.

Second, the world has undergone a conceptual revolution. In contrast with previous beliefs, the experience of the 1960s and 1970s has revealed that there is no long-term tradeoff between inflation and unemployment. Accordingly, one cannot produce permanent jobs and accelerate growth on a sustainable basis by creating inflation. Attempts to exploit this tradeoff have failed and have resulted in disappointment, frustration, and costly economic distortions. The conceptual revolution has yielded the conclusion that price stability contributes to good economic performance, while inflation is a source of instability and economic cost.

Third, there has been a fundamental change in views about the role that governments and economic policy can and should play in the market economy. There is now growing skepticism about the effectiveness of central planning. There is also skepticism about the capacity and the ability of governments to be effective participants in the marketplace. There is a growing conviction that free enterprise led by the private sector is the best framework within which one can generate investment and sustainable growth. Finally, there is also a growing conviction that to promote investment and growth one needs to generate price stability. Thus, the new view about the role of government and the desire to promote sustainable growth within a market economy brought about renewed interest in the conditions necessary for price stability.

Four important historical developments have taken place in the past few years that have contributed to a growing interest in central-bank independence. First, the creation of the European Union brought about negotiations for the creation of a new European central bank. The Maastricht Treaty specified the key characteristics of the law of the new central bank: the central bank must be independent, its main objective must be price stability, it must keep its distance from the governments, it should be kept free from political pressures, and so on. The European countries that have signed this treaty have adjusted their own central-bank legislation so as to conform with the provisions of the law of the new European central bank. This process heightened the official interest in and the public's awareness and familiarity with the topic of central-bank independence.

The second development that stimulated interest in the subject was the urgent need to create several new central banks due to the collapse of the Soviet Union, which brought about the creation of independent republics. These republics have realized the need to have a new central bank that is independent. The third development arose from the experience of several countries in Latin America that recognized that their suffering from high inflation was associated with having weak and not sufficiently independent central banks. The fourth development has been the emergence of globalized capital markets. More and more countries have realized that to succeed in the new highly competitive global environment, countries must be held in high regard by the various rating agencies that grade the economies' risk. These ratings depend heavily on the countries' track record of fighting inflation and on the institutional setting that governs the economic policy-making process. Therefore, the conclusion that has emerged is that a country that wishes to maintain access to the international capital market must aim at achieving price stability and must exhibit a good inflation track record. In addition, it must also have the appropriate institutional and legal frameworks that underlie the policy-making process. Prominent among such institutions is the presence of a independent central bank. In the next section it is argued that there are incentives that produce an intrinsic bias toward a higher rate of inflation than is socially desirable and that an independent central bank can remove this bias.

Inflation and the Inflation Bias

The economic costs from inflation are well known. Even if inflation is fully anticipated, it brings about a substitution of real resources for money services. This substitution is costly since it results in excessive time and resources that are spent on increased frequency of transactions. Since in practice inflation is not fully anticipated, there is the added cost arising from uncertainty. In an inflationary environment, the price mechanism as a con-veyer of information is damaged, and the efficient functioning of labor and financial markets is hurt. Nominal contracts are signed for periods of time that are shorter than is socially optimal, planning horizons are also shortened, and investment plans focus on the near rather than the longer term. An inflationary environment also hurts the credibility of government policy and thereby diminishes the ability of governments to adopt and implement programs of comprehensive economic reforms. Inflation also affects adversely the distribution of income and wealth. It erodes the competitiveness of the economy in international markets and damages the economy's standing in world capital markets.

This partial list of the economic cost of inflation poses the questions of why inflation, being such a bad thing, still exists and why in many cases the broad political support for the disinflation process is still lacking. The answer lies in great measure in the structure of the political process. We know that in the long run the Phillips curve is vertical (implying that one cannot reduce unemployment permanently by means of inflation), but even so, in the short run, due to reasons such as nominal rigidities and long-term contracts, a sharp reduction in inflation may result, for a while, in higher recorded unemployment. Therefore, many governments, wishing to encourage economic activity, are tempted to be "soft" in their anti-inflation position.

In view of inflation that is costly and the possible employment gains from accelerating inflation that may vanish in the long run, the question remains as to why many governments do not resist the temptation to obtain short-term gains in spite of the large long-term losses. To answer this question one must recognize that governments, especially those that are democratically elected, tend to have a high rate of time preference relative to the social optimum. This does not imply that government officials are bad or insensitive. It reflects the reality of the incentive system. Since governments wish to be popular to be reelected, they tend to search for policies that boost their popularity and that produce immediate results in the short run.

In addition, the theory of optimal taxation implies that governments will occasionally resort to the use of the inflation tax. Because such a tax does not require a legislative process, they are likely to rely excessively on this form of taxation. Indeed, as emphasized by John Maynard Keynes (1923): "A government can live for a long time by printing money . . . it is the form of taxation which the public finds hardest to evade and even the weakest government can enforce, when it can enforce nothing else." There is a growing understanding that in addition to its other drawbacks, the inflation tax does not satisfy the basic principles of orderly democratic procedures: it is a tax that is levied without any explicit approval of the legislative body (Congress or Parliament), and it is a tax that, although being levied on everyone, no legislator has to explicitly stand up and vote for it. This form of taxation is highly immoral. As indicated by John Stuart Mill (1848/1995), "depreciation of currency is a tax on the community and a fraud on creditors." In spite of this, the short-term employment gains, the easy collection of inflation-tax revenues, together with the possible short-term boost to the financial system provide the incentives for governments to be soft on inflation for its short-term benefit, even at the expense of the long term. The result of this softness is a higher rate of inflation. The political incentives that bring about the higher rate of inflation is referred to as the *inflation bias*.

It is important to reiterate the fact that the reason that governments in our democratic societies possess an intrinsic bias toward inflation is not because people in government are less moral or less sensitive than the ordinary citizens. In fact, it is very likely that if individuals presently in the government were to be replaced by outsiders, then the new members of government would soon act according to the same incentive structure and would exhibit the same inflation bias. In view of the presence of this fundamental inflation bias, the challenge facing policymakers is to design and create institutions that can overcome this problem. Meeting this challenge has been one of the major rationales for the creation of an independent central bank that is free of the political pressures that generate the inflation bias and thereby that has a longer-term view.

The concept of the inflation bias is familiar from the economic literature. Works by Barro and Gordon (1983) and by Kydland and Prescott (1977), as well as the ample literature on the subject of *time inconsistency*, help us understand analytically why there is an inflation bias and what mechanisms need to be in place to remove it.

The search for appropriate institutions that generate optimal policies marks a fundamental departure from the conventional debate on macroeconomic policies. Whereas in the past, the debate focused on the choice of *policies*, the appropriate mix of fiscal and monetary policies, and the relative effectiveness of these policies, the present approach recognizes that macroeconomic policies are carried out within a well-defined institutional context. The new focus, therefore, is on the choice of institutions. This choice is implemented through the search for the desirable *institutional structure* that is conducive to the promotion of the socially optimal policies. In the context of monetary policy, the search for the appropriate institution leads to the specification of the characteristics of the independent central bank that produces policies that are free of the inflation bias.

Different Forms of Central-Bank Independence

One mechanism for removing the inflation bias was proposed by Kenneth Rogoff (1985), who developed the concept of the *conservative central banker*. According to this approach, a government that wishes to ensure that its own inflation bias does not translate itself into an inflation rate that is higher than desirable should appoint a central-bank governor who is particularly sensitive to the inflation problem and who is sure to carry out policies that reflect this special sensitivity. Using Rogoff's terminology, he should be a conservative central banker.

Another mechanism proposed to offset the inflation bias suggests that the government should sign an *explicit contract* with the governor of the central bank, according to which the latter is obliged to achieve price stability. The contract includes a penalty clause in case that price stability is not achieved. An example of such a contract can be found in the case of New Zealand.

A variety of this approach underlies that logic of the strategy of setting *inflation targets* adopted in many countries in their anti-inflation efforts. According to this approach, the government sets inflation targets and grants the responsibility and authority for meeting the targets to the central bank, which is equipped with the instruments necessary to meet the target and which is granted the complete independence in using these instruments as it deems to be appropriate.

The key concept in this context is independence. There are two concepts of independence. One focuses on goal independence, and the other on instrument independence. *Goal independence* is found for example in the German case, in which the Bundesbank does not get *any* instructions from the government. The Bundesbank sets its own goal and then uses the available instruments in order to meet the goal.

With *instrument independence*, the targets are set by the government, and the central bank is completely free to use the policy instrument at its disposal in order to meet the assigned target. In addition, the central bank is free from any obligation to finance the government's budget. The complete separation between the policies of the central bank and the budgetary needs of the government is put in place to ensure that the intrinsic government's inflation bias does not have any monetary consequences and, therefore, does not result in an *actual* inflation bias.

In addition to the distinction between goal and instrument independence, the very concept of independence requires further classification. One needs to distinguish between *legal independence* that can be inferred from language of the law and *actual independence* that depends on the actual practice and on the way in which the law is being interpreted and implemented. For example, in many developing countries, it is difficult to assess the actual degree of central bank independence from analyzing only the language of the central bank law because the text of the law is often very convincing but the record of implementation is not. In other countries, on the other hand, the provisions contained in the formal central bank law are not so strong, but the actual degree of independence is nevertheless impressive. In summary, the issue of independence is not just a juridical issue but, rather, is a practical one.

Studies that were carried out to examine the issue of independence defined various indices of independence, including the provisions of the law as well as the actual practices. The following questions were examined in this context:

- the length of the term of the governor,
- the dependence of the governor's term on the timing of changes in governments,
- whether a new government has the power to replace the governor prior to the end of his term,
- whether the interest-rate decision should be taken by a board,

- the number of persons who should be included on such a board,
- the number of board members who should be insiders and outsiders,
- whether members of the Board can earn salaries from the other sources,
- who determines the budget of the central bank,
- what happens when there is disagreement between the government and the bank,
- who determines the inflation target,
- whether the bank is endowed with all the instruments needed for the conduct of monetary policy or needs to get government approval at each case,
- how and to whom the bank is accountable.

Those are some of the issues involved. An examination of the data reveals strong evidence that in general countries with an independent central bank have enjoyed better economic performance and in particular have had a much better inflation record than countries with a lesser degree of independence.

Credibility and Central-Bank Independence

One of the important assets of a central bank is its credibility. How can credibility be established? There is a famous dictum according to which "credibility is never owned, it is only rented." One must continually invest in credibility and thereby establish a track record. This track record is the only way to accumulate credibility, which should be viewed as an *asset* that is a form of *capital*. With this perspective it is evident why every mistake may be very costly because it may result in a rapid depreciation. This asset is also referred to as *reputation*. That reputation is an important precondition for the adoption of a long-term approach to economic policy. To provide the incentives for a reputation-based long-term approach, the length of the tenure of the board and of the governor need to be relatively long. This perspective is of special relevance in the context of monetary policy aiming at price stability. Due to the long lags of the effects of monetary policy, and due to the fact that the disinflation process is a long one, it is essential that monetary policy is provided with the incentive to focus on the medium and long terms. This can be provided only if the central bank is granted strong independence. If this is not done, there is the danger that policy will focus on the short term and thereby reintroduce the inflation bias. To keep the inflation bias at bay, one must provide the incentives for having a long-term perspective.

Indeed, studies that compared the turnover of governors in industrial countries with the turnover in developing countries found that typically the length of the tenure is much longer in industrial countries than in developing countries and also that the inflation performance is much better in industrial countries than in developing countries.

When the monetary authority enjoys credibility, it gains an additional degree of freedom in carrying out its monetary policy. The key point that must be realized is that the channels through which monetary policy affects the economy do not constitute only the mere printing of money. Monetary policy impacts the economy also through its announcements, which, in turn, affect market expectations. This channel operates by means of communication with the markets. When the monetary authority transmits a message (or a signal), its effect depends on whether it is believed. If the policymaker is credible, then he is believed, and thereby he gains another important instrument. With credibility, announcements on policy intentions reinforce actual policy measures and impact on market expectations and thereby speed up the transmission mechanism. Furthermore, with credibility the actions of monetary policy are perceived as long lasting rather than transitory and erratic, and, as a result, the effects of any given policy action are amplified and their impact is more pronounced. In other words, to achieve a given objective, policies that enjoy credibility do not need to be as harsh as they would have had to be if they did not enjoy credibility. It follows that to achieve a given degree of disinflation, the credible central bank can afford having a somewhat lower interest rate than less credible banks if monetary policy is credible and is expected to last for long enough time. As the saying goes: "The one who is credible does not need to raise his voice to be heard and listened to." Thus, credibility enhances the effectiveness of monetary policy, and central-bank independence enhances credibility.

In general, the special attention granted to the concept of credibility reflects the new style of modern policy making. Until some years ago, to be effective, policy had to *surprise* the markets. Policy discussions were highly secretive, the public was not informed about the precise issues of debate, minutes of policy meetings were secret, mystery prevailed, and if there was a leak, so that the markets could anticipate the course of policy, this leak nullified the effectiveness of the policy. The name of the game was drama. To be effective, policymakers found it useful to make dramatic news on prime-time television. This style of policymaking has changed significantly. The newstyle of economic policymaking reflects the recognition by policymakers that the depth and breadth of modern financial markets have grown to such an extent so as to put limits on the capacity and effectiveness of policies. Markets are just too big and too liquid to be controlled or manipulated by anyone, including policymakers.

In view of these developments, there is a growing consensus that the role of policy in the modern age is not to surprise the market but to *communicate* with it. The relationship between policy and markets should not be adversarial. Policy should not try to beat the markets through surprises but rather try to join them through communication. Effective communication requires a *dialogue*. Effective dialogue requires *clarity*. To be clearly understood policy must be *transparent*. To be sufficiently transparent, policy should have well-defined *objectives* that can be stated and assessed easily. Clear objectives facilitate transparency, which facilitates clarity, which is essential to the effective long-term dialogue and communication between markets and policymakers, a dialogue that enhances the effectiveness of policy. This is the rationale for the need to invest and accumulate credibility.

Accountability and Transparency of an Independent Central Bank

In an environment of transparency, in which the communication between policymakers and the market is in the form of a dialogue, one must have *accountability* for at least two reasons. First, by creating an incentive, accountability spurs policymakers to improve their performance. The very knowledge that policymakers are held accountable and that they are being judged on their achievements in meeting the targets is likely to increase their efforts.

Second, it is only natural in a democratic society that civil servants and elected officials should deliver an account of their actions. This is achieved through the provisions of transparency and accountability. One mechanism for implementing this requirement is through the periodic publication of an inflation report, as is done in many central banks that see the fighting of inflation as their main objective.

Effective accountability and transparency require that the central bank presents its views and analysis to the public, the government, and the parliament and that such presentations and reporting are required by the law. It should be emphasized and stressed that the requirements of transparency and accountability do not imply in any way a loss of independence, since the latter, of course, must be secured by the central-bank law. In fact, these requirements should be viewed as contributing to independence since they help to clarify the logic behind central-bank policy and thereby may broaden and solidify the public support for the positions of the bank.

Bank Supervision and an Independent Central Bank

One of the issues that is subject to a debate in the context of designing an independent central bank is whether the function of bank supervision should be part of the central bank. In most countries bank supervision is part of the jurisdiction of the central bank, but in some the practice differs. In Germany, for example, bank supervision is not under the auspices of the Bundesbank. The German view is that since the main objective of the bank is the attainment and maintenance of price stability, and other considera-tion (like those introduced by the responsibility of bank supervision, which has to be concerned with the stability of the banking system) may com-promise the main goal and thereby upset the focus of the central bank on price stability. This, however, is only one approach but not necessarily the only acceptable one. An alternative approach, which is favored by most central banks, puts emphasis on the fact that to be effective monetary policy must be based on the most updated data and information about the banking sector. The only way that the central bank can ensure timely access to this information is by including the responsibility for bank supervision under its jurisdiction.

The rationale for the inclusion of bank supervision within the central bank goes beyond the availability of current data and information. There is a strong complementarity between the objective of macroeconomic stability—which is the main responsibility of the central bank—and the objective of promoting a sound and stable banking system—which is the main responsibility of bank supervision.

The interrelationship between these two objectives goes both ways. On the one hand, banking crises inflict high cost and lead to macroeconomic disruption. On the other hand, macroeconomic disruption, especially in an environment of globalization of capital markets, can be transformed into a banking crises. This two-way relationship implies that to reduce the likelihood of banking crises emanating from macroeconomic dis-ruptions, one needs to follow stable macroeconomic policies and that to reduce the likelihood of macroeconomic crises emanating from dis-ruptions to the banking system, one needs to follow sound banking princi-ples. The latter necessitates effective regulation, effective supervision, strict maintenance of capital adequacy ratios, timely disclosure, and effective regulation.

Regulations that are effective facilitate governance and market discipline through improved information and better transparency of the financial conditions of banks. It is relevant to note, however, than sound banking is not a static concept because globalization itself is dynamic. And if globalization is a dynamic concept, so are the innovations in the capital markets. And if financial instruments and practices are evolving, so must the regulatory and the supervisory capacity evolve. Therefore, the concept of sound banking itself should always be dynamic. Thus, the dynamism and innovations that characterize financial markets reflect themselves at the same time in new instruments to be used in the conduct of monetary policy and new supervisory approaches to ensure the soundness of banks.

The relation between macroeconomic stability and sound banking is also relevant for the effectiveness of monetary policy. Since the banking system is one of the major channels through which monetary policy operates, it is crucial that this important channel of the transmission mechanism is robust and sound. If such conditions are met, monetary policy can perform its role effectively.

In addition, if the banking system is weak and vulnerable, the central bank, being concerned with the stability of the banking system, might be timid and reluctant to impose the appropriate degree of monetary tightness. The result of this concern would be a higher rate of inflation than would have prevailed if monetary policy were conducted in an unconstrained manner. As a result, these circumstances yield another form of an inflation bias. An effective way to overcome this bias is the promotion of sound banking principles. Once the banking system is sound, the central bank is able to conduct its anti-inflation monetary policy without having to compromise its commitment to price stability due to being saddled by the concern for the safety of the banks.

The inclusion of bank supervision within the responsibilities of the central bank can strengthen the hand of the supervisory authority by providing it with an incentive for prompt reactions. Experience has taught us that regulators should never let a problem in the banking sector become too big because then the syndrome called "too big to fail" arises. Powerful political interest groups typically attempt to protect banks that are in trouble, and inevitably a crisis blows up as the syndrome of the "too big to fail" gives way to the syndrome of the "too big to save." Many crises could have been avoided had the underlying problem been addressed head on in an early stage.

One of the main lessons to be learned from these crises is that one must deal with banking problems promptly. Otherwise, the difficulties get worse, and the central bank—which by that stage, will have lost credibility—needs to adopt stronger measures just to achieve any given result. Typically, by that stage the banking problems become "too big," and many excuses are offered as rationale for delaying the necessary but painful measures. Such delays reinforce the loss of credibility and make the adjustment more difficult. A central bank wishing to defend its credibility will see to it that the banking problems are dealt with at an early stage.

The preceding arguments imply that the monetary authorities that wish to protect their credibility and enhance the effectiveness of policy have a strong incentive to ensure that the banking system is sound. It follows that the two objectives of price stability and sound banking are complementary to each other and that the inclusion of the function of bank supervision within the central bank can reinforce rather than contradict the attainment of the main objective of the bank.

Multiyear Inflation Targets

One of the mechanisms that can be used by a government that wishes to overcome the inflation bias is the adoption of a long-term commitment for price stability. On its way to price stability, the government can underscore its commitment to the disinflation process by setting a *multiyear* inflation target (on inflation targets, see Leiderman and Svensson, 1995). Such a target should be set for the medium term rather than focus on the short term (such as a single year) to avoid a temptation of giving excessive weight to short-term considerations.

If the government announces a multiyear inflation target, then it gives the central bank a mandate to use the policy instruments to achieve it. The mandate is long term, and therefore the government sends the message to the market that short-term consideration will not override the long-term goals. Multiyear targets that are credible can influence market expectations. Thereby, agents who negotiate forward price and wage contracts will embody these targets into the contracts and thereby support the realization of the inflation targets. Furthermore, by having nominal contracts that are consistent with the socially desired path of inflation, the cost of rigidities associated with the disinflation process is reduced.

The advantage of having multiyear inflation targets is especially pronounced in countries that suffered in the past from very high inflation and that as a result developed mechanism of wage and price indexation so as to enable them to "live with inflation." Indexation makes the disinflation process more complicated and costly since, by linking the evolution of current prices and wages to past inflation, it introduces inertia into the inflationary process. Credible inflation targets could help in removing this inflationary inertia since agents, in setting nominal contracts of wages and prices, would be forward looking and, in effect, "index" the contracts to the credible path of the inflation target rather than to past inflation.

Another reason for having multiyear targets is the fact that monetary policy operates with a time lag. This is unfortunate but a fact of life: the lag is not only long but also variable. The lags in the effects of monetary policy imply that a significant determinant of the rate of inflation for any given year is the policy that was followed in the previous year; by the same token, a significant part of the effects of policy followed in any given year is felt only in the subsequent year. This lack of synchronization between the timing of policy actions and effects imply the need for a multiyear framework.

Furthermore, if you make a mistake in a multiyear program, you can correct it slowly rather than abruptly. Making a correction within a short period of time may be too difficult. The situation is similar to that of a driver; if he sees that he is sliding toward the side of the road, he can correct his course slowly if he has time; if not, he must turn the driving wheel abruptly. To allow for a smooth and gradual correction of deviations (arising from errors or from external shocks), it is often desirable to adopt a strategy of gradualism.

The problem with the strategy of *Gradualism* is, however, that it may be interpreted by the public as reflecting hesitancy and lack of commitment on the part of the authorities. As a result, when the government adopts a path of slow adjustment on grounds of prudence, the public might greet the program with skepticism. The adoption of a multiyear frame-work with preannounced target dates for the completion of the implementation of policy actions enables the government to achieve the desired credibility while at the same time proceeding with a prudent and a gradual pace.

These issues were also raised in the context of the European economic integration. During the 1980s it was difficult to believe that Europe would become a single market during the 1990s. The politicians, however, were willing to undertake a long-term view and adopted a commitment for the unification of markets by 1992. With the benefit of hindsight it now is evident that the strategy was brilliant. By making commitments for the distant future, governments did not need of adopt sharp measures immediately, while at the same time a new reality was created that tied the hands of future governments. Indeed, with a passage of time subsequent governments have found it costly to renege, and thus credibility was built. The precommitment with the explicitly announced date of completion ensured the success of the program. This is just one more example of the benefits from having a multiyear framework for policymaking.

Who Should Set the Inflation Target?

Once a multiyear inflation target strategy has been adopted, there is still the question of who should set the target, the government or the central bank? In addition to the issues raised in the distinction between goal independence and instrument independence as characteristics of central-bank independence, there is a fundamental reason as to why, in my judgment, the quantitative targets should be set by governments. It is important that fighting inflation is viewed as a joint objective and responsibility of governments and central banks. When governments set targets and the central bank uses the instruments in its disposal to achieve the targets, the jointness of the commitment of fight inflation is evident, and the anti-inflation strategy gains legitimacy. On the other hand, if the targets are set by the central bank alone, there is a danger that the government might not be viewed as being a full partner in the fight against inflation.

The lack of full and explicit partnership might be reflected at times by expressions of criticisms of central-bank policies by the government. Such criticism, which typically takes the form of (implicit or explicit) objections to high interest rates, hurts the effectiveness of monetary policy by casting doubts on the capacity of the central bank to sustain its policies. Furthermore, such criticism may also cast doubt on the willingness of government to adopt a policy mix consistent with the attainment of the preannounced inflation target. This potential loss of effectiveness imposes an extra burden on monetary policy, which, to regain the loss of effectiveness, must be tighter than what it would have been otherwise.

When the government and the central bank are viewed as fighting inflation in joint partnership, it becomes clear that price stability is a national priority in conjunction with other economic objectives rather than an esoteric goal of the central banks alone. This makes it easier for the central bank to explain to the public and markets the rationale behind its policies and thereby to gain and consolidate the public support necessary for a sustained anti-inflation effort.

Transparency is crucial for an effective communication between monetary policy and the markets. Such communication is critical for the transmission mechanism and for the effectiveness of monetary policy. Therefore, it is important to institutionalize the obligation for communication and transparency in central-bank legislation. This is the reason that modern central bank laws pay explicit attention to the provisions governing the required flow of information between the central bank, the government, the parliament, and the public.

Policy Cooperation

Central-bank independence does not imply lack of cooperation with the government. Such cooperation is necessary to ensure that monetary policy is not overburdened and that the broad range of economic policy objectives is attained at minimal cost.

In this regard it is worth to distinguish between the concept of coordination and the concept of cooperation. This distinction was emphasized in the debate on the G-7 international policy coordination process. The experience gained from that process showed that in the present democratic systems, national governments are unlikely to adopt policy measures that are not consistent with domestic policy objectives even if they serve global interests. It became clear that coordination—which implies significant changes in the fiscal stance of any given country—is unlikely to materialize if it emanates only from the G-7 meeting; it must be decided at home through the conventional domestic policymaking process. At the same time it also became clear that cooperation—which implies exchange of information, data, and analysis—can contribute significantly to harmony and mutual understanding in the globally integrated economic system. On the issues related to policy coordination and cooperation, see Frenkel and Goldstein (1990) and Shimizu (1996).

In the context of domestic policymaking the distinction between the concepts of coordination and cooperation is also relevant as it characterizes the different layers of policymaking. Economic targets have to be set in coordination between the various agencies reflecting their respective authorities. Once these targets are set, each agency should use the instruments at its disposal so as to attain the targets under its responsibility. The efforts of each agency in meeting the targets under its responsibility are supported by an effective process of cooperation with other agencies.

Applied to monetary policy that is carried out by an independent central bank, these principles imply that once the targets for monetary policy are set (such as multiyear inflation targets), policy cooperation requires an effective dialogue between the central bank and the other agencies (such as government and the parliament). This dialogue takes the form of exchange of information, data, and analysis, all carried out within the context of transparency. It is important to emphasize that the required cooperation should not be viewed as impinging on the indigence of the central bank; rather it should be viewed as an important mechanism designed to support the central bank in its responsibilities while reducing the risk of overburdening.

This perspective on the division of responsibilities between the various agencies (such as the ministry of finance and the central bank) provides a guide as to the appropriate reaction of monetary policy to deviations from fiscal targets. It should be evident that to have a successful central bank one must be sure that other policy instruments are also performing—first and foremost the government's budget. A recent example of the consequences of excessively large budget deficits is provided by the experience of some of the major industrial countries in the late 1980s, which brought about an overburdening of monetary policy. For example, the United States had big budget deficits, and monetary policy was largely overburdened. In addition to performing its usual responsibilities, monetary policy had also to partially offset the expansionary consequences of the large deficits. As a result, the overall economic performance was suboptimal. Obviously, central-bank independence could not guarantee optimal overall performance since greater harmony among the various instruments of economic policy was required. In addition to suffering from the lack of harmony from policy instruments, the performance of the economy also suffered from the fact that the overall credibility, and thereby effectiveness of economic policy in general, was damaged. The adverse effects of the loss of credibility was amplified by the reduced effectiveness of the already overburdened monetary policy due to the lack of understanding and consensus about its role.

In addition to the dependence of the effectiveness of monetary policy on fiscal consolidation, on its transparency, and on its capacity to master public support, a crucial factor determining the ultimate effectiveness of monetary policy is the flexibility of the economic system. To facilitate the reallocation of resources consequent on macroeconomic policies, it is important that good and labor markets are competitive and flexible. The policies that bring about competitiveness, flexibility, reduced distortions, and a liberal economic system are referred to as *structural policies*.

Using a metaphor from the world of music, it is clear that ultimately the harmony of the music depends on cooperation among all members of the orchestra. The violin must play the music written for the violin, the piano must play the music written for the piano, as must be the case for the other musical instruments. The job of the conductor of the orchestra is to ensure that each musician plays correctly his own music, that the harmony is maintained, and that the right tempo is kept. Only then will the performance be successful. If the violinist is not playing his music right, the harmony is destroyed. It is clear that under such circumstances the conductor should insist that the violinist should improve his playing and restore harmony by sticking to the music that was originally written for him. By the same token it is clear that no good conductor would attempt to restore harmony by asking the rest of the musicians to deviate from playing their music and adjust to deviations of the violinist. This analogy is relevant for assessing the question of restoring the appropriate balance to the macroeconomic policy mix along side with structural reforms.

The experience in some of the industrial countries in the late 1980s taught us that when faced with deviations characterized by excessively large budget deficits and inflexible economies, it is much better to address the lack of harmony head on and focus on the restoration of fiscal balance and structural reform, rather than accept the fiscal imbalances and structural rigidities as given and attempt to restore (illusionary) harmony through excessive reliance on monetary policy. Monetary policy should not deviate from attempting to achieve its main objectives (typically price stability or multiyear inflation targets). Central-bank independence provides the mechanism that permits monetary policy to focus on its assigned targets. Thereby, this independence also increases the likelihood that harmony is restored and that the cooperation between the various agencies brings about the optimal policy mix.

Acknowledgment

A previous version of this chapter was presented at the Japan Society of Monetary Economics, on May 31, 1997. I am indebted to Dr. Ohad Bar-Efrat of the Bank of Israel for very useful comments and suggestions.

References

Barro, Robert J., and Gordon David. (1983). "A Positive Theory of Monetary Policy in a Natural Rate Model." *Journal of Political Economy* 91: 589–610.

Central Bank Study Group. (1996). "Reform of the Central Bank System—in Pursuit of Open Independence." Tokyo: CBSG.

Cukierman, Alex. (1992). *Central Bank Strategy, Credibility and Independence: Theory and Evidence.* Cambridge, MA: MIT Press.

Cukierman, Alex. (1996). "The Economics of Central Banking." Working Paper No. 36–96, Tel-Aviv University.

Finance System Research Council. (1997). "Report on the Revision of the Bank of Japan Law." Tokyo: FSRC.

Fischer, Stanley. (1995a). "Central-Bank Independence Revisited." *American Economic Review* 85(2) (May): 201–206.

Fischer, Stanley. (1995b). "Modern Central Banking." In F. Capie, C. Goodhart, S. Fischer, and N. Schnadt (eds.), *The Future of Central Banking, Cambridge University Press*. Cambridge.

Fischer, Stanley. (1996). "Why Are Central Banks Pursuing Long-Run Price Stability?" Washington DC: International Monetary Fund.

Frenkel, Jacob A., and Morris Goldstein. (1990). "The Rationale for, and Effects of International Policy Coordination." In William H. Branson, Jacob A. Frenkel, and Morris Goldstein (eds.), *International Policy Coordination and Exchange Rate Fluctuations*. Chicago: University of Chicago Press.

Fukui, Toshihiko. (1993). "Missions and Responsibilities of a Central Bank in a Contemporary Context." Bank of Japan *Quarterly Bulletin* (August).

Goodhart, Charles. (1994). "Central Bank Independence." London School of Economics, London.

Keynes, John M. (1923/1946). *A Tract on Monetary Reform*. London.

Kydland, Finn E., and Ed Prescott. (1977). "Rules Rather than Discretion: The Inconsistency of Optimal Plans." *Journal of Political Economy* 85: 473–492.

Leiderman, Leonardo, and Lars Svensson (eds.). (1995). *Inflation Targets*. London: CEPR.

Mill, John Stuart. (1848/1996). *Principles of Political Economy*. London.

Rogoff, Ken. (1985). "The Optimal Degree of Commitment to a Monetary Target." *Quarterly Journal of Economics* 100: 1169–1190.

Shimizu, Yoshinori. (1996). "International Policy Coordination and Central Bank Independence." Working Paper No. 15, Hitotsubashi University, Tokyo.

Volcker, Paul A. (1990). "The Triumph of Central Banking." Per Jacobbson Lecture, International Monetary Fund, Washington, DC.

Volcker, Paul A. (1993). "The Independence of Central Banks: Its Value and Its Limits." Banca D'Italia, Rome.

3 CENTRAL BANKING IN A DEMOCRATIC SOCIETY
Implications for Transition Countries

Frederic S. Mishkin

Columbia University and National Bureau of Economic Research

Introduction

In recent years we have seen the emergence of two important trends: an increase in the number of countries operating on democratic principles, especially with the abandonment of communism in the transition countries, and an increase in the independence of central banks. Indeed, many of the transition countries have granted their central banks a higher degree of legal independence than is seen in many other countries. At a glance, the independence of central banks seems to be in conflict with the democratic principle that government policies should be controlled by elected officials rather than by an elite group that is insulated from the political process. On the other hand, there is a strong case for independence of central banks to ensure that they take a long-run view and conduct monetary policy in an effective manner. This apparent conflict between these two views immediately raises the question of what the role of a central bank should be in the emerging democracies of the transition countries. What form should central-bank independence take? Can central-bank independence and democratic principles be reconciled? How can the central bank be made sufficiently accountable in a democratic society? Answering these questions not only is of importance in countries that have been democratic for a substantial period but is especially relevant in the transition countries of Eastern Europe, which are now in the process of designing their political and governmental frameworks.

This chapter seeks answers to the above questions by first discussing what principles should guide the conduct of monetary policy. Using these principles, it goes on to discuss what form the independence of central banks should take and the how independent central banks can be made accountable to the democratic process. Then it examines different monetary policy regimes in different countries and evaluates where these regimes stand in terms of central-bank independence and accountability. Finally, it looks at issues of independence and accountability for the European Central Bank that is coming into existence in 1999 and ends with some implications for transition countries.

Basic Principles for Monetary Policy

Recent theorizing in monetary economics suggests five basic principles that can serve as useful guides to the successful conduct of monetary policy: (1) monetary policy should focus on promoting price stability, (2) monetary policy should avoid the time-inconsistency problem, (3) monetary policy should be forward looking, (4) policymakers should be accountable, and (5) fiscal policy should be aligned with monetary policy. We look at each of these principles in turn.

Price Stability

In recent years a growing consensus has emerged that price stability—a low and stable inflation rate—provides substantial benefits to the economy. Price stability prevents overinvestment in the financial sector, which in a high-inflation environment expands to profitably act as a middleman to help individuals and businesses escape some of the costs of inflation (see, for example, English, 1996). Price stability lowers the uncertainty about relative prices and the future price level, making it easier for firms and individuals to make appropriate decisions, thereby increasing economic efficiency (see Briault, 1995). Price stability also lowers the distortions from the interaction of the tax system and inflation (see Fischer, 1994; Feldstein, 1997).

All of these benefits of price stability suggest that low and stable inflation can increase the level of resources productively employed in the economy and might even help increase the rate of economic growth. While time-series studies of individual countries and cross-national comparisons of growth rates are not in total agreement, there is a consensus that inflation is detrimental to economic growth, particularly when inflation is at high level (see the survey in Anderson and Gruen, 1995). Therefore, both theory and evidence suggest that monetary policy should focus on promoting price stability.

Avoiding Time Inconsistency

One of the key problems facing monetary policymakers is the time-inconsistency problem described by Calvo (1978), Kydland and Prescott (1977), and Barro and Gordon (1983). The time inconsistency problem arises because there are incentives for a policymaker to try to exploit the short-run tradeoff between employment and inflation to pursue short-run employment objectives, even though the result is poor long-run outcomes. Expansionary monetary policy will produce higher growth and employment in the short-run, and so policymakers will be tempted to pursue this policy even though it will not produce higher growth and employment in the long-run because economic agents adjust their wage and price expectations upward to reflect the expansionary policy. Unfortunately, however, expansionary monetary policy will lead to higher inflation in the long run, with its negative consequences for the economy.

McCallum (1995) points out that the time-inconsistency problem by itself does not imply that a central bank will pursue expansionary monetary policy that leads to inflation. Simply by recognizing the problem that forward-looking expectations in the wage- and price-setting process creates for a strategy of pursuing expansionary monetary policy, central banks can decide not to play that game. From my firsthand experience as a central banker, I can testify that central bankers are very aware of the time-inconsistency problem and are indeed extremely adverse to falling into a time-inconsistency trap. However, even if central bankers recognize the problem, there still will be pressures on the central bank to pursue overly expansionary monetary policy by politicians. Thus overly expansionary monetary policy and inflation may result, so that the time-inconsistency problem remains. The time-inconsistency problem is just shifted back one step; its source is not in the central bank but rather resides in the political process.

The time-inconsistency literature points out both why there will be pressures on central banks to pursue overly expansionary monetary policy and why central banks whose commitment to price stability is in doubt are more likely to experience higher inflation. To prevent high inflation and the pursuit of a suboptimal monetary policy, monetary policy institutions need to be designed to avoid the time-inconsistency trap.

Alignment of Fiscal Policy with Monetary Policy

One lesson to be learned from the "unpleasant monetarist arithmetic" discussed in Sargent and Wallace (1981) and the recent literature on fiscal theories of the price level (Woodford, 1994, 1995) is that irresponsible fiscal policy may make it more difficult for the monetary authorities to pursue price stability. Large government deficits may put pressure on the monetary authorities to monetize the debt, thereby producing rapid money growth and inflation. Restraining the fiscal authorities from engaging in excessive deficit financing thus aligns fiscal policy with monetary policy and makes it easier for the monetary authorities to keep inflation under control.

Forward-Looking Policy

The existence of long lags from monetary policy actions to their intended effects on output and inflation suggests that monetary policy should be forward looking. If policymakers wait until undesirable outcomes on inflation and output fluctuations actually arise, their policy actions are likely to be counterproductive. For example, by waiting until inflation has already appeared before tightening monetary policy, the monetary authorities will be too late; inflation expectations will already be embedded into the wage- and price-setting process, creating an inflation momentum that will be hard to contain. Once the inflation process has gotten rolling, the process of stopping it will be slower and costlier. Similarly, by waiting until the economy is already in recession, expansionary policy may kick in well after the economy has recovered, thus promoting unnecessary output fluctuations and possible inflation.

To avoid these problems, monetary authorities must behave in a forward-looking fashion and act preemptively. For example, if it takes two years for monetary policy to have a significant effect on inflation, then even if inflation is quiescent currently but with an unchanged stance of monetary policy policymakers forecast inflation to rise in two years time, then they must act today to head off the inflationary surge.

Accountability

A basic principle of democracy is that the public should have the right to control the actions of the government: "government of the people, by the people, and for the people." Thus the public in a democracy must have the capability to "throw the bums out" or punish incompetent policymakers through other methods to control their actions. If policymakers cannot be removed from office or punished in some other way, this basic principle of democracy is violated. In a democracy, government policymakers need to be held accountable to the public.

A second reason that accountability of policymakers is important is that it helps to promote efficiency in government. Making policymakers subject to dismissal from office makes it more likely that incompetent policy-makers will be replaced by competent policymakers. In addition, making policymakers subject to dismissal or subject to other punishments creates better incentives for policymakers to do their jobs well. Knowing that they are subject to punishment when performance is poor, policymakers will strive to get policy right. If policymakers are able to avoid accountability, then their incentives to do a good job drop appreciably, making poor policy outcomes more likely.

Armed with these five principles of monetary policy, we can now go on to look at two key issues of the design of monetary policy institutions: the degree of independence of the central bank and how central banks might be held accountable.

Central-Bank Independence

Together, the first three principles for monetary policy outlined above suggest that the overriding, long-run goal of monetary policy should be price stability. A goal of price stability immediately follows from the benefits of low and stable inflation, while an institutional commitment to price stability is one way to make time-inconsistency of monetary policy less likely. An institutional commitment to the price stability goal provides a counter to time inconsistency because it makes it clear that the central bank must focus on the long run and thus resist the temptation to pursue short-run expansionary policies that are inconsistent with the long-run, price-stability goal.

The third principle that fiscal policy should be aligned with monetary policy provides another reason that price stability should be the overriding, long-run goals of monetary policy. As McCallum (1995) has emphasized, "unpleasant monetarist arithmetic" arises only if the fiscal authorities are the first mover. In other words if the fiscal authorities are the dominant player and so can move first, thus setting fiscal policy exogenously knowing that the monetary authorities will be forced to accommodate their policies to maintain the long-run government budget constraint, then fiscal policy will determine the inflation rate. Indeed, this is the essence of the fiscal theory of the price level. On the other hand, as McCallum (1996) points out, if the monetary authorities are the dominant player and move first, then it will be fiscal policy that will accommodate to satisfy the long-run government budget constraint and monetary policy that will determine the inflation rate. An institutional commitment to price stability as the over-riding, long-run goal is just one way to ensure that monetary policy moves first and dominates, forcing fiscal policy to align with monetary policy.

Although there is a strong rationale for the price stability goal, who should make the institutional commitment? Should the central bank independently announce its commitment to the price-stability goal, or would it be better to have this commitment be mandated by legislation?

Here the distinction between goal independence and instrument independence made by Debelle and Fischer (1994) and Fischer (1994) is quite useful. Goal independence is the ability of the central bank to set its own goals for monetary policy, while instrument independence is the ability of the central bank to independently set the instruments of monetary policy to achieve the goals. The basic principle of democracy that the public must be able to exercise control over government actions strongly suggests that the goals of monetary policy should be set by the elected government. In other words, a central bank should not be goal independent. The corollary of this view is that the institutional commitment to price stability should come from the government in the form of an explicit, legislated mandate for the central bank to pursue price stability as its overriding, long-run goal.

Not only is a legislated mandate and goal dependence of the central bank consistent with basic principles of democracy, but it has the further advantage that it makes time inconsistency less likely, while making alignment of fiscal policy with monetary policy more likely. As we discussed above, the source of the time-inconsistency problem is more likely to be embedded in the political process than it is in the central bank. Once politicians commit to the price stability goal by passing central-bank legislation with a price-stability mandate, it becomes harder for them to put pressure on the central bank to pursue short-run expansionary policies that are inconsistent with the price-stability goal. Furthermore, a government commitment to price stability is also a commitment to making monetary policy dominant over fiscal policy, ensuring a better alignment of fiscal policy with monetary policy.

An alternative way to solve time-inconsistency problems has been suggested by Rogoff (1985): grant both goal and instrument independence to a central bank, and then appoint conservative central bankers to run it who put more weight on controlling inflation relative to output than does the general public. The result will be low inflation, but at the cost of higher output variability than the public desires. There are two problems with this solution. First, having "conservative" central bankers impose different preferences than the public on the conduct of monetary policy is inherently undemocratic. Basic democratic principles indicate that the preferences of policymaking should be aligned with those of the society at large. Second, in the long run a central bank cannot operate without the support of the public. If the central bank is seen to be pursuing goals that are not what the public wants, support for central-bank independence is likely to erode. Thus appointment of "conservative" central bankers may not be stable in the long run and will not provide a permanent solution to the time-inconsistency problem.

Although an institutional commitment to price stability helps solve time-inconsistency and fiscal-alignment problems, it does not go far enough because price stability is not a clearly defined concept. The definition of price stability has many elements in common with the commonly used legal definition of pornography in the United States: you know it when you see it. Constraints on fiscal policy and discretionary monetary policy to avoid inflation might thus end up being quite weak because not everyone will agree on what price stability means in practice, providing both monetary policymakers and politicians a loophole to avoid making tough decisions to keep inflation under control. A solution to this problem is to have the government and central bank adopt an explicit nominal anchor that ties down exactly what the commitment to price stability means.

There are several forms that an explicit nominal anchor can take. One is a commitment to a fixed exchange rate. For example, in 1990, Argentina established a currency board that required the central bank to exchange U.S. dollars for new pesos at a fixed exchange rate of one to one. A second nominal anchor is for the central bank to have a money-growth target, as in Germany. A third nominal anchor is for there to be an explicit numerical inflation goal as in inflation-targeting countries such as New Zealand, Canada, and the United Kingdom, among others. All these forms of explicit nominal anchors can help reduce the time-inconsistency problem, as the success of countries using them in lowering and controlling inflation demonstrates (Mishkin, 1998b). These nominal anchors help restrain fiscal policy and are also seen as an important benefit of inflation targeting in countries such as New Zealand and Canada (Mishkin and Posen, 1997; Bernanke, Laubach, Mishkin, and Posen, 1998).

The same principles that suggest that the central bank should be goal dependent, with the commitment to the price-stability goal mandated by the government, also suggest that the commitment to an explicit nominal anchor should be made by the government. In the case of an exchange-rate target, the government should set the target, as in Argentina, or in the case of an inflation target, the government should set the numerical inflation goal. The fact that the government sets these targets so that the central bank is goal dependent does not mean that the central bank should be cut out of the decision-making process. Because the central bank has both prestige and expertise in the conduct of monetary policy, governments will almost always be better served by setting these targets in consultation with the central bank.

Although the arguments above suggest that central banks should be goal dependent, the principles for monetary policy in the previous section provide a strong case that central banks should be instrument independent. Allowing central banks to control the setting of monetary policy instruments provides additional insulation from political pressures to exploit short-run tradeoffs between employment and inflation. Instrument independence means that the central bank is better able to avoid the pursuit of time-inconsistent policies.

The important principle that monetary policy needs to be forward looking to take account of the long lags in the effect of monetary policy on inflation provides another rationale for instrument independence. Instrument independent insulates the central bank from the myopia that is frequently a feature of the political process arising from politicians' concerns about getting elected in the near future. Instrument independence thus makes it more likely that the central bank will be forward looking and adequately allow for the long lags from monetary policy actions to inflation in setting their policy instruments.

Recent evidence seems to support the conjecture that macroeconomic performance is improved when central banks are more independent. When central banks in industrialized countries are ranked from least legally independent to most legally independent, the inflation performance is found to be the best for countries with the most independent central banks (see Alesina and Summers, 1993; Cukierman, 1992; and Fischer, 1994; among others.) However, there is some question whether causality runs from central-bank independence to low inflation or, rather, whether a third factor is involved, such as the general public's preferences for low inflation that create both central-bank independence and low inflation (Posen, 1995).

The bottom line is that basic principles for monetary policy and democracy suggest that central banks should have instrument but not goal independence. This degree of independence for central banks is analogous to the relationship between the U.S. military and the government during the successfully prosecuted Gulf War in 1991. The military had instrument independence: it had complete control over the prosecution of the war with little interference from the government (in contrast to the less successfully waged Vietnam War). On the other hand, the military did not have goal independence: it was the commander in chief, George Bush, who made the decisions as to what the objectives and goals of the war would be.

Central-Bank Accountability

The basic principle that policymakers should be accountable indicates that the central bank should be subject to government and public scrutiny. One way of ensuring accountability is to make the independence of the central bank subject to legislative change by allowing the act that created the central bank to be modified by legislation at any time. Another way is to mandate periodic reporting requirements to the government, as was done in the Humphrey-Hawkins legislation, which requires the chairman of the Federal Reserve to testify to Congress twice a year. Stronger accountability can be enforced by making the central-bank governor subject to dismissal if he or she breaches the goals set by the government, as is the case in New Zealand.

Increased transparency of monetary policymaking is another important way to increase central-bank accountability. Central banks need to communicate clearly their monetary policy strategy to explain their objectives and how they plan to achieve them. Each time they change their policy instruments, such as the interbank interest rate, they also need to clearly state the decision and then explain the rationale for it. Furthermore, they need to pursue many outreach vehicles to communicate with the public. These include the continual making of speeches to all elements of society, more openness with the press and media, and the development of brochures and reports that are accessible to the public. Particularly noteworthy in this regard are the *Inflation report* type documents initially developed by the Bank of England but now emulated by many other central banks. These documents depart from the usual, dull-looking, formal reports of central banks to take on the best elements of textbook writing (fancy graphics, use of boxes) to better communicate with the public.

Increasing transparency and accountability not only help to align central banks with democratic principles, and thus are worthy in their own right, but they also have benefits for the ability of central banks to conduct monetary policy successfully. Transparency reduces the uncertainty about monetary policy, interest rates, and inflation, thus making private-sector planning easier. Transparency and communication also promotes a better public understanding of what central banks can do—promote price stability, which has the potential to enhance economic growth in the long run— and what central banks can't do—create permanent increases in output and employment through expansionary policy. Better public understanding of what central banks can and cannot do is then likely to generate more public support for monetary policy, which is focused on price stability as the long-run, overriding goal.

Although central bankers find their life to be a more comfortable one when they are not accountable and can avoid intense public scrutiny, increased transparency and accountability have important benefits for central bankers. Because transparency and accountability can increase the public support for the price-stability goal, they can reduce political pressures on the central bank to pursue inflationary monetary policy. In addition, transparency and accountability can increase support for independence of the central bank. An instructive example is provided by the granting of instrument independence to the Bank of England in May 1997. Prior to this date, monetary-policy decisions in the United Kingdom were made by the government (the Chancellor of the Exchequer) rather than by the Bank of England. When, on May 6, 1997, the Chancellor of the Exchequer, Gordon Brown, announced the granting of instrument independence to the Bank of England, giving it the power to set the overnight interest rate, he made it particularly clear at the press conference that, in his view, the action had been made possible by the increased transparency and accountability of policy under the recently adopted, inflation-targeting regime.

Different Monetary Policy Regimes

There are four basic types of policy regimes that are used in the conduct of monetary policy: (1) exchange-rate targeting, (2) monetary targeting, (3) inflation targeting, and (4) preemptive monetary policy without an explicit nominal anchor. It is well beyond this chapter to discuss the relative merits of these regimes, and so the interested reader is referred to Mishkin (1998b) or our forthcoming book, Bernanke, Laubach, Mishkin, and Posen (1998).

Here we focus on how well these different regimes stack up in terms of central-bank independence and accountability.

Exchange-Rate Targeting

In exchange-rate targeting regimes, whether it is an fixed exchange rate or a crawling peg regime, the target is typically set by the government, with the central bank in charge of setting policy instruments to achieve the target. In this type of setup, the central bank has instrument but not goal independence, which is in line with the basic monetary-policy and democratic principles outlined earlier.

At first glance, exchange-rate targeting makes the central bank quite accountable because it has a clear-cut goal, an exchange-rate target that is easily monitored by the public. However, an exchange-rate target can actually weaken accountability of the central bank, particularly in emerging-market countries, because it eliminates an important signal that can help keep monetary policy from becoming too expansionary.

In industrialized countries, and particularly in the United States, the bond market provides an important signal about the stance of monetary policy. Overly expansionary monetary policy or strong political pressure to engage in overly expansionary monetary policy produces an inflation scare of the type described by Goodfriend (1993), in which long-term bond prices tank and long-term rates spike upwards. In many countries, particularly emerging market countries, the long-term bond market is essentially non-existent. In these countries, the daily fluctuations of the exchange rate can, like the bond market in the United States, provide an early warning signal that monetary policy is overly expansionary. Thus, like the bond market, the foreign-exchange market can constrain policy from being too expansionary. Just as the fear of a visible inflation scare constrains central bankers from pursuing overly expansionary monetary policy and also constrains politicians from putting pressure on the central bank to engage in overly expansionary monetary policy, fear of exchange-rate depreciations can make overly expansionary monetary policy less likely.

An exchange-rate target has the important disadvantage that it removes the signal that the foreign-exchange market provides about the stance of monetary policy on a daily basis. Under an exchange-rate-target regime, central banks often pursue overly expansionary policies that are not discovered until too late, when a successful speculative attack has gotten underway. The problem of lack of accountability of the central bank under an exchange-rate-target regime is particularly acute in emerging-market countries where the balance sheets of the central banks are not as transparent as in developed countries, thus making it harder to ascertain the central bank's policy actions.

One exchange-rate targeting regime that does not suffer from this problem of lack of transparency and accountability is the currency board arrangement like the one adopted in Argentina. The currency board in Argentina clearly is one in which the goals are not set by the central bank but rather by the convertibility law passed in 1990, which fixed the exchange rate of new pesos to the U.S. dollar of one to one. The currency board is an especially strong and transparent commitment to an exchange-rate target because it requires the note-issuing authority, whether the central bank or the government, to stand ready to exchange the domestic currency for foreign currency at the specified fixed exchange rate whenever the public requests it. Although the central bank in theory has instrument independence, in practice it does not because its requirement to exchange the domestic currency for foreign currency at the fixed rate means that it is the demand for domestic relative to the foreign currency it is pegged to (and the interest rates in that foreign country) that determines interest rates, not the central bank. This loss of control of monetary policy is not a problem with the currency board arrangement when independent domestic monetary policy in the past has been irresponsible, and thus it is felt that it is the only way to break a country's inflationary psychology and alter the political process so that it no longer leads to continuing bouts of inflation.

Despite some of the advantages of a currency board in terms of its transparency, accountability, and consistency with democratic principles, it does suffer from some severe problems. Shock, such as the tequila crisis of 1995, can result in the public's pulling their money out of banks and exchanging them for the foreign currency, thus causing a dramatic decline in the money supply and with it a sharp contraction in economic activity, as happened in Argentina in 1995. These and other problems with currency boards are discussed more extensively in Mishkin (1998a).

Monetary Targeting

The second monetary policy regime, monetary targeting, is currently pursued seriously by only two countries: Germany and Switzerland. In both countries, the central banks are both goal and instrument independent. Although legislation has mandated price stability as the primary goal for the Bundesbank, this is not the case for the Swiss National Bank. However, in both countries the central bank, on its own, determines the numerical inflation goal and money growth targets and also has complete control over its monetary policy instruments. Thus by our criteria that central banks should be only instrument but not goal independent, the Bundesbank and the Swiss National Bank appear to be too independent. However, it must be noted that both central banks are well aware that central-bank legislation can be modified at any time and that without the support of the public they will not retain their independence. Indeed, as documented in Mishkin and Posen (1997) and Bernanke, Laubach, Mishkin, and Posen (1998), both banks have demonstrated a very strong commitment to the communication of their monetary policy strategies to the general public, going well beyond what is required of them by law.

One potential advantage of monetary targeting is that information on whether the central bank is achieving its target is known almost immediately: announced figures for monetary aggregates are typically reported periodically with very short time lags—within a couple of weeks. Thus monetary targets can provide almost immediate accountability of the central bank. However, this advantage of monetary targeting depends on a big *if*— that there is a strong and reliable relationship between the goal variable such as inflation and the targeted aggregate. If there is velocity instability so that the link between the goal variable and the monetary aggregate is weak, then the aggregate will no longer provide an adequate signal about the stance of monetary policy. This has not only been a problem in countries like the United States (see Stock and Watson, 1989; Friedman, 1995; Friedman and Kuttner, 1993, 1996; Estrella and Mishkin, 1997), but it also has been a problem in Switzerland and possibly even Germany (Estrella and Mishkin, 1997; Bernanke, Laubach, Mishkin, and Posen, 1998).

The problems with monetary aggregates suggest an important reason why even the most avid monetary targeters, the Bundesbank and the Swiss National Bank, do not rigidly hold to their target ranges but rather allow undershoots and overshoots for extended periods of time. The Bundesbank, for example, misses its target ranges on the order of 50 percent of the time (e.g., see Von Hagen, 1995; Neumann, 1996; Bernanke and Mihov, 1997; Clarida and Gertler, 1997; Mishkin and Posen, 1997; Bernanke, Laubach, Mishkin, and Posen, 1998). The unreliable relationship between monetary aggregates and goal variables also calls into question the ability of monetary targeting to serve as a communications device that both increases the transparency of monetary policy and makes the central bank accountable to the public.

Thus despite its potential advantages, monetary targeting may not enhance central-bank accountability. Indeed, Bernanke, Laubach, Mishkin, and Posen (1998) argue that the monetary targeting strategy of the Bundesbank and the Swiss National Bank has worked only because of the clarity of the explanations emanating from the Bundesbank and the Swiss National Bank and because the policy framework for these central banks includes an explicit long-run inflation goal and regular evaluations of the progress made toward that goal.

Inflation Targeting

Inflation targeting has been adopted by New Zealand, Canada, the United Kingdom, Sweden, Finland, Spain, Australia, and Israel and involves several elements: (1) public announcement of medium-term numerical targets for inflation; (2) an institutional commitment to price stability as the primary, long-run goal of monetary policy and to achievement of the inflation goal; (3) an information inclusive strategy, with a reduced role for intermediate targets such as money growth; (4) increased transparency of the monetary policy strategy through communication with the public and the markets about the plans and objectives of monetary policymakers; and (5) increased accountability of the central bank for attaining its inflation objectives (for detailed analyses of experiences with inflation targeting, see Goodhart and Vinals, 1994; Leiderman and Svensson, 1995; Haldane, 1995; McCallum, 1996; Mishkin and Posen, 1997; Bernanke, Laubach, Mishkin, and Posen, 1998).

In all inflation-targeting regimes to date, the inflation goal is set by the government, in consultation with the central bank. Except in the case of the United Kingdom before May 1997, in all inflation-targeting regimes the central bank sets the monetary policy instruments. Thus inflation-targeting regimes satisfy the criteria from monetary-policy and democratic principles that the central bank should focus on price stability and be instrument but not goal independent.

Inflation-targeting regimes also put great stress on making policy transparent—policy that is clear, simple, and understandable—and on regular communication with the public. Inflation targeting, like exchange-rate targeting, has the key advantage that it is readily understood by the public. Monetary targets are less likely to be easily understood by the public than inflation targets, and as mentioned above, if the relationship between monetary aggregates and the inflation goal variable is subject to large unpredictable shifts (as has occurred in many countries including a long-standing monetary targeter, such as Switzerland), then monetary targets lose their transparency because they are no longer able to accurately signal the stance of monetary policy. However, inflation targeting does have some important disadvantages in terms of accountability: in contrast to exchange rates and monetary aggregates, inflation is not easily controlled by the monetary authorities. Furthermore, because of the long lags of the effects of monetary policy, inflation outcomes are revealed only after a substantial lag. Thus, an inflation target is unable to send immediate signals to both the public, politicians, and markets about the stance of monetary policy.

The central banks engaging in inflation targeting have frequent communications with the government, some mandated by law and some in response to informal inquiries, and their officials take every opportunity to make public speeches on their monetary policy strategy. These channels are also commonly used in countries that have not adopted inflation targeting, Germany, Switzerland and the United States being prominent examples. But inflation targeting central banks have taken public outreach a step further: not only have they engaged in extended public information campaigns, even engaging in the distribution of glossy brochures, but they have engaged in publication of *Inflation Report* type documents (originated by the Bank of England) described earlier.

Another key feature of inflation-targeting regimes is the tendency toward increased accountability of the central bank. Indeed, transparency and communication go hand in hand with increased accountability. The strongest case of accountability of a central bank in an inflation-targeting regime is in New Zealand, where the government has the right to dismiss the Reserve Bank's governor if the inflation targets are breached, even for one quarter. In other inflation-targeting countries, the central bank's accountability is less formalized. Nevertheless, the transparency of policy associated with inflation targeting has tended to make the central bank highly accountable to both the public and the government. Sustained success in the conduct of monetary policy as measured against a preannounced and well-defined inflation target can be instrumental in building public support for a central bank's independence and for its policies. As Bernanke, Laubach, Mishkin, and Posen (1998) find, this building of public support and accountability occurs even in the absence of a rigidly defined and legalistic standard of performance evaluation and punishment.

Inflation targeting stands up well on both the principles of monetary policy outlined earlier, but especially on the democratic principle that policymakers should be accountable to the political process. Under inflation targeting, the central bank is highly accountable to the public and elected officials, who in turn typically have primary responsibility for setting the goals for monetary policy and then monitoring the economic outcomes. At the same time, the inflation-targeting framework ensures that the objectives set by the government are feasible and that they are considered within the appropriate long-run perspective.[1] In terms of independence and accountability, inflation-targeting central banks seem to have it just about right.

Just Do It: Preemptive Monetary Policy Without Explicit Targets

In recent years, the United States has achieved excellent macroeconomic performance without using an explicit nominal anchor such as a target for the exchange rate, a monetary aggregate target, or inflation. Although in the U.S. case no explicit strategy has been articulated, a coherent strategy for the conduct of monetary policy exists nonetheless. This strategy consists of careful monitoring for signs of future inflation, coupled with periodic "preemptive strikes" by monetary policy against the threat of inflation.

This preemptive monetary policy strategy is clearly also a feature of inflation-targeting regimes because monetary policy instruments must be adjusted to take account of the long lags in their effects in order to hit future inflation targets. However, the policy regime in the United States, which does not have a nominal anchor and so might best be described as a "just do it" policy regime, differs from inflation targeting in that it does not officially have a nominal anchor and is much less transparent in its monetary policy strategy.

The "just do it" strategy in the United States is one where the goals of monetary policy are not clearly defined by the government, with potentially conflicting goals a feature of the central bank mandate. Thus the central bank retains a fair degree of goal independence, while it also has complete control over the setting of policy instruments. The substantial goal independence of the Federal Reserve creates a fair amount of tension in a democratic society because it allows an elite group to set the goals of monetary policy. Indeed, recent criticism of the Federal Reserve may have been prompted by the impression that the Federal Reserve, and particularly its chairman, has become too powerful. Although the Fed is currently riding high because of the recent successes of its monetary policy, a political backlash against a highhanded Federal Reserve could have adverse consequences on its independence and ability to successfully conduct monetary policy in the future.

Another important disadvantage of the "just do it" strategy is a lack of transparency. The opacity of its policymaking is hardly conducive to making the Federal Reserve accountable to Congress and the general public because there are no predetermined criteria for judging its performance. In addition, the lack of clarity of the Fed's monetary policy strategy results in a public debate that puts pressure on the Fed to focus more on the short-run creation of jobs and growth, rather than the long-run goal of producing a healthy economy through price stability. The Fed currently has a very positive working relationship with the executive branch of the government. However, in a different economic or political environment, the Fed could be more susceptible to the time-inconsistency problem, whereby it could be pressured into pursuing short-term objectives at the expense of long-term ones.

Thus although the "just do it" regime has worked quite well for the United States in recent years, there is no guarantee that it will continue to do so in the future. In the past, after a successful period of low inflation, the Federal Reserve has reverted to inflationary monetary policy—the 1970s are one example—and without an explicit nominal anchor, this could certainly happen again in the future. In addition, the lack of accountability of the "just do it" framework could cause increased attacks on the independence of the Federal Reserve. We have already discussed how inflation targeting can increase the likelihood that time-inconsistent policies will be pursued and can protect the independence of the central bank. Thus, although many commentators take the attitude that "if it ain't broke, why fix it," as argued in more detail in Bernanke and Mishkin (1997), Mishkin (1998b) and Bernanke, Laubach, Mishkin and Posen (1998) there are strong reasons for a switch in the United States from the "just do it" monetary policy regime to a regime of inflation targeting.

Issues for the European Central Bank

In 1999, we will see the birth of a new central bank for the European Monetary Union. As it is currently designed, how does this new institution, the European Central Bank, compare to other existing central banks with regard to its independence and accountability?

A key feature of the European Central Bank (ECB) is that its statutes cannot be changed by legislation but only by alterations to the Maastricht Treaty. Furthermore, the Maastricht Treaty specifies that the overriding, long-run goal of the ECB is price stability but does not specify exactly what this means. Thus the European Central Bank not only has instrument independence but goal independence as well. Indeed, the ECB will be the most independent central bank in the world since its statues are specified in a treaty and are thus far harder to change than statutes that are embedded in legislation. Moreover, it is not clear to whom the European Central Bank would be accountable. Although the president of the ECB is required to testify once a year to the European Parliament, this requirement may not guarantee sufficient oversight of ECB policies. Since the European Parliament is currently significantly less powerful than the national parliaments of the countries that make up the Monetary Union, scrutiny by that organization would not influence ECB behavior as strongly as would oversight by a more powerful body (such as a consortium of national parliaments) or the individual parliaments themselves.

The European Central Bank will thus an inherently undemocratic organization, and this could be highly problematic in the future. Indeed, recent fights over whether there needs to be additional oversight of the ECB and over who should be the first president suggest that these tensions will be serious ones in the future.

The European Monetary Institute, the precursor to the European Central Bank, is currently debating whether the European Central Bank should adopt one of two possible monetary policy strategies: monetary or inflation targeting. As we have seen, both strategies involve specifying an explicit numerical inflation goal, and there is an important question of who should decide on this goal. Although the Maastricht Treaty gives the ECB the authority to specify the numerical goals, some mechanism for consultation between the ECB and the constituent governments should be developed.

Enabling the national governments to participate in the setting of inflation goals would yield several benefits. First, it would keep the European Central Bank from being viewed as a nondemocratic institution indifferent to the concerns of the public, helping to preserve its independence in the long run. Second, having the governments in the Monetary Union participate in setting inflation goals would help focus the political debate on monetary policy on long-run issues, such as price stability, rather than on the need for short-run monetary stimulus to create jobs. Third, allowing the governments to take part in the setting of inflation goals would tend to sensitize them to the fact that large increases in public-sector wages or unduly expansionary fiscal policies might interfere with these goals.

Because the accountability of the European Central Bank under the Maastricht Treaty seems insufficient, the ECB should be required or voluntarily agree to justify its policy actions though periodic testimony not only in the European Parliament but in the national parliaments of the EMU countries as well. Besides increasing the Bank's accountability, such testimony would demonstrate to the public in each EMU country that the ECB is accountable to them, as well as to EMU as a whole, which should help increase popular support for the Bank's independence. This testimony would also provide the European Central Bank with an additional public forum in which to explain its policy and to emphasize the need for central bankers to adopt a long-run perspective when making policy decisions. In taking up the mantle of the Bundesbank, the ECB should make a concerted effort to communicate regularly and comprehensively with the public as the Bundesbank has done. Production of an *Inflation Report* type document, as well as the ECB's taking every opportunity to explain its policy actions and monetary policy strategy in public forums, should be important elements of this process.

Implications for Transition Countries

This chapter has argued that the institutional design of a central bank most consistent with its role in a democratic society and with basic monetary-policy principles is one in which the central bank is instrument but not goal independent. In addition, central banks should be highly accountable in a democratic society. Making sure that the central bank performs a role in the society that is perceived by the public as consistent with democratic principles is particularly important in transition countries. Because their institutional framework is in some sense starting from scratch, having a central bank that is perceived as undemocratic may undermine support for this institution that may prevent it from carrying out its job properly in the future. Thus, the degree of independence of the Bundesbank, which has an element of goal independence, but especially of the new European Central Bank, which I have argued is far too independent, may be inappropriate for the transition countries.

An evaluation of the four basic monetary policy regimes in terms of central-bank accountability and independence leads to the following conclusions for transition countries. The "just do it" strategy of preemptive monetary policy without explicit targets is highly problematic even for the United States but is clearly inappropriate for transition countries. Given the newness of the independence of central banks in these countries, their central banks do not yet have a high degree of credibilty. Thus the "just do it" strategy is unlikely to be effective because it requires a high degree of credibility to produce good economic outcomes. Furthermore, because it allows too much goal independence for the central bank, the "just do it" strategy is not fully consistent with democratic principles and thus could create tension in a transition country that would ultimately lead to a weakening of support for the central bank.

Because monetary targeting has been associated with goal independence for the central bank and because monetary aggregates may provide poor signals about the stance of monetary policy if the relationship between the aggregate and the inflation goal is weak, monetary targeting may result in a central bank that is too independent and not sufficiently accountable for its actions. The problem of instability of the relationship between monetary aggregates and inflation is likely to be severe in transition countries because the institutional changes they are undergoing is substantial. Thus, monetary targeting is unlikely to be an effective strategy for transition countries and may not lead to sufficient accountability of the central bank.

Exchange-rate targeting, which has been a basic monetary policy strategy for many transition countries, can be consistent with both monetary policy and democratic principles, but only if the commitment mechanism is both strong and transparent. However, exchange-rate targets can weaken the accountability of the central bank because it removes the signal that the foreign-exchange market provides about the stance of monetary policy on a daily basis. Also, for the reasons described in Mishkin (1998a), exchange-rate targeting can be dangerous for emerging market and transition countries because it can promote financial fragility and lead to foreign-exchange crises that can lead to full-fledged financial crises with disastrous consequences for the economy.

Inflation targeting, with instrument but not goal independence and its high accountability, meets the criteria set by both democratic and monetary-policy principles. Indeed inflation-targeting regimes are likely to strengthen the independence of the central bank because it provides an appropriate role for a central bank in a democratic society. Inflation targeting is not without its problems, however. In contrast to exchange-rate and monetary targeting, inflation is not easily controlled by the monetary authorities. This can be a particularly severe problem for a transition country that is trying to bring down inflation from a previously high level and so is more likely to experience large inflation forecast errors. In addition, inflation targets may not provide a sufficient nominal anchor until a central bank in a transition country has established credibility by showing some ability to reduce inflation to reasonable levels. These problems suggest that hard targets from inflation might be worth phasing in only after there has been some successful disinflation. This is exactly the strategy followed by Chile (see Morande and Schmidt-Hebbel, 1997), which adopted a weak form of inflation targeting in September 1990. Initially, inflation targets were announced and interpreted as official inflation projections, rather than as hard targets. However, over time as inflation fell, this procedure was changed, and inflation targets came to be viewed by the central bank and the markets as hard targets. Waiting to harden targets until after some success has already been achieved on the inflation front is also consistent with what inflation-targeting industrialized countries have done: in every case, inflation targeting was not implemented until after substantial disinflation has previously been achieved (see Mishkin and Posen, 1997; Bernanke, Laubach, Mishkin, and Posen, 1998). The discussion above therefore suggests that transition countries should seriously consider inflation targeting as a monetary strategy but may need to choose an alternative monetary policy strategy initially, such as exchange-rate targeting, to obtain the requisite amount of credibility to make inflation targeting a success.

Acknowledgments

Any views expressed in this chapter are those of the author only and not those of Columbia University or the National Bureau of Economic Research.

Note

1. Nominal GDP targeting has many features of inflation targeting and is closely related to it. It is not discussed in this chapter because no country has to date adopted this monetary policy framework. For a discussion of nominal GDP targeting, see Taylor (1985), Hall and Mankiw (1994), Mishkin (1998b), and Bernanke, Laubach, Mishkin, and Posen (1998).

References

Alesina, Alberto, and Lawrence H. Summers. (1993). "Central Bank Independence and Macroeconomic Performance: Some Comparative Evidence." *Journal of Money, Credit, and Banking* 25(2) (May): 151–162.
Andersen, Palle, and David Gruen. (1995). "Macroeconomic Policies and Growth." In Palle Andersen, Jacqueline Dwyer, and David Gruen (eds.), *Productivity and Growth* (pp. 279–319). Sydney: Reserve Bank of Australia.
Barro, Robert J., and David Gordon. (1983). "A Positive Theory of Monetary Policy in a Natural Rate Model." *Journal of Political Economy* 91(4) (August): 589–610.
Bernanke, Ben S., Thomas Laubach, Frederic S. Mishkin, and Adam S. Posen. (1998). *Inflation Targeting: Lessons from the International Experience.* Princeton, NJ: Princeton University Press.
Bernanke, Ben S., and Ilian Mihov. (1997). "What Does the Bundesbank Target?" *European Economic Review* 41(6) (June): 1025–1053.

Briault, Clive. (1995). "The Costs of Inflation." *Bank of England Quarterly Bulletin* 35 (February): 33–45.

Calvo, Guillermo. (1978). "On the Time Consistency of Optimal Policy in the Monetary Economy." *Econometrica* 46(6) (November): 1411–1128.

Clarida, Richard, and Mark Gertler. (1997). "How the Bundesbank Conducts Monetary Policy." In Christina D. Romer and David H. Romer (eds.), *Reducing Inflation: Motivation and Strategy* (pp. 363–406). Chicago: University of Chicago Press.

Cukierman, Alex. (1992). *Central Bank Strategy, Credibility, and Independence: Theory and Evidence*. Cambridge, MA: MIT Press.

Debelle, Guy, and Stanley Fischer. (1994). "How Independent Should a Central Bank Be?" In Jeffrey C. Fuhrer (ed.), *Goals, Guidelines, and Constraints Facing Monetary Policymakers* (pp. 195–221). Federal Reserve Bank of Boston Conference Series 38.

English, William B. (1996). "Inflation and Financial Sector Size." Board of Governors of the Federal Reserve System Finance and Economics Discussion Series, No. 96-16, April.

Estrella, Arturo, and Frederic S. Mishkin. (1997). "Is There a Role for Monetary Aggregates in the Conduct of Monetary Policy?" *Journal of Monetary Economics* 40(2) (October): 279–304.

Feldstein, Martin. (1997). "The Costs and Benefits of Going from Low Inflation to Price Stability." In Christina D. Romer and David H. Romer (eds.), *Reducing Inflation: Motivation and Strategy* (pp. 123–156). Chicago: University of Chicago Press.

Fischer, Stanley. (1994). "Modern Central Banking." In Forrest Capie, Charles A.E. Goodhart, Stanley Fischer, and Norbert Schnadt (eds.), *The Future of Central Banking: The Tercentenary Symposium of the Bank of England* (pp. 262–308). Cambridge: Cambridge University Press.

Friedman, Benjamin M. (1995). "The Rise and Fall of the Money Growth Targets as Guidelines for U.S. Monetary Policy." Paper prepared for the Bank of Japan Seventh International Conference. Preliminary draft.

Friedman, Benjamin M., and Kenneth N. Kuttner. (1993). "Another Look at the Evidence on Money-Income Causality." *Journal of Econometrics* 57: 189–203.

Friedman, Benjamin M., and Kenneth N. Kuttner. (1996). "A Price Target for U.S. Monetary Policy? Lessons from the Experience with Money Growth Targets." *Brookings Papers on Economic Activity*, no. 1: 77–125.

Goodfriend, Marvin. (1993). "Interest Rate Policy and the Inflation Scare Problem: 1979–1992." *Federal Reserve Bank of Richmond Economic Quarterly* 79(1) (Winter): 1–24.

Goodhart, Charles A.E., and José Viñals. (1994). "Strategy and Tactics of Monetary Policy: Examples from Europe and the Antipodes." In Jeffrey C. Fuhrer (ed.), *Goals, Guidelines, and Constraints Facing Monetary Policymakers* (pp. 139–187). Federal Reserve Bank of Boston Conference Series 38.

Haldane, Andrew G. (ed.). (1995). *Targeting Inflation*. London: Bank of England.

Hall, Robert E., and N. Gregory Mankiw. (1994). "Nominal Income Targeting." In N. Gregory Mankiw (ed.), *Monetary Policy* (pp. 71–94). Chicago: University of Chicago Press.

Kydland, Finn, and Edward Prescott. (1977). "Rules Rather Than Discretion: The Inconsistency of Optimal Plans." *Journal of Political Economy* 85(3): 473–492.

Leiderman, Leonardo, and Lars E.O. Svensson. (1995). *Inflation Targeting*. London: Centre for Economic Policy Research.

McCallum, Bennett T. (1995). "Two Fallacies Concerning Central-Bank Independence." *American Economic Review* 85(2) (May): 207–211.

McCallum, Bennett T. (1996). "Inflation Targeting in Canada, New Zealand, Sweden, the United Kingdom, and in General." NBER Working Paper No. 5579, May.

Mishkin, Frederic S. (1998a). "Exchange-Rate Pegging for Emerging Market Countries?" *International Finance*.

Mishkin, Frederic S. (1998b). "International Experiences with Different Monetary Policy Regimes." Mimeo prepared for the Sveriges Riksbank-IIES Conference on Monetary Policy Rules, Stockholm, Sweden, June 12–13.

Mishkin, Frederic S., and Adam S. Posen. (1997). "Inflation Targeting: Lessons from Four Countries." Federal Reserve Bank of New York *Economic Policy Review* 3 (August): 9–110.

Morande, Felipe, and Klaus Schmidt-Hebbel. (1997). "Inflation Targets and Indexation in Chile." Unpublished paper, Central Bank of Chile, August.

Neumann, Manfred. (1996). "Monetary Targeting in Germany." Paper prepared for the Bank of Japan Seventh International Conference.

Posen, Adam S. (1995). "Declarations Are Not Enough: Financial Sector Sources of Central Bank Independence." In Ben S. Bernanke and Julio J. Rotemberg (eds.), *NBER Macroeconomics Annual, 1995* (pp. 253–74). Cambridge, MA: MIT Press.

Rogoff, Kenneth. (1985). "The Optimal Degree of Commitment to an Intermediate Target." *Quarterly Journal of Economics* 100(4) (November): 1169–1189.

Sargent, Thomas, and Neil Wallace. (1981). "Some Unpleasant Monetarist Arithmetic." *Federal Reserve Bank of Minneapolis Quarterly Review* (Fall): 1–17.

Stock, James H., and Mark W. Watson. (1989). "Interpreting the Evidence on Money-Income Causality." *Journal of Econometrics* 40: 161–182.

Taylor, John B. (1985). "What Would Nominal GNP Targeting Do to the Business Cycle?" *Carnegie-Rochester Conference Series on Public Policy* 22: 61–84.

Von Hagen, Jürgen. (1995). "Inflation and Monetary Targeting in Germany." In Leonardo Leiderman and Lars E.O. Svensson (eds.), *Inflation Targets* (pp. 107–121). London: Centre for Economic Policy Research.

Woodford, Michael. (1994). "Monetary Policy and Price Level Determinacy in a Cash-in-Advance Economy." *Economic Theory* 4: 345–380.

Woodford, Michael. (1995). "Price Level Determinacy with Control of a Monetary Aggregate." *Carnegie-Rochester Conference Series on Public Policy*.

4 CENTRAL-BANK INDEPENDENCE AND POLITICAL BUSINESS CYCLES
A Critical Reexamination

Allan Drazen

University of Maryland and National Business of Economic Research

Introduction

The political business cycle, by which one means fluctuations in economic activity that correspond to the electoral cycle, can be observed in many countries. The classic study of the political business cycle is Tufte (1978), in which he presented basic evidence of cyclical movements in policy instruments and in measures of economic activity that correlate with the political cycle and peak around election time. (We discuss below more formal econometric evidence.) For example, for the United States from 1948 to 1976, he argues that, with the exception of the Eisenhower years in the 1950s, political business cycles have consisted of a two-year cycle in "real disposable income, with accelerations in even-numbered years and decelerations in odd-numbered years," as well as four-year cycle "in the unemployment rate, with downturns in unemployment in the months before a presidential election and upturns in the unemployment rate usually beginning from twelve to eighteen months after the election" (Tufte, 1978, p. 27) He similarly argues there is clear evidence of a political cycle in outcomes in other democratic countries as well, in that "short-run accelerations in real disposable income per capita were more likely to occur in election years than in years without elections" (p. 11) in a sample of twenty-seven countries.

Formal models of political business cycles generally fall into one of two classes—*opportunistic* and *partisan*. Opportunistic models stress the use of economic policy by incumbents who attempt to manipulate economic outcomes to improve their chances of reelection. Nordhaus (1975) presented one of the first formal models of a political business cycle due to the behavior of opportunistic policymakers who stimulate the economy before the election to reduce unemployment, with the inflationary cost of such a policy coming only after.[1] Partisan models stress the role of ideological differences in desired macroeconomic outcomes as the driving force of the political business cycles. In the earliest partisan model of Hibbs (1977), changes in the party in power will induce unemployment and inflation fluctuations. For example, the replacement of a left-wing party, which favors low unemployment and high inflation, by a right-wing party with the opposite preferences will imply a cycle in these two variables. In partisan models in which only unanticipated monetary policy has an effect, as in Alesina (1987), uncertainty about who will hold power drives a cycle in the early part of an administration's term. For example, a victory by the left-wing party that was not fully anticipated will lead to inflation being higher than was anticipated in the early part of their term, implying below-average unemployment.

These models sharply differ both in their modeling of the motivations of policymakers and in their implications for observed fluctuations. Much research has been done focusing on these differences in the attempt to determine which of the approaches best describes the political business cycle. These differences, and the stress that proponents of different models place on them, tend to divert attention away from their similarities. First, all three models mentioned above rely on a Phillips curve as the vehicle by which the economy is manipulated. Inflation, particularly when it is unanticipated, induces movements in unemployment, as the economy moves up or down the Phillips curve. Hence, active monetary policy is the key driving force. Second, monetary policy is basically chosen by politicians according to their desires—an incumbent facing a reelection in the opportunistic models or a newly elected administration with specific macroeconomic goals in the partisan models. The monetary authority is subservient to the politicians, and in no sense does it make independent monetary decisions.

These two characteristics—activist monetary policy as the driving force and control of monetary policy by politicians—do not very well describe either political business cycles or central bank behavior, as we detail below.

The purpose of this chapter is to reexamine models of the political business cycle in terms of the role of monetary policy and the central bank to argue for a different view of central bank behavior, a view that is both more logically appealing and more consistent with the data. The plan of the chapter is as follows. We review the Nordhaus model of opportunistic political cycles and then models of partisan political cycles, showing that both types of models share some common problems. On the basis of these problems, in we suggest a revised view of monetary policy in models of the political business cycle. We review econometric studies, arguing that they support this revised view, which in fact can clarify what appeared previously to be contradictory results. Finally, a summary and conclusions are presented.

The Nordhaus Model of the Political Cycle[2]

Nordhaus (1975) presented one of the first formal models of the political business cycle in which opportunistic policymakers stimulate the economy before the election to reduce unemployment, with the inflationary cost of such a policy coming only after. By *opportunistic* one means that the policymaker himself has no preferences over inflation and unemployment. The structure of the economy is summarized by four equations: a standard loss function, whereby voters have a preference for both low unemployment and low inflation; a vote function, relating votes the incumbent receives as a function of past losses; a downward-sloping Phillips curve, yielding a tradeoff between unemployment and unexpected inflation; and adaptive expectations, meaning slow adjustment of inflation expectations to actual inflation. The objective of the policymaker is to maximize his probability of reelection, where voting behavior is retrospective in that it depends on economic performance under the incumbent in the past. We now make these points more specific.

The loss function representing voter dissatisfaction represents their assessment of economic performance—namely,

$$L_t = U_t + \theta \frac{(\pi_t - \pi^*)^2}{2},$$ (4.1)

where p^* is the electorate's target rate of inflation and q is the relative weight the electorate puts on inflation deviations relative to unemployment.

A retrospective voting function for an election at the end of period t is of the form

$$V_t = \sum_{s=0}^{3} \gamma^s L_{t-s} + \eta_t, \qquad\qquad (4.2)$$

where the exogenous length of time between elections is four periods, $0 < g < 1$ is the discount rate on past incumbent performance, and ht is a mean-zero stochastic term relating economic performance to electoral outcomes. The electoral mechanism is not made more specific. The standard opportunistic model assumes that g is large, in the sense that recent economic performance counts far more heavily in influencing voter choices than economic performance in the more distant past. The stochastic element is added to allow for the possibility of an incumbent losing the election. Otherwise, if policymakers cared only about staying in office, in the Nordhaus model they could choose policies such that reelection would be ensured.

The structure of the economy is summarized by a nonstochastic, expectations-adjusted Phillips curve. The divergence of the unemployment rate Ut in any period from the natural rate of unemployment (zero, by our measurement convention) depends on the difference between the actual rate of inflation and the economywide expected rate of inflation pe,t:

$$U_t = -(\pi_t - \pi_t^e). \qquad\qquad (4.3)$$

We further assume that the monetary authority has perfect control over the rate of inflation, so that pt can be taken as its control variable.

The model is closed by specifying the formation of inflation expectations. Crucial to the main results of the Nordhaus model is some adaptive expectations. We assume a fairly simple formulation that could be derived from the general adaptive expectations model—namely, the expected rate of inflation pe,t is (where 1 is a coefficient between 0 and 1 representing the speed with which expectations adapt to past inflation)

$$\pi_t^e = (1 - \lambda)\pi_{t-1} + \lambda \pi_{t-2}. \qquad\qquad (4.4)$$

What is crucial in the formation of expectations is that pe,t does not depend on the expectation of future policies, so that expectations are not rational. It is this characteristic (combined with the absence of any other connections between periods) that gives the incumbent policymaker an exploitable tradeoff between inflation and unemployment in the attempt to affect election outcomes. Combining the above four equations, the expected vote total as a function of current and past inflation policy is given by

$$EV_t = \frac{\theta}{2}\pi_t^2 - \pi_t + (1-\lambda)\pi_{t-1} + \lambda\pi_{t-2}$$
$$+ \gamma\left(\frac{\theta}{2}\pi_{t-1}^2 - \pi_{t-1} + (1-\lambda)\pi_{t-2} + \lambda\pi_{t-3}\right),$$
$$+ \gamma^2\left(\frac{\theta}{2}\pi_{t-2}^2 - \pi_{t-2} + (1-\lambda)\pi_{t-3} + \lambda\pi_{t-4}\right)$$
$$+ \gamma^3\left(\frac{\theta}{2}\pi_{t-3}^2 - \pi_{t-3} + (1-\lambda)\pi_{t-4} + \lambda\pi_{t-5}\right). \tag{4.5}$$

Voter behavior in the Nordhaus model is backward looking in two dimensions: voting depends on past incumbent performance, and inflation expectations depend on past inflation. The incumbent policymaker elected at $t - 3$ chooses inflation rates $pt - 3, pt - 2, pt - 1$, and pt to maximize his expected vote (4.5) in the next election. The implied path of inflation has p being lowest in the two periods just after an election and rising thereafter to reach a peak in the election year, at which point unemployment hits a trough. That is, immediately preceding the election, an opportunistic incumbent stimulates the economy via expansionary monetary policy, unemployment falling due to high unanticipated inflation. The levels of inflation and unemployment are those that maximize voter satisfaction in the election period. Immediately after the election, the government reverses course, engineering a recession via contractionary monetary policy to bring down inflationary expectations. The incumbent keeps economic activity low to keep expected inflation low until the period immediately before the next election, so that a given rate of economic expansion (induced by a monetary surprise) can be obtained at a relatively low rate of inflation. In the next election cycle, the same behavior is repeated. The principal criticism of the Nordhaus model has been its reliance on irrational behavior on the part of voters. Voters are naive, both in the way they form expectations of inflation and in the way they assess government performance, being "fooled" into voting for an opportunistic, manipulative policymaker. Moreover, central banks don't get higher marks for their wisdom in the model, as the Nordhaus economy exhibits repeated inflation cycles. If the world is one of politically opportunistic governments, something more subtle must be going on.

Partisan Political Cycles

An alternative approach is to stress the role of ideology as the driving force in political business cycles. The basic *partisan* model is due to Hibbs (1977), who started from the observation that left-wing and right-wing parties have different positions on economic issues. In terms of the business cycle, they have different preferences over inflation and unemployment, so that the relative dislike of inflation versus unemployment is party specific, as are the inflation and unemployment targets themselves. These differences reflect the fact that left- and right-wing parties in a given country represent constituencies with different views about the costs of inflation and unemployment. This difference in the interests of their constituencies lead the parties to prefer different policies. To represent this difference in interests, one replaces the social loss function (4.1) by a partisan loss function:

$$L_t^j = \frac{(U_t - U^{*j})}{2} + \theta^j \frac{(\pi_t - \pi^{*j})^2}{2}, \tag{4.6}$$

for party j, where π^{*j} is party j's target rate of inflation, U^{*j} is party j's target unemployment rate, and θ^j is the relative weight put on inflation deviations relative to unemployment deviations by party j. There are two parties—a left-wing party, denoted L, and a right-wing party, denoted R—that are characterized by the following possible differences in their objectives. First, the Ls may have a lower unemployment target than the Rs. Second, the Ls may assign a larger cost to deviations of unemployment from their target level than to deviations of inflation from the target. Finally, the Ls may have a higher inflation target than do the Rs, *independent* of the effects on unemployment via the Phillips curve, which could reflect other effects of inflation viewed differently by the two parties. To summarize the difference between the parties:

$$U^{*L} \ le \ U^{*R}$$
$$\theta^L \ le \ \theta^R$$
$$\pi^{*L} \ ge \ \pi^{*R}. \tag{4.7}$$

To obtain the partisan cycles, at least one of these must hold with strict inequality.

The Hibbs model shares two key characteristics with the Nordhaus model: fluctuations in economic activity induced by these partisan differences are generated by movements along an exploitable Phillips curve, and expectations are not rational. Thus, the left-wing party will pursue a more expansionary monetary policy throughout its term, especially if expectations adjust slowly. The economic working of the model could be represented in terms of the expectations-adjusted Phillips curve (4.3) combined with adaptive expectations as in (4.4). One could then derive the unemployment and inflation rates that obtain over the whole term of office when each party is in power, with the difference in policies reflecting the difference in goals in (4.7). Hence, there will be a cycle in unemployment and inflation mirroring the cycle of office-holding across the two parties, with unemployment being high and inflation low whenever party R is in office, and vice versa whenever L is in office.

The main criticisms of the Hibbs model are the same as those applied to the Nordhaus model: it relies on mistaken expectations of what policy will be to get real effects, and it assigns the key role to monetary policy that is politically dictated, though here for ideological rather than opportunistic reasons. An alternative approach to modeling partisan cycles is to retain monetary policy as the driving force, but to assume rational inflation expectations, combined with a Phillips curve where only unanticipated inflation affects output. This is the approach of Alesina (1987), who considers a partisan model with rational expectations. The driving force for fluctuations in inflation and unemployment is not partisan differences per se, but these differences combined with uncertainty about election outcomes.

The Alesina model can be represented by a similar three-equation model to that used by Nordhaus, retaining the expectations-augmented Phillips curve (4.3) but changing the motivation of policymakers and the assumptions about formation of inflation expectations. Alesina divides a term of office into two periods and assumes that there is an election every other period—say, at $t, t+2, t+4$, and so on—to represent the difference between economic effects in the early part and the latter part of the term of office. It is assumed that a party cares only about its own term of office, so that the objective function of party j at time t may then be represented by an extended version of (4.6)—namely,

$$\Lambda_t^j = \frac{(U_t - U^{*j})}{2} + \theta^j \frac{(\pi_t - \pi^{*j})^2}{2} + \beta\left[\frac{(U_{t+1} - U^{*j})^2}{2} + \theta^j \frac{(\pi_{t+1} - \pi^{*j})^2}{2}\right]$$

$$(4.8)$$

for party j, where π^{*j}, U^{*j}, and θ^j are as in (4.7).

The other crucial change, relative to both the Nordhaus and Hibbs models, is that Alesina replaces the assumption of adaptive expectations by rational expectations, so instead of (4.4), expected inflation $\pi e, t$ is given by

$$\pi_t^e = \pi_t. \qquad (4.9)$$

In determining the evolution of inflation and unemployment during a term of office—say, t and $t+1$—the key variable in the model is expected inflation in those periods, this expectation formed before the election in period t. Conditional on expected inflation in each half-term, the party in power chooses its optimal policy (denoted $\pi L, t$ and $\pi R, t$ for the left-wing and right-wing parties, respectively) by maximizing (4.8) subject to (4.3), retaining the assumption from earlier models that the government has perfect control over inflation. In turn, expectations of inflation depend on the expectation of who will win the upcoming election. If outcomes were fully known, there would be *no* cycle. The existence of a cycle depends on uncertainty about election outcomes. Alesina analyzes the implications of a probability q^L that the left-wing party wins the election at t, where q^L is taken as exogenous, restricted only to be between zero and one. Before the election at t, expected inflation is a weighted sum of the policies of the two parties, with q^L and $1 - q^L$ as the weights.

One can then calculate optimal policy for each party at t on the basis of uncertain election outcomes and may easily show that for any $0 < q^L < 1$, for the first half of a term, one obtains

$$\pi_t^L > \pi_t^e > \pi_t^R, \tag{4.10}$$

as long as at least one of the equalities in (4.7) is strict. Hence, at the beginning of a left-wing administration, there will be a boom, with high inflation and with unemployment below the natural rate, while at the beginning of a right-wing administration, there will be a recession, characterized by low inflation and by unemployment above the natural rate. In the second part of the term, there will be no partisan differences in real economic activity. With expected inflation equal to actual inflation, unemployment will be equal to the natural rate no matter which party is in power. Note that a right-wing administration will have a recession in the first part of its term not because it likes recession but because it prefers a *less* expansionary policy than does a left-wing administration.

Though the Alesina model is be quite different than the earlier models in some respects, it shares the characteristic that cycles are driven by monetary policy dictated to the central bank by politicians. In fact, it also shares the characteristic of a crucial irrationality in regard to inflation, even though expectations are literally rational. This characteristic reflects the underlying microeconomic structure such that unanticipated monetary policy can have a real effect. The question of microfoundations is often raised about models in which policymakers exploit an expectations-augmented Phillips curve, but the importance of electoral effects gives it added importance here. A standard argument, used also by Alesina, is that nominal wage contracts are signed at discrete intervals (due perhaps to costs of negotiating such contracts). Nominal wage increases reflect rationally anticipated inflation at the time the contract is signed, so that surprise inflation between contract dates can have real effects even when agents are rational.[3] Hours of work are demand determined, so that the fall in the real wage induced by surprise inflation implies that workers are supplying a different level of labor than they would under full information, ostensible leading to lower utility.

The basic problem is that, on the one hand, elections are an important source of fluctuations due to their outcomes being less than fully anticipated, but, on the other, the election date is fully known. The magnitude of the changes in inflation and unemployment the model is meant to explain are sufficiently large that there should be a large utility payoff to eliminating the uncertainty that leads to these fluctuations. But that is easy to do. To the extent there is a significant effect on unemployment, old contracts should be timed to expire and new contract signing postponed until just after an election, so that they can reflect the election results.[4] (If a contract had to be signed before an election whose outcome were highly uncertain and hence likely to have large real effects, a simple state-contingent contract would similarly eliminate unemployment fluctuations.) Hence, the main driving force of the model would seem to depend on less than rational behavior of workers and unions, not in the formation of their expectations per se but in their labor-supply behavior. A simple change in the timing of contract behavior would eliminate the political cycle.

To summarize, the three models that we have considered in this section and the previous section have quite different implications for the dynamics of the political business cycle. A significant amount of research, especially empirical, has concentrated on these differences. In contrast to much of the literature, I have stressed their shared characteristics, specifically that all three models suffer to a greater or a lesser extent from some common problems. These problems suggest the need for an alternative interpretation of the working of the political business cycle. In the next section we summarize the problems with these models and suggest a different approach.

A Revised View of Monetary Policy in Models of the Political Business Cycle

Both of these characteristics common to most models of political cycles—activist monetary policy as the driving force and control of monetary policy by politicians—do not really match much of what we now about political cycles and about the setting of monetary policies in the economies in which they occur. There are three key problems. First, there is the problem of *rationality*. To the extent that political cycles are recurrent, the central role played by monetary surprises is, to say the least, surprising. This criticism of less than fully rational behavior applies not only to the Nordhaus model of monetary surprises but also, as I will argue, to Alesina's model.

Second, there is the emphasis on *monetary versus fiscal policy*. The central role assigned to monetary policy as the driving force seems misplaced for at least two reasons. First, as numerous authors have argued, our current views on the relation of inflation to economic activity make it doubtful that the effects are via moving along the Phillips curve to reduce unemployment. Second, a key factor in preelectoral cycles appears to be fiscal rather than monetary policy. Authors such as Tufte (1978) and Keech and Pak (1989) find significant preelectoral cycles in transfers in the United States, with the 1972 election getting special attention from Tufte. Two weeks prior to the election there was a 20 percent increase in social security benefits, announced in a letter from President Nixon to 24,760,000 social security recipients.[5] Ben-Porath (1975) finds similar evidence for Israel for the period 1952 to 1973. Fluctuations in fiscal policy will have real effects, whether anticipated or not.

The third problem with most models of the political business cycle is their reliance on a lack of *central bank independence*. Countries in which political cycles are observed are often countries seen as having highly independent central banks. Hence, the view of monetary policy as being dictated by politicians doesn't sound right. Note that this criticism applies equally to the opportunistic and the partisan models. In short, if one accepts the basic premises of many models of the political business cycle, one has to throw out the idea of central bank independence.

I therefore want to suggest a different view of the role of monetary policy and the central bank in models of the political business cycle. This view is based on a more realistic view of the role of the central bank relative to the rest of government. The central bank is independent of the executive and the legislature but must take political pressures into account when formulating policy. This implies the need for the central bank at times to accommodate partially the desires of politicians, especially immediately before and after elections. Hence, though politicians do not control the central bank, monetary policy may partially reflect the desires of politicians at various points.

With regard to the political cycle, following Wooley (1984) and Beck (1987), I argue that monetary policy may be passive rather than active before elections, accommodating fiscal stimuli that opportunistic policymakers may employ to affect election outcomes. As these fiscal stimuli may be targeted to particular groups of voters, their effects may not show up strongly in aggregate economic variables, though they will influence votes. The stress on fiscal policy, especially as targeted to specific groups, also explains why fully anticipated manipulations have a real effect. Finally, this approach may help to make sense of empirical findings previously interpreted as contradictory.

A Closer Look at the Evidence

We now turn to an examination of existing empirical studies and suggest how the alternative view set out in the previous section may be used to interpret the results of these studies. Though empirical studies are often seen as yielding conflicting results, there are in fact a number of clear results, once the empirical findings are interpreted carefully. Though the bulk of studies find relatively little support for the literal Nordhaus model, there appears to be significant evidence of opportunistic pre-electoral manipulation in careful econometric studies. More specifically, I argue as follows: first, there is little evidence on output or unemployment; second, there is, however, evidence of a cycle for inflation and monetary policy that is consistent with the both the opportunistic and the partisan models; and, third, there is extremely strong evidence on fiscal policy. I suggest that this evidence suggests a clear interpretation—namely, one of opportunism and some partisanship in which the government manipulates fiscal policy but doesn't control the central bank. The central bank, anxious to avoid criticism by the government before elections or right after with the election of a new government, accommodates fiscal shocks so that unemployment isn't too strongly affected by the government's choice of policy, but before an election, votes are affected.

Economic Activity

The simplest negative evidence on the basic Nordhaus model comes from running an autoregression of a measure of economic activity on itself, a small set of economic variables, and a dummy variable that is 1 in the election quarter and in the $N-1$ quarters before the election, and 0 otherwise, where N may take on values from four to eight quarters. Alesina, Cohen, and Roubini (1992) perform this type of test on a sample of OECD countries over the period 1960 to 1987 for different measures of economic activity, considering both pooled (with country fixed effects) and individual country regressions. Their evidence is quite negative. They find no significant effects in the pooled regression, no matter what lag length is used for the dummy. In individual country regressions using GNP growth as the economic activity measure, they find significant effects of the correct sign for only four of the OECD economies they considered—Germany, Japan, New Zealand, and the United Kingdom.

The main criticism of this work is on the specification of the timing of political effects—specifically, the discontinuous nature of the dummy, which drops from 1 to 0 after $N - 1$ quarters. This argument has been put forward by Grier (1989) and Williams (1990), who argue that there is significant uncertainty about the shape of an economy's response to preelectoral economic stimulation, with no reason to expect a discontinuous falloff immediately after the election. In a similar vector autoregression for the United States to that used by Alesina, Cohen, and Roubini (1992), but with the political dummy being a counter rising from 1 to 16 over the president's term, Williams finds that the three-month Treasury bill rate is in part explained by a political cycle, with no significant effect for other macroeconomic outcomes, except perhaps a marginally significant effect for real GNP. Though some econometric studies, such as Haynes and Stone (1987), find evidence for a political business cycle in macroeconomic outcomes, the general consensus is that the opportunistic political business cycle model receives little support in the pre-electoral behavior of GNP or unemployment.

The evidence for partisan effects after an election is somewhat stronger, though not uncontroversial. Consider, for example, the Alesina model, which predicts an expansion at the beginning of a left-wing administration, a recession at the beginning of a right-wing administration, the deviation of unemployment from the natural rate being greater the greater is the electoral surprise, with no unemployment effect in the latter part of either party's term. Alesina's (1988) finds nonparametric evidence for the United States, while Alesina and Roubini (1992), in more formal econometric tests, find supportive evidence for a sample of OECD countries over the period 1960 to 1987.

In contrast, Sheffrin (1989), for example, finds the evidence for both the United States and other countries to be weak. For example, he argues that economic fluctuations following Republican presidential victories in the United States are generally inconsistent with the rational partisan theory, postelectoral recessions often coming as a surprise. The weakness of the results, he suggests, reflects at least two problems. First, in the United States, partisan differences are simply not that strong. Second, Sheffrin strongly argues that the rational partisan model is limited by the assumption that only unanticipated money matters. Hibbs (1992) and Gärtner (1994) question the possibility of econometrically distinguishing the different versions of the partisan model,[6] while other researchers have questioned whether it is other factors that account for empirically observed partisan differences.[7]

Inflation and Monetary Policy

Evidence consistent with the Nordhaus model *can* be found in the behavior of inflation, where the prediction of the model is that after an election inflation will begin to increase (see, for example, Alesina, Cohen, and Roubini, 1992; Haynes and Stone, 1987). Overall, there is evidence in support of a political cycle in inflation, with the inflation rate exhibiting a postelectoral jump in many countries. Unfortunately, these results appear to suggest a contradiction between the inflation and output results in terms of the predictions of the Nordhaus model.

To better understand what is going on, one must look at the results for policy instruments. Let's begin with monetary policy. Alesina, Cohen, and Roubini (1992) find a significant political effect for the yearly M1 growth rates in pooled cross-section, time-series regressions over the period 1960 to 1987, with money growth being for the year to year and a half before elections. They find that the evidence of a political monetary cycle is weak for the United States. In contrast, Grier (1989) and Williams (1990) both find significant support for an office-motivated model of monetary policy in the United States over samples covering earlier time periods (see note 8 for an explanation of this difference in results).

How should one interpret the results of a significant cycle in money growth? What light, if any, might be shed on the apparent contradiction, at least as far as the Nordhaus model is concerned, between the results on a postelectoral inflation cycle but the absence of preelectoral output effects? The view advanced in the previous section suggests an interpretation. The key is in distinguishing between active monetary policy and money growth per se, especially in view of the apparent preelectoral manipulation of fiscal instruments already discussed, to be documented below. The distinction between active and passive monetary policy follows Beck's (1987) discussion of Grier's results. Beck argued that there is a political cycle in the money supply in the United States but no cycle in monetary instruments, such as reserves or the Federal Fund rate. The reason is that the Federal Reserve accommodates fiscal policy in an election year, so that there is a passive political monetary cycle caused by a political cycle in fiscal instruments, but the Fed does not actively induce a political cycle. Beck argues that this accommodation is why the monetary cycle that both he and Grier find peaks in the election quarter itself, when the monetary expansion shouldn't affect outcomes. Beck regresses M1 on its on lags and on fiscal indicators to confirm this argument.

Why does the Fed accommodate shock during an election year? The argument, put forward by several authors, is that the Fed is not so much interested in pushing the reelection of the incumbent as in simply "laying low" during the election so as not to be subsequently criticized. Wooley (1984), for example, argues that during election years highly visible monetary policy actions are much more likely to be expansionary than contractionary. In short, monetary aggregates before an election (and inflation after the election) exhibits behavior consistent with an opportunistic cycle, but only because monetary policy is accommodating fiscal policy, so that the Fed is not criticized during the election period.

Fiscal Policy

What then is the evidence on an electoral cycle in fiscal policy? In fact, the strongest econometric evidence by far supporting an opportunistic political business cycle is in the behavior of fiscal policy, both in the postwar United States, as well as in number of OECD economies. Several papers find evidence of a political budget cycle. Tufte (1978), as already discussed, documents a number of clear incidents of preelectoral opportunistic manipulation of fiscal transfers, both social security payments, and veterans benefits. Keech and Pak (1989) found an electoral cycle for veterans' benefits in the United States between 1961 and 1978 but argue that it has subsequently disappeared.[8] Alesina, Cohen, and Roubini (1992), as well as Alesina and Roubini (1992), similarly find evidence for an opportunistic cycle in transfers, though they argue that there is no evidence of fiscal cycle for instruments other than transfers. As with monetary policy, they find no significant difference between Republicans and Democrats in their preelection choices for fiscal policy.

Summary and Conclusions

To summarize the econometric evidence, taken as a whole it presents a very strong case for the existence of opportunistic, preelectoral manipulation of economic policy and for the effects of that manipulation on some, though not all economic variables. However, the evidence is quite weak that this cycle is of the form suggested by Nordhaus, in which expansionary monetary policy and high inflation before an election reduce unemployment before the election, followed by a postelection contraction to cool down the economy. Instead, manipulation occurs via transfer payments, a policy most likely to affect disposable income before an election, as originally argued by Tufte (1978). Monetary policy does not appear to be the driving force for the politically induced cycle, but money growth moves before an election to accommodate fiscal policy, the inflationary effects being seen in the quarter of the election and subsequently.

This view of monetary policy accords far better with central bank independence than what is implied about central bank behavior by several existing models of the political business cycle. The stress on fiscal policy makes voter behavior appear far more rational. Finally, this approach may help to make sense of empirical findings previously interpreted as contradictory.

Notes

1. Kalecki (1943) presented an early explicit model of the political business cycle. The political nature of economic fluctuations was recognized by Schumpeter (1939) in his monumental work on business cycles. Simultaneously presented a formal model of the political business cycle.

2. The material in this section, Portions Political Cycles, and A Closer Look at the Evidence is based on Drazen (forthcoming).

3. There are many theoretical objections that have been raised to this framework. See Cukierman (1992) for a strong critique of the microfoundations of the expectations-adjusted Phillips curve when applied to political models.

4. This problem has been pointed out by Rogoff (1988), among others.

5. The letter read, "Your social security payment has been increased by 20 percent, starting with this month's check, by a new statute enacted by the Congress and signed into law by President Richard Nixon on July 1, 1972. The President also signed into law a provision which will allow your social security benefits to increase automatically if the cost of living goes up. Automatic benefit increases will be added to your check in future years according to the conditions set out in that law."

6. Alesina, Cohen, and Roubini (1992) attempt to distinguish the original partisan theory from Alesina's partisan theory with rational expectations on the basis of persistent versus temporary effects of elections on real economic activity. Since one cannot reject the hypothesis of a unit root in the unemployment data for many countries over the period of analysis, Hibbs (1992) and Gärtner (1994) argue that one cannot confidently base a rejection of one model and acceptance of the other on tests of persistence.

7. For example, in the United States, Democrats have been in power more often than Republicans during wars, which may account for their tenures more often being associated with booms.

8. The disappearance of a political cycle for veteran's benefits after the late 1970s may help explain why Grier (1989) and Williams (1990) find a significant political monetary cycle

in data up to or through the early 1980s, while Alesina, Cohen, and Roubini (1992), using a longer time series find weaker evidence. To the extent that the political monetary cycle is induced by a political fiscal cycle, a weakening of the latter would weaken the former as well.

References

Alesina, A. (1987). "Macroeconomic Policy in a Two-Party System as a Repeated Game." *Quarterly Journal of Economics* 102: 651–678.

Alesina, A. (1988). "Macroeconomics and Politics." In *NBER Macroeconomics Annual*. Cambridge, MA: MIT Press.

Alesina, A., G. Cohen, and N. Roubini. (1992). "Macroeconomic Policy and Elections in OECD Democracies." *Economics and Politics* 4: 1–30.

Alesina, A., and N. Roubini. (1992). "Political Cycles in OECD Economies." *Review of Economic Studies* 59.

Beck, N. (1987). "Elections and the Fed: Is There a Political Monetary Cycle?" *American Journal of Political Science* 31: 194–216.

Ben-Porath, Y. (1975). "The Years of Plenty and the Years of Famine: A Political Business." *Kyklos* 28.

Cukierman, A. (1992). *Central Bank Strategy, Credibility and Independence: Theory and Evidence*. Cambridge, MA: MIT Press.

Drazen, A. (forthcoming). *Political Economy in Macroeconomics*. Princeton: Princeton University Press.

Gärtner, M. (1994). "The Quest for Political Cycles in OECD Economies." *European Journal of Political Economy* 10: 427–440.

Grier, K. (1989). "On the Existence of a Political Monetary Cycle." *American Journal of Political Science* 33: 376–389.

Haynes, S., and J. Stone. (1987). "Political Models of the Business Cycle Should Be Revived." *Economic Inquiry* 28: 442–465.

Hibbs, D. (1977). "Political Parties and Macroeconomic Policy." *American Political Science Review* 71: 1467–1487.

Hibbs, D. (1987). *The American Political Economy: Macroeconomics and Electoral Politics in the United States*. Cambridge, MA: Harvard University Press.

Hibbs, D. (1992). "Partisan Theory After Fifteen Years." *European Journal of Political Economy* 8: 361–373.

Keech, W., and K. Pak. (1989). "Electoral Cycles and Budgetary Growth in Veterans' Benefit Programs." *American Journal Of Political Science* 33: 901–911.

Nordhaus, W. (1975). "The Political Business Cycle." *Review of Economic Studies* 42: 169–190.

Sheffrin, S. (1989). "Evaluating Rational Partisan Business Cycle Theory." *Economics and Politics* 1: 239–259.

Tufte, E.R. (1978). *Political Control of the Economy*. Princeton: Princeton University Press.

Williams, John T. (1990). "The Political Manipulation of Macroeconomic Policy." *American Political Science Review* 84: 767–795.

Wooley, John T. (1984). *Monetary Politics: The Federal Reserve and the Politics of Monetary Policy.* Cambridge: Cambridge University Press.

5 POLITICAL CULTURE AND THE POLITICAL ECONOMY OF CENTRAL-BANK INDEPENDENCE

Arye L. Hillman

Bar-Ilan University

The Empirical Evidence on the Transition Economies

In the substantial literature on central-bank independence (see the comprehensive surveys by Eijffinger and de Haan, 1996, and Alex Cukierman, 1998), two primary empirical issues are (1) measurement of central-bank independence to be able to determine the degree to which a central bank is independent and (2) evaluation of the relation between a measure of central-bank independence and policy performance.

Measures of legal central-bank independence have been subjected to qualification (for a compelling critique, see Forder, 1998; Eijffinger, Schaling, and Hoeberichts, 1998, study the sensitivity of results to uses of different measures). Subject to qualification about the measures, the evidence on transition economies reveals quite high legal independence (see, for example, Cukierman, Miller, and Neyapti, 1998).

The evidence also reveals (see Lougani and Sheets, 1997; Cukierman, Miller, and Neyapti, 1998) that greater legal independence is associated with reduced rates of inflation, *provided that at the same time the economy ranks high by a measure of economic liberalism*. Simple regressions of measures of central-bank independence for the transition economies on inflation gives the result that greater independence is associated with greater inflation. This is contrary to the idea that independence of a central bank will allow responsible policies and will restrain political opportunism. That is, the empirical evidence indicates that in the transition economies central-bank independence is not sufficient for policy discipline. Rather, a necessary accompanying condition is a sufficiently liberal policy orientation. In accepting these results, we need to rely on the empirical studies as having resolved inherent multicolinearity problems if

$$Inflation = f\ (CBI,\ liberalization)$$
$$CBI = F\ (liberalization).$$

Taking this not to be a problem, and taking the results at face value, the conclusion points us in the direction of the influence of political culture.

The political culture determines how central-bank independence is applied. Where politicians' motives are to serve the public interest, the empirical results confirm that central-bank independence also yields more responsible policy. Where however the political environment is self-serving, this is also expressed in the way in which central-bank independence is utilized. Central-bank independence is then also utilized in a self-serving manner. And indeed the higher the degree of central-bank independence, the less disciplined is policy.

The empirical evidence in the transition economies is thus open to a consistent interpretation. Where rent seeking and personal self-advancement and self-enrichment are the norms of political life, the central bank is consistently used for self-serving purposes, and the greater the measure of legal independence, the more so this is the case.

Democratic Accountability

The issue of central-bank independence raises questions of democratic accountability. A starting point for considering these questions is provided by Frederic Mishkin in Chapter 3 in this volume. Mishkin observes that an independent central bank is run by persons who are not elected by the people and hence who are not directly accountable to the electorate. His recommendation for transition (and other) economies is that they should not compromise their newly established (in some cases reestablished) democratic principles by giving to an independent central bank the discretion to determine policy objectives. Government, which is accountable to the people, should choose the policy objectives. Mishkin proposes therefore that the independence of a central bank should be limited to the discretion to choose the means or instruments whereby the policy objectives set by the government are achieved.

Mishkin thus asks that a central bank not be treated differently from any other government bureaucracy. Its task should be efficient and competent implementation of the policy objectives that decided by accountable government. The professional expertise of the central bank staffers can be relied on for determination of how objectives should be achieved, but democratic accountability requires that government set the policies. The government should therefore, for example, set an inflation target and leave it to the central bank to achieve the target. The independence of the central bank is that, with the policy objectives given, a government should not be permitted to act manipulatively behind the scenes to give rise to a policy outcome that is different from the one it is formally committed to.

I shall use the terminology or definition of central-bank independence to refer to independence with regard to policy objectives. The case that a central bank should be independent in this sense implies violation of basic principles of democratic accountability.

The Motives Underlying Policy

In a consideration of central-bank independence, political economy is invariably present, implicitly if not explicitly. Let us consider the implicit foundations of the political economy of central-bank independence. I begin at the beginning, with the distinction between normative and positive analysis. Normative analysis considers what ought to be, and positive analysis seeks to explain what we observe. Mishkin's observations are, for example, broadly normative, since he is providing recommendations about what ought to be. The empirical evidence is positive, in seeking to explain empirically what has been observed. Normative and positive aspects can be related. Normative recommendations might *follow* the positive empirical analysis. If central-bank independence is empirically revealed to result in superior economic performance, central-bank independence might be concluded to be desirable, even if violates the principle of democratic accountability. Can however central-bank independence be desirable *because* it violates the principle of democratic accountability?

Related to normative-positive distinctions are conceptions of exogenous and endogenous economic policy. The theory of *exogenous* policy is normative: the body of economic theory makes recommendations about how to achieve the social good. The theory of *endogenous* policy is positive: this body of theory seeks to explain why observed policy decisions have been made or seeks to predict political decisions. Both perspectives encompass the institutional framework for collective decision making, which we know from the studies of Douglass North (1990) and others to be important. The normative perspective recommends institutions and rules. The positive perspective asks why institutions and rules have been chosen or explains why the chosen institutions and rules give rise to observed outcomes.

Different conceptions of government are also involved. Exogenous-policy recommendations have in the background a benevolent government, which listens to and implements the recommended policies. Or the exogenous-policy recommendations point to the democratic accountability of government as the discipline that will ensure that the socially best policies are adopted, once they are only identified—that is, the people will wise enough to elect wise and benevolent representatives.

The theory of endogenous policy takes quite a different view of government. Politics is personalized rather than idealized. Policy is explained as endogenous with reference to private interests and personal objectives of the persons in government who are in a position to make the policy decisions (see Ursprung, 1991, for a review of the different approaches). The private interest can involve direct personal benefit, or there may political objectives associated with personal electoral success (see, for example, Ursprung, 1990; Potters and Sloof, 1996; Potters, Sloof, and van Winden, 1997).

The case for policy independence of central banks presumes such endogenous policy. The case is based on the idea that politicians have reason to, and indeed have been observed in the past, to behave opportunistically in ways that depart from the public interest. When the recommendation is made that a country's central bank should be independent, we understand that the intention is independence of the potential for undesirable political opportunism.

The Forms of Political Opportunism

Opportunism can take the form of selective income and wealth redistribution, influenced by special interests who benefit from policies that are disadvantageous for the population at large. For example, the business sector may seek lower real interest rates when a lowering of interest rates would compromise a policy of sustained stabilization. We also know that inflation has income-distribution consequences, in general benefiting borrowers at the expense of lenders, which is another reason for business to urge less restrictive monetary policy than the policy that is in the public interest. The supposition underlying the proposal for central-bank independence is that, while politicians may be susceptible to pressure from special interests, a central bank *will be* independent of such demands (a positive proposition since it is a prediction), and therefore it follows that a central bank *should be* independent of political interests (a normative proposition since it is a recommendation).

Central-bank independence is also a component of the theory of political business cycles. The theory of political business cycles proposes that governments have self-interested incentives to act opportunistically to manipulate macroeconomic policy, to ensure reelection prospects are maximized, or at least to ensure that some maximal desired level of political support is attained. The theory has a number of variants. Some variants impute rationality and memory to voters. Other models make allowance for partisan preferences of political parties, and other variants of the theory acknowledge that surplus political support allows ideological indulgence. A concise review of the different theories is provided by Garratt and Jackson (1996). In each variant of political business-cycle theory, the types of policies over which a central bank has discretion can be instruments of opportunistic macroeconomic manipulation. To avoid such opportunistic manipulation of the business cycle, the recommendation is that a central bank should be independent of politicians.

A third case for an independent central bank in the context of endogenous-policy analysis points to the ability of *well-intentioned non-opportunistic governments* to withstand pressures of interest groups, by pointing to the independence of the central bank. The political costs of policies that are unpopular in the short-term but beneficial in the long-term are thereby reduced, so permitting good policies to be pursued. That is, the idea is that if special interests and voters believe that the central bank is truly independent, they cannot blame the government.

The above case for central-bank independence supposes a benevolent government seeking to avoid short-term pressure-group manipulation. Another related view of the benefits of central-bank independence points to the weakness of political will and has a parallel in the story of Ulysses and the sirens. Ulysses binds himself to the mast (and also places wax in the ears of his sailors) to avoid the inevitable temptation that, if he could freely choose, he would approach the sirens. The ship would then sink and all would drown, as happened to many before who fell under the spell of the sirens and could not help themselves. Central-bank independence is, from this perspective, a form of credible commitment in the face of the inevitability of politicians' inability to resist succumbing to short-term electoral (or private) interest.

The Political Principal-Agent Problem

The theory of central-bank independence is therefore based on the declaration that we cannot trust politicians to be socially responsible. This declaration cannot, however, be institution-free. And it cannot be free of considerations of political culture. It is nonetheless a clear expression of the public-choice perspective on economic policy. The public-choice perspective (in the 1990s becoming a more orthodox perspective; see Hillman, 1998) on political behavior applies the same theory of self-interested behavior that economic theory applies to people when they make decisions as consumers and producers, to behavior when the same people come to make political decisions. That is, the public-choice perspective takes the view that people do the best they can for themselves in life generally, whether in private or public domains of decision.

As consumers and as producers, people make decisions that affect their personal lives (they purchase private goods and also make decisions that have collective consequences regarding public goods and the like). A liberal perspective is happy with people making economic decisions in their own interest. Adam Smith's invisible hand should ensure that the outcome is satisfactory for society at large.

Yet the same principle of self-interested behavior, when applied to personal decisions in the domain of politics, does not ensure good outcomes for society at large. For an individual voter has limited control over the behavior of elected representatives. And, since a voter cannot control representatives, there may be no incentive for the voter to acquire knowledge that would be useful in monitoring the behavior of representatives. That is, voters may choose to be "rationally ignorant" of political mechanisms and political decisions. Yet even if they are sufficiently informed to know what is going on, voters may still be ineffective in setting bounds on personal political discretion such are required to ensure socially desirable policies. Hence, the case is that, *because of a principal-agent problem* (voters cannot discipline or control their elected representatives), the policies of the central bank should be independent of the personal political discretion *that voters cannot control.*

Policy independence of the central bank means independence from the democratic process of collective choice. The political principal-agent problem makes this independence virtuous. Indeed, the entire literature on central-bank policy independence is a statement of lack of trust of the democratic political process. The literature says: we should separate the central bank from the domain and from the consequences of the democratic political process.

Yet if the central bank is independent of the democratically elected representatives of the people, what has become of democratic accountability? What replaces the democratic political process? And how will the central bankers who have the policy independence be appointed? Such question have arisen, for example, for a most independent central bank, the Bundesbank (see the interchange between Vaubel, 1997a, 1997b, and Berger and Wiotek, 1997).

The Desirable Attributes of Central Bankers

The problem of finding the persons who can safely be appointed as independent central bankers under conditions where there is no democratic accountability has a heritage in similar problems of choice. We can begin to look for an answer in Jethro's advice to Moses in the Torah (the book of Shemot or Exodus). Jethro tells Moses to delegate responsibility to "men of ability, such as fear heaven, are men of truth, and are hateful of greed." Rashi points out that in the original Hebrew the word for *ability* can also be interpreted to mean *wealth*; men of wealth would have no or less incentive to seek additional wealth from their positions of responsibility and have less reason to flatter or ingratiate themselves to others. Men of truth are, according to Rashi, men who command the confidence of the people and who are deserving to be relied on. Men who hate greed are not preoccupied with their personal property. The Torah reports that Moses heeded the advice of Jethro and delegated responsibility to "men of ability (wealth?)" whom he choose from among the people. There is an ambiguity in interpretation here. Did Moses succeed in finding men with only the attributes of "ability or wealth" but not with the sought attributes of "fear of heaven," "truth," and "hateful of greed"? Or are we to understand *ability* to encompass the other attributes?

There is also another unofficial commentary. When told by Jethro of the attributes required of the people whom he must seek out to delegate responsibility, Moses asks: "How can I ever find such people?" And the answer is, "Pay them enough, and you will find them."

The independent central bankers that society seeks need to be wise persons who are not susceptible to political pressures, who cannot be manipulated by promises of personal material reward, and who will adhere to the principle of the quest for the good of society. That is, the governor of the central bank should be socially responsible, apolitical, and not corruptible—and competent.

There are two steps in the process. First, such people must be found. Second, they must be chosen. Let us take these steps in turn.

Of course, before we proceed, someone might wish to interject that the governor of a central bank can be made subject to monitoring and regulation by a board of people. But then everything we have said about the governor applies just as well to the people who are selected to monitor the governor.

Let us then consider the question of finding the right person to be governor. Such a person will have a *personal objective* of choosing socially optimal policies and will be able to resist political pressures and pressures from special-interest groups to do otherwise.

For this purpose, we require someone whose personal esteem is directly measured by his professional competence and performance. Personal esteem matters in particular when a person keeps the company of peers and when a well-defined respected peer group would socially and personally ostracize him (or her) for opportunistic behavior.

This is, we need a person for whom professional self-esteem and the regard of his peers matter highly. The personal costs of complicity in opportunism of such a person are high. Similarly, the personal benefits of maintained social responsibility are high. There is therefore a signal in *who* is appointed central bank governor—whether it is someone whose ladder of personal progress in life has been political or someone who brings with him a professional reputation, professional self-esteem, and a reference peer group that are the consequences of a to-date successful professional career path.

If the appointment process does not ensure that such a person is chosen, then the conception of central-bank independence is compromised.

This becomes a very personal approach to a basis for predicted benefit from central-bank independence. A less personal, more objectively scientific, criterion would be preferable. Yet we are here in the domain of political culture. A legal standard that permits independence is not sufficient to ensure socially responsible behavior. This is indeed what the empirical studies reveal for the transition economies. And so we should expect. For the independence is the independence to make decisions, and we have to consider how the independence to make these decisions will be exercised. An independent central bank can be an instrument of self-aggrandizement or can be captured, just as any other regulatory authority can be captured, by politicians or by special interests.

We require an assurance that this will not happen. If the assurance cannot be provided, then a democratically elected government should retain accountability for policy. But then we are back in the world of the representative-democracy principal-agent problem, with rational ignorance and political opportunism. We will have therefore come the complete circle—unless we can be assured of a wise and morally principled central banker.

Why Were Independent Central Banks Chosen in the Transition Economies?

The fact that former socialist economies have overall, by the various measures, chosen high formal degrees of central independence reflects a virtue of the process of beginning from nowhere. Without the encumberment of a status quo, decisions could be more freely made. In the immediacy of the transition, high ideals could dominate individual opportunism. Time horizons could be sufficiently long and aspirations could be sufficiently idealistic for perceived socially responsible decisions to be made. The decisions made could reflect the benefits of an independent bank that have become part of received policy advice (see Cukierman, 1992, 1998).

The international institutions also had a role, via aid conditionality.

Central-banking legislation was also part of the broader theme of a desire to emulate the successful West. Consequently, with a focus on the Bundesbank in particular, central-bank independence become a measure of success in complying with the requisites of transition. A country such as Estonia, which set out to recreate itself in a liberal market image, could thus be expected to choose the manifestation of a (non) central bank, in the form of a currency board that followed rules that provided no opportunities for political manipulation. Yet also illiberal Belarus has given its central bank a high degree of central-bank independence—but here the governor of the central bank was jailed and replaced by the finance minister, whose expenditure policies had generated the high inflation that was the attributed failure of the governor. As Mario Nuti observed, "The governor was independent but not free."

Self-esteem and self-respect of the legally independent governor may therefore have little role in the performance of an "independent" central banker. If a central-bank governor takes pride in the display of professional competence, this can be expected to mean much more than the significance attached to a measure of formal central-bank independence, but this may not be sufficient given the practicalities of life.

The independence of the central bank may moreover not be necessary for good performance. A central banker who is not so independent by the different legal measures that are proposed, but who is guided by self-esteem and self-respect (and who is competent in making decisions or following advice), will also perform well, if the political culture is appropriate.

If political culture matters, there should be an important unexplained residual in the cross-country empirical estimations that link competence with measures of central-bank independence. The unexplained residual is attributable to the difficult-to-measure attributes that enter into political culture. So, perhaps, paradoxically, if the cross-country regressions are too successful and do not show significant residuals, we might be surprised rather than impressed. Or else we have to conclude that the regression results show that there is no variation in political culture over the sample of prior socialist economies. Yet this may not be a comfortable conclusion looking at countries that range from Croatia, the Czech Republic, and Estonia on the one hand, to the Ukraine, Belarus, and Turkmenistan on the other.

Let me try to be more specific about what I mean by political culture. My intention is to examine the mind-set of people, their way of thinking after they achieve political power, and why people choose to go into politics or seek public office (such as governor of a central bank)—whether they do so with the intention of benefiting their fellow men and women or whether the decision to follow a political career is a natural progression of an objective of seeking private wealth. There is compelling evidence that in some countries politics and business are inexorably tied (see, for example, Gelb, Hillman, and Ursprung, 1996, 1998, and the recent study on politics and corruption in Russia by Levin and Satarov, 1998).

When the political culture places quest for personal gain as predominant in people's minds, how is formal independence of the central bank to be interpreted? Do the norms of behavior regarding the exercise of power apply to the senior people in the central bank? Have they been selected for the weight of self-esteem and regard for peer evaluation of competence *in their personal calculations of their own state-of-being*? Or, in the scramble for positioning for claims to prior social property and political power, have some people simply found their way to the central bank, when they could just as well have ended up elsewhere in a politicized system of economic decision making and business activity? These are important questions for a study of central-bank independence in the transition.

Will Performance Provide an Answer?

The performance of the central bank can provide an answer to these questions, if the performance is good. If the performance is not good, we cannot be sure of the answers. For in the adverse conditions of the transition, even the best of intentions are not always enough. We see this in particular from the evidence of the most opportune conditions that have been provided for transition, where (to use Horst Siebert's terms) the big brother has brought into his home the little prodigal brother. In the united Germany after a decade of reunification there remain differentials in unemployment, and social and culturally based distinctions persist between west and east. The German experience allows a simple statement that the transition is not easy under the best of conditions. Yet here a political culture of low inflation and social responsibility accompanied transition. Elsewhere, the accompaniment of transition has often been a political culture of private gain.

The Thomas-a-Beckett Affect

The literature in central-bank independence talks about a Thomas-a-Beckett effect. Henry VIII was certain that his friend Thomas-a-Beckett would issue the divorce he was seeking when he appointed him Archbishop of Canterbury. Yet once he took the position, Thomas-a-Beckett refused to comply to comply with the king's request, at the ultimate cost of his life. The analogy is that people who are self-interestedly opportunistic and from whom the central bank requires protection, undergo a personality transformation to become socially responsible once they find themselves in the independent central bank.

In the circumstances of some transition economies, the opposite can, however, readily happen. People who have a sense of self-esteem and social responsibility can over time be transformed to self-serving and be led to participate in the quest for personal wealth that they see taking place around them. It can make little personal sense to continue to be socially responsible while others in positions of power are seen to place little regard on social responsibilities and see their prime objective as enriching themselves.

Political Culture as an Explanation

Economic theory prefers to explain economic and political behavior without including a role for culture. This is because of the difficulty of objectively specifying and measuring variables that reflect cultural differences. Also, when we use recourse to culture to explain behavior, there is a certain inevitability about the decisions that people make. "Culture" leads people to decide as they do. Yet cultural variables do appear to affect a central banker's behavior, as shown in the empirical study of inflation culture by Bernd Hayo (1998). Collective memories give rise to an anti-inflation culture in some societies. When people are asked what they wish of government, people in such societies rank price stability very highly. These tend to be countries with experiences of social and economic disruption due to of high inflation. An independent central bank with a successful policy of price stability is then an expected consequence of such an anti-inflation culture. The explanatory variable is the culture. An anti-inflation culture can override rational ignorance and can be expected to punish politicians by the political process, without regard for measures of an index of legal central-bank independence. Price instability is inconsistent with a culture based on a sense of order. The Weimar Republic was an aberration in many ways, including the inflation. Here, as elsewhere, culture pushed more immediate satisfaction to prominence over longer-run consequences of lack of discipline in behavior.

Does the culture prevail to express broad social norms? Or does the culture prevail expressed in the narrower domain of that which it is permissible to do, once political power or administrative office has been attained? And is there a contradiction between the broader cultural basis of the behavioral norms of the society and the norms of political and bureaucratic office holders? Rational ignorance and the impotency of the individual in influencing political decision making can imply that the latter is the case, and people do not have the outcomes they want and perhaps deserve.

The Preeminence of Markets

In the transition economies, central banks are legally highly independent, but their performance reflects the political culture. In an integrated global economy, however, markets are preeminent and eventually prevail over political culture. Whatever central bankers' perceived goals, the source of those goals, the interests they might reflect, and the incentive structures that might be designed (see Walsh, 1995; Waller and Walsh, 1996), the reaction of international capital markets provides an ultimate discipline on policy opportunism and self-interest. If the market is punishing an undesirable political culture, the outcomes can, of course, be rather unfortunate for the population of the country. This is, however, in the end the cost of external discipline when markets judge internal discipline to be lacking.

References

Berger, Helge, and Ulrich Wiotek. (1997). "How Opportunistic Are Partisan German Central Bankers? Evidence on the Vaubel Hypothesis." *European Journal of Political Economy* 13: 807–821.

Cukierman, Alex. (1992). *Central Bank Strategy, Credibility, and Independence: Theory and Evidence*. Cambridge, MA: MIT Press.

Cukierman, Alex. (1998). "The Economics of Central Banking." In Holger C. Wolf (ed.), *Contemporary Economic Issues* (pp. 37–81). Houndmills, UK: Macmillan.

Cukierman, Alex, Geoffrey P. Miller, and Bilin Neyapti. (1998). "Central Bank Reform, Liberalization, and Inflation in Transition Economies." Mimeo, Department of Economics, Tel-Aviv University.

Eijffinger, Sylvester C.W., and Jakob de Haan. (1996). "The Political Economy of Central Bank Independence." *Special Papers in International Economics*, International Finance Section, Department of Economics, Princeton University.

Eijffinger, Sylvester C.W., Eric Schaling, and Marco Hoeberichts. (1998). "Central Bank Independence: A Sensitivity Analysis." *European Journal of Political Economy* 14: 73–88.

Forder, James. (1998). "The Case for an Independent European Central Bank: A Reassessment of Evidence and Sources." *European Journal of Political Economy* 14: 53–71.

Garratt, D., and P.M. Jackson. (1996). "Political Business Cycles: A Literature Survey." In D. Piacentino and P.M. Jackson (eds.), *Developments in Public Finance*. Aldershot: Edward Elgar.

Gelb, Alan, Arye L. Hillman, and Heinrich W. Ursprung. (1996). "Rents and the Transition." *World Development Report Background Paper*. Washington, DC: World Bank.

Gelb, Alan, Arye L. Hillman, and Heinrich W. Ursprung. (1998). "Rents as Distractions: Why the Exit from Transition Is Prolonged." In Nicolas C. Baltas, George Demopoulos, and Joseph Hassid (eds.), *Economic Interdependence and Cooperation* (pp. 21–38).

Hayo, Bernd. (1998). "Inflation Culture, Central Bank Independence, and Price Stability." *European Journal of Political Economy* 14: 241–264.

Hillman, Arye L. (1998). "Political Economy and Political Correctness." *Public Choice* 96: 219–239 (Presidential Address, European Public Choice Society, Prague, 1997).

Levin, Mark I., and Giorgory Satarov. (1998). "Russia vs. Corruption: Who Wins?" Report of the Council on Foreign Defense Policy and the IDEM Foundation, Moscow.

Lougani, and N. Sheets. (1997). "Central Bank Independence, Inflation, and Growth in Transition Economies." *Journal of Money, Credit, and Banking* 29: 381–399.

Mishkin, Frederic S. (1998). "Central banking in a Democratic Society: Implications for Transition Countries." This volume, Chapter 3.

North, Douglass. (1990). *Institutions, Institutional Change, and Economic Performance*. Cambridge: Cambridge University Press.

Potters, Jan, and Randolph Sloof. (1996). "Interest Groups: A Survey of Empirical Models That Try to Assess Their Influence." *European Journal of Political Economy* 12: 403–442.

Potters, Jan, Randolph Sloof, and Frans van Winden. (1997). "Campaign Expenditures, Contributions, and Direct Endorsements: The Strategic Use of Information and Money to Influence Voter Behavior." *European Journal of Political Economy* 13: 1–31.

Ursprung, Heinrich W. (1990). "Public Goods, Rent Dissipation, and Candidate Competition." *Economics and Politics* 2: 115–132.

Ursprung, Heinrich W. (1991). "Economic Policies and Political Competition." In Arye L. Hillman (ed.), *Markets and Politicians: Politicized Economic Choice* (pp. 1–25). Boston: Kluwer.

Vaubel, Roland. (1997a). "The Bureaucratic and Partisan Behavior of Independent Central Banks: German and International Evidence." *European Journal of Political Economy* 13: 201–224.

Vaubel, Roland. (1997b). "Reply to Berger and Wiotek." *European Journal of Political Economy* 13: 823–827.

Waller, Chrisopher J., and Carl E. Walsh. (1996). "Central Bank Independence, Economic Behavior, and Optimal Term Lengths." *American Economic Review* 86: 1139–1153.

Walsh, Carl E. (1995). "Optimal Contracts for Central Bankers." *American Economic Review* 85: 150–167.

III DEFINING CENTRAL-BANK FUNCTIONS

6 CENTRAL BANKING AND ECONOMIC DEVELOPMENT

Maxwell J. Fry

*University of Birmingham and Bank
of England*

Introduction

In most countries, central banks are responsible for monetary policy, financial stability, and the national or wholesale payment systems. For example, the Bank of England's mission statement specifically recognizes the promotion of sound and efficient payment and settlement arrangements as an important element of the Bank's core purposes. Gerry Corrigan, former president of the Federal Reserve Bank of New York, also recognized this important role when referring to the trilogy of central banking functions and responsibilities: monetary policy, banking supervision, and payment systems.

If price stability accelerates economic growth, as much recent empirical work suggests, then a central bank can promote economic development by delivering price stability. However, two prerequisites must be satisfied to enable the central bank to conduct effective monetary policy—(1) safe and efficient payment system and (2) financial stability. In this way, good monetary policy, financial stability, and efficient payment systems all contribute to economic development.

Central banks in transitional economies are considerably more involved in their countries' payment systems than are central banks in industrial countries, in part because they cannot implement any monetary policy through indirect market-based monetary policy instruments without first developing a payment system: the payment system always constitutes the first link in the transmission mechanism. In fact, over the last two decades, there has been global tendency for central banks to play a more active role in payment systems than they did in earlier years. The most important reasons for this development are rapid technological changes, growth of financial activity and consequent growth in volumes and values of payment transactions, and the integration or globalization of financial markets. Consequently, liquidity and credit risks for central banks, commercial banks, and other participants involved in payment systems have increased dramatically. Payment systems have become an important potential source of domestic and cross-border financial crises. The payment system is to the financial sector what nuclear power is to the energy sector. Both exhibit very small probabilities of very large accidents.

Why financial stability is essential can be illustrated most dramatically in the case of insolvent banks (and other economic agents). Insolvent economic actors exhibit upward-sloping demands for credit. At higher interest rates, they demand more credit with which to pay the higher interest costs. Because they are insolvent, the issue of repayment is irrelevant. They borrow simply to stay in business for as long as lenders are prepared to lend. This implies that tighter monetary policy increases credit demands, raises interest rates, and eventually drives out potentially solvent agents that are no longer profitable at exorbitantly high real interest rates. Here is the extreme form of adverse selection. Clearly, financial stability necessitates the removal of insolvent banks and businesses and the imposition of hard budget constraints on all players in a market economy before monetary policy can dampen credit demand through higher interest rates.

The extent to which a central bank can choose and implement appropriate monetary, financial stability and payment system policies varies considerably across countries. Monetary policy may be constrained or thwarted by inconsistent fiscal and exchange-rate policies. Financial stability may be jeopardized by the gaps that exist in transitional and developing countries' financial landscapes when compared with the constellation of financial institutions and markets that typically constitute the industrial countries' financial sectors. Vital infrastructure in terms of telecommunications, legal provisions, and transport may be inadequate to support the development of a modern payment system. In the transitional economies, expertise formed one serious constraint in the early years (Knight et al., 1997). Expertise was scarce not only in the central bank but also within the financial sector as a whole. Rapid transformation from a monobanking system into a two-tier banking system faced not only lack of expertise and experience but also little understanding of fundamental economic concepts such as opportunity cost and time value of money. Central bankers in transitional economies also faced uncompetitive and uncooperative commercial banking systems.

Much has changed over the past decade in the transitional economies. But some transitional economies have adapted to their new environments more quickly and successfully than others. So there is perhaps more diversity now than there was at the outset. Nevertheless, there are several common features of the process of financial liberalization and financial development. First, whatever legal independence is assigned, central banks have been constrained by their countries' fiscal situation and exchange rate regime (Fry and Nuti, 1992; Koch, 1997). Second, the prevalence of insolvent commercial banks pose serious threats of systemic instability and hinder the adoption of indirect, market-based instruments of monetary policy. Third, central banks in the transitional economies are more heavily involved in their countries' payment systems than are central banks in the industrial countries. Since good monetary policy, financial stability, and efficient payment systems all contribute to economic development, I examine some aspects of each of these central banking functions in this chapter.

Central-Bank Roles in Payment Systems[1]

In general, central and commercial bankers now realize that payment and settlement arrangements cannot simply be left for the back office to sort out. In their role as the "plumbing" of the financial and banking system, the efficiency and safety of these arrangements have become issues with wider strategic and policy implications for central banks. So this section has two basic objectives. The first is to examine the reasons why central banks are interested in payment systems. The second is to provide an overview of the role of central banks in the payment system reforms in transitional economies; Poland is used for illustrative purposes.

Central-Bank Ownership and Oversight of Payment Systems

Table 6.1 Records ownership of the major payment systems across a sample of seventy countries that responded to a recent questionnaire (Fry et al.).

Table 6.1. Central bank ownership of payment systems (percent of countries in each group)

Type	Industrial	Transitional	Developing
Real-time gross settlement:			
Sole	56	86	100
Joint	6	14	0
None	38	0	0
Deferred net settlement:			
Sole	6	44	47
Joint	44	44	37
None	50	12	16

Table 6.2. Central-bank oversight over payment systems (percent of countries in each group)

Type	Industrial	Transitional	Developing
Formal	71	77	75
Informal	48	23	28
Both	19	0	3

Ownership is particularly important to the extent that payment systems pool or absorb participants' payment risks. Unsurprisingly, there is considerably less central-bank ownership of payment systems in the industrial countries than in the transitional and developing countries. While 62 percent of central banks in industrial countries own or part-own their country's real-time gross settlement (RTGS) systems, central banks in transitional and developing countries own or part-own all the existing RTGS systems. Similarly, 50 percent of deferred net settlement (DNS) systems in industrial countries are entirely privately owned, but a large majority of DNS systems in transitional and developing countries are owned or part-owned by their central banks.

The questionnaire collected information on the role of the central bank in the country's payment arrangements. Table 6.2 provides an overview of the nature of central-bank involvement in the payment systems in this country sample. The majority of central banks possess formal powers of oversight over their country's payment systems, a minority use informal arrangements, while some exert both formal and informal powers.

Table 6.3. Pricing of central-bank payment services (percent of countries in each group)

Type	Industrial	Transitional	Developing
Free	5	8	61
Subsidized	0	25	3
Full-cost recovery	90	42	27
Target rate of return	0	17	0
Other	5	8	9

Table 6.3. shows the questionnaire answers on pricing of central-bank payment services. Central banks in the industrial countries tend to price their services on the basis of full-cost recovery, whereas central banks in developing countries typically provide their services free of charge. The distortions so created may appear small at present. Experience from the industrial countries suggests, however, that the sooner such distortions are removed, the less likely are a country's inhabitants to fall into expensive and socially inefficient habits, such as writing checks for sums smaller than the costs of the check processing.

Increasing Central-Bank Involvement in Payment Systems

As suggested in the introduction, central banks have tended to play a more active role in payment systems over the past two decades than they did in earlier years. In large part, this is due to rapid technological changes, dramatic growth of financial activity, and consequent enormous growth in both volumes and values of payment transactions and in the integration or globalization of financial markets. As a result, liquidity and credit risks for central banks, commercial banks, and other participants involved in payment systems have increased dramatically. Furthermore, payment systems have become a serious potential source of domestic and cross-border financial crises.

In this new environment, promoting stability and efficiency of payment systems, developing measures to reduce risk, and ensuring that payment system arrangements and changes in such arrangements do not jeopardize monetary management have become crucial central-bank objectives. An efficiency of a country's payment system is one determinant of its rate of economic growth. Here the speed and certainty of fund transfers from the payer's account to the payee's account are the key elements.

Central banks can promote such efficiency in two ways: by operational involvement or through a regulatory role. The degree to which central banks are involved in operational activities differs across countries. But as an important part of the financial sector, the payment system undoubtedly requires oversight and prudential supervision. Here the role of central banks usually consists of developing rules of operation for the system that are designed to reduce systemic risk. In some countries, the central bank oversees payment systems in a regulatory role. In others, the central bank takes a much more active part in developing and running payment systems, particularly large-value transfer systems (LVTS). Where commercial banks have existed for centuries, central banks tend to play a more passive role than they do in countries that until recently possessed a monobanking system.

In general, central-bank interest in the stability of payment systems is manifested in attempts to reduce the probability of a large participant in the payment system becoming unable to meet its obligations. Such inability can cause serious difficulties for the safe functioning of the system and for other participants. Reducing this risk, known as systemic risk, is the primary central-bank objective in the field of payment systems.

In implementing monetary policy, central banks pursue intermediate targets such as growth rates of monetary aggregates or, in many cases, short-term interest rates. On the one hand, the effectiveness of indirect instruments of monetary policy depends on the stage of development of financial markets used to transmit monetary policy signals. On the other hand, the type of payment instruments used in payment systems, the payment facilities available for market participants, as well as the rules and procedures for payments influence the speed, risk, and cost of transactions in financial markets. For example, while open-market operations necessitate well-developed markets, they also require payment and settlement systems that can transfer securities through book entries and settle transactions accurately, speedily, and with finality.

Some central-bank objectives with respect to the country's payment system may be incompatible with others. For example, one way of reducing systemic risk is to adopt an RTGS system. However, such adoption may have implications for monetary policy implementation. One important issue here involves the cost of liquidity. There are also issues relating to granting intraday overdrafts for RTGS payments, pricing, and guaranteeing payment finality. The choice of payment system may involve a tradeoff between risk reduction and the effectiveness of monetary policy. An additional link between the payment system and monetary policy is produced by required reserves maintained by commercial banks for monetary policy purposes.

Since such reserves can usually be used for settlements during the day, they contribute to the smooth functioning of the payment system. Furthermore, changes in payment systems can cause changes in the velocity of money and banks' demand for reserves. So central banks must take such changes into account when implementing monetary policy.

Another important issue relating to the efficiency of payment systems is payment float. Float is created, in the main, because of delays in the execution of payment transactions. To some extent, availability of funds depends on the instrument used by the participants involved in the transaction. For cash this availability is immediate, while for large-value electronic transfers it is usually less than one day, but for other instruments it is generally two or more days.

There are two kinds of float—credit float and debit float. Credit float is created when a bank debits a client's account before transferring the funds to the beneficiary's bank or when the receiving bank delays crediting the beneficiary's account. Because credit float represents an interest-free loan from bank customers to their banks, banks have an incentive to delay the processing and crediting of payments to customer accounts (Veale and Price, 1994, p. 147). Debit float arises from processing checks or other debit instruments when a bank credits the payee before receiving money from the payer's bank or when the payer's account is debited with delay after funds are paid to the payee's bank. In such case bank customers receive the benefit of float at the expense of the banks.

Both kinds of float can also exist in the central-bank and commercial-bank account relationship. Inefficient processing of transfers by the central bank could cause the delay, such as when instructions have to be transmitted from one central-bank branch to another. Hence, commercial banks may provide interest-free loans to the central bank if the central-bank debits the account of a bank instructing it to transfer funds before crediting the payee bank's account. Conversely, the central bank provides an interest-free loan to the banking system when it credits a bank's account for funds owed before it debits the payer bank's account.

In any event, one of the parties to a payment transaction is either granting or receiving interest-free credit. John Veale and Robert Price (1994, p. 149) construct the matrix reproduced in Table 6.4 distinguishing credit-debit, central bank-bank and central bank-customer float. The volume of float can be important for several reasons. For example, lenders may be unable to charge borrowers for the credit they have extended, borrowers can decide when and how much they borrow, and banks may use float to cover some of their costs. From the central bank's viewpoint, float can affect the level and volatility of banks' reserves and complicate the operation of

Table 6.4. Credit and debit float

Relationship	Credit Float	Debit Float
Commercial banks and their customers	Generated by credit payments such as giro or payment orders. The commercial bank benefits at the expense of the customer.	Generated by debit payments such as checks. Customers benefit at the expense of commercial banks.
A central bank and commercial banks	Generated by credit payments when the account of the payer bank at the central bank is debited before the account of the payee bank is credited. The central bank benefits at the expense of the commercial banks because commercial bank reserves are decreased.	Generated by debit payments when the account of the payer bank at the central bank is debited after the account of the payee bank is credited. The commercial banks benefit at the expense of the central bank because commercial bank reserves are increased.

Source: Veale and Price (1994, table 1, p. 151).

monetary policy. Central banks have a strong preference to minimize payment float, especially in industrial countries where the principle of time value of money (TVM) is well understood. Typically, central banks attempt to reduce float by accelerating paper processing procedures and introducing funds' availability schedules.

The effectiveness of a payment system is also vital for financial stability. Disruption in the payment system reduces public confidence in the financial sector. So to maintain confidence in the financial sector, the central bank must promote a sound and efficient payment system. The payment system constitutes one source of risk to commercial banks. Liquidity problems of one of the participants may cause problems for other participants and so for the entire system.

On the one hand, timely information from the payment system may provide warning signals. On the other hand, some information about an individual bank may produce reactions that exacerbate the difficulty if published by the supervisory authorities. Hence, cooperation between payment system and supervisory specialists is essential. Such cooperation can help central banks to distinguish between serious problems (which may cause insolvency) and temporary liquidity problems. For example, central banks usually have information about whether a commercial bank is experiencing difficulty in maintaining reserve balances at the required level and about its reliance on intraday credit to fund payments. Although reducing systemic risk has been an important central-bank objective for some years, central banks have also been concerned about the relationship between payment arrangements and monetary policy. This springs from the fact that the first link in the transmission mechanism of monetary policy involves payments of one kind or another. Hence, the efficiency of the payment system is essential for monetary policy implementation and for its effective transmission through the economy.

The increasing volume and value of transactions through their payment systems in many economies explain why central banks have become increasing involved in payment system issues in recent years. But is this true for all countries? Maybe only central banks in industrial countries with developed financial sectors and strong economies that are integrated into the global economy focus on their countries' payment systems. To what extent are central banks in transitional and developing countries involved in their payment systems? What is the effect of different levels of central-bank involvement in payment systems? What are the common approaches of central banks to their payment systems?

Views on the role that central banks should play in payment systems are diverse, in large part because different conditions in each country—differences in payment instruments, the domestic financial sector, legal systems, technical infrastructure, stage of institutional development, country size, and go on—make each payment system unique. So in some countries central banks are active providers of payment services, competing with commercial banks, while in other countries, such as Slovenia and the United Kingdom, central banks do not play such a role.

The U.S. Federal Reserve Banks provide a wide variety of payment services that include collection of check payments, electronic fund transfers, securities transfer, and custodial services for U.S. government securities. The Deutsche Bundesbank makes its payment systems available to all credit institutions, many of which operate their own giro systems. The Bundesbank operates an RTGS system (EIL-ZV/EIL system and AZV) as well as a liquidity saving system (EAF2), which combines gross and net features, for large-value payments. The Bundesbank's payment systems are important transfer points for internetwork payments.

At the other end of the spectrum are a number of countries in which the initiative is left primarily to the private sector. In the United Kingdom, for example, the Bank of England's role consists in making accounts available

under certain conditions for settlement purposes, while payment processing is carried out mainly by the private sector. In Slovenia the central bank
does not provide interbank clearing facilities. As the central bank does not
operate a special clearing house for interbank payments, these facilities are
provided by commercial banks.

Roles of the Central Bank in Transitional Economies

Changes in payment systems during the last two decades, globalization,
and growth of both the value and volume of transactions have not been
identical in all countries. Typically, analyses of these issues are made from
the viewpoint of the industrial countries in which sophisticated payment
systems already exist. But countries that have just started to introduce economic reforms and to rebuild their payment systems are usually interested
in basic payment system issues.

The aim of this section is to analyze the role that central banks can play
in payment systems in some transitional countries. Although issues are illustrated for Poland, the situation in most other transitional countries is
similar. While not all the experiences of these countries will be relevant for
other countries that are currently developing their payment systems, many
of the more important problems appear to be.

The political, economic, and financial changes in the 1990s in countries
such as China, Poland, Russia, and Tanzania have placed significant strains
on their payment systems. At the outset of their payment system reforms,
all these countries possessed government-owned monobanking systems.
Initially, there was only one bank (the central bank) in China and Russia.
In addition to the central bank, some government-owned and -controlled
banks that provided agriculture credits, raised domestic saving, and facilitated foreign trade transactions existed in Poland and Tanzania. However,
there was deliberately no competition between these banks.

The role of the central banks in these countries at this stage of development was very different from the role of central banks in market-oriented
economies. Central banks were responsible for issuing money, for fulfilling
the state budget, for maintaining accounts of enterprises and households,
and for providing settlement services and credits to enterprises. In Russia,
the central bank was also involved in collecting taxes. Another major
purpose of the central bank was to monitor the state plan. This plan determined centrally all the production and distribution decisions that are made
independently by individual firms and households in a market economy.
Typically, public saving was channeled to enterprises requiring credit under

the state plan. Credit was automatic and payments were assured through the monobanking system.

Until the start of the reforms in China, Poland, and Russia, payment systems were characterized by a clear separation of cash and noncash circuits. The cash circuit was for households and the noncash circuit for enterprises—usually state-owned and obliged to use a bank account. The main noncash payment instruments consisted of the credit transfer (credit instrument initiated by the payer) and the payment demand order (a debit instrument initiated by the payee following shipment of goods). The central bank debited the payer's bank immediately after receiving a credit transfer order but credited the payee's bank with a lag. In the case of a debit instrument, the payee's bank was credited before the payer's bank was debited.

In both cases this resulted in payment-system float that either decreased commercial bank reserves at the central bank (credit float) or increased commercial bank reserves (debit float). Erratic procedures and delays in processing payments produced large and variable float. In China, Poland, and Russia, payment clearing relied on the physical transport (by postal services) of detailed paper documentation for each transaction. Because of the country size, transport between the initial debit or credit entry and the registration in the books of the other bank involved in the transaction often took several weeks, creating enormous float in China and Russia.

Another common feature of payment systems in these countries was the decentralization of commercial banks' current accounts. Every branch of a commercial bank (where commercial banks existed) kept a clearing account with the local branch of the central bank. Moreover, each branch had to maintain its individual reserve requirements. Reserves were maintained in separate accounts that could not be used for payment purposes. Banks often had large surpluses of funds in some branches and at the same time were paying a penalty for reserve shortfalls in other branches.

The reform of the banking sectors in these countries has required large changes in the arrangements outlined above. This has involved redefining the operational and regulatory roles of the central bank, introducing appropriate accounting procedures and creating new payment systems. Although the starting points in such countries as China, Poland, and Russia were similar, the next section examines the Polish reforms in more detail.

The Case of Poland

In 1990 Poland adopted an adjustment program, known as the Balcerowicz plan, to reduce inflation and liberalize the economy. In parallel with the economic reform, both the National Bank of Poland (NBP) and the financial sector required reform. Under the new Banking Law of 1989 that ended the monobank system, the NBP became the central bank, and its commercial banking functions were spun off into nine state-owned commercial banks. There followed very rapid development of the banking sector: by 1992 some 100 private banks had been established.

One aspect of the reform of this young banking system was the creation of a new payment system. The objectives were to accelerate settlement, to reduce risk, and to increase the efficiency of monetary policy. Although these aims were expressed at the start of the economic reform process, serious discussions about payment-system risk and inefficiencies of the existing payment system—such as large and volatile float, unreliable timing and execution of payment orders, inefficiencies caused by the decentralization of bank funds, problems with operating monetary policy, and so on—started only in 1991 after two large payment frauds.

At that time there was a distinction between the socialized and private sectors. State-owned enterprises were obliged to use bank accounts and to make noncash payments. Households were served by the banks mainly as savings depositories. Banks did not provide households with any payment services. As a result, there was still a noncash circuit for payments in the socialized sector and a cash circuit for payments of the private sector and households. Because of high inflation and demands for cash, the president of the NBP prohibited the use of cash for payments exceeding a certain amount between economic units. The currency per GDP ratio declined considerably from 1989 to 1994.

At the beginning of the banking reform, most noncash payments were executed within the NBP. The NBP operated through independent branches serving their customers and keeping their own books. Each NBP branch maintained accounts for all other branches. Book entries on these accounts were controlled by a centralized computer system working with data delivered by branches. Payment documents were sent directly from branch to branch by standard postal services, which sometimes took several days.

Until 1992, bank branches maintained their current accounts at forty-nine regional branches of the NBP. Banks were obliged to transfer funds between their branches and to maintain reserve balance accounts. For credit transfers, the originating bank debited the customers' accounts and then sent a list of credit transfers to the regional NBP branch, which debited the originating bank and credited an interbank clearing account with the NBP. After some days the branches of other banks received the credit transfers and sent a list to their regional NBP branch. This NBP branch credited the receiving banks' current accounts and debited the interbank clearing account.

Credit transfers were the most popular payment instruments, so the NBP usually had a credit float on its books. Commercial banks had no incentive to speed up the process because they benefited from delaying transmission of the payment document lists. Hence, the banks were able to debit customers' accounts before their own accounts were debited by the NBP.

The transition to a two-tier system transformed what had been an internal float between branches of the central bank into a float involving different institutions. Technical difficulties and the lack of profit orientation on the part of newly created state-owned commercial banks produced long delays in executing transactions. Furthermore, the volume of transactions increased dramatically because of the creation of many new private enterprises. Payment system regulations failed to penalize such delays in processing.

Positive float—an excess of gross debit transfers over gross credit transfers—was less frequent than negative float.[2] This float was reaching 10 percent of reserve money in early 1990 variable.[3] Difficulties in predicting movements in float complicated monetary management in Poland. It was almost impossible to set the size or even the direction of appropriate monetary operations because it was impossible to forecast demand for bank reserves, money, and credit aggregates.

Although net float was negative (credit float exceeded debit float), both the commercial banks and the NBP assumed significant credit risk, especially when banks granted immediate credit to the payee from debit transfers; the payer was debited only after its bank received the cheque. In 1991 a large-scale check-kiting scam was uncovered. A private holding company ART-B used guaranteed checks to finance its activity. They increased the value of the debit float to such an extent that net float in the banking system became positive. When the NBP introduced new rules on checks, which forced banks to receive telecommunication confirmations of balances on payers' accounts before crediting payees, banks realized that there was no money in ART-B's account. The company failed, as did one of commercial banks that had guaranteed the checks.

After the ART-B case, implementation of new arrangements became a matter of urgency. In these circumstances the role of the central bank was crucial, and the NBP implemented the following measures:

- Consolidated banks' clearing accounts into a single account per bank (April 1991 to September 1992). The consolidation of clearing accounts has reduced banks' need for excess reserves, has facilitated banks' liquidity management, and has fostered the development of the money market.

- Implemented a communication infrastructure providing a network between banks.
- Introduced the no-overdrafts rule. This means that banks' payment orders are executed only if there are sufficient funds in the payer's current account. Some rules concerning checks (notification by telex) that decreased debit float from almost 11 percent of reserve money in June 1991 to about 2.6 percent in October 1991 were also introduced. However, there new rules did not change the clearing and settlement mechanism (through branches of NBP) that has deterred almost completely the use of checks in Poland. Float continued but became negative (banks credited the central bank).
- Prepared the rules for the National Clearing House (NCH). The NCH started its activity in April 1993. The NCH operates two clearing systems: paper based and electronic. At the same time, current accounts of the NCH members were moved to the NBP head office.
- Established a new department (Interbank Settlements Department) responsible for managing the new settlement system and overseeing the interbank payment system.
- Established an RTGS system (SORBNET) operated by the Interbank Settlement Department.
- Implemented an automated book-entry securities system for dematerialized treasury bills issued by the Ministry of Finance. Transactions in the treasury bill market are conducted on a delivery-versus-payment (DVP) basis.

Theoretically, the introduction of the new payment system in April 1993 should have accelerated the processing of payment instructions and decreased float in the banking system. There was indeed a significant decrease in the positive float on the central bank's books. However, this was matched by a large increase in the commercial banks' positive float against their customers. This implied that the implementation of the new, much more effective, system shifted float from the central bank to the commercial banks. It also shows that commercial banks did not use the new possibilities to speed up the transfer of funds between their clients. One of the reasons for such behavior was the lack of competition in the banking sector. Nevertheless, these funds did enable banks to create an interbank money market that became the main source of liquidity. Naturally, this had some consequences for the policy of the central bank concerning liquidity in the

RTGS system. The introduction of an RTGS system increases the demand for reserves that central banks may wish to satisfy by creating additional liquidity, such as through intraday credit facilities.

In Poland the policy of the central bank is to decrease bank liquidity because banks are able to use required reserves, which are high in Poland compared with other European countries, for settlement purposes. Hence, reserves and the interbank money market are the main sources of liquidity. In fact, however, Polish banks hold considerable levels of excess reserves that appear to constitute expensive liquidity for payment purposes.

The implementation of these measures took some years. When the NBP started to design a new payment system, there were not enough internal resources and experience to develop a modern payment system quickly. Development of the Polish payment system has been accomplished step by step. The first step was to dismantle the old system and to establish a paper-based clearing-house and gross settlement systems. The second step was to introduce electronic systems both through the Clearing House and the NBP (the RTGS SORBNET system).

Implications for Transitional Economies

For transitional economies one might draw the following conclusions from the material presented above:

- There are some similarities in transitional economies' starting points:
  Monobank or state-owned banking system,

  Cash-based economies,

  Underdeveloped (in technological and institutional terms) payment systems,

  Insufficient recognition of the importance of the time value of money and of opportunity costs in general,

  Absence of competition, and

  Insensitivity to customer needs.
- Initial conditions and changes introduced on a step-by-step basis to date suggest that central banks in transitional economies probably assume, and need to assume, more responsibilities than central banks in market economies in leading and coordinating payment-system reforms. The commercial banks were not strong enough to develop new payment systems on their own. Resources and skilled personnel

were lacking, as was experience in the young private sector. The costs of the reform were too high for new small banks. Furthermore, the central bank was able to receive and coordinate financial help and technical assistance from other central banks and international institutions. Perhaps as a consequence, the similarities in the sequencing of banking system reforms in transitional economies have been quite striking.

- Because of the lack of resources, the shortages of skilled personnel and the lack of experience in the private sector, the central bank is forced to play important roles in all aspects of payment system design and development. Consequently, the central banks in transitional economies typically assume prominent operational roles.
- Emerging economies can adapt successful systems and practices from the industrial countries to suit their own needs. These countries can learn from the experiences of as well as the mistakes made in industrial countries. Furthermore, they can choose design options for modernizing their payment systems that were not available in the past to industrial countries.
- Optimal sequencing of payment system development may be similar—such as accounts in branches of central bank, consolidation of these accounts, paper-based systems, and then RTGS adoption—across transitional economies. Many countries chose an evolutionary approach and did not leap-frog to the latest technology. Users and suppliers in industrial countries possess experience with noncash payment systems and infrastructures that support noncash payments. Such experience did not and still does not exist in many transitional and developing countries. Rapid change in payment systems may not be practical from financial, institutional, or human-resource standpoints. Initial efforts should be implementable and practical. The critical payment design issue is to identify the most important payment applications and develop a system that can be easily installed and used in commercial and central banks.
- Many transitional countries suffer legal deficiencies, such as physical authentication by means of signature as the only legally acceptable method of authenticating a payment.
- In market economies, banks have profit incentives to develop payment services that meet the needs of their customers. So market forces influence the development of payment services. In transitional economies, the profit incentive is still in its infancy. One consequence is that there is little customer pressure for improved payment services.[4]

- The central and commercial banks provide and promote different types of payment services in transitional economies because individuals still rely heavily on cash. This implies that considerable potential exists for commercial banks to expand their markets by developing the banking habit.
- China and Russia still face major management problems within their central banks that necessitate strong centralized control. In the absence of such severe internal management problems, the central banks in Poland and Tanzania have been able to focus on cooperating with the commercial banks to promote reforms in their payment systems.
- Changes in the timing of debits and credits influencing the size and variability of float have caused serious problems for monetary control in the transitional economies.
- Data for transitional countries are still inadequate. Because of insufficient data on the share of cash payments, velocity, and float, large discrete changes in payment-system arrangements in transitional and developing countries necessitate the close attention of central banks to the linkages between payment systems and monetary policy.

For the industrial countries, one general conclusion is that the key lies in regular contact and information sharing among those responsible for payment systems, monetary policy, and supervision and surveillance of banks and financial markets. This is particularly important when major operational changes are contemplated and when markets and systems are under strain. With close cooperation and communication, there should at least be opportunities to prevent problems developing into crises and to reduce the incidence of nasty surprises.

Financial Instability and Fragility from Gaps in Financial Structure

Market Development

Evidence suggests that financial stability is enhanced by the existence of a broad variety of financial markets and financial institutions. As Malcolm Knight (1997, p. 10) points outs:

> Each financial market—as well as the legal and regulatory framework that supports markets—performs a different role that can contribute toward achieving a

robust financial system. If a key market, law, or regulatory practice is missing or does not operate efficiently, financial soundness and the robustness of the system will be adversely affected. . . . most emerging market economies have significant "gaps" in the structure of their financial systems. However, the presence or absence of a given financial intermediary or market, the extent to which it offers close substitutes for bank liabilities and assets, and the degree to which it functions efficiently can affect the soundness of the banking sector. In this sense, gaps in the market can have a large impact on the robustness of a country's financial system—that is, on the financial system's ability to return to a stable equilibrium following a major shock.

Vested interests created under controlled market conditions are bound to oppose reform. Financial restriction involves protecting the commercial banks from which government can expropriate significant seigniorage and discouraging direct markets. Not too surprisingly, when the government develops direct markets not only for its own debt but for private debt as well, commercial banks face a competitive threat. Nonbank investors can be intimidated to some extent from participating in direct markets by fear of reprisals in some form or another from their banks.

This suggests that financial liberalization could be accompanied to advantage by some explicit efforts to develop financial markets. In many developing and transitional countries, establishing voluntary domestic markets for government debt may be particularly efficacious. Markets for government debt provides the central bank with the opportunity to adopt indirect market-based techniques for implementing monetary policy. Abandoning direct controls in favour of indirect market-based techniques can be expected to improve efficiency: all agents face the same market constraint in the form of the market interest rate in their lending and borrowing decisions. This unified market system improves the efficiency with which investible funds are allocated. Formerly, this allocation took place under fragmented market conditions in which agents faced different price signals.

Although government deficits are generally not conducive to economic growth, voluntary private sector purchase of government debt appears to be the least damaging method of financing any given deficit (Fry, 1997a). Both economic and social efficiencies are improved not only though the use of the market-pricing mechanism but also through the transparent presentation of the costs of government expenditures. When the costs of borrowing are borne openly by the public and not hidden through the use of captive buyers, the true resource costs of government spending can be incorporated into both economic and social choices. Even politicians' choices can change when they are properly informed.

A move toward developing voluntary domestic markets for government debt offers benefits in terms of lower inflation and higher saving and growth. High growth, in turn, alleviates the deficit. There is, therefore, some hint of a virtuous circle in which greater use of voluntary domestic markets lowers inflation and raises growth, both of which reduce the government's deficit. In general, developing and transitional country governments make too little use of voluntary private-sector lenders. While the typical OECD country finances about 50 percent of its deficit from voluntary domestic nonbank lenders, the typical developing country finances only about 8 percent of its deficit from this source.

Establishing a voluntary market for government debt involves a fundamental change in the approach to financing the government deficit. Typically, the change occurs from a system in which most institutional interest rates are fixed and the government is financed at favorable fixed rates by unwilling captive buyers of its debt. In such a system, bank rate and all other institutional interest rates, including the treasury bill yield, are simply announced by the minister of finance. Captive buyers hold treasury bills and other government securities to fulfil their ratio requirements and so on, and the central bank takes up any shortfall.

In the process of developing a voluntary market, privileged access and captive buyers are eschewed in favor of a level-playing-field philosophy. Government now competes on the same terms and conditions as private agents for available saving and so faces the economy's opportunity cost of borrowing. It has to accept the interest-cost consequences of its borrowing, and this should exert fiscal discipline that may have been absent when borrowing was kept artificially cheap. The economic principle behind the change is that a level playing field maximizes the efficiency with which scarce resources are allocated throughout the economy. This change in approach necessarily involves many practical changes in the way government debt is sold.

A clean auction in which all bills are sold at whatever price the market yields four advantages:

- It informs the government of the true opportunity cost of its borrowing.
- It avoids recourse to the central bank and so avoids the road back to inflationary finance.
- It provides important feedback signals from the market for monetary policy purposes.
- The treasury bill yield can and soon will be used as a crucial reference rate for the pricing of other financial claims in new markets.

Central banks may well become involved in the debate, since they stand to benefit on at least three counts:

- Getting the government out of the central bank clearly reduces the inflationary threat of deficits.
- Developing voluntary domestic markets for government debt enables the central bank to use indirect market-based instruments of monetary policy.
- By divorcing fiscal and monetary policy in this way, the central bank is bound to attain more independence regardless of any legal provisions.

It is not enough to persuade the main political actors that inflationary finance and financial repression are growth-reducing ways of financing deficits. It is also essential to persuade the main political actors that debts and deficits must be kept within sustainable bounds after inflationary finance and financial repression are abandoned. Hence, the primary macroeconomic prerequisite for developing voluntary domestic markets for government debt is a sustainable government deficit.

The development of markets for government debt has never occurred overnight. The important first step for any country is to gain investor confidence in government debt and to build and maintain a good reputation for issuing and honoring debt. The process is necessarily one of learning by doing as much on the part of the authorities as on the part of the private sector. It is usually also a process of learning from one's mistakes.

David Cole, Hal Scott, and Philip Wellons (1995, p. 19) identify four stages in the typical development process: (1) the controlled system, (2) initial liberalization, (3) retrenchment after crisis, and (4) more aggressive development. The first step invariably takes the form of some interest-rate liberalization. The crisis can take various forms: exchange-rate or balance-of-payments problems, recession, excessive liquidity, or fraud. The reaction is to "shoot the messenger" and reimpose controls. After the crisis abates, a second attempt is launched in the light of the previous experience.

A typical element of sequencing has been the reduction in excessive reserve and liquid asset ratio requirements, although abolition has often been resisted on the grounds that such ratios still serve prudential purposes.[5] To the extent that they remain binding, liquid asset ratio requirements maintain captive buyers and so distort price signals emanating from treasury bill auctions and impede the market development process.

Inevitably, it takes time for any government to establish a new track record of sound finance. At the start of any initiative to develop voluntary domestic markets for government debt, the authorities are bound to face a suspicious and unwilling private sector. Their record is one of confiscation; the promise of attractive market yields is unlikely to be believed before some credibility has been earned. This implies that market yields on government debt will embody a significant risk premium, mainly taking the specific form of an inflation-risk premium. Once the debt has been sold, the private sector may reason, the government will have an incentive to inflate its way out of its obligations returning to the old confiscatory pattern.

Initially, therefore, voluntary lenders demand a risk premium from government. From the government's perspective, it is paying too high an interest rate immediately after the switch to voluntary domestic market financing. From the private sector's perspective, caution dictates the extraction of a risk premium before it can be enticed to lend. One solution that can help reconcile the government's commitment to turn over a new leaf with the private sector's doubts that this has really happened is for the government to issue debt that is automatically adjusted for changes in the price level (index-linked debt) at the outset of its reform.[6]

Aggressive competition among banks should prevent them from intimidating or deterring nonbanks from using direct markets, so measures to ensure vigorous competition may be needed at the start of the market-development program. At the same time, prudential supervision and regulation can play a vital role in maintaining stable rather than unstable competitive conditions.

To enhance competition, measures to broaden the investor base are crucial. These may include advertising as well as improving access for nonbank participants at treasury bill auctions. Indeed, if the major investors remain commercial banks, portfolio adjustments by the banking system as a whole in response to changing business conditions may be constrained or disruptive. If there are no other holders of treasury bills, the banking system will perforce have to hold the same volume even though it would now prefer to reduce such holdings in favor of loans to the private sector. In such case, treasury bill yields must adjust by possibly large amounts. With a broad and deep market for treasury bills, however, banks can use these assets as shock absorbers against fluctuations in both deposits and loan demand. Under such conditions, it is typical to find that banks decrease their holdings of government securities and increase their loans during economic upswings (Fry and Williams, 1984, pp. 92–93).

If the banking system holds the lion's share of government securities, secondary market development is inevitably retarded if not stifled completely because of the lack of diversity amongst the holders of government debt. The homogeneity of banks implies that they will frequently all be on the same side of the market. Hence, trading remains thin, yields fluctuate excessively and spreads stay high. For example, bid-ask spreads are far lower in highly liquid markets, such as Australia (0.03 percent) and Japan (0.02 percent), than they are in illiquid markets, such as India (1 percent), Indonesia (1.5 percent), Malaysia (0.25 percent), and Thailand (0.75 percent) (Lynch 1995, p. 330).

Foreign participation enhances competition and efficiency in several respects. However, before domestic debt markets can be opened to foreign investors with any realistic expectation of foreign participation, they must meet international standards with respect to the market microstructure (such as trading practices, registry, transfer and settlements systems, and so on) and have established a track record.

While no foreign demand exists for some government bonds because of their low yields and high risk, some governments (such as Korea) have restricted foreign acquisition of bonds that yield rates above the world level. Whether due to lack of demand for unattractive fixed-income securities offering yields below the world level or government restrictions on supply, the general pattern of capital account liberalization over the past two decades exhibits a preference for opening the equities market to foreign investors before the debt market. This preference may reflect, in part, a belief that foreign equity participation does not involve payment of a country risk premium to foreigners and, in part, a belief that capital flows into and out of equity markets are less speculative or destabilizing than capital flows into and out of debt markets. In fact, destabilizing capital flows tend to use bank deposits denominated in both local and foreign currency and may be generated just as much if not more by residents than by nonresidents.

One source of reluctance to permit foreign investors to participate in domestic fixed-income securities markets emanates from a concern that the country will pay an unnecessary and expensive currency-risk premium. To the extent that foreign investors are already permitted to participate in equity markets as well as to undertake foreign direct investment (FDI), the relevant comparison is between returns that foreign investors are obtaining in these two markets relative to returns in the bond market. Given the typical incentive package encouraging FDI, the cost to the host country of this form of capital flow may well exceed the cost of funding through domestic bond markets by a considerable margin.

Given the relatively small size of fixed-income markets in most developing and transitional countries, foreign inflows would in any case be limited by their negative impact on yields.[7] While bubbles and herd instincts can produce large stock price rallies under illusions that future dividends will rise too, higher bond prices are necessarily *always* accompanied by the sobering reality of lower yields because coupon payments remain constant.

Foreign participation in domestic bond markets broadens the investor base, permits foreign investors greater diversification than is possible through international bonds, stabilizes aggregate capital flows since more portfolio reallocation can occur among financial assets of the same country, supports bond issuers that are too small for the international market, improves depth and liquidity, improves risk management for investors that simultaneously benefits issuers, increases market sophistication through the transfer of technology, and imposes additional fiscal discipline on the government through the threat of capital withdrawal. In many developing and transitional countries, the main problem is not a potential oversupply of foreign investment into domestic bond markets but rather the lack of a well-functioning bond market into which foreign investment can flow.

Perverse Borrowers and Prudential Supervision

Financial liberalization places an additional burden on prudential regulation and supervision. Several interest-rate liberalization experiments have failed to produce the desired results. The basic problem lies in the perverse reaction to higher interest rates by insolvent (or nonprofit-motivated) economic agents—governments, firms, or individuals. By definition, an insolvent agent (one whose liabilities exceed its assets) or distress borrower is unable to repay its loans. Hence, it is not deterred from borrowing by a higher cost. It simply continues, if it can, to borrow whatever it needs to finance its losses. These inevitably increase with an increase in the interest rate that drives up the agent's cost of servicing its loans. Therefore, such agents exhibit loan demand functions that respond positively to the interest rate.

Perverse upward-sloping demand functions may be responsible, in part, for the observation that real deposit rates in eighty-five developing countries for which any data exist ranged from −458 to +234 percent over the period 1971 to 1995.[8] The standard deviation of these 1,329 annual observations is 32 percent.

José De Gregorio and Pablo Guidotti (1995, pp. 436–437) claim that real interest rates are not a good indicator of financial repression or distortion. They suggest that the relationship between real interest rates and economic growth might resemble an inverted U curve: "Very low (and negative) real interest rates tend to cause financial disintermediation and hence tend to reduce growth, as implied by the McKinnon-Shaw hypothesis. ... On the other hand, very high real interest rates that do not reflect improved efficiency of investment, but rather a lack of credibility of economic policy or various forms of country risk, are likely to result in a lower level of investment as well as a concentration in excessively risky projects" (De Gregorio and Guidotti, 1995, p. 437).

In fact, the point made by De Gregorio and Guidotti holds up well with the data from my sample of eighty-five developing countries. First, I estimated the relationship between the annual rate of economic growth YG and the real rate of interest RR in equations of the basic form $YG = \beta_0 + \beta_1(RR + \beta_2) \times (RR + \beta_2)$. Since the parameter β_2 was not significantly different from zero, although its negative value implies that growth is maximized at some positive real interest rate, I drop it from the estimate reported here. A pooled time-series fixed-effect estimate including both the squared real interest rate and the absolute value of the cubed real interest rate gives the following result (t statistics in parentheses):

$$YG = -0.033RR^2 + 0.088|RR|^3$$
$$(-3.949) \qquad (3.598)$$
$$\overline{R}^2 = 0.163. \qquad\qquad\qquad (6.1)$$

No intercept is reported because the fixed-effect model estimates separate constants for each country; this equation estimates eighty-five intercepts. The effect of a rising real interest rate on growth produced by equation (6.1) is illustrated in Figure 6.1. Evidently, growth is maximized when the real interest rate lies within the normal or nonpathological range of, say, −5 to +15 percent.

Pathologically high positive real interest rates, possibly triggered by fiscal instability, indicate a poorly functioning financial system. Distress borrowing crowds out borrowing for investment purposes by solvent firms, producing an epidemic effect (Fry, 1995, pp. 305–306; McKinnon, 1993, pp. 38–41; Rojas-Suárez and Weisbrod, 1995; Stiglitz and Weiss, 1981). Funds continue to be supplied because of explicit or implicit deposit insurance. Indirect instruments of monetary policy implementation are completely ineffective. The end result is financial and economic paralysis.

There has been increasing recognition that prudential regulation and supervision is a key prerequisite for financial stability. In their absence, financial systems are prone to financial crises, as witnessed by Chile, which experienced high real interest rates in the 1980s: "These incredibly high

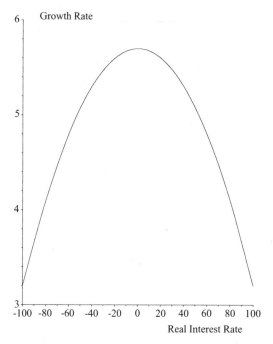

Figure 6.1.   Real interest rates and economic growth rates in 85 developing countries, 1971 to 1995

interest rates on peso loans represented, in large part, the breakdown of proper financial supervision over the Chilean banking system. Neither officials in the commercial banks themselves nor government regulatory authorities adequately monitored the creditworthiness of a broad spectrum of industrial borrowers" (McKinnon, 1991, p. 383).

Before interest-rate liberalization can produce the beneficial allocative and inflation-reducing effects, pathological borrowers with perverse credit demands must be removed from the pool of potential borrowers and banks put on a sound footing. These are tasks for improved prudential supervision and regulation of banks. Essentially, those firms whose liabilities exceed their assets and whose management is not affected positively in some form by better economic performance of their firms should be excluded from the process of credit allocation through the market mechanism. Their behavior in a market environment is inappropriate.

The same criteria—solvency and profit motivation of management— also applies to the banks themselves. Rapid growth in banking creates yet another potential problem in the form of a knowledge bottleneck. For

example, even a short visit makes one immediately aware of the considerable investment in human capital now being undertaken to achieve
the objective of establishing Bangkok as a regional financial center for
Indochina. Obviously, financial expertise and experience cannot beacquired
overnight. This suggests that prudential regulation and supervision are all
the more important in rapidly growing financial sectors than in those
growing less dramatically.

One solution to the knowledge bottleneck lies in foreign banks.[9] If prudential supervision and regulation are weak or stretched, however, wisdom
might counsel granting licences only to large, reputable foreign banks that
would be least likely to risk adverse publicity from sharp, if not illegal, practices (Fry, 1997b). As recognized by Mauritius and the Seychelles, there can
also be some advantages in inviting foreign banks from several different
economies to establish offices. This strategy may not only introduce a
wider range of banking innovations but also deter the formation of
a foreign bank cartel.

In several countries, rapid expansion of lending by newly liberalized
banks has resulted in just as high levels of nonperforming assets as did
directed credit policies under financial repression. Most banking systems
simply lack the expertise needed to make good commercial judgments.
In any case, they cannot acquire more of such expertise at the moment
financial liberalization occurs. Hence, prudential regulation and supervision
are doubly imperative at the outset of financial liberalization to curtail the
worst excesses of inexperienced and untrained bankers (Villanueva and
Mirakhor, 1990; Vittas, 1992).

Experience indicates that interest rate liberalization typically raises at
least two major questions. The first is how to curb or counter an explosion
in consumer lending after financial liberalization, particularly when it takes
the form of the abolition of credit ceilings. The second is how to confront
the herd instinct possessed by bankers throughout the world.

International evidence suggests that easier access to consumer credit
lowers private saving ratios in the medium term (Jappelli and Pagano, 1994;
Liu and Woo, 1994; Patrick, 1994). A burst of consumer lending following
financial liberalization may also jeopardize monetary control or squeeze
out investment lending. Perhaps the pragmatic answer lies in imposing high
downpayment requirements for mortgages and loans for durable consumer
goods at the outset of the liberalization program. Subsequently, such
requirements can be gradually reduced, particularly when the economy is
in no danger of overheating.

Many newly liberalized banking systems have become overly enthusias-
tic about property development, credit card lending, and housing only to

find that expected returns failed to materialize. Loan officers exhibiting such fads and fancies can be compared to a herd of wildebeest moving from one watering hole to another. As one hole runs dry and the surrounding grass is overgrazed, the herd moves on to a new source of water and pastures. The first to arrive at the new watering hole do well; the laggards struggle to survive.[10]

This herd instinct among bankers takes the form of bank lending surging into particular sectors or activities only to withdraw again after delinquency and default rates rise. Loan officers have an incentive to follow the herd when it comes to sectoral lending decisions. To be wrong in the company of most other loan officers is excusable. To be wrong in isolation may not be forgiven so readily.

Occasionally this herd instinct degenerates into lemming-like behavior when bankers all rush into a new activity with virtually no consideration of the risks involved. The macroeconomic problem is that such credit surges produce bubbles in which prices are increased solely as a result of the credit injections. When the bubbles burst, banks are left with collateral worth considerably less than the loans that are now nonperforming. The end result is financial crisis.

Application of risk-weighted capital adequacy requirements provides one specific way of containing systemic risk inherent in overexuberant financial-sector growth, the herd instinct, and herd or lemming-like lending behavior. The aim is to deter excessive lending concentration to (1) a single sector of the economy, such as construction or real estate, (2) a single region of the country, or (3) a single borrower. These capital requirements would gradually raise the marginal cost of excessive growth in loans of all particular types. Thus, a bank that increased risk through rapid expansion of any loan category by either changing the composition of its portfolio or increasing its total portfolio size would incur increased risk weighting on all loans in its high-growth categories.

Such a system could start with an increased risk weighting on all loans in any category whose growth exceeded, say, 15 percent in real terms by, for example, two percentage points by which the actual percentage growth of this loan category exceeded the benchmark. For example, a 20 percent growth of loans in any specific category would involve an increase in risk weighting of ten percentage points on each additional loan of this type. In this way the price mechanism can be used, for example, to increase the financial institutions' marginal cost of property lending, raising interest rates on such loans and deterring speculative real estate booms. A more sophisticated version of this proposal is to assess a bank's portfolio in terms of the covariance of individual loan default probabilities. The score in this exercise would then produce an adjusted capital adequacy requirement.

While capital-adequacy ratios are designed to counteract credit risk, market or interest-rate risk can be equally if not more important in market-based financial systems. Recently, therefore, the Basle Committee for Banking Supervision accepted the use of in-house value-at-risk (VaR) models for determining minimum regulatory capital requirements against market risk and the incorporation of covariances between basic market risk categories (Goodhart, Hartmann, Llewellyn, Rojas-Suárez, and Weisbrod, 1998, ch. 5).

Market VaR models estimate future potential losses on given portfolios caused by fluctuations in interest rates, exchange rates, equity, and commodity prices. The output is an expected maximum loss over a given time period for a given confidence interval. The Basle Committee adopted a two-week holding period, a 99 percent confidence interval, and a one-year data window. Over a one-year period (250 trading days), this implies that expected losses (violations) would exceed the VaR estimate on 2.5 occasions (250 × 0.01). The Basle Committee defines a green zone for zero to four violations, a yellow zone for five to nine violations, and a red zone for ten or more violations. Regulators impose penalties when the number of violations over the past year fall outside the green zone.

While results differ, sometimes considerably, depending on the choices of confidence interval, holding period, and length of data window, they also depend on the model used to predict the frequency distributions of portfolio returns. The three main techniques are the historical simulation based on past outcomes, the variance-covariance approach that assumes a given (usually the normal) distribution, and Monte Carlo simulations that use random-generated risk-factor returns based on either historical data or an adopted parametric distributions (again, usually the normal distribution). In assessing the alternative techniques, Charles Goodhart, Philipp Hartmann, David Llewellyn, Liliana Rojas-Suárez, and Steven Weisbrod (1998, ch. 5) conclude that historical simulation addresses the facts that financial-market returns are not normally distributed and that nonlinear relationships exist between portfolio returns and risk-factor returns. The main disadvantage of historical simulation lies in its sensitivity to the data window. This simply illustrates the point that the past is rarely a good indicator of the future.

Because assessing a bank's in-house VaR model is far from easy, the U.S. Federal Reserve System has suggested an approach that would shift this responsibility on to the banks themselves. Under such a system, the bank commits itself not to exceed a given portfolio loss over some future time period; this precommitted amount then constitutes the bank's regulatory market risk minimum capital requirement. Violation invokes monetary or nonmonetary penalties based on such predetermined graduated ladder of responses. Under this system regulators do not evaluate the model, as they do under the Basle approach, because they focus on the outcomes rather than on the way these outcomes are achieved. Such a scheme can be seen as an incentive contract between regulators and the regulated.

In examining trends in financial regulation, Goodhart, Hartmann, Llewellyn, Rojas-Suárez, and Weisbrod (1998) argue that regulations themselves are becoming more market-based. Specifically, increasing complexity now forces the regulators to adopt systems that attempt to reinforce financial institutions' own internal regulatory structures rather than to superimpose external constraints. For example, the shift from balance-sheet ratio constraints toward capital adequacy provisions recognizes that financial institutions were able with increasing ease to remove activities from their balance sheets. Similarly, the acceptance of institutions' own value-at-risk models for capital adequacy recognises that well-run financial institutions can be steered toward public welfare objectives, such as systemic stability of the financial system, more effectively by regulations based on best-practice internal control mechanisms than on any externally imposed restrictions. Of particular relevance in the present context is the authors' conclusion that the institutional arrangements of national regulatory systems are of second-order importance compared with the substantive issues of how to regulate effectively in a global market environment to protect consumers from poor business practice, fraud, and systemic financial instability.

The Case of China

The end of China's Cultural Revolution in December 1978 heralded a gradual process of economic liberalization and reform. In the financial sector, the monobank system was abandoned in favor of a two-tier banking system in which the People's Bank of China (PBC) became the central bank and its commercial lending activities were transferred to four specialized banks. While China's financial sector has changed since 1978, the credit plan remains the key instrument of monetary policy. Credit ceilings are set for each specialized bank, and subceilings are also imposed for specific types of loans, such as working capital and fixed investment loans. Although banks have some discretion in varying interest rates, China's interest rates are basically determined by administrative fiat (Tseng, Khor, Kochhar,

Mihaljek, and Burton, 1994, pp. 13–18). In large part, reluctance to liberalize interest rates springs from the desire to contain losses in China's
state-owned enterprises, the main borrowers from China's state-owned
financial institutions.

Inconsistencies between the development of a market-based economy
and the use of credit ceilings as the main instrument of monetary policy
have become increasingly apparent. Since 1993, therefore, the Chinese
authorities have accelerated the pace of financial-sector reforms. Part
of these reforms include greater flexibility in, and are scheduled to lead
eventually to market determination of, interest rates (Tseng et al., 1994,
pp. 18–19).

The main problem lies in the fact that the PBC and China's state-owned
banks have undertaken and continue to undertake large quasi-fiscal activities. When these costs are consolidated with the central government deficit,
the consolidated government deficit rises from a reported level of just over
2 percent of GDP to an average of 6 to 7 percent of GDP since 1989, rising
to 7 to 9 percent in 1993 (World Bank, 1995a, pp. xi–xiii). Were the inflation
tax and financial repression as sources of government revenue abandoned
without concomitant increases in conventional tax revenue or reductions in
government expenditure, the government's fiscal position might become
unsustainable and unstable. Furthermore, state-owned enterprises might
well react in a perverse fashion by increasing their demands for credit in
step with increases in the interest rate.

Past quasi-fiscal activities of the PBC and the state-owned banks, here-
after referred to as China's banking system, taking the form of extending
policy loans to state-owned enterprises have produced a legacy of bad
debts. In the form of interest-rate controls that have squeezed spreads
between time deposit and loan rates to zero or even inverted them, these
quasi-fiscal activities have reduced the banking system's reported capital
per asset ratio. Not only has the banking system's balance sheet been
impaired as a result of past quasi-fiscal activities, the government expects
its banking system to continue providing policy loans, either directly or
indirectly, in the future. Hence, the banking system faces both stock and
flow problems. This section questions the sustainability of such quasi-fiscal
activities in the light of proposed interest-rate liberalization.

China's financial system is dominated by its central bank, the PBC, and
its four state-owned specialized banks—the Industrial and Commercial
Bank of China, the Agricultural Bank of China, the Bank of China, and the
People's Construction Bank of China. While they coexist with three policy
banks (the State Development Bank of China, the Agricultural Development Bank of China, and the Export-Import Bank of China), four nation-

wide commercial banks, six regional banks, and numerous deposit-taking nonbank financial institutions (urban credit cooperatives, rural credit cooperatives, financial trust and investment corporations, finance companies, and finance leasing companies), these four state-owned specialized banks distributed 78 percent of all loans and collected 72 percent of all deposits in 1995 (People's Bank of China, 1996, p. 88, and table 6, pp. 93–94).

Despite China's move toward a market economy in several respects, the credit plan still directs financial resources through the state-owned banks to state-owned enterprises to a large extent under a nonmarket allocative mechanism. Hassanali Mehran, Marc Quintyn, Tom Nordman, and Bernard Laurens (1996, p. 69) report that the state-owned enterprises absorb over 80 percent of total bank credit to the economy. These enterprises also post losses of about 6 percent of GDP (Mehran, Quintyn, Nordman, and Laurens, 1996, p. 68).

To contain these state-enterprise losses, the state-owned banks have been used to conduct quasi-fiscal activities in the form of extending loans at subsidised interest rates and to loss-making, insolvent state-owned enterprises. Some loan rates of interest have been held below deposit rates of comparable maturity within the state-owned banking system (Mehran, Quintyn, Nordman, and Laurens, 1996, p. 47). Between April 1990 and January 1995, for example, the margin between deposit and loan rates of maturities exceeding ten years ranged from –0.36 to –4.32 percentage points.

One effect of the wafer-thin spreads between average deposit and loan rates of interest has been a declining profit rate. Eric Girardin (1997, table 6, p. 32) reports a decline in state-bank profits from 1.2 percent of assets in 1987 to 0.3 percent of assets by 1993. A concomitant of declining bank profitability has been the decapitalization of the state-owned banks from a capital to asset ratio of 6.5 to 3.3 percent for the Industrial and Commercial Bank of China and from 7.3 to 2.8 percent for the People's Construction Bank of China between 1989 and 1994 (Girardin, 1997, p. 32). Given an estimate suggesting that 20 percent of state-owned banks' loan portfolios are nonperforming, the current situation raises issues of sustainability and stability.

In effect, the losses of state-owned enterprises have now produced insolvency in all the state-owned specialized banks. While this is not catastrophic because seigniorage revenue and financial repression can still keep the financial sector afloat, continued balance-sheet impairment implies that an increasing proportion of this seigniorage and financial repression revenue must be allocated to bank losses, thus leaving a dwindling proportion available to boost government revenues. As Tamar Atinc and Bert Hofman

(1996, fig. 1, p. 3) demonstrate, government revenue has declined continuously from almost 35 percent of GDP in 1978 to 12.1 percent in 1995 (see also International Monetary Fund 1996, table 38, p. 73). Hence, the fiscal situation is far from buoyant and can ill afford revenue loss from seigniorage or financial repression.

In practice, China has found it impossible to satisfy its intertemporal budget constraint with conventional tax revenue. Indeed, this has been possible only by relying on revenue from the inflation tax and reducing interest costs through financial repression, as do many other developing and transitional countries. In a sample of forty-three developing countries, the inflation tax yielded 2 percent of GDP and financial repression decreased government interest costs by an additional 2 percent of GDP over the period 1979 to 1993 (Fry, Goodhart, and Almeida, 1996, p. 36). In China's case, the inflation tax yielded about 8 percent of GDP with 25 percent inflation in 1994; financial repression reduced interest costs by approximately the same magnitude.

In the Chinese context, it is useful to consolidate central and commercial banks and to treat them for analytical purposes like the monobank they replaced. Hence, the level of and remuneration on required reserves is irrelevent. This will no longer be the case, however, once interest rates are liberalized and private-sector competition introduced into China's commercial banking system. The consolidated balance sheet of China's banking system shows negative values under "other times, (net)" since the first quarter of 1995 (International Financial Statistics, September 1996, CD-ROM). At the end of March 1996, this negative figure had reached −Yuan 159 billion.

In present value terms, the negative net worth of China's banking system produced from the monetary survey can be reduced by the amount of currency in circulation, which has a far smaller present value than its face value, since it pays no interest. The present value of this liability item is the present value of maintaining the currency, preventing forgery, and so on. Here I subtract the entire value of currency in circulation from the monetary survey liabilities making the assumption that currency maintenance costs are zero.

On the other hand, in present value terms, the negative net worth of China's banking system must be enlarged by the amount of nonperforming or bad loans on the banks' books. Taking an estimate of 20 percent of nongovernment loans as effectively uncollectable reduces assets and hence reduces net worth (Girardin, 1997, p. 30). Here I reduce domestic credit by 20 percent of its nongovernment component. I also add the value of bonds issued by banks to quasi-money to obtain an estimate of total interest-paying liabilities. These modifications indicates that the banking system had interest-paying liabilities that exceeded interest-earning assets by Yuan 457 billion, equivalent to about 8 percent of GDP at the end of March 1996.

In one way or another, the cost of servicing the excess interest-paying liabilities must be met through seigniorage revenue or financial repression. In China, seigniorage is currently raised only through currency in circulation because interest comparable to interest paid on deposits and charged on loans is paid on bank reserves. In July 1993, for example, the interest rate on both required and excess reserves was set at 9.18 percent compared with commercial bank rates of 9 percent on six-month working capital loans and 10.98 percent on both twelve-month working capital loans and twelve-month deposits (People's Bank of China, 1996, tables 9–10, pp. 96–97).

The government expects the banking system to provide policy loans to loss-making enterprises at subsidized interest rates as well as to service its negative net worth. A considerable proportion of these policy loans is never repaid. Hofman (1995, table 3, p. 12) estimates that transfers from the Chinese banking system in the form of interest subsidies and loan default averaged over 5 percent of GDP over the period 1992 to 1994. If these transfers continue and, at the same time, depositors were not taxed implicitly through financial repression, the entire cost would have to be met from seigniorage revenue.

That inflation has not risen to over 40 percent, as predicted by the financing model presented in Fry (1998b), is due to the fact that the Chinese authorities have extracted revenue from sight deposits. This has been achieved using the basic instrument of financial repression setting the sight deposit interest rate by administrative fiat. Since July 1993, for example, the sight deposit rate has been 3.15 percent compared with the twelve-month time deposit rate of 10.98 percent and the three-year time deposit partially indexed yield of about 16 percent (People's Bank of China, 1996, table 10, p. 97). These sight and three-year time deposit rates produce almost exactly the twelve percentage point cost-minimizing gap between sight and time deposit rates of interest estimated in Fry (1998b). Hence, China's banking system has extracted the inflation tax from depositors as well as from currency holders.

Proposed interest-rate liberalization in China (People's Bank of China, 1996, p. 82) would undermine the existing method of extracting seigniorage. Seigniorage revenue from deposits would be competed away as sight deposit rates were raised. In the absence of fiscal reform designed to reduce the government's consolidated deficit, financing the policy loan program and debt default equal to about 5 percent of GDP through seigniorage would necessitate an inflation rate in excess of 40 percent. "Good-bye financial repression, hello financial crash" is the verdict of Carlos Diaz-Alejandro (1985) on the Latin American experiments with interest-rate liberalization since the mid-1970s. Were no accompanying measures taken, the same verdict would be applicable to interest-rate liberalization in China.

One solution is to combine interest-rate liberalization with the imposition of a noninterest-earning reserve requirement solely against sight deposits. This reserve requirement retains sight deposits as a source of seigniorage revenue and ensures that, even after interest-rate liberalization, the competitively determined sight deposit interest rate would remain well below time deposit rates. The model presented in Fry (1998b) indicates that such an *intramarginal* tax on currency and sight deposits will not affect the *aggregate* demand for *M2* and therefore will not affect the ability of the banking system as a whole to extend the same real volume of loans as it does under present arrangements. What the noninterest-earning required reserve does is to influence the desired composition of money holding between currency, sight, and time deposits.

Inflation, Growth, Monetary Policy, and Fiscal Dominance

Inflation-Growth Relationships

In the 1960s, much of the economics profession accepted the finding that a tradeoff existed between inflation and growth: higher growth could be achieved at the cost of higher inflation. In the 1970s, more sophisticated expectations-augmented Phillips curves became popular. In fact, David Hume (1752/1958, pp. 46–47) provided one of the clearest expositions of the expectations-augmented Phillips curve in 1752:

> Accordingly we find, that in every kingdom, into which money begins to flow in greater abundance than formerly, every thing takes a new face; labour and industry gain life; the merchant becomes more enterprizing; the manufacturer more diligent and skillful; and even the farmer follows his plough with greater alacrity and attention. . . . To account, then, for this phaenomenon, we must consider, that tho' the high price of commodities be a necessary consequence of the encrease of gold and silver, yet it follows not immediately upon that encrease; but some time is requir'd before the money circulate thro' the whole state, and make its effects be felt on all ranks of people. At first, no alteration is perceiv'd; by degrees, the price rises, first of one commodity, then of another; till the whole at last

reaches a just proportion, with the new quantity of specie, which is in the kingdom. In my opinion, 'tis only in this interval or intermediate situation, betwixt the acquisition of money and rise of prices, that the encreasing quantity of gold and silver is favourable to industry.

In fact, at least above some minimum threshold levels, simple bivariate cross-section and pooled time-series regressions produce *negative* relationships between inflation and growth for various country groups in both long and short runs. Negative sloping long-run expectations-augmented Phillips curve relationships between inflation and growth have also been found, particularly in developing countries (Fry, 1995, ch. 10).

Far from there being any exploitable tradeoff in the medium and longer term between inflation and higher output levels, the accepted view now is that in the longer term this relationship is negative—that is, more inflation is associated with lower growth (Barro, 1995; De Gregorio, 1994; Fischer, 1994). While the deleterious effects of hyperinflation on growth, with the dislocations caused to saving patterns and to the monetary and pricing mechanisms, are fairly obvious, inflation has, so it is claimed, a negative effect on growth even at low or moderate levels. In part, this latter effect may be because a higher level of inflation is generally associated with a greater variability of inflation and hence a greater riskiness of longer-term unindexed contracts. As John Locke (1695/1992, p. 189) wrote:

> I see no reason to think, that a little bigger or less size of the pieces coined is of any moment, one way or the other. The harm comes by the change, which unreasonably and unjustly gives away and transfers men's properties, disorders trade, puzzles accounts, and needs a new arithmetic to cast up reckonings, and keep accounts in; besides a thousand other inconveniencies.

There are a wide variety of potential channels for both negative and positive effects running from inflation to growth, and vice versa. In developing countries, fixed nominal interest and exchange rates may have been particularly harmful (Fry, 1995, ch. 8). As inflation rises, lower real interest rates resulting from fixed nominal rates reduce credit availability and distort resource allocation, while a fixed exchange rate prices exports out of world markets. Both effects are growth-reducing.

All financial systems in market economies, whether they are industrial, developing, or transitional, perform two basic functions: (1) administering the country's payment mechanism and (2) intermediating between savers and investors. On the first function, there is little disagreement that high inflation impairs the domestic currency's attributes not only of a store of value but also of a means of payment. As James Tobin (1992, p. 772) states: "A society's money is necessarily a store of value. Otherwise it could not be an acceptable means of payment." So financial systems are impeded in performing both of their basic functions under high inflation. Society turns to substitute means of payment (foreign currencies or barter trade), thereby bypassing the domestic financial system. This substitution is one manifestation of the law of demand. As the opportunity cost of holding money rises, the demand for money expressed at constant prices or in real terms falls.

In the simplest balance sheet of the banking system, commercial banks hold loans L and reserves R as their assets and deposits D as their liabilites:

Assets	Liabilities
Reserves R	Deposits D
Loans L	

The balance sheet identity implies $R + L = D$. Naturally, this balance-sheet identity is still preserved if one divides both assets and liabilities by nominal GNP Y:

Assets	Liabilites
Reserves R/Y	Deposits D/Y
Loans L/Y	

Ceteris paribus, the ratio D/Y falls as inflation accelerates because households and firms choose to hold smaller money balances in relation to their expenditure levels due to the rising cost of holding money. Therefore, the ratio $R + L/Y$ must also fall.[11] If the ratio R/L remains roughly constant, then both R/Y and L/Y fall as D/Y falls. Since L/Y is the ratio of bank loans to the nominal value of output, business firms find themselves facing a credit squeeze as inflation rises. Unable to obtain the necessary loans to cover the costs of their working capital, some firms may be unable to stay in business. The aggregate level of output in real terms would then fall. In this case, therefore, the deterioration of money reduces the ability of the banking system to administer the country's payment mechanism and to intermediate between savers and investors; performance in both functions is related. Perhaps the former effect reduces income levels while the latter effect reduces income growth.

Fiscal Dominance

Fiscal difficulties frequently lies behind many features and problems of financial systems in developing and transitional countries. Many developing and transitional country governments find it virtually impossible to satisfy their intertemporal budget constraint with conventional tax revenue. Hence, they rely on revenue from the inflation tax, and they reduce their interest costs through financial repression (Agénor and Montiel, 1996, p. 156; Brock, 1989, p. 116; Fry, 1997a, ch. 3; Giovannini and de Melo, 1993). Both the theoretical and empirical findings reviewed in this chapter suggest that financial repression is a particularly damaging quasi-tax from the perspective of economic growth.

Governments can finance their deficits in four major ways:[12]

- Monetising the deficit by borrowing at zero cost from the central bank,
- Borrowing at below-market interest rates by thrusting debt down the throats of captive buyers, primarily commercial banks,
- Borrowing abroad in foreign currency, and
- Borrowing at market interest rates from voluntary lenders in domestic currency markets.

The typical OECD country finances about 50 percent of its deficit in voluntary domestic-currency markets, while the typical developing country finances only about 8 percent of its deficit from this source.

Why this matters is that, for any given persistent government deficit, greater use of the first three sources is associated with higher inflation rates, lower saving ratios, and lower rates of economic growth (Fry, 1997a). Government recourse to the central bank inevitably leads to inflation. Indeed, such inflationary finance can be considered a source of tax revenue in that inflation imposes a tax on money holders.

Financial repression, the second way of financing the government deficit, is also tax-like in that it involves forcing captive buyers to hold government debt at interest rates below market yields. By reducing its interest costs, this method reduces the government's recorded deficit. Foreign borrowing, which for all developing and virtually all transitional countries implies borrowing and repaying foreign rather than domestic currency, constitutes the third method of financing a deficit. Elsewhere, I demonstrate that excessive reliance on these three ways of financing government deficits impedes economic development (Fry, 1997a).

All this conflicts with the views of Robert Barro (1974, 1989) and James Buchanan (1976) on Ricardian equivalence. Barro (1989, p. 39) states that the Ricardian equivalence theorem, proposed only to be dismissed by David Ricardo (1817/19, pp. 336–338) himself, holds that

the substitution of a budget deficit for current taxes (or any other rearrangement of the timing of taxes) has no impact on the aggregate demand for goods. In this sense, budget deficits and taxation have equivalent effects on the economy—hence the term *Ricardian equivalence theorem*. To put the equivalence result another way, a decrease in the government's saving (that is, a current budget deficit) leads to an offsetting increase in desired private saving, and hence to no change in desired national saving.

It also follows that Ricardian equivalence implies that the method of financing government deficits has on impact on the macroeconomy.

While Barro (1989, p. 52) interprets the empirical evidence to provide general support for the Ricardian equivalence theorem, the evidence cited is drawn largely from the United States, where the assumptions of the theorem are perhaps most likely to hold. As Pierre-Richard Agénor and Peter Montiel (1996, p. 127) suggest, "In developing countries where financial systems are underdeveloped, capital markets are highly distorted or subject to financial repression, and private agents are subject to considerable uncertainty regarding the incidence of taxes, many of the considerations necessary for debt neutrality to hold are unlikely to be valid." Hence, the assumptions on which Ricardian equivalence rests (Barro, 1989, pp. 39–48) are almost bound to be violated sufficiently to negate the theorem in these countries. Indeed, Agénor and Montiel (1996, p. 127) conclude that "the empirical evidence [from developing countries] has indeed failed to provide much support for the Ricardian equivalence proposition." The empirical evidence presented in Fry (1997a, pt. 2) confirms the Agénor-Montiel position.

The negative effect of deficit finance on growth is typically demonstrated by estimating a relationship between inflation and economic growth; here inflation *INF* is measured by the continuously compounded rate of change in the consumer price index and growth by the continuously compounded rate of change in GDP measured at constant prices *YG*. To confront the problem that inflation has been far more variable (heteroscedastic) in some countries than in others, I estimate the relationship between economic growth and inflation here using iterative three-stage least squares on a system of equations with the same slope parameters but different intercepts for each country. Furthermore, I deal with the problem of simultaneity by treating inflation as an endogenous variable. Initial tests for nonlinearities indicated that the inclusion of both squared and cubed inflation ($INFG^2$ and $INFG^3$) as explanatory variables for economic growth produced better results than the level (*INFG*). The estimate (with t values in brackets) for a sample of forty-one developing countries for the period 1971 to 1994 (860 observations) is[13]

$$YG = -0.056INF^2 + 0.015INF^3$$
$$(-13.648) \qquad (10.346)$$
$$\overline{R}^2 = 0.154. \qquad\qquad (6.2)$$

I estimate a similar relationship for a sample of twenty transitional economies chosen for this study.[14] Prakash Loungani and Nathan Sheets (1997) also find a strong and robust negative relationship between inflation and subsequent economic growth in a sample of twenty-five transitional economies. Glenn Hoggarth (1997, p. 33) observes that "a sustained recovery of output has only occurred once inflation has been brought down to relative low rates, say below 50 percent per annum."

The problem I have with equation (6.2) and similar estimates is its size. *Ceteris paribus*, could a rise in inflation from zero to 225 percent, the range covering virtually all the observations, really reduce growth by ten percentage points? Since the magnitude of this estimated effect seems nreasonable to me, I suggest that at least not all of this relationship is causal. Rather, I suggest that both economic growth and inflation are both affected in opposite directions by fiscal variables.

To examine the relationship between deficit finance and economic growth more carefully, I obtained data for seventy developing countries for the period 1972 to 1995 and the sample of twenty transitional economies for the past decade.[15] The first sample includes all developing countries with a reasonable number of observations for the relevant fiscal variables. My first examination of the data involves ranking these seventy countries on the basis of various potential discriminating variables. I then select the ten countries with the highest average values of the discriminating variable and the ten countries with the lowest average values of this discriminating variable during the period 1972 to 1995.

Table 6.5. demonstrates some of the relationships between developing countries' fiscal attributes and their inflation and growth performance. Table 6.5 compares the mean values of the fiscal variables when countries are selected on growth rates with their mean values when countries are selected on the fiscal variables themselves. The numbers represent means of all annual values for the country group. In the columns labeled "Low Fiscal" and "High Fiscal," the countries differ for each fiscal factor. So the ten lowest-deficit countries averaged surpluses of 1.6 percent (that is, deficits of −1.6 percent), compared with average deficits of 12.8 percent in the ten highest-deficit countries. Annual changes in reserve money in the ten countries with lowest reserve-money growth averaged 0.7 percent of GDP compared with 6.6 percent in the ten countries with highest reserve-money growth.[16] Finally, the ratio of bank reserves to bank deposits aver-

Table 6.5. Fiscal attributes in high- and low-growth developing countries (average annual percentages, 1972–1995)

Fiscal attribute	Low Growth	High Growth	Low Fiscal	High Fiscal
Government deficit/GNP	9.5	1.4	−1.6	12.8
Δ Reserve money/GNP	4.1	1.4	0.7	6.6
Reserve to deposit ratio	29.2	12.5	6.6	46.9
Growth	0.6	8.1	7.0	3.2
Inflation	40.1	8.2	9.4	27.0

aged 6.6 percent in the ten countries with the lowest ratios compared with 46.9 percent in the ten countries with the highest ratios.

In the columns labeled "Low Growth" and "High Growth," the data relate to the same group of countries.

So in the ten lowest-growing countries, government deficits averaged 9.5 percent of GDP, reserve money growth averaged 4.1 percent of GDP, and bank reserves averaged 29.2 percent of bank deposits. In the ten highest-growing countries, government deficits averaged 1.4 percent of GDP, reserve money growth averaged 1.4 percent of GDP, and bank reserves averaged 12.5 percent of bank deposits. Inflation and growth rates reported in the last two rows are averages for the ten lowest-growth, highest-growth, lowest-deficit, and highest-deficit countries.

All the differences between high- and low-growth countries are highly significant. In all cases, high-growth countries exhibit low averages for fiscal variables—that is, low deficits, low reserve-money growth, and low reserve to deposit ratios. In other words, countries with good fiscal characteristics perform better economically with higher growth and lower inflation than those with poor fiscal characteristics. I conjecture that these fiscal characteristics explain much of the negative association observed between inflation and growth. After conducting formal causality tests, Stanley Fischer (1993, p. 510) concludes that "small deficits are good for growth."

Table 6.6. provides some comparable statistics for the twenty transitional economies.[17] In this table, the column labeled "Low" shows the average values of each variable for the ten lowest countries in each category.

So the ten transitional countries with the lowest government deficits posted deficits averaging 0.5 percent of GDP over the period 1993 to

Table 6.6. Fiscal attributes in twenty transitional countries (average annual percentages, 1993–1997)

Fiscal Attribute	Low	High	Average
Government deficit/GNP	0.5	5.7	2.9
Δ Reserve money/GNP	2.3	7.1	4.7
Reserve to deposit ratio	15.0	34.4	24.2
DCGR	4.1	40.8	22.4
Growth	−10.8	5.3	−2.7
Inflation	22.6	628.4	325.5

1997. Similarly, the ten countries with the highest reserve to deposit ratios produce an average of 34.4 percent for 1993 to 1997. The row labeled "*DCGR*" gives the ratio of net domestic credit to the central government as a percentage of aggregate domestic credit. The ten lowest countries averaged 4.1 percent compared with the ten highest countries that averaged 40.8 percent. The final column gives the simple average for all twenty countries. No data are available for the reserve deposit ratio for Kazakstan.[18] In the ten lowest-growth transitional economies, inflation averaged 451 percent compared with 200 percent in the ten highest-growth economies. The negative relationship between inflation and growth holds for this country group, just as it does for many other country samples.

However, the fiscal variables exhibit far weaker relationships in the transitional economies than they do in the sample of seventy developing countries. This may well be due to large public sectors in some transitional economies. In China, for example, quasi-fiscal activities of the People's Bank of China and the state-owned banks in the form of subsidies to state-owned enterprises explain why a modest government deficit if found alongside a high reserve to deposit ratio (Fry, 1998b).

Elsewhere, I suggest that poor fiscal policy is likely to be accompanied by accommodating or inflationary monetary policy (Fry, 1998a). To examine the relationship between fiscal and monetary policies, I estimate monetary policy reaction functions for groups of countries selected on their fiscal characteristics, drawn from the sample of seventy developing countries used in Table 6.5. The results suggest that, far from offsetting expansionary fiscal policy, monetary policy tends to compound any inflationary fiscal stance in these countries. Larger deficits and greater reliance by governments on the domestic banking system are associated not only with less monetary policy neutralisation (that is, changes in government borrowing from the domestic banking system are not countered by equal and opposite changes in credit to the private sector), but also with less sterilization of increases in foreign-exchange reserves. In other words, more inflationary fiscal policies are accompanied by more accommodating and so more inflationary monetary policies.

Inflation and Central-Bank Independence

István Ábel, Pierre Siklos, and István Székely (1998, ch. 9) point out that new central banking laws in central European transitional economies have been modeled along the lines of the Deutsche Bundesbank's statutes. Ironically, this implies that legal independence is rather modest. By law, the Bundesbank is required to support the government's economic policy. Loungani and Sheets (1997) find a negative relationship between central-bank independence and inflation across twelve transitional economies. However, legal independence provides no predictive power whatsoever in terms of inflationary outcomes in developing countries (Fry, 1998a).

I suggest that measures of central-bank independence constructed and used by Loungani and Sheets and others are endogenous variables. The most important necessary condition for *de facto* central-bank independence is fiscal discipline. In other words, central-bank independence is a luxury that governments in dire fiscal plights cannot afford. Fiscal discipline is not a sufficient condition for central-bank independence because central-bank independence is gained in large part through the central bank's competence and the ability to demonstrate it. Alex Cukierman (1992, pp. 393–394) makes the point that

> A governor who is backed by an absolutely and relatively strong research depart-ment carries more weight vis-á-vis the Treasury and other branches of govern-ment. The r eason is probably that the governor is perceived as a relatively impartial provider of reliable information about the economy. A possible indi-cator of the quality of bank's research department is the quality of the annual report it produces.

Closer and more regular contact with government can provide the central bank with the means to demonstrate its competence, as well as to educate its government in what can and cannot be achieved by the central bank. Specifically, the establishment of a monetary policy committee consisting of, among others, the minister of finance and the central-bank governor may enable the central bank to achieve greater influence over the thrust of monetary policy.

The Mauritian experiment with such an arrangement since June 1994 appeared to increase central-bank independence quite considerably, despite the fact that no other change in personalities or legal powers occurred. The monthly Monetary Policy Committee meetings enabled the Bank of Mauritius not only to set the agenda for the debate between it and the government on possible conflicting objectives of monetary policy but also to explain to the government in analytical fashion matters pertaining to monetary policy. The results were both considerably more harmonious relations between government and central bank as well as, more important, more effective and successful monetary policy implementation.

This experiment also demonstrated the value of a well-staffed central-bank research department. In the Mauritian case, it was given the opportunity to communicate on a regular basis with the Minister of Finance and other government officials through a briefing paper modeled along the lines of the Bank of England's *Inflation Report*. Since briefing papers for these meetings were prepared by the research staff of the central bank, this provided the central bank with a forum for explaining what it believed to be appropriate policy and what consequences would follow from pursuing alternative policies. In this light, expertise within the central bank and an opportunity for regular demonstration of such expertise may well be the keys to independence, regardless of any statutory provisions.

A second key ingredient of central-bank independence in practice lies in an understanding by the government of the macroeconomic effects of its funding activities. Acknowledging the benefits to the economy of competing with other borrowers on a level playing field is the first step to producing marketable government debt. This, in turn, is a prerequisite both for monetary policy to be separated from fiscal policy and for a central bank to implement monetary policy through open-market operations. Perhaps most important is the fact that, once the government accepts the case against financial repression for raising funds at below-market interest rates, the central bank can assume the responsibility of funding the government by auctioning treasury bills.

Again, Mauritius provides an example. After the government accepted the level-playing-field principle, monetary policy was divorced from fiscal policy, and the Bank of Mauritius was able to conduct treasury bill auctions independently from fiscal concerns. By ensuring that the government was not directly affected financially by how its deficit was financed, the Bank of Mauritius could offer the appropriate volume of treasury bills for auction each week without regard to the precise weekly or monthly financing requirements of the government. When sales exceeded the government financing requirement, the balance was placed in a special treasury bill management account at the Bank of Mauritius that earned interest equal to the auction yield. When sales fell short of the government financing requirement, the Bank of Mauritius lent to the government at a rate equal to the auction yield. In this way, the Bank of Mauritius could determine the appropriate volume of treasury bills to offer without consulting the Ministry of Finance over the financing implications (Fry and Basant Roi, 1995).

Cukierman (1992, p. 395) makes a related point in a situation in which the government had not accepted the benefits of marketable debt (which necessitates level-playing-field government borrowing): "The ability of the Bank of Israel to conduct open market operations is seriously restricted despite the fact that it holds a large amount of government securities. The reason is that these securities are not tradable and the Israeli Treasury has consistently refused to make them tradable."

All this suggests, I think, that a move away from inflationary finance, financial repression, and excessive reliance on foreign currency borrowing toward developing voluntary domestic markets for government debt offers benefits in terms of lower inflation and higher saving and economic growth rates. High growth, in turn, alleviates the deficit. There is, therefore, some hint of a virtuous circle in which less financial repression and greater use of voluntary domestic markets lowers inflation and raises growth, both of which reduce the government's deficit. In general, developing and transitional countries make too little use of voluntary lenders in domestic currency markets.

Given fiscal discipline, removing existing distortions and resisting the imposition of new distortions on financial markets constitute growth-enhancing government policies. Undistorted domestic financial markets promote economic growth by enhancing both the quality and the quantity of investment. Well-functioning domestic financial markets facilitate the allocation of capital inflows from abroad to their most productive uses; they also deter capital flight. Central banks can play key roles in fostering these changes in their financial sectors.

Nevertheless, increased vigilance is imperative because of the potential for increased financial system fragility that accompanies the global trend toward market-based financial structures. The convergence hypothesis argues that state-based and bank-based financial systems are becoming increasingly uncompetitive in the global environment (Peréz, 1997; Vitols, 1997, pp. 221–255). The new financial institution is a lightly regulated financial supermarket offering a range of financial products to a mobile pool of consumers seeking short-term relationships on the basis of price competition. The development of direct financial markets, particularly secondary markets for government securities and corporate paper, is increasingly important for the competitive survival of financial systems in this age of globalization.

While the market-based financial structure may dominate international finance at the end of the twentieth century, it tends to substitute efficiency for stability and short-term profit for long-term relationships aimed at sustained productivity gains. Globalization introduces new problems for national financial regulators in terms of surges in international capital flows that can be, and have been in several countries, highly destabilizing. In the belief that financial structures may well be converging on the market-based model, I now focus on aspects of the liberalization and globalization process that may confront transitional economies over the next decade as their central banks introduce further domestic and international financial liberalization.

Conclusion

One common prerequisite for monetary and financial stability is a level playing field. First, in my opinion, central banks in the transitional economies could usefully promote development of a secondary market for government debt; the government should certainly compete with other borrowers on a level playing field. This enables monetary policy to be separated from fiscal policy and promotes financial stability. Second, a level playing field necessitates the exclusion of uneven—that is, insolvent—players. This is the key role of prudential supervision and regulation in the development process. The case study of China indicates that at least this transitional economy still exhibits a Himalayan topology. While an efficient payment system fosters economic development in its own right, it also promotes it indirectly by facilitating monetary policy. A sound payment system contributes to overall financial stability and so, in this way too, promotes economic development.

Acknowledgment

My thanks go to John Bonin for extremely helpful comments on an earlier version of this chapter.

Notes

1. Much of this section is based on Fry et al. (1998).

2. Negative float implies that credit float exceeds debit float, a situation one would anticipate in a system where credit transfers predominate over debit transfers.

3. Tomás Baliño, Juhi Dhawan, and Venkataraman Sundararajan (1994, fig. 6, p. 403) compare float as a percentage of reserve money in Poland and the United States, 1990 to 1992. Float in Poland ranges from 2 to 10 percent of reserve money while float in the United States ranges from 0.05 to 0.5 percent of reserve money.

4. The apposite expression used in Eastern Europe is: "It is easier to get people out of communism than communism out of people."

5. In practice, resistance often springs from reluctance to lose seigniorage revenue.

6. Much of the literature on indexation (e.g., Dornbusch and Simonsen, 1983; Gleizer, 1995; McNelis, 1988) concentrates on its role in a stabilization program rather than as a specific instrument for use in the process of developing voluntary domestic markets for government debt. For articles focusing more on the market-development and fiscal aspects of price-indexed debt in such countries as Australia, Canada, and the United Kingdom, the interested reader may consult the Bank of England (1996).

7. The World Bank (1995b, p. iii) notes that total market capitalization of Pacific Asian bond markets equaled $338 billion (22 percent of GDP or one-third of the size of equity markets) at the end of 1994.

8. Not all countries report data for the entire period. Here I use the geometric average of commercial bank deposit and loan rates, since these are the most prevalent interest-rate data reported in the March 1996 International Financial Statistics CD-ROM. For symmetry, I use continuously compounded rates throughout this chapter. The real interest rate is defined as the continuously compounded nominal interest rate minus the continuously compounded inflation rate.

9. Herbert Grubel (1977) provides one of the most comprehensive frameworks with which to assess the costs and benefits of permitting foreign banks to establish branches.

10. I am grateful to Andrew Mullineux for providing this analogy.

11. Even a competitive banking system cannot raise deposit rates of interest in step with inflation when subject to non-interest-bearing reserve requirements. The reserve requirement tax burden that increases with inflation is passed on to depositors or lenders.

12. Under cash-based budgets, arrears and other deferred payment arrangements together with unfunded future liabilities such as state pensions constitute additional techniques of disguising the true magnitude of a deficit.

13. The instruments are lagged inflation, lagged money and output growth rates, oil inflation, and the OECD growth rate. The estimation procedure, which is asymptotically full-information maximum likelihood, automatically corrects for heteroscedasticity across equations and therefore, in this case, across countries (Johnston, 1984, pp. 486–490).

14. Albania, Armenia, Azerbaijan, Belarus, China, Croatia, Czech Republic, Estonia, Hungary, Kazakstan, Latvia, Lithuania, Moldova, Mongolia, Poland, Romania, Russian Federation, Slovak Republic, Slovenia, and Ukraine.

15. Details of the developing country sample and the data definitions are presented in Fry (1997a). For analytical purposes, I examine data for transitional economies during the period 1993 to 1997.

16. If reserve money represented 10 percent of GDP, this 6.6 percent would correspond to an annual average rate of growth in reserve money of 66 percent.

17. These data were extracted from International Financial Statistics, March 1998, CD-ROM, and World Development Indicators 1997, CD-ROM.

18. No data on government deficits are available for Armenia, Azerbaijan, Belarus, Moldova, Russian Federation, Slovak Republic, and Ukraine. So for the reserve to deposit ratio, figures are for the lowest ten and highest nine countries. For the government deficits, the averages are for the lowest seven and highest six countries.

References

Ábel, István, Pierre L. Siklos, and István P. Székely. (1998). *Money and Finance in the Transition to a Market Economy.* Cheltenham: Edward Elgar.

Agénor, Pierre-Richard, and Peter J. Montiel. (1996). *Development Macroeconoics.* Princeton: Princeton University Press.

Atine, Tamar Manuelyan, and Bert Hofman. (1996). "China's Fiscal Deficits, 1986–1995." Toronto: University of Toronto, AERIL Tax Program, August.

Baliño, Tomás J.T., Juhi Dhawan, and Venkataraman Sundararajan. (1994). "Payment System Reform and Monetary Policy in Emerging Market Economies in Central and Eastern Europe." *International Monetary Fund Staff Papers* 41(3) (September): 383–395.

Bank of England. (1996). *The UK Index-Linked Gilt-Edged Market: Future Development.* London: Bank of England, Papers from the Conference on Indexed Bonds.

Barro, Robert J. (1974). "Are Government Bonds Net Wealth?" *Journal of Political Economy* 82(6) (November/December): 1095–1117.

Barro, Robert J. (1989). "The Ricardian Approach to Budget Deficits." *Journal of Economic Perspectives* 3(2) (Spring): 37–54.

Barro, Robert J. (1995). "Inflation and Economic Growth." *Bank of England Quarterly Bulletin* 35(2) (May): 166–176.

Brock, Philip L. (1989). "Reserve Requirements and the Inflation Tax." *Journal of Money, Credit and Banking* 21(1) (February): 106–121.

Buchanan, James M. (1976). "Barro on the Ricardian Equivalence Theorem." *Journal of Political Economy* 84(2) (April): 337–342.

Cole, David C., Hal S. Scott, and Philip A. Wellons. (1995). "The Asian Money Markets: An Overview." In David C. Cole, Hal S. Scott, and Philip A. Wellons (eds.), *Asian Money Markets* (pp. 3–38). New York: Oxford University Press.

Cukierman, Alex. (1992). *Central Bank Strategy, Credibility, and Independence.* Cambridge, MA: MIT Press.

De Gregorio, José. (1994). "Inflation, Growth and Central Banks: Theory and Evidence." Washington, DC: International Monetary Fund.

De Gregorio, José, and Guidotti, Pablo E. (1995). "Financial Development and Economic Growth." *World Development* 23(3) (March): 433–448.

Diaz-Alejandro, Carlos. (1985). "Good-Bye Financial Repression, Hello Financial Crash." *Journal of Development Economics* 19(1–2) (September–October): 1–24.

Dornbusch, Rudiger, and Mario Henrique Simonsen. (1983). *Inflation, Debt, and Indexation*. Cambridge, MA: MIT Press.

Fischer, Stanley. (1993). "The Role of Macroeconomic Factors in Growth." *Journal of Monetary Economics* 32(3) (December): 485–512.

Fischer, Stanley. (1994). "Modern Central Banking." In Forrest Capie, Charles Goodhart, Stanley Fischer, and Norbert Schnadt (eds.), *The Future of Central Banking: The Tercentenary Symposium of the Bank of England* (pp. 262–308). Cambridge: University of Cambridge Press.

Fry, Maxwell J. (1995). *Money, Interest, and Banking in Economic Development* (2nd ed.). Baltimore: Johns Hopkins University Press.

Fry, Maxwell J. (1996). "How Foreign Direct Investment in Pacific Asia Improves the Current Account." *Journal of Asian Economics* 7(3) (Fall): 459–486.

Fry, Maxwell J. (1997a). *Emancipating the Banking System and Developing Markets for Government Debt*. London: Routledge.

Fry, Maxwell J. (1997b). "Financial Sector Development in Small Economies." In Alison Harwood, and Bruce L.R. Smith (eds.), *Sequencing? Financial Strategies for Developing Countries* (pp. 167–187). Washington, DC: Brookings Institution.

Fry, Maxwell J. (1998a). "Assessing Central Bank Independence in Developing Countries: Do Actions Speak Louder Than Words?" *Oxford Economic Papers* 50:

Fry, Maxwell J. (1998b). "Can Seigniorage Revenue Keep China's Financial System Afloat?" In Donald J.S. Brean (ed.), *Taxation in Modern China*. New York: Routledge.

Fry, Maxwell J., and Ramesh Basant Roi. (1995). "Monetary Policy-Making in Mauritius." *Bank of Mauritius Quarterly Bulletin* 35 (January–March): 11–16.

Fry, Maxwell J., Charles A.E. Goodhart, and Alvaro Almeida. (1996). *Central Banking in Developing Countries: Objectives, Activities and Independence*. London: Routledge.

Fry, Maxwell J., Isaack Kilato, Sandra Roger, Krzysztof Senderowiz, David Sheppard, Francisco Solis, and John Trundle. (1998). "Payment Systems in Global Perspective: Some Views from the Central Bank." London: Bank of England, Report Prepared for the Central Bank Governors' Symposium at the Bank of England on Friday, June 5.

Fry, Maxwell J., and D. Mario Nuti. (1992). "Monetary and Exchange Rate Policies During Eastern Europe's Transition: Lessons from Further East." *Oxford Review of Economic Policy* 8(1) (Spring): 27–43.

Fry, Maxwell J., and Raburn M. Williams. (1984). *American Money and Banking*. New York: Wiley.

Giovannini, Alberto, and Martha de Melo. (1993). "Government Revenue from Financial Repression." *American Economic Review* 83(4) (September): 953–963.

Girardin, Eric. (1997). *The Dilemmas of Banking Sector Reform and Credit Control in China.* Paris: OECD Development Centre.

Gleizer, Daniel L. (1995). "Brazil." In Stephan Haggard, and Chung H. Lee (eds.), *Financial Systems and Economic Policy in Developing Countries* (pp. 212–256). Ithaca, NY: Cornell University Press.

Goodhart, Charles A.E., Philipp Hartmann, David Llewellyn, Liliana Rojas-Suárez, and Steven Weisbrod. (1998). *Financial Regulation: Why, How and Where Now?* London: Routledge.

Grubel, Herbert G. (1977). "A Theory of Multinational Banking." *Banca Nazionale del Lavoro Quarterly Review* 123 (December): 349–363.

Hofman, Bert. (1995). "Fiscal Decline and Quasi-Fiscal Response: China's Fiscal Policy and Fiscal System, 1978–1994." Washington, DC: World Bank, Paper prepared for the CEPR/CEOII/OECD Conference on Different Approaches to Market Reforms, Budapest, October 6–7.

Hoggarth, Glenn. (1997). "Monetary Policy in Transition Space: The Case of Central Europe." *Central Banking* 8(1) (Summer): 32–43.

Hume, David. (1752/19••). "Of Money." In *Political Discourses* (2nd ed.) (pp. 41–59). Edinburgh: Kincaid and Donaldson.

International Monetary Fund. (1996). "People's Republic of China: Recent Economic Developments." Washington, DC: International Monetary Fund, IMF Staff Country Report 96–40, May.

Jappelli, Tullio, and Marco Pagano. (1994). "Saving, Growth, and Liquidity Constraints." *Quarterly Journal of Economics* 109(1) (February): 83–109.

Johnston, Jack. (1984). *Econometric Methods* (3d ed.). New York: McGraw-Hill.

Knight, Malcolm. (1997). "Developing Countries and the Globalization of Financial Markets." Washington, DC: International Monetary Fund, Monetary and Exchange Affairs Department, August.

Knight, Malcolm, et al. (1997). "Central Bank Reforms in the Baltics, Russia, and the Other Countries of the Former Soviet Union." Washington, DC: International Monetary Fund, Occasional Paper 157, December.

Koch, Elmar B. (1997). "Exchange Rates and Monetary Policy in Central Europe: A Survey of Some Issues." Vienna: Oesterreichische Nationalbank, Working Paper 24, September.

Liu, Liang-Yn, and Wing Thye Woo. (1994). "Saving Behaviour Under Imperfect Financial Markets and the Current Account Consequences." *Economic Journal* 104(424) (May): 512–527.

Locke, John (1695/1992). *Further Considerations Concerning Raising the Value of Money* (2nd ed.). London: Churchil.

Loungani, Prakash, and Nathan Sheets. (1997). "Central Bank Independence, Inflation, and Growth in Transition Economies." *Journal of Money, Credit and Banking* 29(3) (August): 381–399.

Lynch, David. (1995). "Links Between Asia-Pacific Financial Sector Development and Economic Performance." Ph.D. thesis, Macquarie University, Sydney.

McKinnon, Ronald I. (1991). "Monetary Stabilization in LDCs." In Lawrence B. Krause, and Kim Kihwan (eds.), *Liberalization in the Process of Economic Development* (pp. 366–400). Berkeley: University of California Press.

McKinnon, Ronald I. (1993). *The Order of Economic Liberalization: Financial Control in the Transition to a Market Economy* (2nd ed.). Baltimore: Johns Hopkins University Press.

McNelis, Paul D. (1988). "Indexation and Stabilization: Theory and Experience." *World Bank Research Observer* 3(2) (July): 157–169.

Mehran, Hassanali, Marc Quintyn, Tom Nordman, and Bernard Laurens. (1996). "Monetary and Exchange System Reforms in China: An Experiment in Gradualism." Washington, DC: International Monetary Fund, Occasional Paper 141, September.

Patrick, Hugh T. (1994). "Comparisons, Contrasts and Implications." In Hugh T. Patrick, and Yung Chul Park (eds.), *Financial Development of Japan, Korea, and Taiwan: Growth, Repression, and Liberalization* (pp. 325–371). New York: Oxford University Press.

People's Bank of China. (1996). *China Financial Outlook* '96. Beijing: China Financial Publishing House.

Peréz, Sofía A. (1997). "'Strong' States and 'Cheap' Credit: Economic Policy Strategy and Financial Regulation in France, and Spain." In Douglas J. Forsyth, and Ton Notermans (eds.), *Regimes Changes: Macroeconomic Policy and Financial Regulation in Europe from the 1930s to the 1990s* (pp. 169–220). Providence, RI: Berghahn.

Ricardo, David (1817/19••) *On the Principles of Political Economy, and Taxation.* London: John Murray.

Rojas-Suárez, Liliana, and Steven R. Weisbrod. (1995). "Financial Fragilities in Latin America: The 1980s and 1990s." Washington, DC: International Monetary Fund, Occasional Paper 132, October.

Stiglitz, Joseph E., and Andrew Weiss. (1981). "Credit Rationing in Markets with Imperfect Information." *American Economic Review* 71(3) (June): 393–410.

Sundararajan, Venkataraman, Arne B. Petersen, and Gabriel Sensenbrenner (eds.). (1997). *Central Bank Reform in the Transition Economies.* Washington, DC: International Monetary Fund.

Tobin, James. (1992). "Money." In Peter Newman, Murray Milgate, and John Eatwell (eds.), *The New Palgrave Dictionary of Money and Finance* (vol. 2 pp. 770–778). London: Macmillan.

Tseng, Wanda, Hoe Ee Khor, Kalpana Kochhar, Dubravako Mihaljek, and David Burton. (1994). "Economic Reform in China: A New Phase." Washington, DC: International Monetary Fund, Occasional Paper 114, November.

Veale, John M., and Robert W. Price. (1994). "Payment System Float and Float Management." In Bruce J. Summers (ed.), *The Payment System: Design, Management, and Supervision* (pp. 145–163). Washington, DC: International Monetary Fund.

Villanueva, Delano P., and Abbas Mirakhor. (1990). "Strategies for Financial Reforms: Interest Rate Policies, Stabilization, and Bank Supervision in Developing Countries." *International Monetary Fund Staff Papers* 37(3) (September): 509–536.

Vitols, Sigurt. (1997). "Financial Systems and Industrial Policy in Germany and Great Britain: The Limits of Convergence." In Douglas J. Forsyth, and Ton Notermans (eds.), *Regimes Changes: Macroeconomic Policy and Financial Regulation in Europe from the 1930s to the 1990s* (pp. 221–255). Providence, RI: Berghahn Books.

Vittas, Dimitri (ed.). (1992). *Financial Regulation: Changing the Rules of the Game.* Washington, DC: World Bank, EDI Development Studies.

World Bank. (1995a). *China: Macroeconomic Stability in a Decentralized Economy.* Washington, DC: World Bank.

World Bank. (1995b). *The Emerging Asian Bond Market.* Washington, DC: World Bank.

IV CENTRAL BANKS AND FINANCIAL SOUNDNESS

7 CENTRAL BANKS, ASSET BUBBLES, AND FINANCIAL STABILITY

George G. Kaufman

Loyola University and Federal Reserve Bank of Chicago

With the rapid disappearance of product (goods and services) inflation as the major policy concern for central banks in many countries over the last decade, asset price inflation (bubbles) and financial stability have increasingly become important concerns. A recent survey by the International Monetary Fund (IMF) reported serious banking and financial market problems in more than 130 of its 180 plus member countries since 1980, and that was before the most recent round of financial crises in Asia (Lindgren, Garcia, and Saal, 1996). The cost of resolving these crises is high. The transfer costs from the use of public (taxpayer) funds to finance the negative net worths of insolvent banks and at times of other financial institutions resulting from the shortfall of the market value of the institutions' assets from the par value of their deposit and other liabilities, which are explicitly or implicitly protected from loss by the government, exceeded 10 percent of GDP in a significant number of countries.

The overall cost of the banking problems is increased further by the costs from any unused labor and capital resources as well as the misallocation of employed resources that reduce GDP, from the depreciation of the domestic currency (which is frequently translated into a higher rate of inflation), and from increased uncertainty that shortens investment time horizons and contributes to slower macroeconomic growth. As a result, financial nstability is an important cause of macroeconomic instability and poor performance. The costs can also spill over to other countries either because of reductions in the values of cross-border financial claims or because downturns in macroeconomic activity or depreciations of local curencies cause slowdowns in imports from other countries. Moreover, industrial countries are often called on to provide direct financial as well as technical assistance to less industrial countries experiencing serious banking difficulties.

On the other hand, evidence also suggests that macroeconomic instability is an important cause of financial instability. In particular, inflation in either or both product prices and asset prices reduces the efficiency and endangers the survival of financial institutions. Although central banks have a long history of targeting and affecting product inflation and both the strategies used and their abilities to do so have been analyzed in depth, the role of central banks in targeting asset prices is less well chartered and considerably more controversial.[1]

This chapter (1) reviews the evidence on the causes and implications of financial instability, in particular the role of asset-price bubbles, (2) discusses the potential role of central banks in preventing financial instability, and (3) describes a prudential regulatory scheme and strategy that could help central banks insulate financial institutions from asset price bubbles and reduce disruptions to the macroeconomy.

Financial Instability

Andrew Crockett, the general manager of the Bank of International Settlements (BIS), has defined financial stability as "stability of the key institutions and markets that make up the financial system." He continues (Crockett, 1997, pp. 9–10):

> Stability in financial institutions means the absence of stresses that have the potential to cause measurable economic harm beyond a strictly limited group of customers and counterparties. . . . [S]tability in financial markets means the absence of price movements that cause wider damage. . . . [S]tability requires (1) that the key *institutions* in the financial system are stable, in that there is a high degree of confidence that they can continue to meet their contractual obligations without interruption or outside assistance; and (2) that the key financial *markets* are stable, in that participants can confidently transact in them at prices that reflect fundamental forces that do not vary substantially over short periods when there have been no changes in fundaments.

This chapter focuses primarily on financial institutions, although institutions and markets are closely interrelated. A major cause of bank instability is instability in financial markets in the form of asset-price bubbles. Conversely, bank instability feeds back onto financial markets, reducing their stability.

In market-oriented economies, financial institutions mobilize savings and channel them to the most potentially productive uses. The more efficient this transfer, the more efficiently are real resources allocated and the greater is the aggregate welfare of the economy. Financial institutions also assist in monitoring the performance of the borrowers for the lenders and in policing corporate governance. Recent empirical evidence supports the theoretical arguments that banking matters—namely, that the more developed is the financial sector in a country, the faster is real per capita macroeconomic growth. (The evidence is reviewed in Levine, 1997a; and Rajan and Zingales, 1998.) Moreover, countries that have both developed banking markets and liquid capital markets appear to grow faster, on average, than countries that have only one developed market, which in turn grow faster than countries in which neither banks nor capital markets are very well developed (Levine, 1997b).

Although the evidence suggests that the behavior of banks importantly affects the macroeconomy for both good and bad, the predominant focus to date has been on the bad—breakdowns in banking spreading to breakdowns in the macroeconomy. A large number of studies report that the frequency of bank failures in industrial countries is inversely correlated with the stage of the business cycle—rising during recessions and falling during expansions—although the relationship appears stronger in the United States. (A review of the literature appears in Benston and Kaufman, 1995; Bordo, 1986; Kaufman, 1994; Mishkin, 1997.) For example, the correlation between annual changes in the number of bank failures and industrial production between 1875 and 1919 in the United States was –0.42, and in only two periods of sharp increases in bank failures did industrial production fail to decline (Benston et al., 1986). The studies differ on how banking crises begin—whether bank problems exogenously ignite the macroeconomic problems or are ignited by the macroeconomic or other exogenous forces and, in turn, feedback on the macroeconomy and intensify the magnitude and duration of the macro problem.

Among more contemporary economists, Hyman Minsky (1977) and Charles Kindleberger (1985, 1996) are the major proponents of banks exogenously igniting problems that spread first throughout and then beyond the banking and financial sectors. Like most economic agents, banks get caught up in the euphoria of budding economic expansions and expand credit rapidly to finance the increase in economic activity, particularly in areas subject to the greatest increase in demand and consequently in prices, such as stock market and real estate. Moreover, the credit is often collateralized by the assets purchased. The credit expansion fuels and accelerates the economic expansion, accelerates asset-price increases, and encourages additional speculation. Both lenders and borrowers fall victim to "irrational exuberance." Through time, borrowers become more highly leveraged and turn increasingly to shorter-term debt. Their margin of safety in covering their debt-service payments from operating revenues or continued increases in asset prices declines and approaches zero. Increasingly, debt servicing is financed out of new debt (in Minsky's terms, *Ponzi finance*). Given the high leverage, a slight decline or even slowdown in expected revenues, and the bursting of asset-price bubbles, even moderate increases in interest rates can cause defaults. The financial system crashes off is own weight. This leads to a self-feeding sequence of distress selling, fire-sale losses, further defaults, business failures, bank runs, and bank failures, and the expansion turns into a macroeconomic downturn. Bank problems precede macroeconomic problems.

Most contemporary analysts, however, view the bank problems during macroeconomic downturns to be caused primarily by the accompanying increase in business failures and rising unemployment, which in turn are often caused by some exogenous shock, including government policies that reduce aggregate bank reserves and therefore the money supply and the bursting of asset-price bubbles (Bordo, Mizrach, and Schwartz, 1998; articles included in Hubbard, 1991). Increased business failures and unemployment and sharply lower asset prices increase defaults on bank loans and also the perceived risk of performing bank loans. The banking problems make it increasingly difficult for depositors to evaluate the financial health of their banks and to differentiate financially healthy from sick institutions (Mishkin et al., 1995). As a result, in the absence of deposit insurance, they are encouraged to run from deposits at their banks into currency outside the banking system rather than to other "safe" banks. Unless the accompanying loss in aggregate bank reserves is offset by a central bank lender of last resort, a multiple contraction in money and credit is ignited (Kaufman, 1988). This, in turn, feedbacks onto the macroeconomy, transmitting and magnifying the initial downturn.

Kaminsky and Reinhart (1996) have recently examined twenty-five banking crises worldwide between 1970 and the early 1990s and developed a series of stylized facts. These are shown in Figure 7.1. Note that, on average, the banking crises are dated a number of months after declines in both aggregate output and the stock market and increases in real

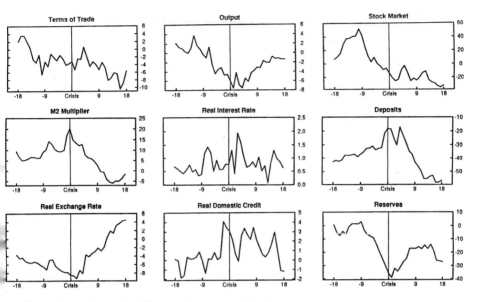

Figure 7.1.   Empirical Regularities during banking crises
Source: Kaminsky and Reinhart (1996, p. 26).
Note: The real exchange rate and the real interest rate are reported in levels while
all other variables are reported in twelve-month changes. All of them are relative
to "tranquil" times. The vertical axes are in percent, and the horizontal axes are
the number of months.

domestic credit and bank deposits. Kaminsky and Reinhart conclude that
"recessionary conditions characterize the periods preceding . . . banking
. . . crises" (Kaminsky and Reinhart, 1996, p. 15).

    Asset-price bubbles have received particular attention in recent years as
evidence has accumulated that they contributed importantly to banking
problems in many countries,—for example, bubbles in real estate and
energy in the United States in the mid- and late 1980s, bubbles in real estate
and stock prices in Japan in the early 1990s, and bubbles in real estate and
stock prices in Korea and Southeast Asia in the mid-1990s.[2] Financial institutions are particularly sensitive to abrupt asset-price declines because
many of them engage in asset-based lending in which the institutions
finance the acquisition of assets, which are pledged as collateral. If asset
prices decline abruptly, the institutions must either require additional collateral or sell the assets to repay the loans. If the asset sales are not quick
enough, the banks may generate insufficient funds to retire the outstanding amount of the loans, and the banks will suffer losses and, if large enough,
may be driven into insolvency.

Capital-impaired banks are likely to cutback on their new lending until their capital is replenished. Moreover, abrupt price declines increase general uncertainty. In such an environment, even solvent banks encounter difficulties in evaluating the value of risky assets and ventures and are likely, in the absence of deposit insurance and other guarantees, to reshuffle their loan portfolios toward safer projects; the more so, the closer the bank is to insolvency. Combined with the cutbacks in total bank lending, this behavior creates a "credit crunch" that makes it more difficult to ignite or sustain recoveries in macroeconomic activity.

As Anna Schwartz has frequently and eloquently argued, financial institutions, and banks in particular, do not do well in periods of uncertainty and macroeconomic instability (Schwartz, 1988). To a great extent these institutions effectively deal in forward contracts. They commit themselves to pay sums of money on deposits and collect sums of money on loans in the future at prices (interest rates) determined today. In the process, they assume a number of risks, including the following:

- *Credit risk*   risk that all future payments are not made in full or on time,
- *Interest-rate risk*   risk that interest rates change differently than expected,
- *Foreign-exchange risk*   risk that exchange rates change differently than expected,
- *Liquidity risk*   risk that assets cannot be sold or liabilities replaced quickly at equilibrium prices,
- *Operational risk*   back office and general management risk,
- *Legal risk*   risk that priorities in default change,
- *Regulatory or legislative risk*   risk that regulations or legislation change abruptly,
- *Fraud risk*.

Banks undertake some or all of these risks because they believe that they can manage them better than others—that is, because they believe that they have a comparative advantage arising from greater knowledge and expertise in both measuring and managing the risks involved. This involves forecasting interest rates, prices, exchange rates, income, and economic activity in the relevant market areas, as well as more specialized factors, such as political stability. As a result, the banks believe that they can sell their risk-taking services for more than the expected losses and generate a positive return on average. But to do so, their forecasts must be right. If they are wrong, any excess losses suffered are charged to capital. Because banks tend to be highly leveraged and have low capital-to-asset ratios, losses, which may appear relatively small to nonbanks that are less highly leveraged, may drive banks into insolvency. On the other hand, if the banks do not engage in any risks, they cannot expect to earn more than a risk-free return on their equity. To fulfill their economic role, banks must manage not eliminate risk taking.

The more volatile the economic, political, or social environment, the greater are the risks assumed in unhedged forward contracts and the greater must be the risk premiums charged in order to avoid losses. Empirical evidence suggests that, although banks fancy themselves as experts in risk management, their record is not exemplary. Their losses are occasionally substantial. Bank failures are highly correlated with volatility in product prices, asset prices, and interest rates. Michael Bordo (1997) has plotted the bank failure rate in the United States since 1870 with the rate of product inflation. This is shown in Figure 7.2. It is evident that, with the primary exception of the post-FDIC period through the late 1970s, bank failures peak after product inflation peaked and prices slowed sharply or declined. For S&Ls in the United States in the 1980s, the failure rate is effectively pushed forward some ten years to when product inflation first accelerated sharply—pushing up interest rates unexpectedly abruptly at a time the institutions were heavily asset long—and then slowed equally sharply.

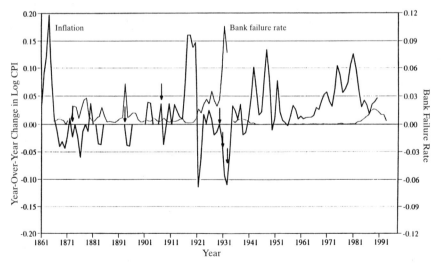

Figure 7.2.   U.S. CPI inflation rate and bank failure rate
Source: Bordo (1986).

Asset inflation plays a similar role. Many analysts have blamed the large increase in U.S. bank failures during the 1929 to 1933 Great Depression on the collapse in stock prices following a sharp run up, which they believed was fueled by excessively liberal bank credit. Earlier studies of banking problems in other countries as well as the United States have also identified collapses or bubbles in asset prices as a major culprit (Kindleberger, 1996; Friedman and Schwartz, 1971; Schwartz, 1988). In only two of the eight periods of sharp increases in bank failures in the United States before the Great Depression of the 1930s did the stock market not decline, and the correlation between bank failures and the annual S&P stock index was − 0.53 (Benston et al., 1986). More recently, as noted, asset-price bubbles have played a major role in producing large banks losses and widespread bank insolvencies in many countries.

In the United States, a large number of the S&Ls and banks that failed in the 1980s and early 1990s experienced large losses from the bursting of energy prices, particularly in the Southwest, and real estate prices, primarily in the Southwest and New England. The institutions had lent heavily to finance both the acquisition of these assets and ventures based on projected increases in these asset prices. When the bubbles burst, defaults increased sharply both directly as the value of the collateral declined and indirectly as economic activity spurred by the asset price runups slowed. The banks victimized included the very large Continental Illinois Bank (the eighth-largest bank in the country at the time), the Bank of New England (Boston), and seven of the largest ten banks in Texas (Kaufman, 1995). Kindleberger summarizes more than thirty banking and financial crises throughout Western Europe and the United States from the early 1600s through 1990, starting with the Thirty Years' War in Europe in the 1620s, Tulipmania in Holland in the 1630s, and the South Sea Bubble in England in the 1720s. In almost all of these, he identifies peaks in asset speculation (asset-price bubbles) as preceding the crisis (Kindleberger, 1996, app. B).

Bank Fragility

Banks are widely perceived as particularly vulnerable to excessive risk taking because they are perceived to be more structurally fragile than other firms and therefore more likely to fail. Their perceived fragility arises from three sources:

- Low cash-to-assets ratio (fractional reserve banking),
- Low capital-to-assets ratio (high leverage),

- High demand debt (deposit)-to-total debt (deposit) ratio (high ability to run).

Each one of these sources by itself is perceived to reflect fragility, but all three in combination are perceived as particularly fragile and dangerous. At the first signs of doubt about the ability of their banks to be able to redeem deposits in full and on time, demand and other short-term depositors can run on the banks to be first in line and withdraw their funds without loss. Because they hold cash equal to only a fraction of their deposits, the banks are likely to have to sell some earning assets quickly to accommodate all fleeing depositors. In the process, they are likely to suffer fire-sale losses, the more so the more opaque are the assets. These losses, in turn, may exceed the small capital base of the banks and drive them into insolvency.

Not only were banks perceived to fail more frequently than other firms, but their failures were perceived to be more detrimental and costly to the economy for a number of reasons. Among other things, the failures would

- Reduce deposits and thereby the aggregate money supply and hamper trade,
- Reduce the most liquid wealth holding of a large number of lower- and middle-income households,
- Reduce the availability of the major source of credit to households, business enterprises, and governments, and
- Give rise to fears that the failures would spread to other banks and beyond to the financial system as a whole, the macroeconomy, and other countries—that is, produce systemic risk.

But fragility per se does not necessarily imply breakage or failure. Rather, it implies "handle with care." And when encouraged to do so, the market does so. As a result, the breakage rate for fine wine glasses and china is likely to be lower than for ordinary drinking glasses and dishware. And the same is true for banking. U.S. experience in this area is useful for a number of reasons. Reasonably long and accurate historical data are available. The United States has had a large number of privately owned banks. Until recently, most were particularly fragile because narrow restrictions on geographic and product-line expansion hindered them from reducing their risk exposures through diversification as much as otherwise. In addition, with the exception of the repudiation of gold contracts in 1933, the U.S. government did not expropriate or devalue deposits, and, with the exception of the South after the Civil War, the United States did not experience changes in governments where the new government repudiated the debt (money) of the old government or confiscated bank balances.[3] This permits us to analyze the performance of the U.S. banking system over a sufficiently long uninterrupted period of time to derive a meaningful number of observations both before and after the introduction of the safety net. The U.S. experience also permits us to analyze the effects of imposing government guarantees on a previously basically uninsured banking system.[4]

From 1870 through 1995, the average annual failure rate for banks in the United States was greater than for nonbanks (Kaufman, 1996b). But all the difference is attributable to the large number of bank failures during the Great Depression from 1929 to 1933, when nearly 10,000 banks failed. In the absence of this period, the annual bank failure rate was about the same as the rate of nonbank failures. Indeed, for the period 1870 to 1914, before the establishment of the Federal Reserve System and the beginning of the federal government safety net under banks, the annual bank failure rate was lower than that for nonbanks.[5] However, for all periods, the variance in the annual bank failure rate was greater; banks failures were clustered in a small number of years. Such clustering is consistent with the presence of bank contagion and systemic risk and contributes to the widespread public fear of bank failures.

Moreover, more thorough analysis of the numerical values of the three bank ratios that are widely perceived to reflect fragility indicates the opposite, particularly in the period before the bank safety net. These values were determined by the marketplace. Despite the perception, bank cash ratios were not lower than for other firms, not were their earning assets necessarily more opaque. Although demand deposits facilitate runs on banks, the very fact that they do serves as a powerful form of market discipline on bank management to curtail risk taking (Calomiris and Kahn, 1991.) That is, while runs may be detrimental to bank stability, the ex-ante threat of runs from demand depositors serves to enhance stability by making management more cautious.

The low capital ratios before deposit insurance (even after adjustment for double liability) could only have existed if the market perceived banks to be less risky rather than more risky than other firms. Indeed, the evidence suggests that in the United States in this period, not only was the bank failure rate lower than for nonbanks, but insolvent banks were resolved more quickly with less loss to depositors or creditors than insolvent nonbanks (Kaufman, 1992, 1994, 1996a). In the United States, insolvent banks then as now were resolved by their chartering regulatory agency. They do not go through the regular corporate bankruptcy process. In the absence of deposit insurance, depositor runs on perceived insolvent banks quickly produced liquidity problems and forced the banks to suspend operations. Bank examiners determined whether the bank was experiencing a liquidity or solvency problem. If they concluded the bank was insolvent, it was resolved by the regulators through recapitalization by existing shareholders, merger, sale, or liquidation. The bank did not have much opportunity to operate while insolvent and increase its losses, as could happen after federal government provided deposit insurance was introduced and the need for depositors to run and force resolution was reduced. The decision to resolve insolvencies and the timing were effectively transferred from the market place to the regulatory agencies. In contrast, nonbank insolvencies are resolved through the bankruptcy process, which both before and after introduction of the safety net is much slower and, in the United States, less favorable to creditors. Thus, creditors demand higher capital ratios at these firms to protect themselves from failures, which are associated with relatively larger losses.

It should be noted that the runs before deposit insurance and the accompanying liquidity problems were largely the result and not the cause of the bank insolvencies. That is, with rare exception, the solvency problems caused the liquidity problems, and the liquidity problems did not cause the solvency problems (Kaufman, 1996a). An analysis of the causes of some 3,000 national bank failures before deposit insurance by J.F.T. O'Conner (1938), who served as Comptroller of the Currency from 1933 through 1938, reported that runs accounted for less than 10 percent of all causes listed for these failures (some failures had multiple causes) and were a cause in less than 15 percent of all failures.

Despite this evidence on the small number and low cost of bank failures on average before deposit insurance, the clustering of large numbers of bank failures in a few years was scary when they occurred and gave rise to fears of systemic risk. The failures were widely perceived to represent serious market failures. This led to calls for improvements. In response, the government imposed a government-provided safety net under the banks, first in the form of a discretionary Federal Reserve lender of last resort and then, when this failed to prevent the severe banking crisis of the early 1930s (less than twenty years after it was introduced), in the form of less discretionary, at least on the downside, deposit insurance by the FDIC. Gerald Corrigan (1991, p. 3), former president of the Federal Reserve Bank of New York, has stated that

> More than anything else, it is the systemic risk phenomenon associated with banking and financial institutions that makes them different from gas stations and furniture stores. It is this factor—more than any other—that constitutes the fundamental rationale for the safety net arrangements that have evolved in this and other countries.

When the government provides deposit insurance, it has, like any insurer/guarantor, a financial stake in the financial condition of the bank and will act to protect its interest through rules or price regulating. Government-provided deposit insurance by necessity begets government regulation.

Government Regulation and Financial Stability

By guaranteeing the par value of deposits, government provided deposit insurance (and other parts of the safety net under banks) changed the banking landscape greatly. Because it relieves some or all depositors of the need to be concerned about the financial health of their banks, deposit insurance, like all insurance, reduced the market discipline that insured depositors previously exerted. But unlike private insurance, it generally did not either price or increase regulatory discipline sufficiently to offset the relaxation in market discipline. As a result, banks engaged in moral-hazard behavior and increased their risk exposures by increasing their asset and liability portfolio exposures to credit, interest rate, and other risks and low-ering their capital-to-asset ratios. Moreover, governments were able to use banks to help pursue their economic and political objectives regardless of the increase in risk imposed on the banks. For example, to foster home own-ership, the government in the United States in the 1960s and 1970s per-suaded the S&L industry to extend progressively longer fixed-rate mortgages funded by short-term insured deposits, which greatly increased their interest-rate risk exposure. Likewise, to support its foreign policy, the U.S. government persuaded large money center banks in the late 1970s to make loans to less developed countries (LDCs). Without deposit insurance, it is highly likely that depositors would have run on these risky institutions and discouraged them from participating in these activities. As it turned out, both policies resulted in large losses (Barth, Brumbaugh, and Litan, 1992). Nor is it likely that Hong Kong and East Asian banks would have had as large portfolios of real estate and stock market loans in recent years in the absence of perceived government guarantees.

In addition, with insurance and little fear of depositor runs, government regulators became less vigilant than their private counterparts in imposing sanctions on troubled institutions and, particularly, in imposing closure on economically insolvent institutions to minimize losses to the healthy banks that contributed premiums to the insurance fund and to the taxpayers who are the ultimate guarantors of the fund. That is, the regulators became poor agents for their healthy bank and taxpayer principals. Regulators frequently tend to be motivated by political forces (such as friendships, bestowing favors, succumbing to pressures from powerful bankers or bank customers, and maintenance of personal reputations) as much if not more than by economic forces. Excessive moral-hazard behavior by banks and poor agency behavior by regulators is, however, not inherent in government-provided deposit insurance. Rather, it is only a likely outcome as governments tend to economically misprice and misstructure their services, including deposit insurance.

The evidence from almost each and every country in recent years is that some government-provided deposit insurance—whether explicit or implicit, direct or indirect (backup to private insurance), and on all depositors or on only some depositors—is a political reality. Except for foreign-owned banks in small countries, only governments are perceived to have the financial resources to stem a loss of confidence in large banks or the banking system as a whole, at least in terms of domestic currency. The evidence also suggests that it is best to provide such insurance explicitly, so that the rules are known in advance and the coverage not fought ex-post on the political battlefield.

Thus, the solution to the deposit insurance and bank safety-net problem is to maintain some government-provided protection, but to structure it in such a way that it is based on economic considerations and restricts both bank moral-hazard behavior and regulator poor agent behavior to what would exist if private firms provided the insurance. This is the objective of a scheme of structured early intervention and resolution (SEIR), which in large measure was enacted in weakened form in the United States in the prompt corrective action (PCA) and least-cost resolution (LCR) provisions of the FDIC Improvement Act (FDICIA) of 1991, which was adopted at the depth of the banking and thrift crises. The particulars of SEIR, its history, and the experience to date have been discussed elsewhere, and there is little need and even less room to review them again in any detail here (Benston and Kaufman, 1997, and 1998; Kaufman, 1997a). Suffice it to say that this structure attempts both to (1) supplement government regulation, required by the limited and explicit government deposit insurance provided, with market regulation and (2) structure the government regulation to mimic private market regulation. In the process, SEIR introduces explicit regulatory sanctions on financially troubled banks that become both progressively harsher and progressively more mandatory as a bank's performance deteriorates and it approaches insolvency. The major provisions are shown in Table 7.1.

In addition, and probably most important, SEIR introduces a mandatory "closure" rule, through which banks are resolved by recapitalization,

Table 7.1. Summary of prompt corrective action provisions of the federal deposit insurance corporation improvement act of 1991

Zone	Mandatory Provisions	Discretionary Provisions	Capital Ratios (percent) Risk-Based Leverage		
			Total	Tier 1	Tier 1
1. Well capitalized			>10	>6	>5
2. Adequately capitalized	• No brokered deposits except with FDIC approval		>8	>4	>4
3. Undercapitalized	• Can suspend dividends and mangement fees • Can require capital-restoration plan • Can restrict asset growth • Approval required for acquisitions, branching, and new activities • No brokered deposits	• Can order recapitalization • Can restrict interaffiliate transactions • Can restrict deposit interest rates • Can restrict certain other activities • Any other action that would prompt corrective better carry out action	<8	<4	<4

			<6	<3	<3
4.	Significantly undercapitalized	• Same as for Zone 3 • Can order recapitalization[a] • Can restrict interaffiliate transactions[a] • Can restrict deposit interest rates[a] • Pay of officers restricted	• Any Zone 3 discretionary actions • Conservatorship or receivership if fails to submit or implement plan or recapitalize pursuant to order • Any other Zone 5 provision if such action is necessary to carryout prompt corrective action		
			<2		
5.	Critically undercapitalized	• Same as for Zone 4 • Receiver/conservator within 90 days[a] • Receiver if still in Zone 5 four quarters after becoming critically undercapitalized • Can suspend payments on subordinated debt[a] • Can restrict certain other activities			

Source: Board of Governors of the Federal Reserve System.
a. Not required if primary supervisor determines action would not serve purpose of prompt corrective action or if certain other conditions are met.

merger, sale, or liquidation before their capital is fully dissipated—say, when their capital declines to some small but positive percentage of their assets.[6] In theory, if a bank could be resolved at such a point, losses are confined to shareholders and do not affect depositors. Deposit insurance is effectively redundant. Moreover, if losses from bank failures can be eliminated or at least minimized, fears either of a competitive banking system (which encourages the failure of individual inefficient banks) or of systemic or contagion risk (which occurs only when losses are sufficiently large to wipe out a bank's capital, and the resulting large negative net worths cascade from bank to bank wiping out the next counterparty's capital) are no longer warranted. Unlike other insurance companies, which can limit but not eliminate all losses (such as fire and automobile insurance), a government deposit insurance agency can effectively eliminate its losses completely by monitoring and strictly enforcing its closure rule at no lower than zero economic capital. That is, except for major fraud, losses from bank failures are effectively under its own control.

The incentive for banks to engage in excessive moral-hazard behavior is restrained by copying the constraints that private insurance companies impose through insurance contracts and creditors on debtors through covenants. Risk exposure is priced by risk-based insurance premiums. The ability of the bank to shift its losses to its creditors or insurance firms is reduced by imposing increasingly harsher and broader sanctions as insolvency approaches. The use of multiple performance zones or tranches, measured by capital-to-asset ratios or such, permits the sanctions to be graduated in strength rather than increased sharply and abruptly. This increases the credibility of regulators imposing the sanctions and decreases the incentive for the institution to increase its risk exposure as its performance deteriorates to near the bottom of a particular zone. To supplement the sanction sticks, carrots in the form of additional powers, fewer and faster examinations, and so on are specified to encourage banks to perform well.

Regulatory discipline is reinforced by market discipline exerted by uninsured larger depositors and other creditors, who both may be reasonably assumed to be informed or at least informable creditors and make credit quality decisions regularly in the normal course of their business. They may be expected to require higher interest rates as the financial condition of a bank deteriorates or run from these to safer banks. In contrast, small depoitors are less likely to be very knowledgeable in credit-evaluation procedures and efforts to force them to do so would be inefficient and represent a dead-weight loss to the economy. In addition, small depositors are the only depositors who can operate with currency and therefore are likely to run into currency instead of other, safer banks and to drain reserves from the banking system as a whole. The definition of "small" depositors is as much political as economic. It may be defined as those depositors to whom any loss from bank failure represents a significant loss in their wealth and who are likely to take to the political battlefield to protest the loss and gain the sympathy of the country in the struggle.

Evidence from the United States and Canada before deposit insurance strongly indicates that at least many larger depositors are able to differentiate financially strong from weak banks (for example, Calomiris and Mason, 1997; Kaufman, 1994; Carr, Mathewson, and Quigley, 1995). Likewise, a comparative analysis of deposit behavior during the 1994 to 1995 banking crises in Argentina, which had limited deposit insurance, and in Mexico, which guaranteed all deposits, showed that deposits declined more at banks with progressively greater nonperforming loans in Argentina but not in Mexico (Moore, 1997). This is shown in Figure 7.3.

SEIR restrains the incentive for regulators to delay and forbear in imposing sanctions in response to political pressures or other agendas by specifying loss minimization from bank insolvencies as effectively the sole objective of prudential regulation and imposing explicit and visible rules that mandate sanctions, including resolution, when banks fail to respond to earlier discretionary sanctions. The sanctions become progressively more mandatory as the performance of a bank deteriorates. The threat of mandatory sanctions increases the credibility and effectiveness of discretionary sanctions and serves to supplement rather than to replace the discretionary

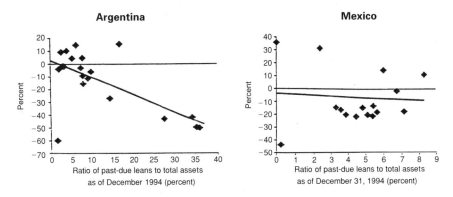

Figure 7.3. Real deposit growth and bank asset quality in Argentina and Mexico, December 1994–June 1995
Source: Moore (1997, pp. 18–19).

sanctions. The mandatory sanctions also increase certainty, treat all banks equally, and help free regulators from political pressures. Identifying insolvency loss minimization as the objective of prudential regulation establishes the same objective as private insurers and creditors have. By aligning the objectives and achieving objective compatibility, deposit insurance becomes incentive compatible, so that all players—private and government—will row in the same direction. At the same time, increased transparency enhances regulatory agency compliance and accountability. While SEIR should reduce the number of bank failures, it is particularly designed to reduce, if not to eliminate, the costs of bank failures. The exit of banks that fail through either bad management or bad luck is required to attain and maintain an efficient banking industry.

To date, the PCA and LCR structure in FDICIA appears to have been successful in the United States. However, because the combined effects of the prolonged recovery of the U.S. economy, the virtual elimination of product inflation, the avoidance of asset-price bubbles in energy and real estate (where U.S. banks are big lenders), and an upward-sloping yield curve have enhanced the recovery of banks and thrifts from the debacle of the 1980s to their healthiest level since the 1960s, the precise contribution of FDICIA is difficult to isolate. But both the rapid build up in bank capital ratios through the sale of new shares in the early 1990s, before renewed bank profitability was established, to the highest levels since the 1960s and the imposition of shared losses on uninsured depositors at resolved banks in almost all resolutions in which the FDIC suffered a loss, indicates strongly that market discipline had been awakened (Benston and Kaufman, 1997, 1998). On the other hand, because no major money center bank has failed since 1992 or even deteriorated sharply in performance, a true test of "too big to fail" (TBTF)—or, more accurately, too big to impose pro-rata losses on uninsured deposits—has not yet occurred.

It is important to note, however, that TBTF has become substantially more difficult for the regulators to impose. With one exception, the FDIC is prohibited from protecting uninsured depositors at insolvencies where doing so will increase its losses. To protect uninsured deposits at such insolvent institutions, a determination must be made in writing by two-thirds of the FDIC directors and the Board of Governors of the Federal Reserve System and by the Secretary of the Treasury in consultation with the President of the United States that not protecting the uninsured depositors "would have serious adverse effect on economic conditions or financial stability" and that protecting these depositors would "avoid or mitigate such adverse effects." If afterward the protection results in a loss to the FDIC, a special assessment must be levied on all banks based on their total assets. Thus, most of any cost would be borne by other large and likely competitor banks, who may be unenthusiastic about using their monies to keep an insolvent competitor in operation. In addition, the documentation underlying the decision must be provided by the Secretary of the Treasury to the Congress and reviewed by the General Accounting Office. This requirement should discourage aggressive use of the TBTF exception. Moreover, TBTF would be invoked only if a very large bank had been unresponsive to the series of PCA sanctions that had been imposed on it earlier to prevent it from failing. If the sanctions were imposed on a timely basis, few if any banks should be in a position to require such protection.

It is also important to understand how prorata losses could be imposed on uninsured deposits without affecting the economy adversely. As noted earlier, in the United States, insolvent banks are resolved by federal regulators without going through the bankruptcy courts. The FDIC generally also acts as the receiver. Insured depositors have full and complete access to their funds on the next business day at either the bank that assumed these deposits or at the bank in receivership until liquidated. Because under FDICIA's PCA requirements regulators become increasingly involved with a troubled institution before it requires resolution in an attempt to turn it around, including identifying and notifying other banks that may be potential bidders of the possible insolvency of the bank, the FDIC has the opportunity to value its assets before resolution. Thus, at the time of resolution, it is in a position to make a reasonably accurate estimate of the recovery value of the assets and of the loss it will incur in protecting insured depositors. It then provides an advanced dividend of the prorata, albeit conservative, estimated recovery value to the uninsured depositors available the next business day. In effect, the uninsured depositors will have immediately available funds equivalent to the par of their deposits amount less the prorata estimated loss, which under FDICIA should be relatively small. If such provisions were not in place, it is likely that long delays would result in uninsured depositors' receiving their funds, that substantial unnecessary economic harm may occur, and that political pressure to protect uninsured deposits fully become too strong to resist.

SEIR has a large number of advantages over other prudential regulatory structures that also makes it desirable for countries other than the United States (Kaufman, 1997b). These include the following:

- Maintains existing banking structure,
- Maintains insurance for "small" depositors only,

- Reduces number of failures,
- Reduces losses from failures (makes deposit insurance effectively redundant),
- Reduces bank insurance premiums and incorporates risk-based premiums,
- Reduces probability of systemic (contagion) risk,
- Reduces too big to fail (protection of uninsured depositors),
- Treats all banks equally,
- Encourages market discipline from "large" depositors to supplement regulatory discipline,
- Reduces moral hazard behavior by banks,
- Reduces agency problem for regulators,
- Provides for carrots as well as sticks to improve bank performance,
- Permits wide range of product powers for well-capitalized banks,
- Reduces regulatory micromanagement of banks.

But because countries differ in significant ways, it is important to tailor the structure to the particular economic, political, social, legal, and cultural characteristics of the country (see Working Party of Financial Stability, 1997). To be effective, SEIR depends on the abilities of both the regulators and the market place to impose sufficient discipline to curtail bank risk taking and losses, of bankers to manage their operations in a way to maximize value to both shareholders and the economy, and of governments to accept loss minimization in insolvencies as the primary goal of bank regulation. If these parties can agree to these preconditions, SEIR may be modified to be effective in the particular countries. The more important modifications required depend on the country's

- Macroeconomic instability,
- Political instability,
- Strength of private market and tradition of market discipline,
- Structure of banking, including solvency and the importance of SOBs and SCBs,
- Sophistication of bankers,
- Sophistication of bank regulators, supervisors, and examiners,
- Sophistication of market participants,
- Credit culture,
- Equity culture,
- Bank control of nonbanks and nonbank control of banks,
- Loan concentration in banks,
- Quality of accounting information and disclosure,

- Bankruptcy and repossession laws,
- Bank reliance on foreign currency deposits.

More specifically, the following features need to be tailored carefully to the country:

- Values of the tripwires for PCA and LCR,
- Types of regulatory sanctions,
- Division between regulatory rules and discretion,
- Definition of "small" depositors,
- Regulation of foreign currency exposure,
- Bankruptcy (resolution) process for insured banks.

The greater the macro and political instability in a country, the higher need be the numerical values of the tripwires for the PCA and LCR tranches, particularly for resolution of potential insolvencies. If these zones are stated in terms of capital-to-asset ratios, it is important to note both that assets must include both on- as well as off-balance-sheet activities and that the Basle capital ratios are minimum requirements for large, international banks in industrial countries with relatively high macroeconomic and political stability. For most other banks and countries, the capital ratios for each zone need to be considerably higher. These values need also be higher, the poorer is the quality of accounting information. Although poor-quality accounting information may either overstate or understate the true information, incentives are to overstate. Thus, banks almost universally under reserve for loan losses and find additional ways of at least temporarily hiding losses. Because the value of the final tripwire for resolution determines the potential for losses to the insurance agency, assigning a value that is too low to prevent or minimize losses can defeat the objective of SEIR.

What is the appropriate capital ratios for banks in a particular country? Because deposit insurance insulates banks from full-market discipline, the market solution in an insurance environment implicitly incorporates a provision for loss sharing and therefore understates the private capital ratio that the market would require in the absence of the insurance. A proxy for this value may be obtained in each country by observing the ratio the market requires of noninsured bank competitors, such as independent finance companies, insurance companies, and so forth. In most countries, these ratios are significantly higher. Thus, increasing bank capital ratios to these levels does not increase their costs unfairly but primarily removes a subsidy. Moreover, because capital is effectively any claim that is subordinated to the insurance agency, it can consist of such subordinate debt, which in some countries has tax advantages over equity. Resolving a bank before its capital becomes negative does not represent confiscation. Current shareholders are given first right to recapitalize the institution. It is only if they prefer no to do so, most likely because they believe that the bank's true capital position is even worse than the reported position, that resolution through sale, merger, or liquidation proceeds. Any proceeds remaining after resolution are returned to the old shareholders.

It also follows that the values of the tripwires for each zone need to be higher, the weaker the credit and equity cultures in a country; the less sophisticated the bankers, regulators, and market participants; the more concentrated bank loan portfolios; the larger the definition of "small" depositor; and the greater bank reliance on foreign-currency deposits. Likewise, these conditions also suggest greater emphasis on regulatory rules than on regulatory discretion.

Foreign-currency-denominated deposits are particularly important in smaller, open economies. Exchange-rate (currency) problems and banking problems are often interrelated and easily confused. Foreign-currency problems can spillover and ignite banking problems. Banks that offer deposits denominated in foreign currencies assume exchange-rate risk, unless offset by foreign-currency-denominated assets or hedged otherwise. And the shorter term the deposits—the "hotter" the money—the greater the risk. Banks are particularly tempted to raise funds in foreign currencies when domestic interest rates greatly exceed those on the foreign currencies. Economic theory, however, indicates that in equilibrium such rate differences should be matched by equal differences in the opposite direction between spot and forward exchange rates. This condition is referred to as *interest-rate parity*.[7]

Any downward pressure on the country's exchange rate will impose losses on unhedged banks and, if large enough, may cause banking problems in previously strong banking systems or exacerbate problems in weak banking systems, such as in many Asian countries in the past year. In addition, downward pressure on the exchange rate in a country with a financially strong banking system may encourage depositors in domestic currency to run into deposits in foreign currencies, possibly even at the same "safe" banks. This is a run on the domestic currency, not on banks. The run exerts downward pressure on the country's exchange rate. If the country attempts to protect its exchange rate (maintain fixed exchange rates), it needs to sell foreign reserves. This reduces aggregate bank reserves.[8] Unless this decrease is offset by infusions of reserves from other sources by the central bank, which would be difficult in these countries without intensifying the problem, it will ignite a multiple contraction in money and credit. This is likely to impair the financial solvency of the banks and may possibly ignite bank runs.

Such a scenario is visible in the stylized facts on banking and balance-of-payments crises compiled by Kaminsky and Reinhart. As shown in Figure 7.1, foreign reserves begin to decline before the banking crises. The banking impact, however, is offset temporarily by increases in the money (deposit) multiplier that permit both deposits and credit to continue to increase. At some point, the banking crises occurs and sets in motion the series of adverse effects. In some countries, there is evidence that the rapid increases in deposits and credit before the banking crisis were fueled by increased bank reserves resulting from large capital inflows and government policies of maintaining fixed exchange rates, which required purchasing the foreign currency.

Conversely, if a country with a strong foreign-currency position but a financially weak banking system experiences depositor runs to domestic currency deposits at "safe" banks or into domestic currency, the banking problem will not spread to foreign-currency (exchange-rate) problems. But if the runs are from domestic currency deposits to foreign-currency deposits even at the same "safe" banks, downward pressure will be exerted on the exchange rate and ignite an exchange-rate problem. Thus, exchange-rate problems can cause banking problems, and banking problems can cause exchange-rate problems.[9] But because the causes differ, the solutions also differ.

Banking problems require first the recapitalization of insolvent or under-capitalized banks and then the introduction of SEIR-like deposit insurance provisions. Because state-owned banks (SOBs) and at times also state-controlled banks (SCBs) are perceived to have complete government protection, they provide unfair competition to other private banks and are likely to prevent these banks from gaining or even maintaining market share, unless equal protection is provided them either explicitly or implicitly. Indeed, it is difficult to have a system of limited deposit insurance in a banking system that includes major SOBs or SCBs.

Major SOBs and SCBs should be completely privatized with sufficient capital to be both economically solvent and politically independent. Because their insolvencies or negative net worth are likely to be greater than their going concern or franchise values, it is unlikely that private parties will bid on these banks unless the capital deficits are reduced. This requires the use of public (taxpayers') funds. Because the sale will change bank management and ownership and value will not accrue to the old shareholders, such a use of public funds is necessary and appropriate and differs significantly from the inappropriate use of public funds to prop up existing shareholders and managers as is being practiced in a number of countries including Japan.[10] Permitting well-capitalized foreign banks to purchase SOBs in competitive bidding is desirable for at least four reasons. One, in some countries, the foreign banks will be relatively small units of much larger and well-capitalized organizations that may be perceived to be able to protect their small affiliates more securely than the domestic government can protect deposits at domestically owned banks through deposit insurance. Two, foreign banks are likely to bid a higher premium for insolvent or barely solvent institutions to get a toehold in the country, thereby reducing the need for any public funds to lower the negative net worth position of insolvent institutions to a level that domestic private parties are willing to absorb. Three, the foreign banks are likely to enhance competition and encourage a more efficient domestic banking system, particularly in countries that are dominated by a few large domestically owned banks. Four, large international banks are likely to be better diversified than smaller domestic banks and will reduce the vulnerability of the banking sector to adverse shocks.[11]

Foreign-currency problems generally reflect macroeconomic problems with which central banks have traditionally dealt. The solution does not require changes in prudential bank regulations, although the scheme discussed in this chapter is helpful if governments permit these problems to deteriorate into banking problems.

Central-Bank Policies to Enhance Financial Stability

As discussed earlier in this chapter, financial instability is often ignited by instability in product and asset prices. Stabilizing product prices is a time-honored, traditional central-bank operation that most banks appear to have achieved successfully in recent years, at least temporary. Affecting asset prices is a less well-traveled path for central banks. Indeed, although the harm both to financial institutions and markets and to the macroeconomy from instability in asset prices has been well documented, the theoretical and policy links between the central bank and asset prices have only rarely been developed.

This is not to argue that central banks have not had a long-standing interest in asset prices and preventing asset-price bubbles. The uncertainty focuses on when asset price changes become undesirable and what central banks should and could do about them when they to occur. In the late 1920s, the Federal Reserve became greatly concerned about the rapid increase in stock prices in the United States and directed policy actions at slowing the increase (Friedman and Schwartz, 1971). The discount rate was increased to increase the cost of credit used in the stock market and to reduce its amount. Some analysts have blamed these actions for the severity and long duration of the subsequent Great Depression. They argue that while stock prices may have been rising rapidly, the rest of the economy was not over-heated and the Federal Reserve's restrictive actions were unwarranted and dangerous. More recently, again in response to rapidly rising stock prices, Federal Reserve Chairman Alan Greenspan has attempted to "talk-down" any potential bubble by cautioning market participants about the possibility of "irrational exuberance" and the unsustainability of the current rate of price increases. However, unlike in the 1920s, the Federal Reserve did not take any specific policy actions directed at the stock market, and, after briefly dipping in response to the comments, market prices have continued their upward spiral to date before declining sharply in response to the intensification of the banking and financial problems in East Asia and Russia.

The recent Japanese experience resembles the U.S. experience of the 1920s and 1930s, at least in terms of monetary policy and asset bubbles. As shown in Figure 7.4, stock prices and real estate prices both surged rapidly in the mid- and late 1980s to far above their trend values. At first, the Bank of Japan did not respond, in part because product inflation was moderate. Moreover, the asset-price increases and in particular the land prices were believed to be fueled by sharp increases in bank credit following liberalization of bank deposit rates and portfolio restrictions. Only when product inflation started to accelerate in early 1989 did the Bank tighten policy (Bordo, Ito, and Iwaisako, 1997). It increased its discount rate sharply from 2.5 percent to 6 percent and restricted bank credit extensions to real estate. At least in partial response, both stock and land prices started their sharp and prolonged declines. However, the real economy remained strong for another year or two before it weakened, and monetary policy remained restrictive over that period.

In its *1997 Annual Report*, which devotes considerable attention to the issue of asset prices and financial stability, the BIS lists three reasons that central banks may wish to respond to sharp movements in asset prices. Such movements (1) may lead to financial instability, (2) play a major role in the transmission mechanism for monetary policy by being a major component of changes in aggregate wealth, and (3) contain valuable information about expectations of future prices, income, and policies, such as the yield curve on Treasury bonds.

But the BIS is nevertheless uncertain about what central banks can or should do with this information: "While asset prices may be useful

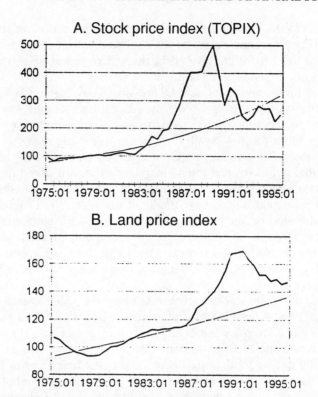

A. Stock price index (TOPIX)

B. Land price index

Figure 7.4.   Japanese stock and land prices, 1975–1995
Source: Bordo, Ito, and Iwaisako (1997).
Notes: Semiannual data, observations at the ends of March and September each
year. Trend line is the exponential of the fitted values from the following regression: $\ln(X) = a + \beta \cdot t$; X = original asset price; period: 1975:01 to 1985:01; stock-
TOPIX (the average of the first section, Tokyo stock exchange); land-land price
index of cities (Japan Real Estate Institute) (both series are nominal, and are n
ormalized in the way that 1980:01 = 100).

indicators, gearing policy directly to them could give self-validating asset
price movements" (BIS, 1997, p. 75). Unlike product inflation, which experience has shown should be targeted to be low and the harm caused by not
constraining it has been amply verified, appropriate targets for asset
inflation have not been developed, and the harm caused by asset inflation
before prices bubbles burst has not been demonstrated. Asset-price bubbles
are recognized only after they occur—ex-post. While asset prices are
rising—bubble? What bubble? One person's bubble is another's equilib-

rium price based on solid fundamentals. Current asset prices to a large extent reflect future asset prices or future prices of the goods or services generated by the assets. Without knowing the future and disagreeing with it, it is difficult for a central bank to argue that the current asset prices are either too low or too high—that is, that the stock market or real estate are either over- or undervalued. Nor do asset prices necessarily move in high correlation with product prices. Although the energy-price bubble of the early 1980s in the United States occurred simultaneously with the sharp acceleration in product inflation, the real estate bubbles in the energy belt and New England in the mid- and late 1980s occurred while product inflation was slowing. Likewise, as noted, the sharp runup in real estate and stock prices in Japan in the late 1980s occurred in a period of slow product inflation, as did the real estate and stock market bubbles in Southeast Asia in the late 1990s.

Although central banks may not target asset prices directly, their actions directed at product prices and other targets affect asset prices. Decreases in interest rates increase asset prices, and increases in interest rates decrease asset prices. At times, conflicts may arise between central-bank polices required to achieve product price and macroeconomic stability and to achieve asset-price and financial and banking stability. For example, in periods after asset-price bubbles have contributed to both a weakened banking system and a macroeconomic recession, central banks pursue expansive monetary policies. But undercapitalized banks are constrained from expanding leading and likely even to curtail it. To stimulate lending and energize its expansive measures, central banks may be tempted to ease prudential standards before the commercial banks have recovered. In contrast, in periods of accelerating product inflation and income growth, the central bank needs to pursue restrictive polices but may be constrained by fear that the accompanying higher interest rates might induce sharp reductions in asset prices and financial instability. Thus, it is likely that the strategy of relatively low interest rates to avoid choking off the current macroeconomic expansion in the United States in light of the low rate of product inflation may have contributed to the acceleration in stock prices as well as accelerating a budding rise in real estate prices. The conflicts and pitfalls facing central banks at times of asset-price bubbles are well summarized in the following two statements by long-time students of monetary policy. In reviewing recent central bank policy in Japan, Bordo, Ito, and Iwaisako (1997, pp. 12, 19) write:

> In the second half of the 1980s, partly preoccupied by the exchange rate fluctuations, Japanese monetary policy ignored the speculation in domestic

asset markets. After mid-1989, containing the asset price boom became an objective for the monetary authorities. Admittedly, many economists were supportive of the Bank of Japan in its policy toward stopping a bubble during this period. However, both Japanese monetary authorities and academic economists may have underestimated the effects of asset deflation on the Japanese economy. So we learned an old lesson once again in a hard way: the monetary authority should pay regard to the asset markets, but stopping short of including asset prices as one of the objectives policy.... [As a result] the Japanese monetary authorities repeated the mistake the U.S. authorities made; using monetary policy to end speculation in asset markets carries a risk of subsequent deflation.

Likewise based on his analysis primarily of the U.K. and U.S. economies, Goodhart (1995, p. 294) concludes that

> macro-policy has been systematically mishandled.... This was partly because they [central banks] were concentrating on a limited index of inflation, current service flow prices, and ignoring the message about inflation given by asset prices. ... The monetary authorities, therefore, share responsibility, along with the commercial banks, for the recent asset price/banking cycle.
>
> There is an inbuilt conflict ... between the imposition of generalized prudential regulations and macro-monetary stability, since the former, almost by definition, must bite harder at times of (asset price) deflation, and hence must, to some extent, aggravate the accompany credit contraction. But it would make a mockery of such regulations, and negate their impact, if they were to be regularly relaxed at such times; though I would advocate that Central Banks should have a, carefully restricted, right of override of these regulations at times of severe, unforeseen shocks. Faced with this conflict, the correct response for the Central Banks is to take more aggressive expansionary action during such deflations, while still using their traditional rescue policies to prevent systemic panics, in the time-honored fashion.

Insulating Banks from Price Bubbles

In the absence of agreement on stabilizing asset prices to avoid financial instability, central banks can protect the financial sector and thereby the macroeconomy from asset bubbles by adopting a version of SEIR and permanently increasing the numerical values of all capital-asset tripwires to provide greater protection against losses from the increased risk exposures of banks when asset inflation accelerates. Because capital absorbs losses before they are charged to depositors and other creditors, the higher the ratios, the less likely is the probability of bank insolvency. Excessive leverage has been identified as a major cause of failure in most banking debacles, particularly in the recent Asian banking crises. However, its is unlikely and undesirable to raise required capital ratios for all banks to levels that would absorb all shocks and prevent all insolvencies. But as discussed earlier, government-provided deposit insurance and other forms of the safety net encourage banks to substitute public for private capital and to hold smaller private capital-to-asset ratios than either the market requires of noninsured bank competitors or that is consistent with the degree of instability in the macroeconomic in the absence of deposit insurance. Thus, increases in private capital ratios to these levels would not be inappropriate.

The higher capital ratios would not impose an unfair competitive disadvantage on banks or reduce their potential return on equity below that of comparable noninsured firms. Rather, the increases reduce any subsidy that banks may be deriving from underpriced deposit insurance or would be matched by decreases in insurance premiums if the probability of failure and losses are reduced. Nor would the higher capital requirements necessarily encourage banks to increase their risk exposures unduly. To the extent the higher requirements match the requirements the market would impose in the absence of insurance, the risk exposures should also be comparable (see Esty, 1998, for historical evidence). Moreover, the banks remain subject to the SEIR sanctions when losses from any greater risk taking occur and their capital deteriorates through the multizones. In addition, the regulators could subject excessively risky banks to harsher or earlier sanctions. Lastly, as long as the performance of the banks can be monitored by the regulators on a reasonably accurate and timely basis, and, in the absence of large abrupt declines in asset values (jump processes), the severe penalty of resolution at no less than zero economic capital also serves to constrain bank risk-taking behavior.

At least until the theory and practice of central-bank intervention in asset prices is better developed, increasing capital ratios is a relatively costless but effective way of insulating banks and the macroeconomy from the bursting of asset price bubbles that are associated with larger losses and defaults than otherwise.

Unfortunately, many banks and bank regulators have a strong aversion to requiring additional private capital of banks, despite the overwhelming evidence of recent years that insufficient capital was a major cause of the widespread bank failures in effectively every country. Indeed, regulators appear schizophrenic on the issue. On the one hand, ex-post, they identify insufficient capital as an important factor in almost every banking crisis. On the other hand, ex-ante, they oppose increasing it. As argued above, banks currently maintain private capital ratios well below those that would be required in a nonsafety-net environment. Part of the hostility may be due to a misunderstanding of the cost of bank capital. Basic finance theory tells us that in the absence of mispriced deposit insurance, taxes, and other institutional details, the overall cost of bank funding is independent of the source of the funding. The lower the proportion raised through capital, the higher is the cost of debt financing and vice versa. With fairly priced deposit insurance, the premiums paid should approximate the reduction in interest rates paid on deposits, as the risk is shifted from the depositor creditor to the insurance agency. Again, the total cost of funds to the bank remains basically unaffected. Only if deposit insurance were underpriced for the protection provided would reductions in capital reduce the total cost of funds and lead to higher returns on equity than otherwise.

Under SEIR, sufficient capital is required to validate that a strictly enforced closure rule at some low positive capital ratio that would, at best, eliminate or, at worst, minimize losses to depositor creditors. The stronger the validation, the lower would be the insurance premiums charged on insured deposits and the interest rates on uninsured deposits and other funds.

Capital is sometimes confused with assets or number of banks, particularly in discussions of excess capacity in banking. Because deposit insurance and other government guarantees to banks permit insolvent banks to continue to operate and thus prevent exit from the industry through failure, there are more assets in the banking industry in some countries than can earn a competitive return and than would exist without these guarantees. But this "overbanking" does not imply that there is also too much private capital in banking. Indeed, the presence of insolvent banks in such environments indicates that there is too little capital. Requiring additional private capital would encourage exit by banks that cannot generate a competitive return. This distinction is also missed by others. A recent article in the prestigious *Economist* argued that the problem with the Japanese banking system was too much, rather than too little, capital ("How to Waste $250 Billion," 1998). Nor does the presence of such overbanking suggest that there are too many banks. Reducing the number of banks without reducing the amount of aggregate banking assets will only reduce the intensity of competition and be counterproductive and dangerous public policy.

Another reason that increases in capital are opposed is that capital is perceived to be a flawed measure of the health of a bank. Many banks that failed had high reported capital ratios.[12] But this reflects primarily problems with the measurement of capital rather that the concept of capital per se. Reported capital often differs significantly from economic capital, or the capital that is available to absorb losses before they must be charged to depositors. Regulators frequently permit banks to underreserve for loan losses and underreport nonperforming loans. Adjustments frequently are not made for loans made to the holders of a bank's capital (bank owners), or "connected credit." Such credit needs to be subtracted from the bank's capital to obtain a measure of the net funds that capital providers have at risk. Losses (and gains) in securities due to increases (decreases) in interest rates are also generally not recorded in accounting measures of capital, so that market values of capital differ from book or historical values of capital (Benston, 1990).[13]

Moreover, in many countries, regulators permit, if they do not outright encourage or require, reported capital to be inflated by accounting trickery, to deliberately project a misleading image of a stronger than actual banking system to ease public fears of a banking crisis or the need for public (taxpayer) funding support. Such trickery includes capitalizing loan losses and amortizing them slowly over time, recording guarantees of support by the government as assets, and recording upward adjustments for increases in the market values of bank buildings or securities but not requiring reporting of comparable losses (that is, reporting the higher of market or book values). A description of the fast footwork practiced during the 1980s by U.S. regulators to increase the reported official capital ratios of S&Ls is reviewed by Kane (1989) and Barth (1991) and of banks by Barth, Brumbaugh, and Litan (1992). Bank regulations in Japan are currently promoting such accounting trickery, as well as using government funds to purchase bank stock. Neither strategy is likely to fool many anymore and only postpones and very likely increases the cost of the ultimate resolution.

Some reduction in the meaningfulness of reported capital is brought about by the regulators themselves. The amount of capital a private noninsured firm is required to hold by the marketplace is determined by the market's evaluation of its risk exposure. The riskier the market evaluates the operation of a firm, the greater will be the capital demanded by its creditors to preserve a given level of credit risk. In recent years, bank regulators in industrial countries have attempted to mimic the market and require capital adjusted for, at least, the bank's credit risk. Major banks in industrial countries that prescribe to the Basle Accord are subjected to a minimum 8 percent risk-adjusted capital requirement. Similarly risk-adjusted capital-to-asset ratios are used to partially define the capital zones for PCA under FDICIA. But while worthy in objective, the Basle risk-based capital measures are badly flawed and possibly counterproductive in implementation. The risk categories and weights assigned to each asset by the regulators are determined not by the market but by relatively arbitrary and broad classifications and political pressure. The less risky regulators classify a particular activity relative to the market-assigned risk, the lower is the regulatory required capital relative to the market-determined capital and the more profitable is it for banks to extend credit for the activity. The potential distortions have been described in the literature by Grenadier and Hall (1995), Kane (1995), and Williams (1995), among others. Until better, more objective risk measures are developed by regulators (on which they are currently working), risk-adjusted capital measures are less useful for regulatory purposes than simple market value and even book-value (adjusted for off-balance sheet entries) capital-to-asset leverage ratios that may be interpreted more easily. FDICIA requires that the performance zones be defined by both unadjusted and risk-adjusted capital measures.

Basle regulators also divide capital between what is permanently provided (basically equity) (Tier 1) and what has a maturity date and needs to be repaid (Tier 2). Tier 1 is rated higher than Tier 2. But this division not only fails to recognize the basic function of capital and is inconsistent with any accepted financial theory but discourages the use of an efficient type of capital in the form of subordinated debt. The basic function of capital is to absorb losses to avoid charging them against other higher-priority claims. What serves as capital depends on the legal rank of a particular claimant in insolvency. The more senior the claim, the more other types of claims serve as protection or capital (Kane, 1992; Benston, 1992; Kaufman, 1992; Miller 1995). From the vantage point of bank regulators, capital should be any financial claim that is junior to the government's claim through deposit insurance, regardless of whether it is equity or debt, with the exception that the debt must have a sufficiently long remaining maturity (say, two years) so that it cannot run and disappear at times of trouble and that interest payments may not be made if they reduce remaining capital below the resolution tripwire value.

In countries that have developed capital markets, such subordinated debt is a particularly useful type of capital for a number of reasons. Knowing its junior standing and its inability to participate in the bank's upside earnings potential beyond the amount of the coupons, holders of the debt will monitor the issuing bank carefully and sell the debt if they perceive undesirable increases in risk taking. This reaction increases interest rates on the debt and signals other participants and the regulators. In the United States, FDICIA prohibits critically undercapitalized banks from making any payment of principal or interest on their subordinated debt after sixty days from the date of their being so classified. The market discipline so induced will supplement and reinforce regulatory discipline. In addition, to the extent the debt is not perpetual and is issued in staggered maturities, the bank must refinance it periodically, and any difficulties encountered in doing so would be visible to the market and the regulators. In response to its banking crisis of 1994 and 1995, Argentina required all banks to issue subordinated debt equal to 2 percent of their deposits. At least in the United States, failure to give full regulatory weight to subordinated debt discourages banks from holding as much capital as otherwise as interest on the debt is tax deductible while dividends on equity is not. Thus, subordinated debt is a cheaper but just as effective source of capital for banks in some countries for protecting the insurance agency as is equity.[14]

At times, regulators also appear to lose sight of the fundamental role of capital–to absorb losses—and view it only as a high-cost source of funds to penalize banks. In the United States, for example, they appear to be wedded to the numerical values for the FDICIA capital zones that they set in 1992, regardless of the changes in conditions since. It may credibly be argued that the values set in 1992 were set deliberately low in order not to identify too many banks as poorly capitalized in a period in which the industry was still in crisis. But now that the industry is healthier. Almost all banks are not only classified as "well capitalized" but are maintaining capital well in excess of this criterion. Nevertheless, the regulators are still hesitant to increase the tripwire values, even though it would downgrade few banks. At the same time, reductions in the capital ratios of large banks are beginning to be reported as a concern in the press (Padgett, 1998).

Regulators need not be concerned about all losses in banking, even losses that may periodically exceed one or a few banks' capital and threaten insolvency. Indeed, market discipline requires periodic losses to remind participants of the penalties for being wrong and to encourage them to operate prudently. Periodic small losses are the best deterrent to large losses and market failures in the future that are likely to give rise to calls to replace market regulation with government regulation. If the market does not enforce proper corporate governance of financial institutions and markets, governments will, and many countries will find themselves back in the periods of broad government intervention and subsequent regulatory failures from which they are now trying to escape through financial liberalization.

In many countries, financial deregulation or liberalization is being introduced at the same time as deposit insurance reform and for the same reasons. The two reforms are not independent of each other. Because SEIR retains some government-provided deposit insurance, it retains the need for some government regulation, in particular for government supervision and examination to be able to monitor banks on an adequate basis. Deregulation does not imply desupervision.

Indeed, supervision may need to be intensified as many banks, after laboring for years under a repressed system, are often ill prepared to suddenly operate in a market structure with penalties as well as rewards. In particular, they are likely to have weak if any credit cultures and engage in insufficient credit analysis and monitoring. Moreover, many borrowers have also been protected and are not used to either operating profitably on an unsubsidized basis or repaying loans promptly. Thus, bank risk exposures and subsequent losses are likely to virtually explode following a sudden changeover from financial repression to financial liberalization, unless the liberalization is structured correctly (Working Party of Financial Stability, 1997). Unfortunately, this was not recognized sufficiently in many countries, including both in the United States in the early 1980s and in Japan in the late 1980s, and was an important cause of the banking debacles. Banking liberalization must be phased in or sequenced in such a way that at any one-time regulatory discipline is not reduced by more than market discipline is reasonably able to replace. The weaker is the sum of market and regulatory discipline, or total discipline, on banks, the higher need be the required private capital ratios to achieve the same degree of stability.

Other Short-Term Assistance

Although the role of central banks in targeting asset prices is both largely unchartered and controversial, its role in preventing the adverse effects of a bursting of asset-price bubbles is better chartered and less controversial, although not entirely without controversy. This role has been explored, at least in industrial countries, even before Bagehot in 1873 (Humphrey, 1989; Kaufman, 1991). As discussed earlier, burstings of important asset-price bubbles are highly disruptive to both the financial system and the macroeconomy. Not only do the sudden and sharply falling prices trigger losses and defaults, but they destroy valuable price information necessary for economic agents to allocate resources efficiency and to be willing to trade in financial markets. If price information becomes too uncertain and unreliable, agents increasingly tend to make their portfolio adjustments in quantities (withdrawals and runs) rather than in prices. It is better to be safe than sorry at almost any price until conditions settle! This further reduces liquidity and reinforces the tendency for price declines to temporarily overshoot their new lower equilibrium levels and increase fire-sale losses. Information processing and decision making are not instantaneous, even in the current high-tech world, and the more uncertain the environment, the longer the delays. In addition, trade clearing and settlements systems also slow when price information becomes less reliable and both delivery and payment failures increase.

As is well recognized, at such times, central banks need to act as active or standby lenders of last resort, injecting sufficient liquidity into the markets to avoid trading stalls. However, this is not straightforward for three reasons. One, central banks are unlikely to know the new lower equilibrium prices and thus how much liquidity support to provide. Although they may reasonably be expected to err on the side of too much rather than too little liquidity, they should not attempt to support the old prices. In addition, excessive liquidity to slow or offset the asset-price declines carries the risks of both igniting product inflation and misallocating resources. Any excess liquidity needs to be withdrawn quickly (Mishkin, 1997).

Two, at least in developed countries with viable money and capital markets, central banks are unlikely to know the financial condition of individual institutions better than the market does. Thus, any liquidity assistance in these countries should be provided to the market as a whole through open market operations rather than directly to individual institutions through the discount window (Kaufman, 1991). That is, in developed economies the lender of the last resort and the discount window can and should be separated. Bagehot was writing in a very different environment. In countries with less developed financial markets, the discount window remains as the primary channel for lender of last resort funding. As a result, the central bank incurs the risk of misallocating resources through error or political pressure.

Three, central banks have unlimited capabilities of providing liquidity only in their own domestic currency. As discussed earlier in the chapter, in smaller, open economies, banking and foreign-currency problems are often interconnected, so that the bursting of asset-price bubbles could require liquidity support in both domestic and foreign currencies. However, sufficient foreign currency support is unlikely to be provided by the domestic central bank and is likely to require multinational agreement or an international lender of last resort. This is a highly complex, controversial, and charged issue and will not be discussed in this chapter.

Summary and Conclusions

Financial stability is a prerequisite for macroeconomic stability in market economies. Recent experiences in many countries, differing widely in economic, political, legal, and cultural characteristics, have clearly demonstrated the high cost of bank crises both to the countries themselves and often also to other countries. Asset-price bubbles have increasingly been a cause of banking crises. In contrast to product price stability, which is widely accepted as a legitimate goal of central-bank policy and whose attainment is reasonably well known, asset-price stability is clouded in controversy. Disagreement surrounds its definition, its causes, the role of central banks in targeting it, and the mechanism by which the central bank can affect asset prices, if indeed the bank wished to do so, without triggering major disruptions to the macroeconomy. To date, central banks have not been very successful in containing the damage from asset-price bubbles. This chapter argues that central banks can protect the financial system and the macroeconomy from much of the adverse effects of asset-price bubble bursts through appropriate prudential and lender-of-last-resort policies.

Commercial banks are particularly susceptible to asset price bubbles as their primary ongoing reason for being is the management of risk. The ability to manage bank risk successfully becomes more difficult, the less stable is the price and income environment. Ironically, government attempts to stabilize banking in the form of safety nets under the industry have unintentionally released powerful destabilizing forces that have to date rarely been held in check and have been counterproductive at least as frequently as they have been productive.

This chapter examines the sources of these counterproductive forces and recommends a scheme for prudential regulation of banking that curtails these forces and promises to produce a more efficient and safer banking system. The scheme was recently enacted in the United States, following its banking crisis of the 1980s, and with relatively minor changes appears adaptable to other countries. The scheme permits the regulators to protect both the banking system and the macroeconomy from the full adverse effects of asset-price bubbles by focusing on bank capital sufficient to absorb the greater losses and defaults that typically arise when asset-price bubbles burst. The particulars of this strategy are dependent on a number of important characteristics of the country to which it is applied and may be expected to vary across countries. Nevertheless, higher ratios of economic capital to total bank assets represent a relatively costless and effective means of neutralizing asset-price bubbles until effective strategies are developed for asset-price stabilization by central banks.

Finally, central banks need to act as lenders of last resort, if sudden asset-price declines appear to overshoot their new lower equilibrium levels. But as central banks are unlikely to know these new levels and likely to err on the side of excessive ease, this policy could result in misallocating resources and igniting product inflation. It would be best to avoid asset-price bubbles beforehand, if only we knew how.

Acknowledgments

This chapter was prepared for presentation at the Fourth Dubrovnik Conference of Transitional Economies in Dubrovnik, Croatia, on June 24–26, 1998, sponsored by the Croatian National Bank. It was also presented at the annual meeting of the Western Economic Association in Lake Tahoe, CA, June 29–July 1. I am indebted to the participants at both conferences and, in particular, to the assigned discussants, John Bonin (Wesleyan University) and Richard Nelson (Wells Fargo Bank) as well as to Douglas Evanoff and James Moser (Federal Reserve Bank of Chicago) for their helpful comments and suggestions.

Notes

1. Economists have only recently devoted much attention to either incorporating asset prices into measures of the general price level theoretically (Goodhart, 1995) or even to developing aggregate asset price indexes for a wide range of countries (Borio, Kennedy, and Prowse, 1994).

2. The BIS has estimated that, after the bursting of property price bubbles in industrial countries in recent years, commercial property traded at near 30 percent of its peak values and residential proterty at near 70 percent in real terms (BIS, 1998).

3. Much fear of bank failures in many countries appears to stem from government actions that devalue, tax, expropriated, or freeze bank deposits and often also currency in some way, even though the banks may be healthy. That is, the fear of banks in these countries often stems more from fear of government intervention than of bank insolvency.

4. Nonfederal government—provided deposit insurance schemes had been introduced in a number of states before 1933, and national bank notes issued by nationally chartered banks were required to be fully collateralized and any deficit paid by the U.S. Treasury Department. Thus, early national banks had some of the characteristics currently proposed by proponents of "narrow banks" (Calormiris, 1989; Kaufman, 1987).

5. The low bank failure rate appears to have existed even before the Civil War. Alan Greenspan, chairman of the Board of Governors of the Federal Reserve System as recently observed that "the very early history of American banking was an impressive success story. Not a single bank failed until massive fraud brought down the Farmers Exchange Bank in Rhode Island in 1809" (Greenspan, 1998, p. 2). Schwartz (1988) reports similar evidence for other countries.

6. Liquidation or physically closing and liquidating insolvent banks should be employed only rarely when the demand for banking services at the locations involved appears insufficient to promise competitive returns.

7. Before the recent crisis, banks in a number of Asian countries were borrowing heavily

in short-term foreign currencies (primarily dollars) at low interest rates and lending in domestic currency much higher rates in amounts that may have suggested that they were operating under the illusion that their governments could and did repeal the law of interest-rate parity. The BIS recently estimated that nearly 60 percent of the international interbank borrowing by banks in Indonesia, Korea, Malaysia, the Philippines, and Thailand in 1995 and 1996 were denominated in dollars and most of the rest in yen. Two-thirds had a maturity of less than one year (BIS, 1998).

8. The same effect is encountered if the run on the domestic currency takes the form of a run from bank deposits denominated in domestic currency to currency, which is then shipped to banks in foreign countries for redeposit into foreign-currency deposits.

9. Kaminsky and Reinhart (1996) find that banking crises predict balance-of-payments (exchange-rate) crises, but balance-of-payments crises do not predict banking crises.

10. The use of taxpayer funds in supporting banks is often misunderstood (see, for example Working Party of Financial Stability, 1997, p. 41).

11. As some countries break up into smaller countries, the ability of banks to diversify geographically domestically is reduced further.

12. The BIS, for example, notes that many Asian banks had much higher reported capital ratios before the crisis than required by the Basle Accord (BIS, 1998).

13. Because of the difficulty in measuring and monitoring capital correctly, some countries, particularly developing and transitional economies, partially shift prudential emphasis to cash reserves, which are easier to measure and monitor. The larger is the percentage of cash reserves required, the less important is capital, although banks could attempt to offset the loss in earnings from high reserve requirements by selecting riskier earnings assets. Problems of connected lending may also be reduced by requiring arm's-length types of transactions between the bank and the owners' entities. But caution still suggests that the amounts lent be excluded from regulatory capital.

14. Recently, some Basle and other industrial countries have permitted large banks to use additional subordinated debt with a minimum maintained maturity of two years as a newly added Tier 3 capital against market risk in trading accounts.

References

Bank for International Settlements. (1997). *Sixty-Seventh Annual Report.* Basle: BIS.

Bank for International Settlements. (1998a). *The Transmission of Monetary Policy in Emerging Market Economies.* BIS Policy Papers No. 3. Basle: BIS.

Bank for International Settlements. (1998b). *Sixty-Eighth Annual Report.* Basle: BIS.

Barth, James R. (1991). *The Great Savings and Loan Debacle.* Washington, DC: American Enterprise Institute.

Barth, James R., R. Dan Brumbaugh, Jr., and Robert E. Litan. (1992). *The Future of American Banking.* Armonk, NY: Sharpe.

Basle Committee for Banking Supervision. (1997). *Core Principles for Effective Banking Supervision.* Basle: BIS.

Benston, George J. (1990). "Market-Value Accounting by Banks: Benefits, Costs and Incentives." In George Kaufman (ed.), *Restructuring the American Financial System* (pp. 35–56). Boston: Kluwer.

Benston, George J. (1992). "The Purposes of Capital for Institutions with Government-Insured Deposits." *Journal of Financial Services Research* (April): 369–384.

Benston, George J., Robert A. Eisenbeis, Paul M. Horvitz, Edward J. Kane, and George G. Kaufman. (1986). *Perspectives on Safe and Sound Banking*. Cambridge, MA: MIT Press.

Benston, George J., and George G. Kaufman. (1995). "Is the Banking and Payments System Fragile?" *Journal of Financial Services Research* (December): 209–40.

Benston, George J., and George G. Kaufman. (1997). "FDICIA After Five Years." *Journal of Economic Perspectives* (Summer): 139–158.

Benston, George J., and George G. Kaufman. (1998). "Deposit Insurance Reform in the FDIC Improvement Act: The Experience to Date." *Economic Perspectives* (Federal Reserve Bank of Chicago) (2nd qtr.): 2–20.

Bordo, Michael. (1986). "Financial Crises, Banking Crises, Stock Market Crashes and the Money Supply: Some International Evidence 1870–1933." In Forrest Capie and Geoffrey E. Wood (eds.), *Financial Crises and the World Banking System* (pp. 190–248). New York: St. Martin's Press.

Bordo, Michael D. (1997). "Financial Crises and Exchange Rate Crises in Historical Perspective." Working Paper, Rutgers University, August.

Bordo, Michael D., Takatoshi Ito, and Tokuo Iwaisako. (1997). "Banking Crises and Monetary Policy: Japan in the 1990s and U.S. in the 1930s." Working Paper, University of Tsukuba (Japan).

Bordo, Michael D., Bruce Mizrach, and Anna J. Schwartz. (1998). "Real vs. Pseudo International Systemic Risk: Some Lessons from History." *Review of Pacific Basin Financial Markets and Policies* (March): 31–58.

Borio, C.E.V., N. Kennedy, and S.D. Prowse. (1994) *Exploring Aggregate Asset Price Fluctuations Across Countries*. BIS Economic Papers No. 40. Basle: BIS.

Calomiris, Charles W. (1989). "Deposit Insurance: Lessons from the Record." *Economic Perspective* (Federal Reserve Bank of Chicago) (May/June): 10–30.

Calomiris, Charles W., and Charles M. Kahn. (1991) "The role of Demandable Debt in Structuring Optimal Banking Arrangements." *American Economic Review* (June): 497–513.

Calomiris, Charles W., and Joseph R. Mason. (1997). "Contagion and Bank Failure During the Great Depression: The June 1932 Chicago Banking Panic." *American Economic Review* (December): 863–883.

Caprio, Jr., Gerald, and Daniela Klingebiel. (1996). "Bank Insolvency: Bad Luck, Bad Policy, or Bad Banking." Working Paper, World Bank.

Carr, Jack, Frank Mathenson, and Neil Quigley. (1995). "Stability in the Absence of Deposit Insurance: The Canadian Banking System 1890–1966." *Journal of Money, Credit, and Banking* (November): 1137–1158.

Corrigan, E. Gerald. (1991). "The Banking: Commerce Controversy Revisited." *Quarterly Review* (Federal Reserve Bank of New York) (Spring): 1–13.

Crockett, Andrew. (1997). "Why Is Financial Stability a Goal of Public Policy." In

Maintaining Financial Stability in a Global Economy (pp. 7–36). Kansas City: Federal Reserve Bank of Kansas City.

Esty, Benjamin. (1998). "The Impact of Contingent Liability on Commercial Bank Risk Taking." *Journal of Financial Economics* (February): 189–218.

Friedman, Milton, and Anna J. Schwartz. (1971). *A Monetary History of the United States, 1867—1960*. Princeton. NJ: Princeton University Press.

Goodhart, Charles, A.E. (1995). "Price Stability and Financial Fragility." In C.A.E. Goodhart (ed.), *The Central Bank and the Financial System* (pp. 263–302). Cambridge, MA: MIT Press.

Greenspan, Alan. (1998). "Remarks." Washington, DC: Board of Governors of the Federal Reserve System, May 2.

Grenadier, Steven R., and Brian J. Hall. (1995). "Risk-Based Capital Standards and the Riskiness of Bank Portfolios: Credit and Factor Risk." Working Paper 5178, National Bureau of Economic Research, July.

"How to Waste $250 Billion." (1998). *The Economist*, January 24, p. 16.

Humphrey, Thomas M. (1989). "Lender of Last Resort: The Concept in History." *Economic Review* (Federal Reserve Bank of Richmond) (March/April): 8–16.

Kaminsky, Graciela L., and Carmen M. Reinhart. (1996). "The Twin Crises: The Causes of Banking and Balance of Payments Problems." International Finance Discussion Paper 544. Washington, DC: Board of Governors of the Federal Reserve System.

Kane, Edward J. (1989). *The S&L Insurance Mess.* Washington, DC: Urban Institute Press.

Kane, Edward J. (1995). "Difficulties in Transferring Risk-Based Capital Requirements to Developing Countries." *Pacific Basin Finance Journal* (September): 193–216.

Kaufman, George G. (1987). "The Federal Safety Net: Not for Banks Only." *Economic Perspectives* (Federal Reserve Bank of Chicago) (November–December): 19–28.

Kaufman, George G. (1988). "Bank Runs: Causes, Benefits, and Costs." *Cato Journal* (Winter): 539–587.

Kaufman, George G. (1991). "Lender of Last Resort: A Contemporary Perspective." *Journal of Financial Services Research* (October): 95–110.

Kaufman, George G. (1992). "Capital in Banking: Past, Present, and Future." *Journal of Financial Services Research* (April): 385–402.

Kaufman, George G. (1994). "Bank Contagion: A Review of the Theory and Evidence." *Journal of Financial Services Research* (April): 123–150.

Kaufman, George G. (1995). "The U.S. Banking Debacle of the 1980s: An Overview and Lessons." *The Financier* (May): 9–26.

Kaufman, George G. (1996a). "Bank Failures, Systemic Risk, and Bank Regulation." *Cato Journal* (Spring/Summer): 17–45.

Kaufman, George G. (1996b). "Bank Fragility: Perception and Historical Evidence." Working Paper Series 96–18. Chicago: Federal Reserve Bank of Chicago.

Kaufman, George G. (1997a). "Banking Reform: The Whys and How To's." Working Paper, Loyola University Chicago, August.

Kaufman, George G. (1997b). "Lessons for Transitional and Developing Economics from U.S. Deposit Insurance Reform." In George M. von Furstenberg (ed.), *Regulation and Supervision of Financial Institutions in the NAFTA Countries and Beyond* (pp. 16–55). Boston: Kluwer.

Kindleberger, Charles P. (1985). "Bank Failures: The 1930s and 1980s." In *The Search for Financial Stability: The Past Fifty Years* (pp. 7–34). San Francisco: Federal Reserve Bank of San Francisco.

Kindleberger, Charles P. (1996). *Manias, Panics, and Crashes: A History of Financial Crises* (3rd ed.). New York: Wiley.

Levine, Ross. (1997a). "Financial Development and Economic Growth: Views and Agenda." *Journal of Economic Literature* (June): 688–726.

Levine, Ross. (1997b). "Stock Markets, Economic Development, and Capital Control Liberalization." *Perspective* (Investment Company Institute) (December): 1–7.

Lindgren, Carl-Johan, Gillian Garcia, and Matthew I. Saal. (1996). *Bank Soundness and Macroeconomic Policy.* Washington, DC: International Monetary Fund.

Miller, Merton H. (1995). "Do the M&M Propositions Apply to Banks?" *Journal of Banking and Finance*, (June): 483–489.

Minsky, Hyman P. (1977). "A Theory of Systematic Financial Fragility." In Edward Altman and Arnold Sametz (eds.), *Financial Crises: Institutions and Markers in a Fragile Environment* (pp. 138–152). New York: Wiley.

Mishkin, Frederic S. (1997). "The Causes and Propagation of Financial Instability: Lessons for Policy Makers." In *Maintaining Financial Stability in a Global Economy.* Kansas City: Federal Reserve Bank of Kansas City.

Mishkin, Frederic S., et al. (1995). "The Monetary Transmission Mechanism." *Journal of Economic Perspective* (Fall): 3–96.

Moore, Robert R. (1997). "Government Guarantees and Banking: Evidence from the Mexican Peso Crisis." *Financial Industry Studies,* Federal Reserve Bank of Dallas (December): 13–21.

O'Conner, J.F.T. (1938). *The Banking Crisis and Recovery Under the Roosevelt Administration.* Chicago: Callaghan.

Padgett, Tania. (1998). "Capital Slide Could Spur Big Banks to Debt Market." *American Banker*, March 12, pp. 1–2.

Rajan, Raghuram G., and Luigi Zingales. (1998). "Financial Dependence and Growth." *American Economic Review* (June): 559–586.

Schwartz, Anna J. (1988). "Financial Stability and the Federal Safety Net." In William S. Haraf and Rose Marie Kushmeider (eds.), *Restructuring Banking and Financial Services in America* (pp. 34–62). Washington, DC: American Enterprise Institute.

Williams, Michael G. (1995). "The Efficacy of Accounting-Based Bank Regulation: The Case of the Basel Accord." Working Paper 95–9. Santa Monica, CA.: Milken Institute.

Working Party of Financial Stability in Emerging Market Economies. (1997). *Financial Stability in Emerging Market Economies.* Basle:

8 THE CONDUCT OF MONETARY POLICY AND BANKING SOUNDNESS
A Slovenian Episode
Velimir Bole

Introduction

In transition economies, necessary market institutions and instruments were only partly in place during the first years of transition to market economies. So monetary policy faced serious nonstandard challenges when stabilizing the macroeconomic environment. A weak and insolvent banking sector further complicated the attainment of monetary control objectives. As the banking sector is the basic transmission mechanism of monetary policy, weak and insolvent banks prevented the efficient and sustainable usage of more restrictive monetary policy measures, which were necessary to stabilize the macroeconomic environment and to spur essential restructuring of the financial sector.

Specific domestic and foreign shocks during the transition period made the conduct of monetary policy even more difficult. Almost complete product and market reshuffling of the economy and a fast increase in private consumption, driven by catching up to the living standards in developed countries,[1] were the most important domestic shocks. Strong financial inflows, predominantly driven by *push factors*[2] (further accelerated by privatization *stock adjustment* and corresponding low prices of assets) presented the most challenging foreign shocks, at least in more advanced transitional economies. Macro management of such foreign shocks probably need some specific adjustments in the conduct of policy, especially monetary policy, to mitigate the effects of the lack of institutions and instruments—namely, existing micro distortions in some markets, especially labor markets, and shallowness of financial intermediation prevented sustainable absorption of financial flows without seriously aggravating macroeconomic stability.[3] At least to get time to increase the robustness of the financial sector against the mentioned severe longer-term shocks infinancial flows, adjustment of monetary and fiscal policy seems indispensable.

It is generally true that in the medium run, an anti-inflation monetary policy can be carried only if fiscal policy does not overburden the budget and banking soundness is secured (see Frenkel, 1997). Both conditions were tight in economies in transition. The weak and underdeveloped sector of financial intermediation and severe shocks only strengthened the role of financial sector robustness, and therefore also the banking soundness, for increasing the scope and the potential effectiveness of monetary policy. It could be expected that only after actual steps in rehabilitation of banks, correction of shortcomings in accounting, implementation of legal and regulatory framework, and supervision are made, the scope and efficiency of the monetary policy in transition economies would be enhanced.

Standard models of monetary policy assume that policymaker objective function consists of inflation and unemployment. Given a theoretical econometric model of the economy, optimal feedback rules for monetary policy are established. Monetary policy effects, especially the tradeoff between inflation and output growth, are additionally studied in an uncertain environment, in which random disturbances (which are usually supposed to be uncorrelated and equally distributed) are disrupting the steady-state path of the economy. In such a theoretical framework general comparisons are made between rules and (optimal) discretion policies and between different targets and exchange-rate regimes (see, for example, Fischer, 1990).

Leaving aside the necessary simplification of theoretical analysis as well as different theoretical arguments, pro and cons, different optimal monetary policies (such as time inconsistency, instrument instability, insulation of the central bank from political pressures, and so on), it still seems that basic theoretical guidelines from such an analysis cannot be really relevant for economies in transition if at least two specific (transitional) facts are not explicitly taken into account. The first, shocks are large, correlated, and autocorrelated in time, so there is no steady-state path from which disturbances are pushing away the economy. And second, for transition countries it is crucial to take into account explicitly the constraints put on the conduct of monetary policy by banking-sector soundness.

This means that guidelines for optimal policies would have to be conditional on financial- (banking-) sector soundness so that the optimal policy would not reduce banks' ability to control their balance sheets and therefore significantly decrease their responsiveness to the volatility of exchange and interest rates. Then also conduct of optimal policy would not prevent sustainability of the monetary policy by aggravating excessive distortions of the transmission mechanism of monetary policy.

The Slovenian economy is small and very open. It started the transition with large-market reshuffling, negligible foreign-exchange reserves, and almost 40 percent of the banking sector insolvent. In stabilization, key macroeconomic variables have been normalized sustainably although not very quickly (see, for example, Bole, 1997b). However, the robustness of the economic system (especially of its financial part) has not been improved enough to be able to contain and neutralize some important macro disturbances impinging on the economy without adjustments of macroeconomic policy. So the scope of macroeconomic policy has been considerably constrained by a rather fragile economic and especially financial system.

In this chapter two-way effects among the monetary transmission mechanism fragility and the conduct of monetary policy are analyzed for the Slovenian economy. Analysis is made for the period 1995 to 1997—that is, for the period after a significant drop in foreign-exchange risk premiums took place. That period was characterized by large and exceptionally volatile foreign financial inflows and stubborn distortions on the micro markets (especially on the labor market). The robustness of the financial system is studied against macroeconomic disturbances originating in financial flows. Potential banking system risks originating in the high volatility of foreign financial flows are identified. The break point in the scale of volatility is documented, and the escalation of crises described. To increase the shockproofness of the banking system, modifications in prudential regulation and the central-bank safety net were made. Those less standard changes are explicitly discussed, and possible effects evaluated. It is illustrated that both modifications enabled monetary policy to overcome serious liquidity problems in the banking system after a sudden drop in foreign-exchange inflows.

The rest of the chapter is structured as follows. In the second part, a brief overview of the macroeconomic environment and the conduct of monetary policy is given. Some important risks originating in the volatility of foreign-exchange flows, which have been endangering banking soundness, are identified in the same part. The mechanism of crises triggered by a big shock in foreign-exchange flows and the weakness of monetary policy are documented in the third part of the chapter. Then reshaping of prudential regulation and the central-bank safety net are described, and possible effects on the conduct of monetary policy illustrated. Conclusions are presented at the end of the chapter.

Volatility of Foreign-Exchange Flows and Monetary Policy

Macroeconomic Policy and Performance

From the very beginning of stabilization, exogenous money and a managed floating exchange rate have been the basic pillars of the monetary policy. In all years of transition, the fiscal stance was strong, in comparison with other more advanced economies in transition.[4] The pension system has been by far the most fragile part of the general government fiscal position.

By the end of 1994, monthly inflation leveled off at around 0.8 percent, and growth of the economy stabilized at 3.5 percent to 4 percent. In the first years of transition, extremely high real interest rates were caused by perverse transmission of the weak banking system and the eradicated information capital of banks, after collapse of their clients' markets (in the former Yugoslavia) (see Bole, 1996).[5] After the third year of stabilization (1994), when stubbornly high real interest rates started to fall, distortions on the labor markets (wage pres-sures) remained the most important macroeconomic problem of the policy-makers. The wage pressures were especially dangerous because the bulk of social transfers (such as pensions) were pegged to average wage dynamics.[6]

At the very beginning of transition, *distress exporting* gave a strong push to foreign-exchange inflows. Driven by differences in interest rates (*push factors*), short-run macroeconomic adjustment (credit squeeze), and labor market distortions, capital inflows took the lead in increasing foreign-exchange inflows after the first half of 1994, when liquidity and currency risk started to drop. Net medium- and long-term capital inflows exceeded, on average, 4.5 percent of GDP. Facing significant micro distortions on the labor market, policymakers decided to contain and neutralize net financial inflows to prevent larger appreciation of the exchange rate, early in the transition period (see Bole, 1997a).

Monetary Policy and Volatility of Foreign-Exchange Flows

Real appreciation of the exchange rate and consequent reduction of foreign competitiveness are usually the major sources of concern to policymakers in countries facing huge financial flows. However, banking crisis episodes triggered by high financial flows prove that banking fragility to intermediation of huge volatile financial flows might not be less important.[7]

The volatility of foreign financial flows intermediated by banks can significantly increase the risks faced by banks. The nature of risks depends on the kind of monetary policy (targets and instruments), foreign-exchange regime (floating or fixed), and foreign-exchange intervention (sterilized versus nonsterilized).

In Slovenia, the volatility of foreign-exchange flows originated from capital flows as well as the current account dynamics. Both components are presented (in terms of GDP) in Figure 8.1. To further illustrate volatility of financial flows, a basic term structure of capital inflows is presented in Figure 8.2. Obviously, volatility was considerable for both components.[8]

In the process of intermediation of financial flows, high volatility of

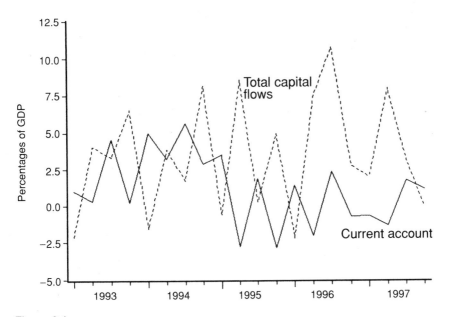

Figure 8.1.

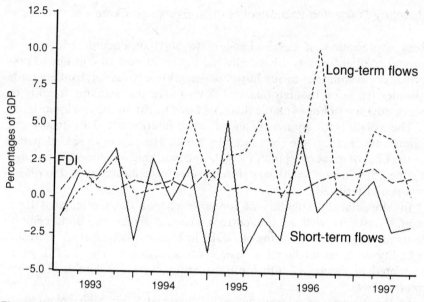

Figure 8.2.

foreign-exchange flows could be transmitted into exchange rates, interest rates, or money-supply volatility. However, depending on the characteristics of monetary policy, exchange-rate regime, and foreign-exchange intervention, volatility of effected variables can vary greatly.

As mentioned, the central bank tried to contain and neutralize swings in foreign-exchange flows. Nevertheless, it kept monetary policy unchanged because of its commitment to disinflation and still present (wage and transfers) inflationary pressures.[9]

The effects of volatility of financial flows impinging on the sector of financial intermediation (and, therefore, corresponding risks) are illustrated by Figures 8.3 and 8.4. Exchange rates and interest rates are given.

Exchange-Rate Volatility

Huge inflows of foreign exchange have been continuously pushing the foreign-exchange rate toward real appreciation,[10] since 1992. In five years, real appreciation attained around 13 percent in cumulative terms; the trend in real appreciation was therefore around 2.5 percent per year. Using wholesale (or producer) prices instead of retail prices in measuring appre-

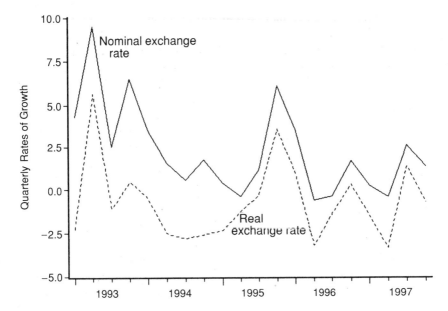

Figure 8.3.

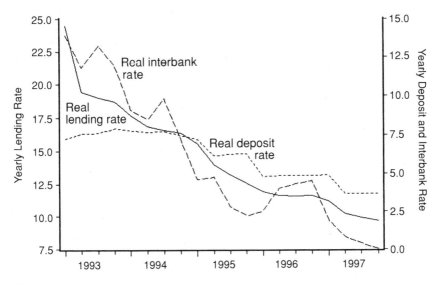

Figure 8.4.

ciation, there was no cumulative real appreciation in the period after 1992 in Slovenia (see, for example, Bole, 1997a). Namely, the basket for retail prices does include services whose relative prices significantly increased in the period of transition.

Because money was exogenous (it was an explicit target of monetary policy), it could be expected that volatility in foreign-exchange flows would be transformed into volatility of exchange rate. However, because of sterilized foreign-exchange interventions, paths of money and those of exchange rate were more independent than one would have been expected.[11] The central bank has persistently tried to influence portfolio decisions of residents in favor of foreign-exchange-nominated instruments. (see Bole, 1997a).

Deviation from the trend was the biggest in 1995 and 1996 (around 5 percent), when also volatility of foreign-exchange flows was the greatest. The volatility of the nominal exchange rate was also considerable; the biggest amplitude of oscillation around the trend attained over 5 percent in the period after 1992. Although a wholesale policy of containing and neutralizing financial flows was used, obviously policymakers did not succeed in preventing long-term real appreciation or in stabilizing completely the volatility of exchange rate. Nevertheless, the scale of swings in exchange rate did not exceed the standard width of the band used in pegged or crawling pegged exchange-rate regimes in other more developed economies (such as economies in transition).

Although monetary policy dampened the volatility of exchange rate through sterilized foreign-exchange interventions, amplitudes were big enough to expose banks to serious exchange-rate risks in cases when they do not have closed foreign-exchange position. To avoid such foreign-exchange risk, banks used instruments in domestic currency but indexed by exchange rate.

Interest-Rate Volatility

To detect possible effects of banking intermediation of foreign-exchange inflows as well as possible side products of a sterilization policy on interest rates, on the Figure 8.4 real (short-term) lending rate, real (time) deposit rate, and interest rate on the interbank market are given.

After 1992, real interest rates dropped significantly. Decrease of lending and interbank market interest rates was almost the same, cumulatively for around fourteen percentages points in real terms, by the end of 1997. Deposit rates fell significantly less, in cumulative terms by 4 percent.

Two changes could be identified in the trend dynamics of real interest rates. In both cases, falling of real interest rates became steeper. The first change took place in the middle of the second quarter of 1993, when rehabilitation of almost 35 percent of the banking system was launched.[12] The second happened at the end of 1994, when the central bank started to penalize free-riding behavior of individual banks on the market for deposits. The central bank penalized individual banks if they increased deposit interest rates significantly over the average of the banking system.[13] By making this, the central bank reduced strategic uncertainty on the market for deposits. By doing that, the central bank increased also the banking competition on the lending side and, therefore, decreased lending rates. After 1995, an interbank agreement on the highest deposit rates enabled the same mechanism of cutting lending rates (see Bole, 1996).[14]

The dropping of lending rates was more smooth than those of deposit rates and interest rates on the money market. Intermediating the volatile foreign-exchange flows, considerable swings in flows made the liquidity position of banks significantly more uncertain than the liquidity position of other economic units. The same fact is illustrated also in Figure 8.5, where base, narrow, and broad money per unit of GDP are presented. After inflation finally leveled off at around 8 to 9 percent per year

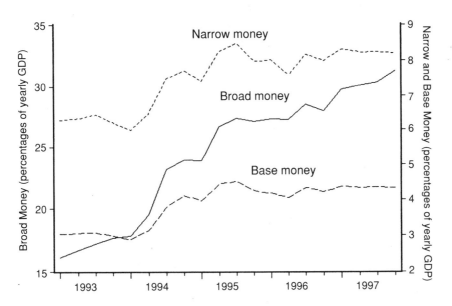

Figure 8.5.

in the first quarter of 1995 and remonetization of the economy was stabilized, base money per unit of GDP stayed almost constant for three years (around 0.044). So volatility of the interbank market interest rates in the same period would have to originate from the changing of the expected demand for base money—that is, from the uncertain liquidity position of the banks.

Amplitudes in the real interest rates on the interbank market around a decreasing trend (of 2.8 percentages points per year) attained the greatest values (around 2.5 percentages points) in the period 1995 to 1996. The greatest volatility of interest rates on the interbank market was, therefore, in the same period when there was the greatest swing in the (current and capital part of) foreign-exchange flows. Liquidity uncertainty (liquidity risk) faced by banks would have to increase greatly in that period because the decreasing dynamics of real interest rates on the interbank market was reversed for a year and a half, while the trend dynamics of base money, narrow money, and broad money per unit of GDP did not change significantly after remonetization was finished in 1995/I (see Figure 8.5).

Volatility of Foreign-Exchange Monetization on the Retail Foreign Exchange Market

The size and volatility of foreign-exchange inflows impinging on the economy is illustrated on the Figure 8.6. Net monetization on the retail foreign-exchange market (per unit of GDP) is presented.[15]

The creation of money through monetization of foreign-exchange flows had a slight falling trend during transition period. From 5 percent of GDP, at the beginning of transition, trend values dropped to 1.5 percent GDP in 1997. Because money had opposite-growing trend, monetization of foreign-exchange flows had a large share in increments of money in the first phases of stabilization (yearly monetization was over 30 percent of broad money), while the later corresponding share dropped considerably (yearly monetization came to 5 percent of broad money by 1997).

While trend values of monetization have become negligible, disturbances to money supply caused by extreme volatility of monetization did not abate after 1992. Amplitudes of quarterly oscillations attained values as high as 7 percent of (quarterly) GDP. Because a significant part of oscillations originated in capital flows (especially after mid-1995), high volatility and unpredictability of short-term as well as long-term financial flows directly

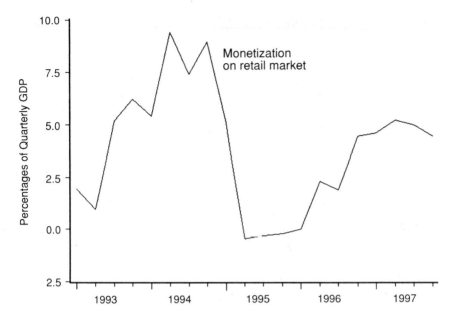

Figure 8.6.

increased uncertainty of the environment of banking intermediation and therefore also risks faced by banks (see Figure 8.1).[16]

When inflation leveled off at around 8 to 9 percent and after the remonetization of economy was completed, the dynamics of money became more stable in terms of GDP (see Figure 6.5); because of still present inflationary pressures, only small oscillations in money were tolerated by monetary policy. However, keeping money on track (narrow money was targeted), high volatility of financial flows (and therefore high volatility of monetization of foreign-exchange flows) caused considerable volatility in the credit supply of money.

After 1992, there were large swings in monetization of foreign-exchange flows. Especially pronounced drop of foreign-exchange monetization was in 1995 (see Figure 8.6). Large swings in monetization caused strong acceleration (or decceleartions) in credits growth.

High oscillations of credits increased credit and liquidity risks faced by the banking sector. The phases of fast-increasing credits, necessary to offset the sudden fall of foreign-exchange monetization (net foreign-exchange inflows) were especially dangerous. A fast increase in credits necessary to offset the quarterly oscillations in foreign-exchange monetization (which topped over 7 percent of quarterly GDP or over 9 percent of broad money) could well trigger a banking crisis.

"Big" Shock in Foreign-Exchange Flows and the Banking Sector

Plummeting of Foreign-Exchange Flows and Credit Taking Off

It is a well-known fact that a too rapid increase of real credits is one of the basic factors causing banking crises (see, for example, Caprio and Klingebiel, 1996). Strong acceleration of credit growth increases the iquidity and credit risks faced by the banking sector. Acceleration of credit disbursement prolongs average effective maturity of credits (although maturity of individual credits is not changed) and so increases pressure on the current liquidity of banks and, especially, makes prospective liquidity less certain. Fast growth of credits causes decline of credit standards. Namely, the very lack of on-time information makes it much more difficult for supervisors (and bankers) to keep loan quality unchanged when credits accelerate their growth considerably (see, for example, Caprio and Klingebiel, 1996). If lack of on-time infor-mation because of considerable acceleration of credits is combined with increased variance of relative prices (of particular group of enteprises), the increase in credit risk would be even considerably greater. Increased volatility of relative prices (of a particular group of banking sector clients) makes prospective solvency of those clients of the banking sector more uncertain—the information capital of the banking sector decreases.[17]

Empirical estimates (using international evidence on a sample of economies) reveal that real growth of credits faster than twice the growth of GDP significantly increases the probability of banking crises. (see Caprio and Kligebiel, 1996).

In 1995, net foreign-exchange inflows dropped significantly. Considerable real appreciation of the exchange rate in the period after the fourth quarter of 1993 depressed the current account balance by more than 3 percent GDP (from surplus it came to zero) in 1995.[18] Capital inflow decreased by additional 0.5 percent GDP (from 2.6 percent GDP in 1994 to 2.1 percent GDP in 1995). A considerable fall in net foreign-exchange inflows squeezed quarterly creation of money through foreign-exchange monetization to zero from over 8 percent of quarterly GDP (8.7 percent of broad money) in the middle of 1994 (see Figure 8.6).

In 1995, there was no significant change in dynamics of any variable figuring in the monetary rule.[19] So the stance of the monetary policy (determined by the target narrow money path) was not changed. The more gentle slope of money (per unit of GDP) after the beginning of 1995 resulted mainly from the already completed remonetization of the economy, after inflation dropped from around 5 percent quarterly to around 2 percent quarterly at the end of 1994 (see Figure 8.7, where base money and inflation are presented).

Because of unchanged monetary policy and actual demonetization driven by foreign-exchange flows, credit supply of money (in terms of GDP) started to grow faster than money. This credit taking off is illustrated in Figure 8.8, where broad money and total credits (per unit of yearly GDP) are given. Strong acceleration pushed growth rates of real credits over 40 percent per year after the first quarter of 1995.

Structure of Banks That Participated in the Credit Stampede

Credit expansion was not uniform across the structure of banks. To reveal the banking structure characteristics of the credit stampede, shares in credit

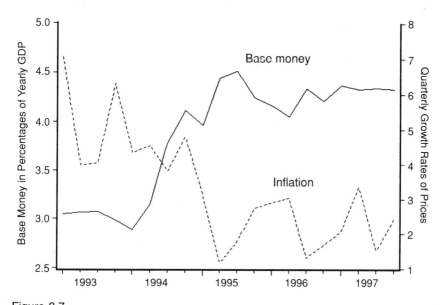

Figure 8.7.

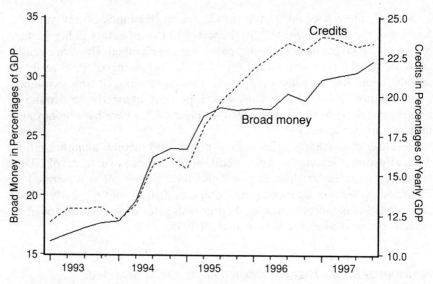

Figure 8.8.

Table 8.1. Increments in credits (shares in credit increments in total banking sector)

	1995	*1996*	*1997*
First percentile	0.088	0.052	0.014
Second percentile	0.083	0.063	0.056
Second decile	0.096	0.123	0.019

Source: Internal data of Bank of Slovenia; own calculations.
Note: Distribution of banks by the size of balance sheet.

increase for the first two percentiles and second decile of the banking system are presented in Table 8.1 for 1995, 1996 and 1997.[20]

Figures in the Table 8.1 show that in the first decile of the banking system the increase of credits per unit of balance sheet was almost twice as high as for the whole banking sector. Smaller banks had had much higher capital adequacy before the stampede of credits started in 1995. So they took their advantage and pushed credits up, only to increase their market share.

Informational capital in smaller banks had been far smaller than in-balance capital (in comparison with bigger banks). Besides, they were without good enough screening and monitoring capabilities for making

Table 8.2.   Increments in deposits of nonhousehold sector (shares in increments of deposits of nonhousehold sector in total banking sector)

	1995	1996	1997
First percentile	0.089	−0.019	0.050
Second percentile	0.070	0.075	0.052
Second decile	0.010	0.188	0.108

Source: Internal data of Bank of Slovenia; own calculations.
Note: Distribution of banks by the size of balance sheet.

Table 8.3.   Increments in deposits of household sector (shares in increments of deposits of household sector in total banking sector)

	1995	1996	1997
First percentile	0.079	0.114	0.065
Second percentile	0.052	0.067	0.049
Second decile	0.066	0.066	0.077

Source: Internal data of Bank of Slovenia; own calculations.
Note: Distribution of banks by the size of balance sheet.

credits to the business sector. Therefore, small banks were active chiefly in accelerating consumer credits, especially because consumer credits could be insured at insurance companies and also qualitative (very liquid) collateral were available.

To sustain the fast increase of credits, smaller banks also increased deposit rates to the ceiling rate of the interbank agreement (on maximal deposit rates) and so attracted sufficient deposits (liquidity) from other banks. Their marketing was especially aggressive toward bigger (very liquid) enterprises from retail trade, gasoline trading, and so on. However, those enterprises were buying only short-term deposits. The banks' structure of new deposits acquired from the household sector and from the nonhousehold sector are presented in Tables 8.2 and 8.3. Again, percentages of total increase in deposits are given for the first two percentiles and second decile of the banking sector. Obviously, banks in the first percentile attracted (per unit of balance sheet) almost 80 percent more deposits from nonhousehold and 60 percent from household sector[21] in 1995 compared to the banking sector average. Actually, morally hazardous behavior of smaller banks was curbed only by the interbank agreement on maximal deposit rates.

Powerlessness of Monetary Policy to Curb the Credit Stampede

Although base money was almost stable (in terms of GDP) and narrow money on the target track (see Figure 8.5), the ratio of increments in credits over increments of broad money increased from 0.4 at the beginning of 1995 to as high as 1.7 in the last quarter of 1995 (see Figure 8.9). Although the bulk of credit increase balanced the drop of foreign-exchange monetization to zero, there was also a small part that was the counterpart of falling net foreign assets of banks. Although banks already had liquid enough foreign assets (in deposits and foreign-exchange bills of the central bank), they additionally took credits abroad and extended credits in domestic currency to sell foreign exchange.[22] After the fall of foreign-exchange risk in 1994, banks were able to get credits abroad under pretty favorable conditions.

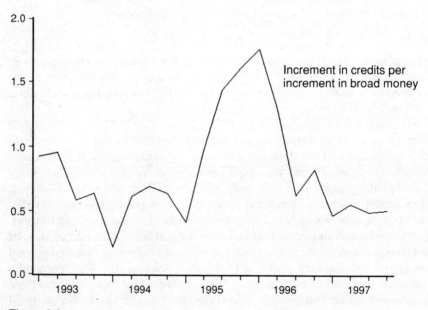

Figure 8.9.

Increased demand for foreign exchange resulted in a strong depreciation of the real exchange rate in the last quarters of 1995 (see Figure 8.3). Depreciation of exchange rate was actually the only curb for fast-increasing credits. Namely, for the credit increase, funded by foreign credits, the banking sector did not need any additional liquidity to proceed with the fast growth of credits.[23] Depreciation of the (floating) exchange rate was, however, too slow to stop the credit stampede. That is, depreciation was too slow to significantly increase current account and (tolar) costs of foreign credits (and so increase creation of money through monetization of foreign exchange on the retail foreign-exchange market) in a short period.

Because the bulk of the credit increase actually offset a drop in monetization of foreign exchange to zero, monetary policy could not mitigate credit growth without severely endangering the liquidity of the economy. Besides, base money and narrow money (per unit of GDP) were already falling in 1995. In the last three quarters of 1995, base money dropped by 0.3 percent GDP (7 percent of base money) and narrow money by 1 percent GDP (12 percent of narrow money).

Because in some (predominantly smaller) banks increasing of credits was almost twice as fast as the banking system average, additional squeezing of base money would be especially dangerous for a considerable number of smaller banks.

There is also a principal question: did monetary policy have to intervene at all? Namely, monetary policy kept the money strictly on the target track. So fast credit growth could endanger stability of the economy only if such an acceleration in intermediation of loanable funds endangered the soundness of banks. It would be more appropriate to adjust prudential regulation, to make the banking sector more robust to such shocks, than to use discretion in monetary policy.

Reversed dynamics of financial flows and liquidity of banks. In the first quarter of 1996 short- and long-term capital flows started to pick up (see Figure 8.2). In the same quarter, the dynamics of the real exchange rate reversed to appreciation. Net foreign-exchange monetization also accelerated immediately. In the second quarter 1996 it already attained 2.5 percent of quarterly GDP (around 30 percent of quarterly increment in broad money).

The stance of monetary policy remained unchanged in 1996. As it is apparent from Figure 8.5, base money per unit of GDP did not change. Although ratio of increments in credits (per increments in broad money) also dropped (to around 1) in the second quarter of 1996, the squeeze on bank liquidity accelerated. So real interest rates on the interbank market increased considerably; by 1996/II they almost doubled in real terms to around 4 percent (see Figure 8.3).

The liquidity squeeze was concentrated only in a part of the banking sector. Those (mainly smaller) banks with fastest increase of credits in 1995 faced severe liquidity pressure already in the second quarter 1996. Some of smaller banks completely rationed credits. Still, their liquidity was so squeezed that on the interbank market they had to give collateral for getting deposits from other banks. Knowing the praxis of banks, bigger enterprises also started to condition their (even only short-term) deposits with corresponding collateral.

The same (mainly smaller) banks with liquidity problems also did not have enough assets eligible for using lender-of-last-resort refinancing. One of the small banks became illiquid at the beginning of the third quarter 1996.

Deposits started to move, and uncertainty increased. At the time of this bank failure, there were several smaller banks with similar liquidity problems. They had not enough qualitative assets for refinancing with the central bank.[24] At the same time they also needed good collateral to get deposits from other banks. Knowing the squeezed liquidity position of particular banks, "bigger" depositors from the nonfinancial and nonhousehold sector started to move their deposits to other more safe (bigger) banks. Namely, only household deposits were insured by the state in Slovenia. The liquidity of some banks became highly volatile and uncertain.

Figures in Tables 8.2 and 8.3 confirm the moving of deposits. Nonhousehold deposits in the first percentile of banks dropped, while those in the second decile increased (per unit of balance sheet) almost 90 percent more than in the total banking sector. Quite the opposite happened with the time deposits of the household sector, which were insured by the state. Those deposits in the first percentile of banks increased by twice as much as in the total banking sector. Smaller banks raised deposit rates to the upper ceiling for deposit rates, fixed by interbank agreement. To mimic a better liquidity position, banks with liquidity problems still extended credits, but in normal dynamics. Bigger banks accelerated their share in new credits.

Avoiding Deterioration of Crises by Improving Prudential Regulation and the Central-Bank Safety Net

Prudential Regulation Practice Until 1995

In Slovenia, prudential control was performed by the central bank from the very proclaiming of monetary independency. It practiced almost all key prudential requirements followed also in European Union (minimum capital for new banks, minimum capital adequacy ratio, maximum loans to one borrower, lending to related parties, and new bank licensing).[25] On- and off-site supervision was practiced.

Because of the risks caused by the high volatility of the business environment, some requirements of prudential regulation were very restrictive in Slovenia. Volatility of the business environment was mainly caused by foreign financial flows and prices on foreign trade markets. So the minimum capital for new banks with a full license (enabling activity abroad) was raised to 60 million DEM. The minimum capital requirement was adjusted as early as 1992. However, banks had to adjust (increase) their capital in two phases until 1995. It was shown elsewhere that by increasing capital expected solvency risks was actually reduced. So the lending rate margin was also significantly squeezed (see Bole, 1996). Actual capital adequacy ratio in the banking sector was also much higher (21.5 percent of risk-weighted assets by end of 1997) than the standards in developed economies (for example, Basle standards). It goes without saying that in an economy facing wholesale restructuring and an extremely volatile environment default probabilities cannot compare with those in the Group of Ten.[26]

Among key prudential practices probably the liquidity requirements (ratios) were the weakest element in Slovenia. Until 1996, the central bank issued guidelines to banks for measurement and management of liquidity risk. However, such a supervisory approach presumes that the interbank market is deep enough to assist banks in maintaining liquidity (see, for example, Lindgren, Garcia, and Saal, 1996). This silent presumption was not correct, as it was documented by uncertainty on the interbank market and insulation of banks with liquidity difficulties (by conditioning liquidity support with a collateral) in the second and third quarters of 1996.

Facing increased uncertainty because of moving unstable nonhousehold deposits and an inability to support banks through the lender-of-last-resort facility, the central bank made two adjustments in prudential regulation. First, liquidity requirements were implemented by a so-called liquidity ladder. And, second, a restriction was made on possible falling of net foreign assets.[27] The central bank also supplemented its safety net with a special credit facility (so-called *credit with bank's assistance*).

Liquidity Ladder

In developed countries, where the deep interbank market assists banks in managing liquidity, supervision of the liquidity risk is usually enabled by guidelines issued to banks for measurement and management of such risk as well as different statutory requirements and monitoring (see Pecchioli, 1987). In Slovenia, only guidelines of the central bank and monitoring were used before 1996. However, in 1996 it became clear that the interbank market was not stable enough to enable banks to manage liquidity using mainly interbank market. So the additional approach of supervising liquidity risk (through prudential ratios of liquid assets) was launched.

In principle, the liquidity ladder[28] relies on the maturity ladder. It requires balance between maturities of liabilities and assets for three cumulative classes of liabilities and assets. Special treatment is given to "big" deposits and to deposits and credits from banks. Besides, for all assets and liabilities actual (that is residual) maturity is taken into account. As a "cover" for short-term liabilities only those government securities, central bank bills, and foreign-exchange deposits with foreign banks that are not already used as a collateral can figure.

In the time when uncertainty was the largest (third quarter of 1996), the whole banking sector had assets greater than liabilities in all three maturity classes. Problems with maturity mismatch were concentrated in the segment of the smallest banks. Table 8.4 shows the percentage of banks that do not fulfill the requirements of liquidity ladder in the period when bank liquidity was the most uncertain (mobility of deposits the highest). Percentages (of balance sheet) are given for the first percentile, first decile, and total banking sector. Figures in Table 8.4 show that current and prospective liquidity problems were concentrated in the first decile of banks.[29] Almost 54 percent of banks from the first decile had severe liquidity prob-

Table 8.4. Liquidity ladder for quantiles of banking sector (percent of banks not fulfilling corresponding liquidity ratio)

	Class 1	Class 2	Class 3
First percentile	46.5	81.3	73.6
First decile	45.7	62.9	59.1
Upper 90% of banks	13.6	1.5	0.0

Source: Internal data of Bank of Slovenia; own calculations.
Notes: Class 1: sight deposits, big deposits, and deposits of banks with (residual) maturity less than thirty days; Class 2: deposits and securities with (residual) maturity less than thirty days; Class 3: deposits and securities with (residual) maturity less than 180 days.

lems and, in the same time, insufficient volume of assets eligible for refinancing with the central bank. Namely, in the first decile of the banking sector 54 percent of banks had volume of very liquid liabilities[30] greater than the sum of very liquid assets (primary liquidity)[31] and securities eligible for getting credit from the central bank (secondary liquidity). In the rest of the banking system very liquid liabilities were greater than the sum of primary and secondary liquidity only in 16 percent of banks.

When the liquidity ladder was introduced as a part of prudential regulation requirements, the period of adjustment for banks that did not fulfill the ladder at the very launching of the new regulation requirement was determined.

Foreign-Exchange Exposure

Until 1996, the closed foreign-exchange position was not part of prudential regulation. Actually, the banking system as a whole had a short foreign-exchange position until the end of 1997.

Because of huge surpluses in the current account and significant capital inflows, the shortness of the foreign-exchange position (and therefore exposure to foreign-exchange risks) dropped considerably from 1992. In 1992 banks were short for 113 percent of capital, yet by the end of 1996 the shortness of the foreign-exchange position dropped to only 22 percent of capital.[32] In between, banks used instruments in domestic currency with foreign-exchange indexation to close their foreign-exchange position.

The regulators did not enforce a closed foreign-exchange position before 1996 because that could significantly increase the already high volatility of the foreign-exchange rate. There were three reasons for that. First, a huge gap in foreign-exchange position (chiefly caused by household savings in foreign exchange) inherited from the system in the former Yugoslavia, uncertain long-term dynamics of potential foreign-exchange flows, and finally a huge volume of government long-term treasury bills with foreign-exchange-rate indexation. So the central bank tolerated covering exchange-rate risk by using instruments in domestic currency and indexed by exchange rate before 1996.

The credit stampede in 1995 and in the first half of 1996 was partly accelerated by the bank practice known as South Zone—namely, taking credit abroad and extending it on domestic market in tolars. To prevent that, a break was put on a possible deterioration of the foreign-exchange position in 1996/III. Definitive (obligatory) requirements for closing the foreign-exchange position were made in 1997.[33] By the end of 1997, the foreign-exchange position was already closed for the banking system as a whole. The situation in individual banks was, however, different.

Central-Bank Safety-Net Enhancement

Several small banks did not have assets eligible for refinancing with the central bank when their liquidity was endangered in 1996, especially because many of bigger depositors and banks also required collateral for their deposits or credits.

At the same time, banks with liquidity difficulties had an almost unchanged portfolio of no classified (standard) loans in 1996. In Table 8.5 increases in substandard loans are given for some quantiles of the banking sector. Apparently, the increase in substandard loans did vary with the size of the bank; however, increases were not exceptionally high.[34]

The new safety-net scheme would have to enable the central bank to perform the lender-of-last-resort function also for banks without appropriate collateral[35] but still qualitative loan portfolio.

In the 1996/III, the new safety-net scheme was launched. It enabled banks with liquidity problems for refinance with the central bank using assets from the loan portfolio only indirectly as a collateral. Using it directly, the central bank would have required much higher capital. The central bank was doing this with the assistance of other banks because it could not directly use assets from loan portfolios as collateral. Assistant banks gave credit to the bank with problems (getting the qualitative part of loan portfolio as a collateral), while the central bank extended its credit to assistant banks (using eligible assets of assistant banks as a collateral). The qualitative part of the loan portfolio of the bank in trouble was identified in advance by the central bank because more banks took part in the assis-

Table 8.5. Growth rates of substandard loans

	1995	1996	1997
First percentile	27.9	23.0	24.7
Second percentile	0.0	32.9	0.0
Second decile	41.8	6.0	6.6
Third and fourth deciles	30.7	−51.8	28.8

Source: Internal data of Bank of Slovenia; own calculations.
Note: Distribution of banks by the size of balance sheet.

tance. Credit risk thereby stayed with the assisting banks, which take part in the new safety-net scheme. To get such a credit from the central bank (with assistance of other banks), the particular bank with problems had to accept in advance severe restructuring measure enforced by the central bank. If any of the assistant banks would have been interested, merger with the weak bank also could have been enforced. Such assistance contracts between the central bank and assistant banks were made for the longer period to cover the period of uncertainty. For a contracted period, the central bank paid (commitment) fees to assisting banks for being prepared to assist the central bank.

The basic idea behind the new safety-net scheme—to increase refinancing possibilities of banks in distress with the central bank by using support of other banks—is similar to Liko-Bank in Germany, which was established after Herstatt crisis.[36]

The first contract was made for a nine-month period. Later, contracts were prolonged. In the first period, when banks with liquidity problems were almost insulated from the interbank market because of high uncertainty, the commitment fee paid by the central bank was 7 percent yearly. Later it was cut to 1 percent. In the first period, the volume of the bank's commitment for the "credit with bank's assistance" was almost 9 percent of base money. That was enough for potential intervention in the first percentile of the most endangered banks.

Avoiding Credit Crunch and Decreasing Uncertainty

While the liquidity ladder increased banking-sector robustness in the long run, the new safety-net scheme augmented the potential scope of central-bank intervention immediately. So after establishing the new safety-net scheme uncertainty on the interbank market started to abate. Because of high minimum capital requirements, and therefore high capital adequacy ratio of banks, it was obvious that the scope of refinancing with the central bank could be significantly extended if facilitated by the "credit with bank's assistance." On the interbank market, the insulation of banks with liquidity problems started to melt.

Although there were already present signs of credit crunch before the central-bank intervention,[37] credits and money in terms of GDP immediately started to improve after "credit with bank's assistance" was made workable at the end of the third quarter of 1996 (see Figures 8.5 and 8.7). Real interest rates on interbank market also started to fall (see Figure 8.3).

Distribution of deposits also normalized. In 1997, the increase of household- and nonhousehold-sector deposits became almost uniformly distributed among banks of different size. The same happened also with credits, only banks in the first percentile increased credits less because in 1997 they had to adjust their credit expansion to meet the requirements of the liquidity ladder.

Conclusions

In this chapter, two-way effects among the monetary transmission mechanism fragility and the conduct of monetary policy are analyzed for the Slovenian economy in transition. Among the most important disturbances impinging on the Slovenian economy in transition were foreign-exchange flows. Monetary policy facilitated policy of containing and neutralizing financial flows, but policymakers did not succeed either to prevent long-run appreciation or to completely stabilize the volatility of exchange rate.

Intermediating foreign-exchange flows, high volatility of flows was transmitted to increased volatility of interest rates, foreign-exchange rate, and credit supply. Therefore, corresponding risks also increased. The greatest volatility of interest rates and exchange rates around the trend dynamics (respectively, 2.5 and 5 percentages point) was in the period in which there was the greatest swing in the foreign-exchange flows. High volatility of credit supply was the most important effect of foreign-exchange flows intermediation. Quarterly amplitudes in oscillation of monetization of net foreign-exchange flows and those of credit supply attained even 8 percent of quarterly GDP.

In 1995, a sharp drop in current account and financial flows caused fast real credit growth of over 40 percent per year. Monetary policy strictly kept money on the target path; credit increase predominantly offset only a drop in monetization of foreign exchange on the retail part of the foreign-exchange market. Smaller banks increased credits the most.

The exchange rate depreciated significantly in real terms. Exchange-rate depreciation was strong enough to prevent any attack on reserves but too slow to curb the credit stampede.

The liquidity of some banks (predominantly smaller) became endangered when financial flows picked up again. Monetary policy could not intervene because banks with liquidity problems were not able for refinancing with the central bank, as they did not have enough eligible instruments for refinancing. After one bank became illiquid, liquidity uncertainty increased further.

The central bank enhanced its safety net and made two adjustments in prudential regulation. A liquidity ladder was introduced by which balance between maturities of liabilities and assets was enforced. A restriction was put on foreign-exchange exposure, to prevent further falling of net foreign assets. To increase the scope of refinancing with the central bank, "credit with bank's assistance" was offered. The new safety net scheme enabled the central bank to give liquidity support to those banks that did not have assets eligible for refinancing with the central bank.

After adjustments in prudential regulation and central bank safety net, the liquidity situation started to improve sustainably.

Acknowledgment

I would like to thank Evan Kraft and Jože Mencinger for helpful comments. Of course, I am responsible for any errors.

Notes

1. Kornai called it, "goulash postcommunism" (Kornai, 1997).
2. See, for example, Claessens, Dooley, and Warner (1995).
3. Nonstandard adjustments of policy (for example, introducing foreign capital controls) could be even second-best solutions in the context of micro distortions on specific markets (see, Dooley, 1996).
4. General government spending was kept around 46 percent GDP and fiscal deficit under 1 percent of GDP.
5. On "perverse transmission of the weak banking sector," see Fischer (1997).
6. Detailed description of the policy measures and economy performance in transition are given in Bole (1997b).
7. See, for example, Schadler, Carkovic, Bennett, and Kahn (1993) and Calvo, Leiderman, and Reinhart (1993).
8. Coefficients of variability of the term structure of capital flows are similar to some developed economies, such as the German economy (see Bole, 1997a), and Claessens, Dooley, and Warner (1995).
9. Target path of narrow money was determined by a rule that included expected inflation, real interest rates, and volume of transactions; after 1994 financial wealth variable also was included in the rule (see Bole, 1997b).
10. Using retail prices and PPP rule as a criterium for appreciation.
11. Sterilization was therefore at least partly successful (see Obstfeld, 1982).
12. At the very beginning of the operation, nonperforming credits and potential losses were swapped for the government bonds, old management was changed, and procedures for giving and taking credits and disinvestment of banks were made and supervised by the special agency for the rehabilitation of banks.
13. Central banks penalized free-riding banks with reducing possible day-to-day variability in fulfilling monthly obligation for reserve requirements.

14. About strategic uncertainty in financial intermediation, see Yanelle (1989).

15. Foreign-exchange trading among banks is usually dubbed as "wholesale trading on the foreign-exchange market" (see, for example, Bingham, 1994). In analogy, foreign-exchange transactions between banks and their clients can be classified in retail part of the foreign-exchange market. Observing this, net foreign exchange bought by the Slovenian banking sector (including central and commercial banks) from the nonbanking sector will be called *monetization of foreign exchange on the retail (part of the foreign-exchange market* in the chapter. Also the shorters term *monetization of foreign exchange* will be used in this sense.

16. It is documented for a greater sample of economies, that term structure of capital flows does not really mean much for analysis of volatility and predictability of financial flows (see Claessens, Dooley, and Warner, 1995). Coefficients of variability of term structure components of financial flows illustrate that similar conclusion can be made also for Slovenia (see Bole, 1997a).

17. On information capital of banks, see, for example, Caprio (1992).

18. Strong real appreciation of exchange rate accumulated to around 10 percent in a year and a half before drastic deterioration of the current account (see Figure 8.3). That was probably the main reason for squeezing of the surplus.

19. Real volume of all transactions, expected inflation, and real interest rates (see Bole, 1997b).

20. In Table 8.1 and subsequent tables different quantiles are calculated from banks' distribution. Banks are arranged by increasing size of the balance sheet. In the first percentile there are, therefore, the smallest banks, comprising 5 percent of the balance sheet of the total banking sector.

21. Per unit of balance sheet.

22. Fast increasing of credits driven by decreasing of net foreign assets is a well-known characteristic of financial disorder after premature financial liberalization and a weak banking sector, known from banking crises in South Zone (see, for example, Dijiaz-Alejandro (1985), McKinnon (1990), or Corbo and DeMelo, (1985).

23. Banks (partially) covered potential exchange-rate risk caused by falling net foreign assets by extending credits in domestic currency with exchange-rate indexation.

24. The central bank would extend credit against any government security, its own bills, foreign-exchange deposits with foreign banks, government bonds from OECD countries, and commercial paper of appropriate quality.

25. Almost the same practices had been in place already in the former Yugoslavia after 1989.

26. Because of the credit stampede, in only six months the capital adequacy ratio dropped from 21.5 percent (by the end of 1995) to 19 percent (by end of June 1996 (see Bank of Slovenia Annual Report, 1996). According to some authors, the capital adequacy ratio would have to be much higher (possibly over 20 percent) in developing and transitional economies because of higher default probabilities (much lower information capital), underdeveloped supervisory technique (loan classification and provisioning practice), and legal infrastructure (see, for example, Caprio, 1995, or Lindgren, Garcia, and Saal 1996).

27. In the whole period after 1992, banks were not exposed to exchange-rate risk because they systematically closed this risk through offering instruments in domestic currency but indexed by exchange rate.

28. It was introduced in 1996 to 1998.

29. In the first 10 percent of smallest banks measured by the size of balance sheet.

30. Sight deposits, deposits (of banks) with residual maturity less than thirty days, and "big" deposits with residual maturity less than thirty days.

31. Giro account, vault money, reserve requirements account, sight foreign-exchange deposits at foreign banks, and sight foreign-exchange deposits at Bank of Slovenia and other domestic banks.

32. See *Bank of Slovenia Monthly Bulletin.*

33. Foreign exchange exposure can be 20 percent of capital.

34. Total tolar credits for whole banking sector increased by 19.8 percent in 1996.

35. Eligible to get credit from central bank.

36. NLiquiditats-Konsortialbank GMbh (Liko-Bank) is a joint venture between the Bundesbank and banks from all sectors of banking sector. The Liko-Bank can extend credit to banks, deposit funds with them, and purchase from them, which become eligible for refinancing with the Bundesbank due to additional signature of the Liko-Bank (see Pecchioli, 1987).

37. Abrupt slow down in the credit machinery.

References

Bingham, T.R.G. (1994). "Foreign Exchange Markets." In P. Newman, M. Milgate, and J. Eatwell (eds.), *The New Palgrave Dictionary of Money and Finance* (vol. 2) (pp. 154–156). MacMillan.

Bole, V. (1996). "The Financial Sector and High Interest Rates: Lessons from Slovenia." In M.I. Blejer, and M. Škreb (eds.), *Financial Sector Transformation: Lessons form Economies in Transition* (pp. 293–317). Cambridge: Cambridge University Press.

Bole, V. (1997a). "Financial Flows in a Small Open Economy: The Case of Slovenia." In J. Gacs, R. Holzmann, and M. Wyzan (eds.), *The Mixed Blessing of Financial Inflows: Transition Countries in Comparative Perspective* (pp. 195–238). Edward Elgar.

Bole, V. (1997b). "Stabilization in Slovenia: From High Inflation to excessive Inflow of Foreign Capital." In M.I. Blejer, and M. Kreb (eds.), *Macroeconomic Stabilization in Transition Economies* (pp. 172–203).

Calvo, G.A., L. Leiderman, and C. Reinhart. (1993). "The Capital Inflows Problem: Concepts and Issues." IMF Paper on Policy Analysis and Assessment, International Monetary Fund.

Caprio, G.J. (1992). "Policy Uncertainty, Information Asymmetries, and Financial Intermediation." Working Papers, WP853.

Caprio, G.J. (1995). "Bank Regulation: The Case of the Missing Model." Paper presented at the conference on Sequencing of Financial Reforms, mimeo, Policy Research Department, World Bank.

Caprio, G.J., and D. Klingebiel. (1996). "Bank Insolvency: Bad Luck, Bad Policy, or Bad Banking?" Paper presented at the World Bank's Annual Bank Conference on Development Economics, Washington, DC, April 25–26.

Claessens, S., M.P. Dooley, and A. Warner. (1995). "Portfolio Capital Flows: Hot or Cool?" *World Bank Economic Review* 9: 153–174.

Corbo, V., and J. DeMelo. (1985). "Overview and Summary." *World Development* 13: 863–866.

Dijaz-Alejandro, C. (1985). "Good-bye Financial Repression, Hello Financial Crash." *Journal of Development Economics* 19: 1–24.

Dooley, M.P. (1996). "A Survey of Literature on Controls over International Capital Transactions." Staff Papers, International Monetary Fund, 639–687.

Fischer, S. (1990). "Rules Versus Discretion in Monetary Policy." In B.M. Friedman, and H.F. Hahn (eds.), *Handbook of Monetary Economics* (pp. 1156–1182).

Fischer, S. (1997). "Banking Soundness and the Role of the Fund." In C. Enoch, and H.J. Green (eds.), *Banking Soundness and Monetary Policy* (pp. 22–34).

Frenkel, J.A. (1997). "Capital Mobility and Its Impact on the Operations of a Central Bank." In C. Enoch H.J., and Green (eds.), *Banking Soundness and Monetary Policy* (pp. 71–83).

Kornai, J. (1997). "The Political Economy of the Hungarian Stabilization and Austerity Program." In M.I. Blejer, and M. Kreb (eds.), *Macroeconomic Stabilization in Transition Economies* (pp. 172–203).

Lindgren, C.J., G. Garcia, and M. Saal. (1996). "Bank Soundness and Macroeconomic Policy." IMF.

McKinnon, R.I. (1990). "Financial Liberalization in Retrospect: Interest Rate policies in LDC's." In G. Ranis, and T.P. Schultz (eds.), (pp. 386–415).

Obstfeld, M. (1982). "Can We Sterilize? Theory and Evidence." *American Economic Review: Papers and Proceedings* 72(2)(May): 45–50.

Pecchioli, R.M. (1987). "Prudential Supervision in Banking." OECD.

Schadler, S., M. Carkovic, A. Bennett, and R. Kahn. (1993). "Recent Experiences with Surges in Capital Inflows." Occasional Paper 108, International Monetary Fund, Washington, DC.

Yannele, M.O. (1989). "The Strategic Analysis of Intermediation." *European Economic Review* 33: 294–301.

V DISINFLATION AND THE ROLE OF NOMINAL TARGETS

9 MONETARY POLICY STRATEGIES FOR DISINFLATION
Lessons from Recent Experience In Transition Economies and Israel

Academic College of Tel Aviv Yaffo

Leonardo Leiderman

Bank of Israel and Berglas School of Economics at Tel Aviv University

Introduction

Consider a small open economy that—after a long period of chronic inflation, of substantial deficits in the government budget and the current account of the balance of payments, and of a marked accumulation of domestic and foreign debt—implemented a comprehensive exchange-rate-based stabilization program that resulted in a sharp reduction in the rate of inflation to about 15 to 20 percent per year. Although the reduction in the rate of inflation is considered as a major achievement, it is accompanied by real exchange-rate appreciation and weaker competitiveness of exports—say, two to three years after the stabilization, and this trend can not be sustained over time. Given this, and the increasing need to allow for some reaction of the nominal exchange rate in response to capital inflows and outflows, sooner or later policymakers in such a hypothetical economy are likely to consider introducing some degree of exchange-rate flexibility while at the same time avoiding the possible inflationary consequences of nominal exchange-rate depreciation and creating the conditions for a further reduction in the rate of inflation toward world levels.

Faced with the foregoing policy dilemma, several countries have shifted toward increased nominal exchange-rate flexibility in at least one of two forms: the adoption of crawling exchange-rate bands and the adoption of explicit inflation targets. In those countries that adopted them, crawling bands are seen as a regime that partially maintains an anchoring role for the nominal exchange rate yet at the same time provides flexibility to deal with short-term shocks and with the marked volatility of international capital flows. Inflation targets, if credible, are seen as a transparent channel through which the authorities can make commitments and discipline their monetary policy without necessarily incurring the macroeconomic costs of currency pegs. In some countries, the two anchors coexist.

The disinflation experience of various countries with the foregoing characteristics in recent years provides a rich and useful territory for analysis of monetary policy strategies for disinflation. Consider, for example, the case of Israel, where since 1992 monetary policy is based on both a crawling exchange-rate band and inflation targets. As seen in Figure 9.1,

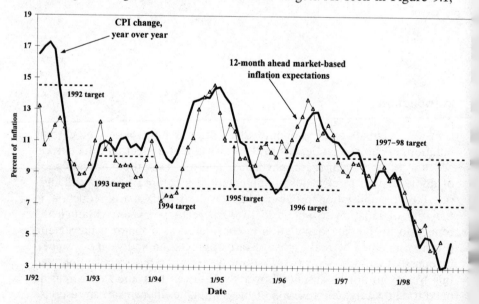

Figure 9.1.   Israel: inflation—targets, actual end-market expectations

the first phase after the 1985 stabilization program exhibited a rate of inflation of about 18 percent per year, up to 1991. Then, from 1992 to 1996 the average rate of inflation was reduced to about 10 percent per year. Lately, there has been a sharp reduction in the rate of inflation, to 7 percent in 1997, and year-over-year inflation to March 1998 was 4 percent. Most forecasts at the moment are that the rate of inflation in the coming twelve months will be of about 3.5 to 4 percent, quite a remarkable disinflation.

In the case of Hungary, where a crawling band is used as main anchor for the nominal system, inflation has declined especially after the March 1995 stabilization, remained at a double-digit level of about 18 percent in 1997, and is forecasted to reach about 13 to 14 percent in 1998 (see Figure 9.2). In September 1998 the Monetary Policy Council of Poland announced a multiyear monetary policy strategy including a 4 percent inflation target for 2003 with an 8 to 8.5 percent target for 1999.

The Czech Republic has shown a remarkable disinflation performance over the years, with inflation rates of about 8 to 10 percent in the last three years (see Figure 9.3). The considerable trend of disinflation was stopped following the speculative attack of mid-1997, yet it is likely to go on in the future. Before this attack, the nominal exchange rate was the key anchor for monetary policy, yet this was followed, from early 1998 onward, by a shift to a managed float and to an inflation target. With the adoption of

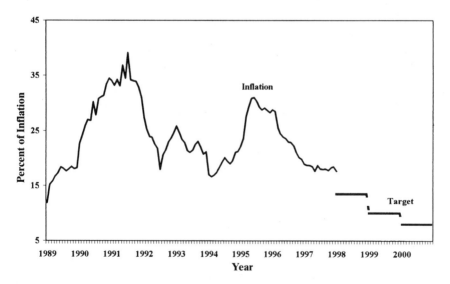

Figure 9.2.   Hungary: CPI inflation (year-over-year change)

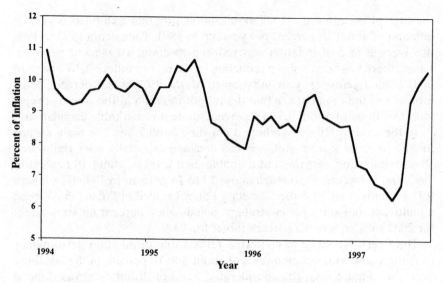

Figure 9.3.   The Czech Republic: CPI inflation (year-over-year change)

inflation targeting, disinflation became not only the main objective but also the direct objective of policy. The inflation target is set as a gradually declining corridor, reaching 3.5 to 5.5 percent by year 2000 with a series of intermediate targets.

Considerable disinflation has also taken place in Poland, where nowadays a crawling band coexists with an inflation target. According to Figure 9.4, the rate of inflation has continuously fallen from about 35 percent in 1993 to a forecasted rate of 12 percent in 1998.

In this chapter we document and analyze the experience of these four countries with monetary policy and disinflation, with particular emphasis on the choice of the nominal anchor: an exchange-rate band and inflation targets. By providing and discussing background and evidence on these countries' experiences, it will be possible to derive policy implications of the strategies adopted, some of which may apply to other transition economies. Moreover, the stylized facts of this chapter could well serve as the basis for future analytical work on these issues.

The chapter is organized as follows. The next section deals with nominal exchange-rate targeting, and it is followed by a section on inflation targeting and one on the evidence of Israel and three transition economies. The final section draws the main lessons.

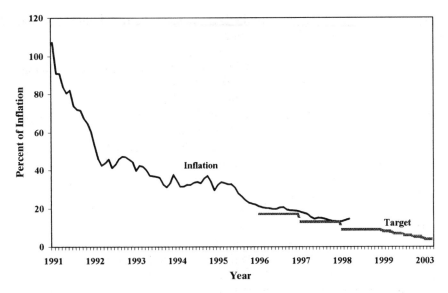

Figure 9.4.   Poland: CPI inflation (year-over-year change)

Nominal Exchange-Rate Targeting

A fixed exchange rate or more flexible forms of nominal exchange-rate targeting have proven to be powerful ingredients of inflation stabilization
strategies in a large number of countries, both industrial and developing. A
nominal exchange-rate target is a relatively simple and verifiable system for
policymakers to make a credible anti-inflation commitment. An exchange
rate can be observed at each point in time, and it is easy to check whether
the commitment is fulfilled or not. Although a fixed exchange rate can be
very effective in helping break previous inflationary inertia and bring about
disinflation, it can weaken the competitiveness of exports and the current
account position to the extent that there remains a considerable domestic-
foreign inflation rate differential. In addition, the advent of substantial
international capital mobility has given rise to a potentially more important role for nominal exchange-rate fluctuations as important shock
absorbers of shifts in capital mobility. Accordingly, an increasing number of
countries have adopted crawling exchange-rate bands as a regime that
resolves the tradeoff posed by the desire to keep a competitive nominal
exchange rate and at the same time avoid the potentially inflationary
consequences of nominal exchange-rate depreciation and allow for some

degree of response of the nominal exchange rate to foreign-exchange market forces, primarily led by capital movements.

A crawling exchange-rate band regime is specified by the authorities' choices in regards to: (1) the behavior of the central parity exchange rate, (2) the width of the band, (3) the degree and form of intramarginal intervention, and (4) the allocation of adjustments among interest-rate changes, exchange rates, and official intervention in supporting the band under various shocks.[1] Various countries differ in their choices about these policy parameters. Consider first the characteristics of the central parity exchange rate. In most cases, the target exchange rate is denominated in terms of a basket of foreign currency, with weights that generally reflect the relative importance of the currencies in the international trade flows of the country under discussion. Basket-type central parities are currently used, for example, in Chile, Hungary, Israel, and Poland. Interestingly, we know of no cases where the choice of specific weights in baskets of foreign currencies reflected also their role in the country's international capital flows. Assuming that it has been specified that the central parity rate will crawl over time, the next issue to be resolved is how to determine the pace of crawl. In a forward-looking regime, the authorities precommit to an announced trajectory for the nominal exchange rate for a specified time period into the future. A plausible option in this context is to set the rate of crawl as equal to the difference between the country's inflation target and a forecast of foreign inflation, such as in Israel. Alternatively, in a backward-looking regime—as in Chile—the announced rate of crawl for some time into the future is a function of the difference between past inflation and either a forecast of, or the past behavior of, foreign inflation.

The main virtue of the forward-looking scheme is that, if credible, it can provide a strong nominal anchor for inflation expectations and for disinflation. The main limitation of the scheme is that it does not allow for automatic adjustment of the rate of crawl to what may prove to be substantial and persistent shocks that may raise doubts about the sustainability of the planned nominal exchange-rate trajectory. Although the backward-looking mode can embody endogenous exchange-rate fluctuations in response the changing economic conditions, it can result in a greater degree of nominal accommodation that the alternative regime, and it can easily transform one-time changes in the price level (or the exchange rate) into permanent changes in the rate of inflation. Most countries operating under crawling exchange-rate bands have done so under a version of the forward-looking regime, which is consistent with a strong desire to reduce inflation, especially via the choice of the rate of crawl of the currency band.

The next issue to discuss is the choice of band width. Existing currency bands exhibit a variety of widths around the central parity, ranging from 2.5 percent in Hungary, through 7 percent in Poland, and up to 15 percent in Israel. This choice has been influenced by at least four main factors. First, bands tend to be wider in those economies subject to a relatively high degree of variability of the underlying nominal and real shocks. In this context, one can expect that a higher degree of international capital mobility would lead to the choice of wider bands. Second, bands tend to be wider when credit markets function relatively well and derivatives are available for the private sector to cope with exchange-rate risk. Third, a relatively high desired degree of autonomy in conducting monetary policy would typically result in wider bands than otherwise. Fourth, other things equal, narrow bands are likely to be subject to frequent realignments. Accordingly, the higher the political and credibility cost to the authorities of reneging on the existing band, the greater will be the attractiveness of adopting relatively wide bands.

Band width represents only the maximal degree of fluctuations of the exchange rate within an existing band. In practice, the existence of intramarginal intervention can limit the room for such fluctuations. As a matter of fact, most countries that adopted currency bands implemented operations within the band at various times, in the context of an inner intervention band. In principle, the same factors that determine band width can be thought of influencing the choice of the extent of intramarginal intervention. In addition, extensive intramarginal intervention might be needed when the central bank is concerned that the broader currency band has relatively low credibility, in which case generating a trajectory of the nominal exchange rate that is close to the path of the central parity can help "persuade" the public that the nominal exchange-rate commitment embodied in the band is credible and is there to stay. Yet heavy intramarginal intervention is costly: it reduces the autonomy of domestic monetary policy and increases the variability of foreign-exchange reserves, it can result in substantial quasi-fiscal costs of sterilization, it prevents the foreign-exchange market from serving—in a broader sense—as a shock absorber for some of the disturbances in the economy, and it can give rise to confusion by market participants about central bank actions, especially when the parameters of the inner band and the intervention actions are kept as confidential. Furthermore, as illustrated by recent currency crises in Europe, Latin America, and Asia, heavy intramarginal intervention can reduce—for some time—the perceived risk in the foreign-exchange market below the "true" level of risk that can prevail in the economy, thus providing an incentive for excessive speculative short-term capital flows.

Last, the specification of the currency band regime is completed by a characterization of the various combinations of movements in foreign-exchange reserves, domestic interest rates, and exchange rates that can be used to deal with exogenous shocks that create pressure on an existing currency band. In some countries, the main burden of the adjustment falls on domestic interest rates, whose changes are subordinated to the sole objective of sustaining and defending the prevailing exchange-rate system. In others, some combination of exchange-rate fluctuations within the band and foreign-exchange market intervention is used to deal with shocks, and interest-rate changes are implemented only if the former are not sufficient to deal with the specific shocks.

Although a nominal exchange-rate commitment—either a fixed exchange rate or a currency band—can be an effective anchor in the process of disinflation, theory and practice indicate that sooner or later severe difficulties may arise. First, fixed exchange rates are fragile and vulnerable, especially when there is a considerable degree of capital mobility and there could be capital-flow reversals or speculative attacks. In many cases, governments may find it excessively costly to tolerate the type of fiscal and monetary policy adjustments, and the loss of foreign-exchange reserves, needed to defend the nominal exchange-rate commitment and may opt to renege on the exchange-rate regime. The public is aware of this possibility, and this knowledge can lead to some loss of credibility about the sustainability of the regime. As a matter of fact, a nominal exchange-rate commitment imposes strong constraints on fiscal policy and monetary policy. Second, fixity (partial or full) of nominal exchange rates can slow down the process of real exchange-rate adjustment to real shocks and can result in wider business cycle fluctuations, especially in shock-prone economies with short-term nominal rigidities in the goods and labor markets. Instead, rapid adjustment could be facilitated by allowing nominal exchange rates to make most of the equilibrating adjustment required for real exchange rates.

A third important problem with nominal exchange-rate targeting is that it may lead to a distortion: the public's perception of exchange-rate risk might become substantially lower than the true (based on the country's shocks and fundamentals) degree of exchange-rate risk in the economy. When there is a nonnegligible differential between domestic and foreign interest rates, this distortion may induce substantial capital inflows, as foreigners attempt to take advantage of the higher domestic yields and as domestic agents find it cheaper to borrow abroad. In principle, the lower the perceived risk of exchange-rate fluctuations, the larger will be the relative size of short-term speculative capital inflows. By itself, this development makes the nominal exchange-rate commitment more vulnerable and less sustainable and may result in a stronger currency crisis, as demonstrated by those in Asian countries, and previously in Latin America (such as Mexico).

Last, nominal exchange-rate targeting may conflict with other objectives of macroeconomic policy and of monetary policy. For the latter, a specific conflict may arise between targeting the nominal exchange rate and targeting inflation. One characterization of this conflict is when higher domestic interest rates might be needed to combat inflation, yet they may result in nominal exchange-rate appreciation that brings the exchange rate to the lower (most appreciated) limit of the band, thus giving rise to foreign-exchange intervention and sterilization. Another characterization is when higher domestic interest rates are needed to defend the upper limit of the exchange-rate band—say, in view of excess demand for foreign exchange— yet from the point of view of inflation and the real economy much lower interest rates can be allowed. The mere presence of these conflicts, or various other forms of them, can damage policy credibility and economic performance. Policy dilemmas could be avoided if the authorities established priorities among their objectives in a clear and transparent manner, which is rarely the case.

Monetary Policy under Inflation Targeting

Recent experience points to an increasing reliance by various countries— both industrial and developing—on explicit inflation targets as a monetary policy regime (see, e.g., Leiderman and Svensson, 1995). This trend reflects important developments in the theoretical and empirical literature on monetary economics, such as the emphasis on price stability as the primary goal for monetary policy and the role of credible commitments (such as inflation targeting) and central-bank independence in reducing the degree of inflation bias. In addition, it reflects a key practical consideration: the increasing dissatisfaction with the performance of either monetary-aggregates targeting or nominal exchange-rate targeting, especially under a considerable degree of international capital mobility as discussed in the foregoing section.

An explicit inflation target may become a key nominal anchor in the economy, and as such it can play two main roles. First, it provides a transparent guide to monetary policy, the commitment, discipline, and accountability of which can be judged according to whether policy actions were taken to ensure that the target is achieved. Needless to say, the existence of a reasonable degree of central-bank independence is an important prerequisite for the efficacy of monetary policy under inflation targeting. Second, if credible, it should serve as a coordination device in the wage- and price-setting process and in the formation of the public's inflation expectations. In an economy with a large public sector as many transition countries, the credibility of the inflation target can be strengthened if the specific target that was chosen serves also as a coordination device in the setting of public-sector wages, of prices of public-sector utilities, and of the price deflator used in the government budget.

Under this regime policymakers typically commit to an explicit quantitative inflation target that specifies the following: (1) the index to which the target applies (such as, the consumer price index or a measure of core inflation, (2) the target level and tolerance interval (such as an inflation target of 5 percent per year with tolerance levels of plus or minus 2 percent), (3) the time frame (such as a multiyear target or a target for a specific year), and possibly (4) escape clauses, or situations in which the targets will be modified or disregarded (such as, natural disasters, large fluctuations in the terms of trade, or the effects of changes in indirect taxes). In most cases, the inflation target is not accompanied by the use of intermediate targets, yet nothing prevents the use of the latter as long as they are ex-ante consistent with the inflation target, and as long as priority is given to the inflation target if a conflict between these targets arises.

Second, at variance with other cases there is a considerable degree of ambiguity about the nature and operational meaning of inflation targets as a precommitment device not only for monetary policy but for fiscal policy as well. In part this reflects the fact that initially inflation targets were introduced in the somewhat technical context of determining the slope of the crawling exchange-rate band. It was only recently that inflation targets have been given more fundamental importance—for example, as indicated by the fact that the target for 1998 has been discussed in detail in several cabinet meetings and has been set jointly for the first time (in July 1997) with the setting of the targets for the government budget for that year. Third, Israel is one of the very few cases where inflation targets coexist with another nominal commitment—namely, the crawling exchange-rate band. Other such cases are Chile, Colombia, and Poland. Accordingly, under a considerable degree of international capital mobility, concrete dilemmas about policy have emerged as a result of shocks and developments that gave rise to conflicts between the monetary policy measures required to achieve each one of these two targets.[2]

Inflation Targeting: Analytical Basis

Since inflation targeting is a relatively new regime for the conduct of monetary policy, it is well to briefly discuss some of the analytical basis underlying such a framework and its policy implications. It is convenient to do so by drawing on the recent important contributions by Lars Svensson (1997a, 1997b) (on the motivation for and application of inflation targets in different countries, see, for example, Leiderman and Svensson, 1995).

Consider the model in Svensson (1997a):

$$\pi_{t+1} = \pi_t + \alpha_1 y_t + \alpha_2 x_t + \varepsilon_{t+1} \tag{9.1}$$

$$y_{t+1} = \beta_1 y_t - \beta_2 (i_t - \pi_t) + \beta_3 x_t + \eta_{t+1} \tag{9.2}$$

$$x_{t+1} = \gamma x_t + \theta_{t+1}, \tag{9.3}$$

where $\pi_t = p_t - p_{t-1}$ is the inflation rate in year t, p_t is the log price level, y_t is the log of output relative to potential output, x_t is an exogenous variable that represents an impulse to aggregate demand (such as fiscal policy), i_t is the monetary policy instrument (say, the interest rate on central bank funds), and ε_t, η_t, θ_t, are i.i.d. random variables with a zero conditional mean. The coefficients α_1 and β_2 are assumed to be positive, the other coefficients are assumed to be nonnegative; β_1 and γ in addition fulfill $\beta_1 < 1$, $\gamma < 1$. The long-run natural output level is normalized to equal zero. Although this is a closed-economy formulation, which can be extended to an open-economy setting (see below), it helps to illustrate the considerations that affect the conduct of monetary policy under inflation targets in both these cases.

From equation (9.1), which is a version of a short-term Phillips curve, the acceleration in the rate of inflation is increasing in lagged output and the lagged exogenous variable. Equation (9.2), which can be viewed as an IS relation, posits that output in the current period depends on output in the previous period, on the lagged real interest rate and the lagged exogenous variable.[3] Equation (9.3) gives the evolution of the exogenous variable as a first-order autoregressive process. It can be seen that here the nominal interest rate set by the central bank affects output with a one-year lag and inflation with a two-period lag. Hence from the standpoint of influencing the path of inflation, the model embodies a two-period policy lag. That this is the case can be verified by expressing inflation at $t + 2$ in terms of time t variables:

$$\pi_{t+2} = \alpha_1 \pi_t + \alpha_2 y_t + \alpha_3 x_t - \alpha_4 i_t + (\varepsilon_{t+1} + \alpha_1 \eta_{t+1} + \alpha_2 \theta_{t+1} + \varepsilon_{t+2}), \tag{9.4}$$

where

$$\alpha_1 = 1 + \alpha_1\beta_2; \quad a_2 = \alpha_1(1+\beta_1); \quad \alpha_3 = \alpha_1\beta_3 + \alpha_2(1+\gamma); \quad \alpha_4 = \alpha_1\beta_2. \quad (9.5)$$

Inflation at time $t+2$ is increasing in the rate of inflation, the output gap, and the exogenous variable at time t, and is decreasing in the nominal interest rate set at time t. Notice that the equation can be rewritten to include the real interest rate on central bank funds in the right-hand side:

$$\pi_{t+2} = \pi_t + \alpha_2 y_t + \alpha_2 x_t - \alpha_4(i_t - \pi_t) + (\varepsilon_{t+1} + \alpha_1 y_{t+1} + \alpha_2 \theta_{t+1} + \varepsilon_{t+2}). \quad (9.6)$$

How should monetary policy be conducted in this model? Assuming, as in Svensson, that government has set an inflation target of π^* (say, 8.5 percent per year), that the central bank acts to minimize the expected sum of the discounted losses from current and future deviations of the rate of inflation from the inflation target set by government, and that the period loss function is quadratic, the first-order condition for this minimization problem can be expressed as

$$\pi_{t+2|t} = \pi^*, \quad (9.7)$$

where $\pi_{t+2|t}$ is the current (that is, time t) conditional forecast of the rate of inflation at $t+2$. Accordingly, the central bank should engage in what Svensson termed "inflation forecast targeting"—that is, *to set the interest rate so as to equate its own two-year forecast of the rate of inflation with the inflation target.* This yields the central bank's optimal interest-rate rule:

$$i_t = \pi_t + b_1(\pi_t - \pi^*) + b_2 y_t + b_3 x_t, \quad (9.8)$$

where

$$b_1 = \frac{1}{\alpha_1\beta_2}; \quad b_2 = \frac{1+\beta_1}{\beta_2}; \quad b_3 = \frac{\alpha_1\beta_3 + \alpha_2(1+\gamma)}{\alpha_1\beta_2}, \quad (9.9)$$

which is a reaction function similar to a Taylor (1994) rule. A central bank equipped with this rule will raise the nominal interest rate on its funds in reaction to any one of the following events: a rise in the rate of inflation (above the inflation target), an increase in output relative to potential, and a rise in the exogenous impulse x_t. As stressed by Svensson, the interest rate depends on current values of inflation, the output gap, and the exogenous variable not because current inflation is targeted but because in the model these current variables have persistent effects and predict future inflation. Absent monetary policy change, an increase in current output above potential or a more expansionary fiscal policy (say, an increase in x_t) predict a future deviation of inflation $(\pi_{t+2|t} - \pi^*)$ from target. Other things equal, these events call for a rise in the current interest rate in order to achieve (in a conditional expectation sense) the inflation target.[4] Svensson shows that inflation targeting via an interest-rate reaction function is more efficient, in the sense of bringing lower inflation variability, than money growth or exchange-rate targeting. On the empirical side, recent research has shown that policy rules such as (9.8) capture relatively well the behavior of leading central banks (see, e.g., Clarida, Gali, and Gertler, 1997).

Although this is a relatively simple model of the economy—one that can be extended to an open-economy framework—it captures the essence of *forward-looking* monetary policy under inflation targets: achieving these targets in the future requires (in the presence of lags) adjusting current monetary conditions in response to current and expected future developments that could lead to deviations of inflation from target. If policy is conducted in this way (that is, via equation (9.4)), the inflation forecast equals the target, and ex-post inflation will differ from the target only because of random shocks whose realization could not be predicted at the time of formulating the policy. Notice that while policy is successful in achieving the target in this case, there will be no simple statistical relation between the interest rate and the rate of inflation: although the inflation rate will be equal, on average, to the target, the interest rate will fluctuate to offset potential deviations of inflation from target that may arise due to movements in the output gap (y_t) and in the exogenous variable (x_t, say due to fiscal policy). Hence, the more fundamental link relates a change in the monetary conditions now with the deviation of future inflation from target that would have taken place in the absence of such an adjustment in current monetary conditions. Put differently, the arrival of new information about inflation forecasts that may imply future deviations of inflation from target can trigger interest-rate adjustments aimed at avoiding the emergence of such deviations.

Potential Difficulties in Implementing Inflation Targets

Although the foregoing discussion depicts a relatively clear and straightforward function for inflation targets, some of the implications might be difficult to implement in practice, especially in the case of developing or transition economies.[5] *First*, in a country that recently adopted inflation targeting there can be a substantial debate about monetary policy because as of that time there are not simple rules (as, for example, equation (9.8)) for how such policy should be conducted under the new inflation target regime. Moreover, since the decision-making process for monetary policy involves an assessment of current and future inflationary trends and their comparison against the inflation target, the process is not likely to end with an agreed specification such as equation (9.6). Instead, the process leaves considerable margin for discretion, which in turn may leave room for substantial debate about the policy. In view of the considerable room for discretion, it is important to strengthen the credibility of the regime by enhancing the transparency and openness about the operating model used by policymakers, such as through the regular publication of an *Inflation Report* including the minutes of the monetary board meetings.[6]

Second, in developing or transition economies there can be a considerable degree of ambiguity about the nature and meaning of inflation targets as a precommitment device not only for monetary policy but for fiscal policy as well. Ambiguity may show up in the form of lack of consensus about the goals of monetary policy, about how seriously inflation targets should be taken by policymakers, and about the extent to which fiscal policy and wage policy need to support the inflation target that was chosen. In some cases, lack of consensus may seriously threat the inflation target regime and can ultimately given rise to inflation bias. *Third*, there are a few cases of developing or transition economies in which inflation targets coexist with another nominal commitment, such as a monetary-aggregates target or an exchange-rate band. These cases may lead to concrete policy dilemmas (or conflicts) between the monetary policy measures required to achieve the inflation target (see, for example, equation (9.8)) and those required to achieve the other target, and the efficacy of policy is likely to be damaged by lack of a clear ordering of targets by priority.

In sum, each one of the foregoing considerations can weaken the credibility of monetary policy under inflation targeting, especially in the initial period after the adoption of such a policy. As a matter of fact, most inflation target policies have faced initially problems of credibility, such as reflected in a persistent positive difference between expected inflation and the inflation target for the relevant time forecasting horizon.

Recent Experience: Israel and Selected Transition Economies

In this section we discuss recent experience from Israel and selected transition economies on the choice of the nominal anchor during disinflation.

Israel

Monetary policy in Israel has gone through major changes in recent years. From a highly accommodative policy in the late 1970s and early 1980s, which supported the escalation of inflation to triple-digit figures, the first phase in the aftermath of the remarkable stabilization program of June 1985 featured a policy oriented toward sustaining a fixed-but-adjustable nominal exchange rate, considered as a key nominal anchor in disinflation. Throughout this first phase after the stabilization program, from 1986 to 1991, the rate of inflation stayed in the range of 16 to 20 percent on average per year. This was followed by a second phase, the period from 1992 to 1996, characterized by the modification of the exchange-rate regime to a crawling exchange-rate band and by the adoption of an explicit inflation target. In this period, the average rate of inflation was reduced to about 10 percent per year.[7] Although it is still premature to reach a decisive conclusion, recent developments point to a third phase in the disinflation process, starting in 1997, featuring single-digit and declining rates of inflation. That is, the rate of inflation was 7 percent for 1997 and 4 percent for year over year to March 1998. Overall, the evolution of the nominal policy regime after 1985 shows a *gradual shift toward increased flexibility of the nominal exchange rate coupled with increased emphasis on inflation targeting.*

From the standpoint of studying an inflation targeting regime in developing or transition economies Israel's case is of interest for three main reasons. First, there are still some institutions and modes of operation in that economy left over from the era of triple-digit inflation, which make the job of disinflation more difficult. Second, there has been a considerable degree of ambiguity about the nature and operational meaning of inflation targets as a precommitment device not only for monetary policy but for fiscal policy as well. And third, inflation targets in Israel coexist with another nominal commitment—namely, the crawling exchange-rate band.

That recent developments featured severe challenges to official inflation targets is evident from Figure 9.1–8. This figure depicts the evolution of the rate of inflation, inflation targets, and market-based expected inflation in Israel from 1992 to the present (March 1998). Although there are no explicit multiyear inflation targets in Israel, when the targets were set for both 1997 and 1998 (at 7 to 10 percent), the government added the objectives of having an inflation target for the year 2001 as that common in OECD countries and of continuing the gradual reduction in the rate of inflation to achieve over time price stability as in the industrial countries. As common in Israel, expected inflation is derived from the yields on indexed and nonindexed bonds traded in the local capital market. It can be seen that there have been several periods in which the rate of inflation deviated from target. Measured from December of a given year to December of the previous year, as in the specification of the target, the largest deviation of inflation from target occurred in 1994, when annual inflation reached 14.5 percent against a target of 8 percent. However, in the following years of 1995 and 1997 the targets were achieved (and any deviations that occurred were quite minimal). Overall, with a multiyear perspective it can clearly be argued that *inflation targets have been achieved on average*: the average annual rate of inflation from 1992 to 1997 was 9.7 percent, which is very close to the average annual inflation target of 9.8 percent. In addition, the year-over-year rate of inflation to March 1998 has declined to about 4 percent, thus giving rise to an important opportunity to make rapid progress in achieving the government's longer-term inflation target of convergence to the rates in industrial countries.

Having established that annual inflation targets were achieved on average in the past six years, it is well to stress that there were two major episodes of acceleration of the rate of inflation *within* the years well above the target: these occurred in late 1994 and in the first half of 1996 (see Figure 9.1). In both these cases the regime was challenged and its credibility was endangered, as captured by the escalation of inflation expectations to about 15 percent per year.

These developments occurred in the face of strong inflationary pressures arising from a relatively overheated economy, in which there was a marked decline in the rate of unemployment, and from a fiscal policy that took an expansionary stance. The fiscal expansion in the period from 1994 to 1996 initially took the form of an increase of government expenditures in 1994 by about 6 billion NIS (2.7 percent of GDP) beyond the originally planned level that was the basis for that year's budget law. Then, the domestic budget deficit reached 3.2 percent of GDP in 1995 compared to the budget target that was set at 2.75 percent of GDP; and subsequently there was an additional, but sharper, overrun of the domestic budget deficit target in 1996 that reached 4.6 percent of GDP compared to a target of 2.5 percent of GDP. At the same time, during the above-mentioned period, the economy rapidly moved toward full employment, and the rate of unemployment declined from a peak of 11.2 percent in 1992 to 7.8 percent in 1994, 6.9 percent in 1995, and 6.7 percent in 1996. This move was accompanied by demand pressures on Israel's domestic resources and by a rapid deterioration in the current account deficit of the balance of payments, which reached 5.6 percent of GDP in 1996.

These circumstances created a situation where restrictive monetary policy was needed to counterbalance expansionary fiscal policy and the demand pressures in an overheated economy and to reduce the implied deviation of the rate of inflation from government's inflation target.[9] There is no doubt that much of the public discussion and debate in Israel about inflation targets has to do with the evaluation of these two salient episodes, which represented a severe challenge to the inflation targets and an overburdening of monetary policy.

In 1997 the rate of inflation was 7 percent, at the bottom of the inflation-target range (7 to 10 percent). During the second half of the year and the first quarter of 1998 inflation was running at an annual rate that was well below the lower limit of the inflation target range for 1998 (7 to 10 percent). Although in principle this points to a within-the-year deviation of inflation from target, this development was understood as potential substantial progress toward achieving government's longer-term target of inflation convergence to rates in industrial countries. In any case, there is an active public controversy and debate as to how policy should proceed under these circumstances and whether the existing inflation target should be modified.

The Crawling Exchange-Rate Band

Figure 9.5 gives the evolution of Israel's nominal exchange rate compared to a basket of foreign currencies and of the crawling exchange-rate band. As in the case of the inflation target, the parameters of the exchange-rate

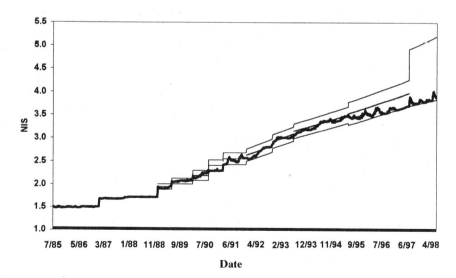

Figure 9.5.   The exchange rate of the NIS, July 1985–July 1986, NIS per U.S. dollar, August 1986 and onward, NIS per currency basket unit

regime are set by the government following consultation with the Bank of Israel. This crawling exchange-rate band was introduced in late 1991 as a part of relaxing the fixity of the previous band system that was based on a fluctuation zone around a fixed central parity rate. The move to a more flexible system came after a series of speculative attacks on the NIS during the 1988 to 1991 period that were mainly based on the perception that a fixed exchange rate was not sustainable in view of the persistent domestic-foreign inflation differential. During this period, the interest rate was used entirely to cope with speculative attacks on Israel's foreign-currency reserves and not as an instrument aimed at achieving a given inflation objective. From 1992 onward there were no major threats to the exchange-rate regime, and the interest rate gradually gained a central role in the effort to meet the inflation target that was introduced, for the first time, in December 1991 as a part of the new crawling exchange-rate band system.[10]

During the majority of the crawling band's life span until 1996, the central bank operated an inner, intramarginal, intervention band, aimed at keeping the exchange rate relatively close to the central parity rate. During the period when capital inflows grew considerably—in part due to the progress in the Middle East peace process from late 1993 onward and in part as a result of financial opening and liberalization measures taken in previous years—this intervention resulted in the Bank of Israel purchasing the considerable excess supply in the foreign-exchange market, with little change in the nominal exchange rate. In late May 1995, the Bank of Israel and the Ministry of Finance announced the widening of the exchange-rate band from 5 percent to 7 percent around the central parity rate. The initial purpose of this step was to adjust the exchange-rate regime so as to potentially allow greater exchange-rate flexibility. In spite of the potential increase in exchange-rate risk, after a few weeks there was a strong tendency for the exchange rate to appreciate within the band, and the central bank returned to large-scale intervention in the foreign-currency market. It is evident that the perceived implicit commitment of the Bank of Israel to the inner band was interpreted by market participants as a signal that there was little risk associated with exchange-rate fluctuations. The combination of this perception and a sizable domestic-foreign interest-rate differential provided an additional incentive for domestic agents to shift from domestic-currency denominated credit into borrowing abroad, thus strengthening short-term capital inflows and their pressure toward nominal exchange-rate appreciation. Overall, throughout the period between late 1994 and early 1998 the Bank of Israel purchased a cumulative sum of about 16 billion thorough foreign-currency market intervention (see Figure 9.6).

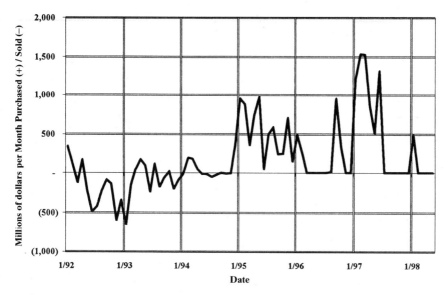

Figure 9.6.   Bank of Israel foreign-exchange intervention: millions of dollars per month purchased (+)/sold (−) by the Bank of Israel

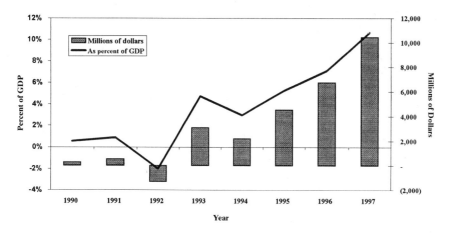

Figure 9.7.   Total capital flows (net) to Israel

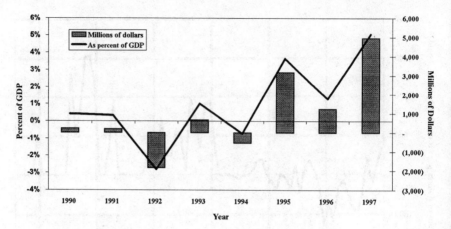

Figure 9.8.   Short-term debt capital flows (net) to Israel

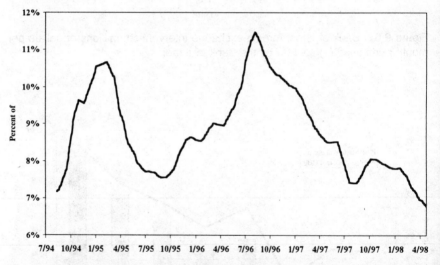

Figure 9.9.   Israel: interest-rate differential (Bank of Israel rate, per weighted basket of interest rates), moving average of 30 days

The sterilization of these operations was carried out by an elimination of monetary loans to the banking sector and the creation of deposits of the banking sector with the Bank of Israel (reverse repo).

The foregoing developments, and the objective to make further progress at capital account liberalization and deepening of the foreign-exchange

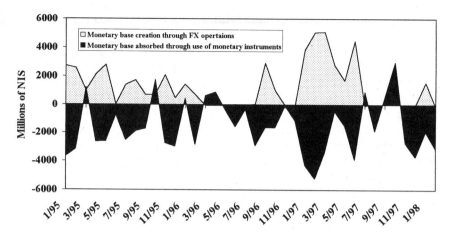

Figure 9.10.   Sterilization of foreign-currency market operations by the Bank of Israel

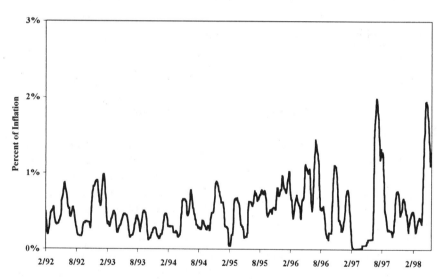

Figure 9.11.   Israel: thirty-day moving standard deviation of the distance of the exchange rate from the lower limit of the band

market, prompted policy decisions that enabled increased exchange-rate flexibility. Specifically, the inner band was abandoned in February 1996, and as a result there was a larger room for movements of the exchange rate within the band. By the summer of 1996 the exchange rate appreciated to the band's lower (strongest) limit. With the background of a continuation of capital inflows and pressure for nominal exchange-rate appreciation, and given the desire to deepen the foreign-exchange market and to make forward progress in liberalization toward capital account convertibility, the next and latest change in the band's parameters occurred in June 1997 when additional room for exchange-rate flexibility was introduced in the form of enlarging the band's width from 14 percent to 28 percent, to be gradually increased later on, until mid-1998, to 30 percent. The increase of the band's width was implemented entirely through the raising of the upper (weakest) limit of the band. Parallel to the upward widening of the band, the rate of crawl of the band's lower limit was reduced to 4 percent per year and leaving the slope of the upper limit at 6 percent per year. The fact that following these changes the stock of foreign-currency-denominated credit did not expand further in the second half of 1997 probably indicates a stronger perception of foreign-exchange risk by the private sector, both in view of the wider exchange-rate band and of the developments in foreign-exchange markets in Asia. As far as pressure on the exchange rate is concerned, to a large extent the reduction in foreign credit capital inflows was offset by a rise in foreign investment and by an improvement in the current account of the balance of payments, thus resulting in an exchange-rate path still close to the lower limit of the currency band.

In sum, it seems that the very slow and gradual move toward increased flexibility of the nominal exchange rate, under considerable capital mobility and strong inflationary pressures in the economy, contributed to the conflict that monetary policy in Israel has faced over the last two to three years in the attempt to support two nominal goals (the inflation target and the exchange-rate band) with one instrument (the interest rate). In other words, the level of the interest rate that was required to ensure meeting the inflation target has been larger than the level of the interest rate that would have resulted in no pressures on the exchange-rate band limits. Since the exchange-rate band limits became a binding constraint a large degree of sterilized intervention of capital inflows was required—sterilization that carried with it a sizable quasi-fiscal cost—and monetary policy could not fully affect inflation developments through the very important exchange-rate channel of the transmission mechanism.

Interest-rate Adjustments

The implications of the interaction between current and expected future developments on current monetary policy adjustments can be discussed in

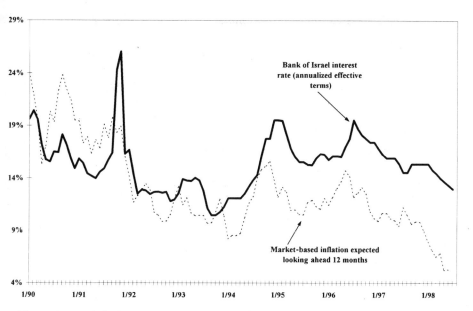

Figure 9.12. Inflation expectations and the interest rate on Bank of Israel funds

terms of developments in Israel with Figures 9.1 and 9.12. From Figure 9.12 are clear the two recent salient episodes of marked interest-rate rises by the central bank that occurred in late 1994 and early 1995 as well as in the second half of 1996. While there is no official or commonly used inflation forecast formulated by the Bank of Israel, there is a wide use of market-based inflation expectations—namely, expectations derived from yields on indexed and nonindexed bonds traded in Israel's capital market. In many cases, these expectations, plotted in Figure 9.12, have served a similar role as the inflation forecast, $\pi_{t+2|t}$, as in Svensson's model. In fact, the above-mentioned interest-rate rises were triggered by a combination of factors included in the reaction function (9.8): a rise in expected inflation, a rise in government's budget deficit, and reductions in the rate of unemployment. Along similar lines, when these factors signaled an easing of inflationary pressures, the central bank adjusted interest rates in the downward direction.

Overall, monetary policy developments in Israel illustrate how monetary policy can become severely overburdened in its attempt to achieve the inflation target when other key factors (such as fiscal policy and the state of the business cycle) exert strong upward pressures on the rate of inflation. In addition, these developments illustrate that, under a high degree of capital mobility, the coexistence of an exchange-rate band and inflation targeting may make the job of monetary policy more difficult than in the absence of an explicit exchange-rate commitment, especially when the level of the interest rate required based on inflation-targeting considerations sharply differs from that consistent with the lack of pressures on the exchange-rate band. To avoid potential conflicts among these nominal targets, it would be useful if the authorities could prioritize their objectives in a clear and transparent manner. One possible arrangement is to make official inflation targets the key objective of monetary policy and to allow for relatively free movements of the exchange rate. Alternatively, if there are any implicit or explicit exchange-rate targets, these could be subordinated to the inflation target. In fact, almost all countries that are implementing inflation targeting have given primacy to the inflation target over any available intermediate targets.

Two Major Episodes in the Disinflation Process

It is worthwhile to focus on two major episodes along the disinflation process in Israel: 1997 to 1998 and 1991 to 1992. In discussing the most recent reduction in the rate of inflation (from the second half of 1997 to the present), it is well to stress the role of monetary policy that since the middle of 1996 maintained an ex-ante, expected, real Bank of Israel rate of about 5 percent per year. Yet, as typical in other cases of rapid disinflation, the fast decline in inflation expectations and a slowly changing nominal interest rate on Bank of Israel funds resulted in a rise in the real rate to about 7 percent per year, which is perceived as a temporary development. In addition, the existence of supportive macroeconomic conditions facilitated the decline of inflation in this episode. More specifically, and as shown in Figure 9.13, falling import prices (which drove imported inflation downward) and a rise in and a decline of domestic demand growth, (which began prior to the tightening of monetary policy) contributed to disinflation in Israel in 1997 to 1998.

Similarly, the favorable role of various key economic variables for disinflation is documented in the six panels in Figure 9.14. It is possible to group the factors into four main categories. Consider first external price impulses in the form of Israel's "imported" inflation. The decline in Israel's rate of inflation was supported by a substantial drop in foreign price pressures to the point that the latter exhibited deflation during the relevant period. As a matter of fact, import prices in U.S. dollar terms fell by an average of 5.6 percent in 1991 and by a further 1.2 percent in 1992. A second set of disinflationary factors was related to the labor market and the state of the economy. Starting in the late 1980s there was a considerable rise in

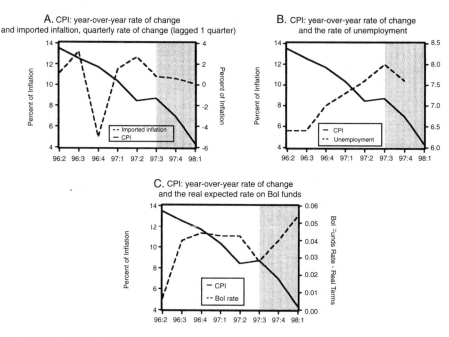

Figure 9.13. The development of inflation and fundamental macroeconomic factors during the 1997 to 1998 inflation stepdown

the rate of unemployment, from 6.4 percent in 1988 to 11.2 percent in 1992, which initially reflected mainly a major restructuring of business activities after the 1985 stabilization and later on the massive inflow of new immigrants into the labor force. It appears that these developments contributed to attenuate existing labor-market rigidities and sharply reduced the extent of price and wage pressures. Accordingly, real wages in the business sector declined by a cumulative 8 percent in the 1989 to 1991 period, and the official minimum wage set by government (which was applicable to most of the new immigrants during their entry into the labor market) declined in real terms for four consecutive years starting in 1990. Third, as documented in the foregoing subsection and in the one that follows, there was an important shift in monetary policy from late 1991 or early 1992 onward. Specifically, policy begun to focus on achieving government's inflation targets, and given other developments it took a tighter stance than in the preceding period. As a result of this shift there was a gradual increase in the real, ex-ante, interest rate on central-bank funds, from negative levels in the preceding periods to positive rate. This was accompanied by a substantial reduction in the rate of growth of M1. Last, but not least, while

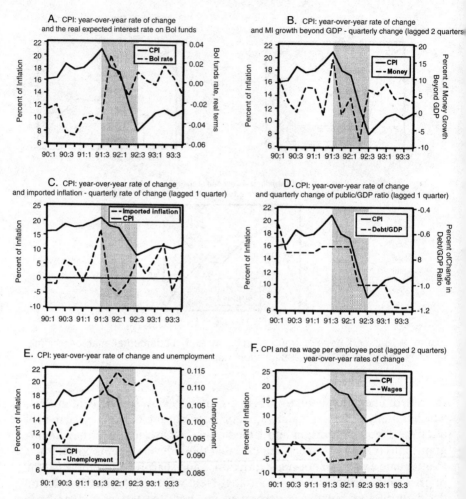

Figure 9.14. The development of inflation and fundamental macroeconomic factors during the 1991 to 1992 inflation stepdown

various fiscal policy indicators pointed to continuous tighter discipline after 1985, fiscal policy credibility was enhanced in 1991 with the passing of the "law of diminishing budget deficits" and with a strengthening in the already existing trend of decline in the ratio of public sector debt to GDP.[11]

In sum, it is hard to find a single economic factor that explains the major reduction in the rate of inflation to about 10 percent in 1991 to 1992, and this reduction cannot be attributed to a single specific decision by the

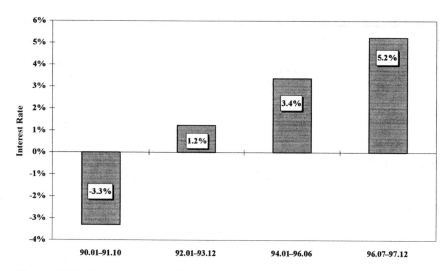

Figure 9.15.   Interest rate on Bank of Israel funds, real ex-ante terms, annualized period averages
Note: The figures for November and December 1991 were not included as these months were characterized by a sharp increase of the interest rate in response to a speculative attack on the NIS at the time.

authorities to that matter. Instead, foreign price deflation, tight fiscal and monetary policies, and a rise in unemployment together with a more flexible labor market and the lack of autonomous wage pressures combined to result in a decline in the rate of inflation, which was then further supported and transformed into a persistent change by the behavior of fundamentals (and in particular, of monetary policy) in the period that followed. The 1997 to 1998 phase of disinflation supports the notion that synchronization of all factors in the process of disinfaltion—monetary, fiscal, labor market, and external factors—is an important element determining both the degree of success in bringing down inflation and the cost of disinflation. Commitment to disinflation seems to be an additional prerequisite for success in disnfation. From the viewpoint of monetary policy this may be translated to willingness to maintain a relatively high real interest rate on central bank funds for an extended period. In other words, a more coherent set of macroeconomic variables and policy actions will allow for an easier and less costly phase of disinflation.

When focusing on monetary policy and strategies for disinflation in transition economies, compared to the Israeli case, it is quite clear that there are several strong similarities. More specifically, the countries discussed

here—Poland, Hungary, the Czech Republic, and Israel—have been trying to reduce inflation from triple- and double-digit rates to single-digit,
industrial-country standards. In all of these countries inflation has been
dropping steadily. In addition, the above-mentioned countries have adopted
inflation targets, explicit or implicit. The issue of the optimal policy mix and
its relation to the success and cost of disinflation has risen, thus in the case
of the Czech Republic and Israel it seems that monetary policy was not
always supported sufficiently by other policies (fiscal, structural), leading to
a sometimes-unbalanced policy mix. In several of the cases discussed here
conflicts between various policy variables have appeared. For example, in
the case of Poland there is strong potential for conflict between the wish to
disinflate and the rate of crawl of the exchange-rate band. Lowering the
rate of crawl may jeopardize the current account deficit, while maintaining
a relatively high rate of crawl may limit the scope of disinflation. An additional point of conflict pertains to the width of the exchange-rate band and
the wish to bring down inflation expectations. A relatively narrow band may
send a clear and transparent message to inflation expectations regarding
the rate of expected depreciation of the currency (that is, a nominal anchor).
A wider band may help to reduce the pressure of capital inflows and also
make the task of dealing with speculative attacks easier. Nonetheless, a
wider band might not serve as a very strong nominal anchor. The following
three subsections present the cases of Poland, Hungary, and the Czech
Republic. These subsections put emphasis on the commonalties of the
dilemmas that these countries have been facing and the relevance of the
accumulated experience in the case of Israel for the formulation of courses
of action for these countries.

Poland

The zloty is pegged to a basket of five currencies. The central parity is
adjusted under a crawling peg at a preannounced monthly rate. In May 1996
a band of +/–7 percent was introduced around the central rate, and the
exchange rate appreciated to about 2 percent from the bottom of the band
(the strong limit of the band). The exchange rate was managed within an
intramarginal intervention band. Over the past few years there were two
important speculative episodes of capital inflows to Poland. The first
episode, in 1995, was caused by the high domestic interest rate combined
with foreign investor and domestic bank expectations for a revaluation of
the currency. In response, in September 1995 the exchange rate was allowed
to appreciate further 1 percent within the band, and the interest rate was
reduced. Nonetheless, in late 1995 rapidly growing capital inflows pinned

the exchange rate to the stronger limit of the band. In response, the central parity rate was adjusted and appreciated by 6 percent. Following the global financial shocks of 1997, the exchange rate moved more widely within the band, mostly on the weak side of the parity. In early 1998 pressures for appreciation of the currency grew once again, the official band and the unofficial inner band were widened, and the exchange rate continued to move toward the stronger limit of the band (see Slawinski, 1998). In addition to the similarity the cases of Poland and Israel as to the tendency of the exchange rate to be on the stronger side of the central parity, the policy of gradually widening both the official and the inner band is highly reminiscent of the development of the Israeli currency band. In both cases the background conditions were those of relatively large capital inflows that required sterilized intervention by the central bank. In the case of Poland it seems that sterilization costs were the main problem from the point of view of monetary policy, while in the case of Israel the problem was more diverse, including attacks on central-bank policy due to the slowdown of economic activity growth.

Given the high degree of central-bank intervention in Poland's foreign-exchange market, it seems that despite growing volumes of trade, the overall picture up until mid-1997 was one of a shallow market. For example, throughout 1996, the central bank limited the deviation of the exchange rate from central parity to 2 percent. The low volume of foreign-exchange trade and the high degree of central-bank intervention further strengthened the incentive for capital inflows. This situation is similar to the one that prevailed in Israel up until mid-1997, in which capital inflows were largely supported by low exchange-rate volatility, a high interest-rate differential, and a notion of relatively low uncertainty as to the future development of the exchange rate. In 1997 the NBP reduced its degree of foreign-currency intervention. This change came as a result of rapidly growing foreign-currency bank loans and a deterioration of the trade account. The central bank was faced with a dilemma: raise the interest rate and get more capital inflows or increase short-term exchange-rate volatility by a sharp reduction of foreign-currency market intervention, which will hopefully curb capital inflows. The NBP opted for the later and in mid-1997 the central bank withdrew from the foreign-exchange market. This step combined with the increase of risk that followed the Asian market crisis in late 1997 helped to curb inflows. A similar type of development took place in Israel from 1995 onward, during which the degree of intermarginal exchange-rate intervention was reduced over time. In the case of Israel, this alone did not have the hoped-for effect on capital inflows. Capital inflows were curbed in mid-1997 only after the width of the exchange rate was dramatically increased to from 14 percent to 30 percent. In

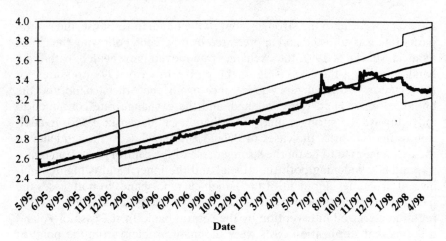

Figure 9.16.   The exchange rate of the Polish zloty (per basket unit)

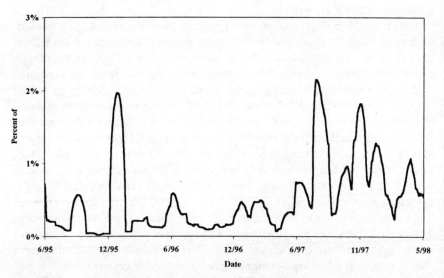

Figure 9.17.   Poland: thirty-day moving standard deviation of the distance of the
exchange rate from the lower limit of the band

addition, following the changes of the exchange-rate band's parameters, the
exchange rate responded with a period of increased volatility that include
a phase of rapid depreciation followed by appreciation of the exchange
rate.

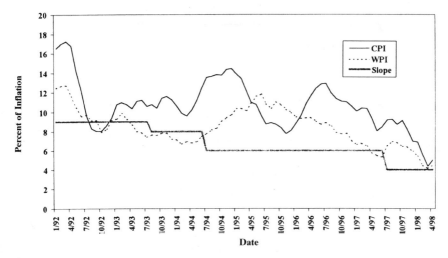

Figure 9.18.   Israel: year-over-year rates of inflation (CPI, WPI) and the rate of crawl of the currency band

Despite the fairly rapid rate of growth of the economy, Poland has seen a consistent drop of inflation to the current level of about 14 percent (see the appendix for money growth figures). The decline of inflation seems to be attributable to structural reforms and also to tighter monetary policy that is evident in the gradual increase of the real interest rate over the past two years. An additional factor that helped the decline of inflation is strong growth of productivity and the decline of the labor-unit cost. As noted earlier in the case of the Israeli disinflation in late 1991 and late 1997, the existence of favorable fundamental conditions is an important factor in determining the degree of success and the short-term cost of disinflating. The forward-looking stance of the crawling exchange-rate band has also been a driving force in disinflation. Nonetheless, as Figure 9.18 implies, that further success in disinflation and in meeting the 1998 inflation target of 9.5 percent should be led by a reduction of the rate of crawl of the currency band. In the case of Poland there is potential for a conflict between the wish to disinflate and the rate of crawl of the exchange-rate band. Lowering the rate of crawl may jeopardize the current account deficit. Nonetheless, it seems that rate of crawl has created a "floor" under which inflation cannot fall very easily. The rate of crawl of the band has been 1 percent per month, equal to 12.69 percent per year, with CPI inflation at about 13 percent in late 1997 and PPI inflation at about 12 percent (see Figure 9.19). A similar phenomenon has emerged in Israel, where since the onset of the crawling

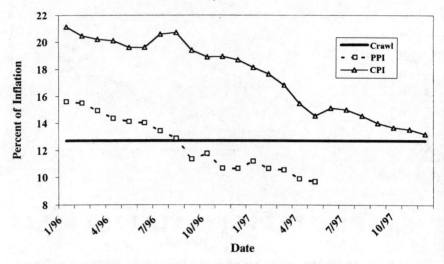

Figure 9.19.   Poland: year-over-year rates of inflation (CPI, PPI) and the rate of crawl of the currency band

band, the year-over-year rate of inflation has been able to go any lower than rate of crawl of the exchange rate band (see Figure 9.18).

An additional point of conflict in the case of Poland is between the width of the exchange-rate band and the wish to bring down inflation expectations. A relatively narrow band may send a clear and transparent signal to inflation expectations regarding the rate of expected depreciation of the currency (that is, a nominal anchor). A wider band may help to reduce the pressure of capital inflows and also make the task of dealing with speculative attacks easier. Nonetheless, a wider band might not serve as a very strong nominal anchor. A similar conflict has arisen in the case of Israel, and as a result the widening of the band to the current +/-15 percent width has been gradual. The main advantage of this gradual approach is that the anchor-type role of the exchange-rate band, which is important in a double-digit inflation environment as in Poland, diminishes at a slow pace.

Capital inflows to Poland have developed at a relatively slow pace compared to the Czech Republic, Hungary, and Israel (Figure 9.20). Nonetheless, since late 1994 FDI to Poland has grown quite sharply to about $3 billion in 1996, and 1997 has exceeded that of the Czech Republic or Hungary. The increase in FDI is attributed to widescale structural reform and strong macroeconomic fundamentals. Similarly, inflows coming from portfolio investment have been of growing importance and have reached a level of $2 billion in 1997. High interest rates and a strong currency have

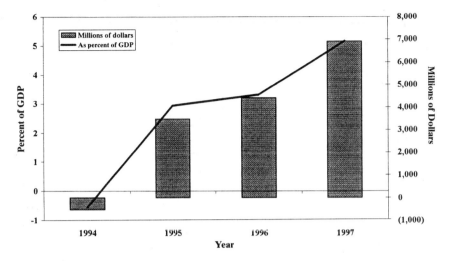

Figure 9.20.   Total capital flows (net) to Poland

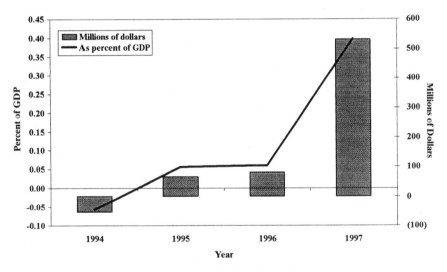

Figure 9.21.   Short-term capital flows (net) to Poland

also encouraged inflows mainly of financial nature (see Figures 9.21 and 9.22). This, plus a 20 percent real appreciation of the currency in 1995 and 1996, contributed to an acceleration of capital inflows to Poland. This appreciation of the currency occurred following the reduction of the rate of crawl of exchange-rate band and the widening of the band since late

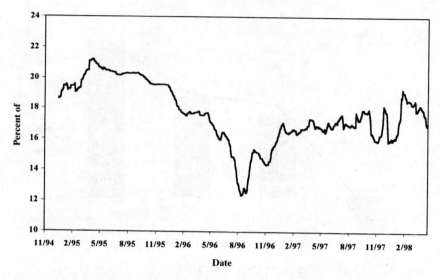

Figure 9.22.   Poland: interest-rate differential (PNB rate/average DM, $ libor) moving average of thirty days

1994. In mid-1996 capital outflow possibilities were widened by the liberalization of foreign-exchange regulations allowing investment abroad. This step helped to temporarily slow down net capital inflows and reduced the magnitude of sterilized intervention needed by the central bank. Favorable fundamental data that started to mount from mid-1997 encouraged capital inflows. Long-term portfolio flows and purchases of treasury bills by foreign parties rose in early 1998. The central bank was once again faced with a dilemma: whether to reduce the rate of crawl of the band or reduce the interest rate. While the reduction of the domestic interest rate poses the threat of undesired bank credit growth and possible destabilization of the foreign–currency market, a reduction of the rate of crawl of the currency band may lead to the deterioration of the trade balance. The NBP preferred to cut the rate of crawl of the band in addition to further increasing the width of the band to increase the degree of foreign-exchange uncertainty and to deter capital inflows. Nonetheless, the response of investors was to futher increase capital inflows, forcing the central bank to intervene in the foreign-currency market. Only in mid-1998 did the NBP reduce the interest rate. This plus the increased instability of world financial markets in mid-1998, and especially in neighboring Russia, helped to curb capital inflows.

Hungary

Until March 1995, the value of the peg of the forint to the currency basket was adjusted periodically, mainly on the basis of the foreign-domestic inflation differential. Since then, the value of the peg is adjusted in accordance with a preannounced forward-looking rate of crawl (see Figure 9.23).[12] The rate of crawl was gradually reduced from 1.9 percent per month in March 1995 to 1 percent per month as of August 1997. In 1998 the rate of preannounced crawl was reduced twice and was set a 0.7 percent per month from October 1, 1998. Throughout the life span of the band, the composition of the currency basket changed several times. The width of the band is narrow (only +/–2.25 percent), and the exchange rate has been on the bottom (strong end) of the band since mid-1995. This situation required heavy sterilized intervention by the NBH in the foreign-exchange market. The NBH foreign-exchange market net intervention amounted to about \$3.5 billion per in 1995 and 1996, an equivalent of 8 to 9 percent of GDP. The combination of a very narrow band with the exchange rate constantly on the limit of the band resulted in extremely low exchange-rate volatility from mid-1995 onward. As in the case of Israel during the first half of 1997 the large interest-rate differential plus the low volatility of the exchange rate provided fertile ground for capital inflows. The case for a widening of the Hungarian band has become stronger for the following reasons. The 1995 stabilization package has helped to reestablish internal and external equilibrium creating a situation where greater flexibility of exchange rate is possible; the widening of the band could help in reducing the magnitude

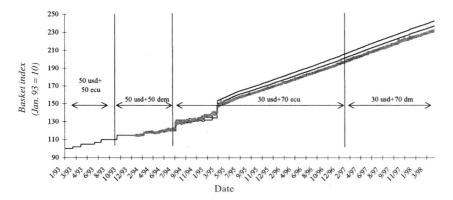

Figure 9.23.   The development of the Hungarian forint exchange-rate index

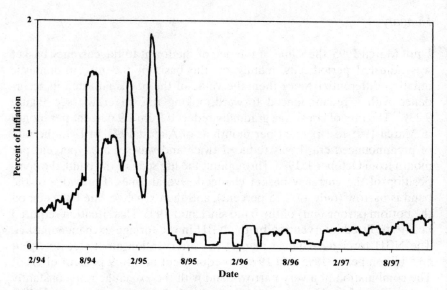

Figure 9.24.   Hungary: thirty-day moving standard deviation of the distance of the exchange rate from the lower limit of the band

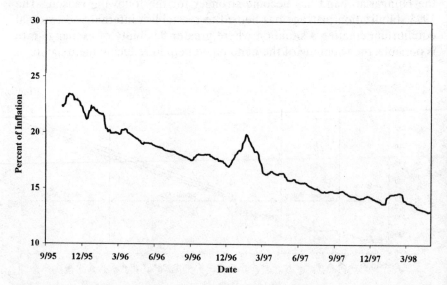

Figure 9.25.   Hungary: interest-rate differential (NBH rate/average DM, $ libor) moving average of thirty days

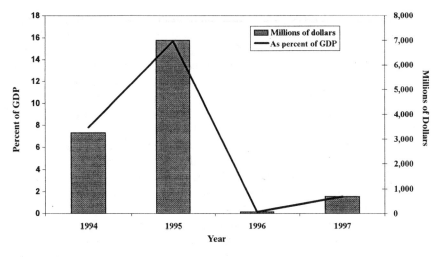

Figure 9.26.   Total capital flows (net) to Hungary

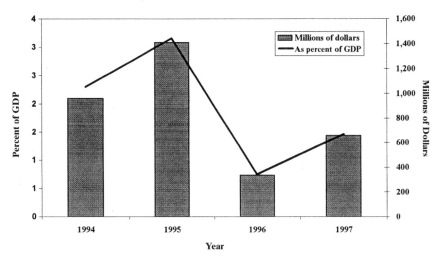

Figure 9.27.   Short-term capital flows (net) to Hungary

of sterilized FX intervention; the widening of the band could be combined with a gradual reduction of the rate of crawl of the exchange rate as part of a disinflation program.

Inflation has declined somewhat and stabilized at a low double-digit level, currently about 14 percent. The interest rate has declined in nominal terms over the past three years while maintaining a constant, but relatively low, real short-term interest rate of about 2 percent (see the appendix for details). Based on the Israeli experience and that of other countries that were able to reduce inflation from double-digit levels to low single-digit levels, it appears that the real interest rate required for disinflation in Hungary is much higher than it is as of now. In addition, money growth at a rate of about 20 percent seems to be too high to support further disinflation.

Hungary has received large capital inflows in the form of FDI, portfolio investment, and private debt inflows. Total capital inflows as a percentage of GDP reached double-digit levels in 1995. This increase is the combined result of short-term private-debt inflows coming close to 10 percent of GDP, FDI reaching the 10 percent of GDP level, and portfolio investment reaching 5 to 6 percent of GDP. Extensive sterilized intervention was used to deal with these inflows. The bulk of capital inflows rapidly developed after the first results of the 1995 March stabilization appeared and credibility of the adjustment had been achieved

The Czech Republic

From 1993 to late May 1997, the Czech koruna was pegged against a basket of two currencies. Perhaps one of the more striking characteristics of the koruna's exchange rate was its long fixed period, of sixty-two months, from early 1991 to early 1996, which stemmed from the very narrow band that existed during that period. In late February, 1996 the exchange-rate band was widened from +/−0.5 percent to +/− 7.5 percent. Nonetheless, the band remained horizontal and not upward sloped, despite a considerable domestic-foreign inflation-rate differential. This may suggest that the CNB was still focusing on exchange-rate-based disinflation. As in Israel and many other countries, horizontal exchange-rate bands despite considerable domestic-foreign inflation rate differential tend to lack credibility. In the case of Israel, this was understood in late 1991, and the system was changed to a crawling one.

In early 1997 the worsening economic situation and current account deficit, compounded by a complicated political situation, put pressure on the Czech koruna, which ultimately caused currency instability in May 1997, followed by abandonment of the fluctuation band mechanism in late May 1997. The first indications of the imminent attack on the currency were changes in the mood of investors leading to a slight drop in the koruna exchange rate from March, an increase in foreign-currency deposits by

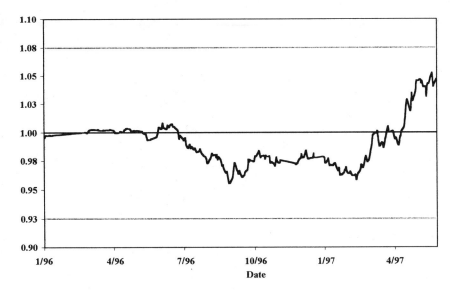

Figure 9.28.   The development of the Czech Koruna exchange-rate index

residents, and less foreign-investor involvement on the domestic capital market (see Figure 9.28). As expected, the attack on the currency led to a marked increase in foreign-exchange volatility. In late May 1997 a managed float was introduced (see Figure 9.29). After the attack, the situation on the foreign-exchange market was relatively quiet. The exchange rate gradually stabilized at a level that was equal to a 12 percent depreciation compared to its former parity and gradually recovered to 9 percent. By the end of July and the beginning of August, interest rates had steadied at a level around 2 percent higher than before the currency turbulence. An important side effect of the move to a flexible exchange rate was the loss of the nominal anchor. To replace this anchor, there was a shift of strategy to inflation targeting from early 1998, thus joining and increasing number of countries that switched to inflation targeting[13]. In many aspects this is also the case of Israel, which shifted to an inflation target regime with a crawling exchange-rate band following a large speculative attack in late 1991.

The Czech Republic went through a period of large capital inflows in the first half of the 1990s (see Figure 9.32). Private debt inflows reached a level of about 10 percent of GDP per year in 1995 and 1996, mostly short term (see Figure 9.33). Foreign investment was also large. Through various measures (such as raising minimum reserve requirements to 11.5 percent, sterilization of privatization investment inflows, and increasing the volume

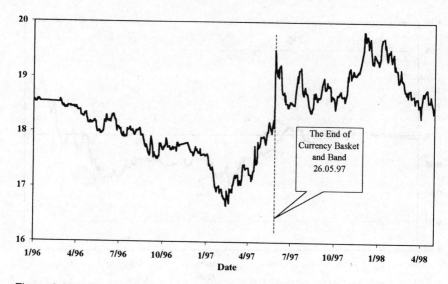

Figure 9.29.   The exchange rate of the CZK against the DM

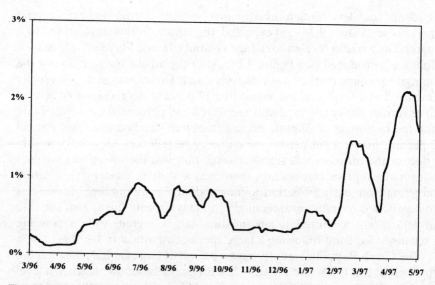

Figure 9.30.   The Czech Republic: thirty-day moving standard deviation of the distance of the exchange rate from the lower limit of the band

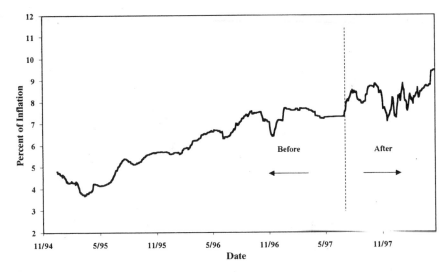

Figure 9.31.   The Czech Republic: interest-rate differential, excluding the speculative attack period (CNB rate/average DM, $ libor), moving average of thirty days

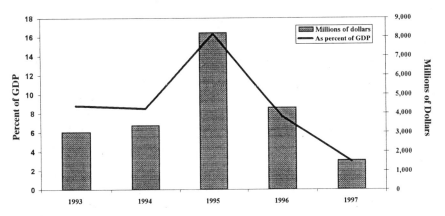

Figure 9.32.   Total capital flows (net) to the Czech Republic

of treasury bills held by commercial banks), the CNB has succeeded over
two years in sterilizing a considerable amount of money (reaching nearly
17 percent of GDP in 1995). Annual growth in the money supply as measured by M2, however, remained near the 20 percent level until the end of
the first half of 1996.

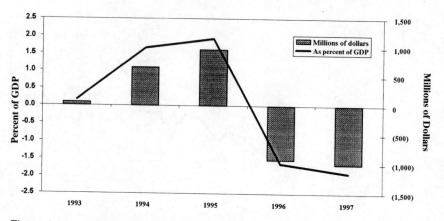

Figure 9.33.   Net private debt flows to the Czech Republic

The rate of inflation has risen following the speculative attack of mid-1997 after being on a downward trend toward 10 percent. Monetary aggregate growth remains relatively low after a period of declining money growth. Nonetheless, based on the Israeli experience, it appears that the real interest rate is relatively low—about 3 percent. In addition the macroeconomic fundamentals seem to be rather problematic, including a large fiscal deficit that has shown up in a large balance of payment deficit.

Capital inflows to the Czech Republic reached a peak of over $8.2 billion in 1995, around 16 percent of GDP. The vast majority of these inflows were private-sector initiated, signaling the rapid transition from the initial phase of transformation to a market economy, where flows from official sources played a key role in foreign-currency financing. In fact, private capital flows became increasingly important and since 1995 have made up more than 80 percent of capital flows. Background conditions were supportive throughout most of the period of inflows to the Czech Republic and included a large interest differential and a stable exchange rate. Additional factors included liberalization of the capital account, new investment opportunities, and a limited supply of domestic-based mid- and long-term financing. Short-term capital flows increased in 1994 and 1995 to about one-quarter of total capital inflows, driven by high domestic interest rates. In response, the government widened the currency band from 1.5 percent to 15 percent to introduce increased currency risk. The measure did succeed to curb capital inflows somewhat, and in 1996 short-term borrowing declined to less that 20 percent of total inflows. In addition, privatization was a driving factor behind FDI, which rose dramatically in 1995 to about $2.2 billion (over 4 percent of GDP) following a large privatization sale of the local telephone company and later declined. Similarly, portfolio flows were an import contributor to capital inflows.

Throughout most of the period of rapid capital inflows, and especially from 1995 onward up until the speculative attack in 1997, the Czech central bank intervened in the foreign-exchange market to defend the limit of the band. The sterilization of this intervention was carried out through open market operations, higher reserve requirements, and depositing privatization proceeds with the central bank. Other side effects of capital inflows included destabilizing inflationary and monetary pressures, a widening of the current account deficit, and an increase of the vulnerability of the domestic economy to exchange-rate shocks.

Policy Lessons

The are so many characteristics in common between the country experiences discussed above—also shared by the experience of countries from other regions, such as Asia and Latin America—that it is possible to draw some conclusions that seem to have a very broad base and applicability.

Lesson 1. Although nominal exchange-rate targeting has been extremely useful at the initial phase of disinflation, as time passed an increasing number of countries found difficulties with this regime, especially when there is a considerable degree of capital mobility. As a result, we have seen a gradual move toward increased flexibility of nominal exchange rates. At the same time, official inflation targets have been taking more and more of the emphasis in monetary policymaking. A number of transition economies, such as Hungary and Poland, may well shift in coming years the anchoring role toward inflation targets and away from exchange-rate targeting.

Lesson 2. The coexistence of multiple anchors—such as a crawling currency band and an inflation target—sooner or later is a source of potential policy conflict and dilemmas, all of which may considerable damage policy credibility. Typical conflicts that have been observed were, for example, that the relatively high domestic real interest rate that was required to combat inflation was accompanied by substantial capital inflows that created strong pressures for nominal exchange-rate appreciation beyond the lower (most appreciated) limit of the band. Also, we have seem many cases where the relatively high domestic real interest rate required for defending the upper limit of the band in the face of demand for foreign exchange could not be supported because it was stronger than required for the planned disinflation. Other types of conflicts that in transition economies may stem from the notion that inflation has several other than monetary sources, which originate in pressures accumulated during the former centrally planned economy regime. The relative price distortions developed in the previous regime make the higher rate of inflation unavoidable for some time (as a transitory phenomenon), taking into account the relatively sticky nature of prices, as well as the fact that relative price corrections only rarely take place through price decreases.

Some of this can be reduced by setting a clear pattern of priorities among the targets. Also, for those maintaining an exchange-rate band it is extremely important that the parameters of various anchors be synchronized. For example, the slope of the crawling band needs to be synchronized with the inflation target. Recent developments in Israel and Poland indicate that the slope of crawl might be larger than what is needed to support disinflation. The experience of Hungary, for example, shows that the coexistence of multiple anchors (both growth and inflation targets) can be a source of confusion and may damage policy credibility. Parameter synchronization is absolutely necessary but not easy.

Lesson 3. The extent to which the exchange rate is allowed to fluctuate, both within a band or in general through foreign-exchange market intervention, has important side effects for the public's perception of exchange-rate risk. This may give rise to a distortion in the form of a much lower perceived risk of exchange-rate fluctuations than the true risk, which in turn may result in larger capital inflows and increased vulnerability than otherwise. The main lesson here is that if bands exist, they need to be broad enough not to create this distortion. True, the associated exchange-rate volatility can be damaging to some sectors, yet this can be attenuated by developing the use of derivatives and other financial instruments to protect against such volatility.

Lesson 4. When inflation targets are used, it is extremely important to determine very clearly the principles of operation, accountability, the role of the central bank, and so an. To gain credibility, the inflation-targeting regime has to be as unambiguous as possible. In addition, the credibility of the regime would be strengthened if there are supporting policies via the government budget, wages, and so on and there is no overburdening of monetary policy. Synchronization of fiscal, monetary, and wage policies is extremely important for generating substantial reductions in the rate of inflation along the disinflation process, as shown by Israeli experience in 1991 to 1992 and 1997 to 1998.

Lesson 5. If operating with inflation targets, due to their discretionary nature problems of credibility may be encountered at the beginning. It is extremely important then how policy reacts. Strong and aggressive response, when needed, can generate credibility. See Israel, where there were two major deviations of inflation from target and there was a strong policy reaction that followed. Israel's experience showed that prompt reactions can contribute to credibility.

Acknowledgments

This chapter was presented as a paper at the Fourth Dubrovnik Conference on Transition Economies, Dubrovnik, Croatia, June 24–26, 1998. 6: Bufman is lecturer at the Academic College of Tel-Aviv Yaffo and a private economic consultant, and Leonardo Leiderman is senior director in the Research Department at the Bank of Israel and professor of economics at the Berglas School of Economics at Tel-Aviv University. We thank Rafi Lipa for his research assistance. The views expressed in the chapter are the sole responsibility of the authors. We would like to thank Pawel Durjasz, Judit Nemenyi, and Daniel Oks for providing very useful information.

Notes

1. See, e.g., Leiderman and Bufman (1996). For related work see Begg (1996) and Masson and Savastana (1997).

2. See Bufman, Leiderman, and Sokoler (1995) for a more detailed discussion of the history of the adoption of inflation targets in Israel.

3. As shown in Svensson (1997a) the model can be extended to incorporate an LM relation through inclusion of the money market. This would enable to determine a "steady-state" value for the rate of inflation. π.

4. As shown by Svensson, to the extent that the loss function of the central bank includes also deviations of output from potential output, the optimal interest rate rule is of the same from as equation (9.8), yet the absolute value of the b_1 coefficient is smaller, and the absolute value of the b_2 coefficient is larger, than for the loss function in the text. Extending the basic model to a small open economy would introduce additional transmission mechanisms for monetary policy, especially through its impact on nominal and real exchange rates.

5. On the scope for inflation targeting in developing countries, see Masson and Savastano (1997).

6. See, e.g., the Bank of England's remarkable *Inflation Report* (various issues).

7. For description and analysis of monetary and exchange-rate policies in recent years, see e.g., Bruno (1993), Leiderman (1993), Helpman, Leiderman, and Bufman (1994), Bufman, Leiderman, and Sokoler (1995), Leiderman and Bufman (1996), and Sokoler (1997).

8. For more detailed discussion of these and related developments, see Bank of Israel, *Annual Report*, issues from recent years.

9. In terms of Svensson's model, it is as if all of the right-hand-side terms in equation (9.8) increased, thus calling for an upward shift in the central-bank nominal interest rate.

10. Specifically, the slope of the crawl (in annual terms) was set equal to the difference between the inflation target and a forecast of foreign inflation.

11. On the role of fiscal policy variables in the inflation process, see Dahan and Strawczynski (1997).

12. For further analysis of developments in Hungary, see Halpern and Nemenyi (1997).

13. For further discussion, see Hrncir (1998).

References

Begg, D.K. (1996). "Monetary Policy in Central and Eastern Europe: Lessons After Half a Decade of Transition." Working Paper WP/96/108, International Monetary Fund, September.

Bruno, M. (1993). *Crisis, Stabilization and Economic Reform: Therapy by Consensus.* Oxford: Oxford University Press.

Bufman, G., L. Leiderman, and M. Sokoler. (1995). "Israel's Experience with Explicit Inflation Targets: A First Assessment." In Leiderman and Svensson (1995).

Cohen, Daniel, and Sara Soreni. (1995). "Identifying an Intermediate Target for Monetary Policy in Israel 1988–1994." Discussion Paper 95.13, Research Department, Bank of Israel.

Crockett, A. (1993). "Monetary Policy Implications of Increased Capital Flows." Paper presented at the symposium on Changing Capital Markets: Implications for Monetary Policy, Federal Reserve Bank of Kansas City, Jackson Hole, August.

Dahan, Momi, and Michel Strawczynski. (1997). "Fiscal Policy and Inflation in Israel." Working Paper, Research Department, Bank of Israel.

Halpern, L., and J. Nemenyi. (1997). "Balance of Payments, Exchange Rates, and Competitiveness in Different Phases of Transition in Hungary." Paper presented at the Third Dubrovnik Conference, June.

Helpmean, E., L. Leiderman, and G. Bufman. (1994). "A New Breed of Exchange Rate Bands: Chile, Israel, and Mexico." *Economic Policy* 19(October): 259–306.

Hrncir, M. (1998). "Transition Stages and Monetary Policy Strategy (Some Lessons from the Czech Case)." Paper presented at the Fourth Dubrovnik Conference, June.

International Monetary Fund. (1995). *International Capital Markets-Developments and Prospects, and Key Policy Issues.*

Kleiman, E., and T. Ophir. (1975). "The Effects of Changes in the Quantity of Money on Prices in Israel, 1955–65." *Bank of Israel Economic Review* 42 (January): 15–45.

Leiderman, L. (1993). *Inflation and Disinflation: The Israeli Experiment*. Chicago: University of Chicago Press.

Leiderman, L., and G. Bufman. (1996). "Searching for Nominal Anchors in Shock-Prone Economies in the 1990s: Inflation Targets and Exchange Rates Bands." In R. Hausmann and H. Reisen (eds.), *Securing Stability and Growth in Latin America: Policy Issues and Prospects for Shock-Prone Economies*. Paris: OECD.

Leiderman, L., and L.E.O. Svensson (eds.). (1995). *Inflation Targets*. London: CEPR.

Masson, P.R., and M.A. Savastano. (1997). "The Scope for Inflation Targeting in Developing Countries." Working Paper WP/97/130, International Monetary Fund, October.

Obstfeld, M. (1995). "International Currency Experience: New Lessons and Lessons Relearned." *Brookings Papers on Economic Activity* 1: 119–196.

Poole, W. (1994) "Monetary Aggregates Targeting in Low Inflation Economies." In J.C. Fuhrer (ed.), *Goals, Guidelines, and Constraints Facing Monetary Policymakers*. Boston: Federal Reserve Bank.

Slawinski, A. (1998). "The Development of the Forex Market in Poland and Its Influence on the NBP Monetary Policy." Paper prepared for Global Tendencies and Changes in East European Banking Conference, June.

Sokoler, Meir. (1997). "Credibility Half-Won in an Ongoing Battle: An Analysis of Inflation Targets and Monetary Policy in Israel." Working Paper, with members of the Monetary Department, Bank of Israel.

Svensson, L.E.O. (1997a). "Inflation Forecast Targeting: Implementing and Monitoring Inflation Targets." *European Economic Review*.

Svensson, L.E.O. (1997b). "Inflation Targets: Some Extensions." Working Paper 5962, NBER. Taylor, J.B. (1994). "Discretion Versus Policy Rules in Practice." *Carnegie Rochester Conference Series on Public Policy* 39(Autumn): 195–214.

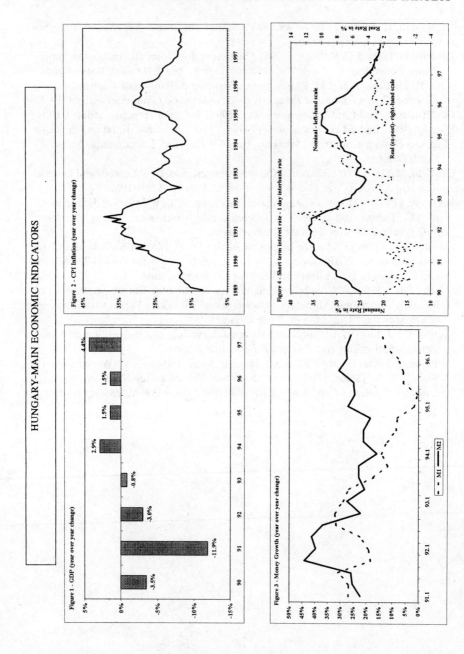

HUNGARY-MAIN ECONOMIC INDICATORS

Figure 1 - GDP (year over year change)

Figure 2 - CPI Inflation (year over year change)

Figure 3 - Money Growth (year over year change)

Figure 4 - Short term interest rate - 1 day interbank rate

HUNGARY-MAIN ECONOMIC INDICATORS

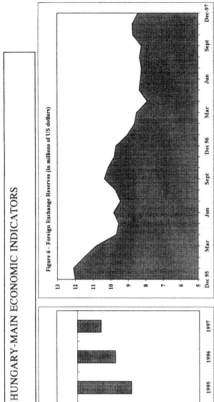

Figure 6 - Foreign Exchange Reserves (in millions of US dollars)

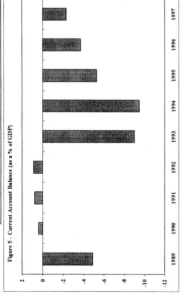

Figure 5 - Current Account Balance (as a % of GDP)

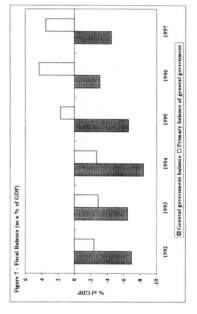

Figure 7 - Fiscal Balance (as a % of GDP)

POLAND-MAIN ECONOMIC INDICATORS

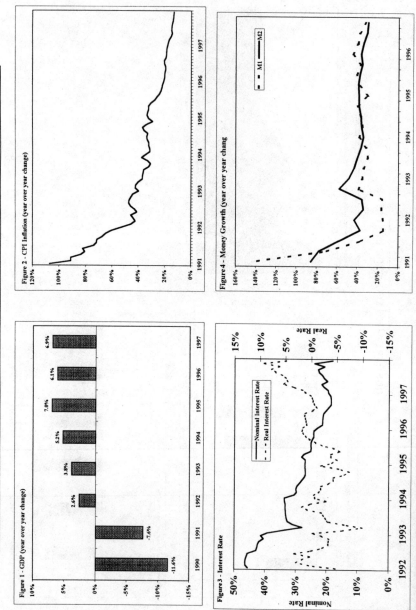

Figure 1 - GDP (year over year change)

Figure 2 - CPI Inflation (year over year change)

Figure 3 - Interest Rate

Figure 4 - Money Growth (year over year chang)

POLAND-MAIN ECONOMIC INDICATORS

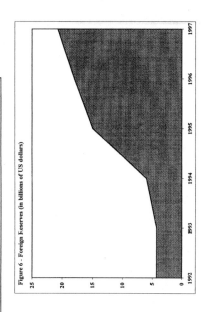

Figure 6 - Foreign Reserves (in billions of US dollars)

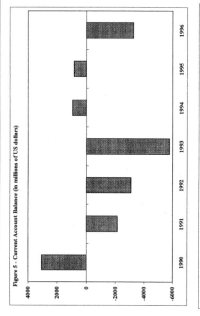

Figure 5 - Current Account Balance (in millions of US dollars)

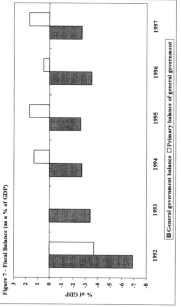

Figure 7 - Fiscal Balance (as a % of GDP)

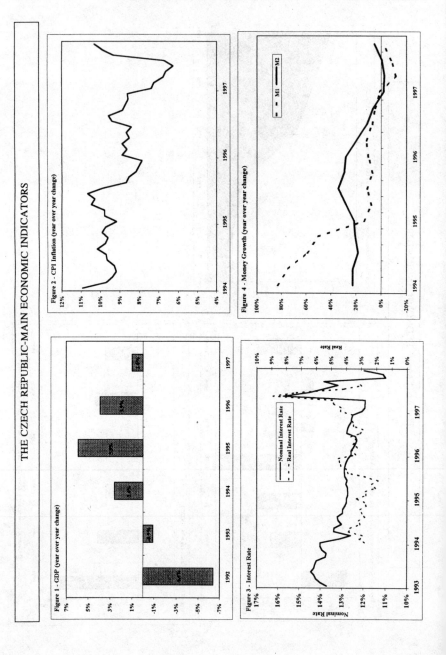

THE CZECH REPUBLIC–MAIN ECONOMIC INDICATORS

Figure 1 - GDP (year over year change)

Figure 2 - CPI Inflation (year over year change)

Figure 3 - Interest Rate

Figure 4 - Money Growth (year over year change)

THE CZECH REPUBLIC-MAIN ECONOMIC INDICATORS

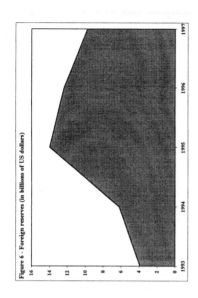

Figure 6 - Foreign reserves (in billions of US dollars)

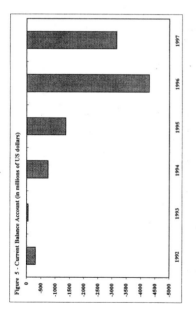

Figure 5 - Current Balance Account (in millions of US dollars)

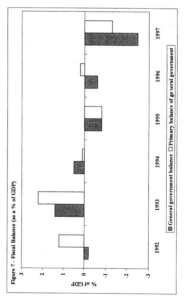

Figure 7 - Fiscal Balance (as a % of GDP)

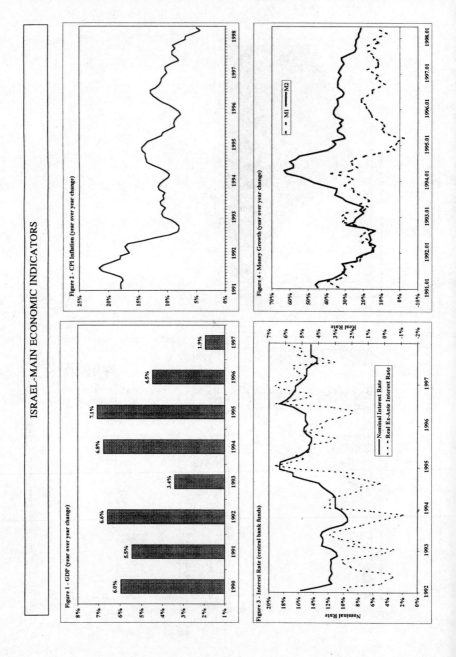

ISRAEL-MAIN ECONOMIC INDICATORS

Figure 1 - GDP (year over year change)

Figure 2 - CPI Inflation (year over year change)

Figure 3 - Interest Rate (central bank funds)

Figure 4 - Money Growth (year over year change)

ISRAEL-MAIN ECONOMIC INDICATORS

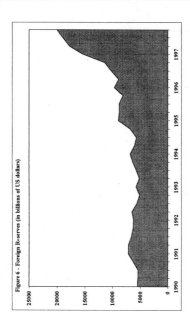

Figure 6 - Foreign Reserves (in billions of US dollars)

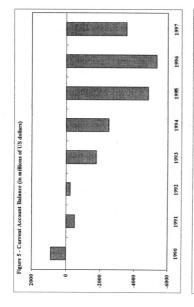

Figure 5 - Current Account Balance (in millions of US dollars)

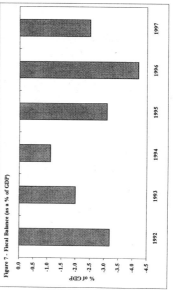

Figure 7 - Fiscal Balance (as a % of GDP)

VI CURRENCY CRISES AND CAPITAL CONTROLS

10 SPECULATIVE ATTACKS AND CAPITAL MOBILITY

Charles Wyplosz

Introduction

Once again speculative attacks have created disasters. The Asian crisis follows on the tracks of Mexico, the European Monetary System, and previous crises in Latin America. Once again, an initial shock has been followed by widespread contagion. Once again, observers have been surprised while commentators have blasted authorities and investors alike for irresponsible behavior. And once again the official reaction has been vigorously criticized.

Much effort is being invested in learning the lessons from the Asian debacle. The International Monetary Fund has published an interim *World Economic Outlook*, and its regular issue of May 1998 devotes a large amount of space to this issue. The explicit message is that the crisis was due to inadequate macroeconomic policies, structural weaknesses in banking and financial systems and supervision, excessive risk taking by foreign investors, a lack of transparency, and political uncertainty. Once the crisis erupted, exchange rates and asset prices crashed for days and weeks: the IMF lays the blame on local authorities that faltered for too long before adopting suitable policies. The required actions spelled out in the IMF programs include the familiar mix of firm monetary policy, disciplined fiscal policies, proper restructuring of the financial systems, and improvements in public and corporate governance.

The IMF also outlines a prevention strategy that emphasizes that the liberalization of capital movements imposes a number of accompanying measures: a more flexible exchange-rate regime, proper regulation and supervision and better information, and the uprooting of corruption and nepotism. Much of the promised effort concerns early warning systems and more openness. This is a traditional tune and, wisely, no miracle is promised: "With the increased globalization of financial markets and the apparent tendency for investors to react exuberantly to success, belatedly to emerging concerns, and eventually to overreact as sentiment changes, it may well be that the risk of crises is rising, including the scope for international contagion" WEO (1998, p. 7).

There is a new, implicit message however. It represents a serious turn-around in official thinking. Up until recently, the liberalization of capital flows was presented as a must to which all the rest has to adapt. Ever so softly, the IMF now recognizes the need for "preconditions for an orderly liberalization of capital movements," which includes "market-based instruments such as reserve requirements on foreign-currency deposits and short-term borrowing" WEO (1998, p. 7). In short, the IMF now admits that financial-market liberalization needs to be preceded by a number of measures. This is an admission that liberalization has proceeded too fast, that some form of restriction is desirable in the transition to full freedom of capital movements, and that the official calls for better information will not hurt but will not help much either.

This chapter explores these two issues further. It starts with a brief overview of what triggers speculative attacks and then argues that tremendous increase in capital mobility is the root source of many of the recent waves of speculative attacks. This argument is used to present the view that currency crises are unlikely ever to be predicted. Finally, it draws some policy implications, in particular for the need for careful capital-account liberalization and the question of restricting capital movements in a market-friendly way.

Theories of Speculative Attacks

It is now well understood that there exist two varieties of financial crises. The early literature described foreign crises triggered by unsustainable poli-cies (Krugman, 1979). What Eichengreen and Wyplosz (1993) have dubbed *first-generation models of crises* correspond to a situation when the fundamentals do not allow the survival of a fixed exchange-rate regime. *Second-generation models* show that crises can be self-fulfilling because there exist multiple equilibria (Obstfeld, 1986). There is a "good" equilibrium where the markets do not attack the currency and the authorities' preference is to maintain the peg, which is possible since the fundamentals allow the survival of the regime. Simultaneously there exists a "bad" equilibrium where an attack, if it were to occur, would succeed. This equilibrium exists because the policies required to defend the regime (raising the interest rate, which may lead to a recession or a bank failures) are less desirable than abandoning the exchange-rate regime. All that is needed is that market participants coordinate themselves and bet that the currency will float and depreciate. When the crisis occurs, the authorities indeed give up. There may exist several (or an infinity of) "bad" equilibria corresponding to various sizes of the postcrisis depreciation. What is needed is that all such equilibria be internally consistent—that market expectation of what the authorities will do in the event of a crisis actually match the authorities' best course of action under the circumstances.

The generic cause of multiple equilibria is that markets act on the basis of expectations of a particular outcome. What makes a crisis occur is the belief that it *can* occur. Expectations that are ex ante unjustified are validated ex post by the outcome that they have provoked. They are self-fulfilling. For a while, self-fulfilling crises have been considered as a theoretical curiosity without practical relevance. The EMS crisis of 1992 to 1993, the Mexican crisis of 1994 to 1995, and the Asian crisis (Thailand excepted) all exhibit features compatible with the assumption of self-fulfilling attacks.[1]

Fundamental-based crises can be predicted. In fact, they typically are. For several months before the attack, it was known that the Mexican peso and the Thai baht were overvalued. The usual signals were flashing: large and growing budget deficits, matched by large and growing current account deficits. For this kind of crisis, early warning signals can work, but they are fairly trivial and hardly missed.

The situation differs considerably when the crises are of the self-fulfilling variety. As noted by Krugman (1996), not every country with a fixed exchange rate is susceptible to fall victim of a self-fulfilling attack. There must preexist some weakness that will prevent the authorities from conducting a full-fledged defense of its currency by raising the interest rate. For example, high unemployment may deter a vigorous defense if it means a recession, especially if the government is politically weak. A weak banking system may collapse, or an asset-price bubble may crash. The preexisting weakness is not be lethal in and by itself, or else this would mean that the fundamentals are bad, but it can become lethal once the situation deteriorates.

It is likely that most countries exhibit some weakness, but under normal conditions such weaknesses are not expected to bring hardship. If all goes well, the weaknesses eventually disappear without further ado. The existence of a weakness is a necessary condition for a speculative attack but not a sufficient condition. Self-fulfilling attacks may affect any country (with a fixed exchange rate and a high degree of capital mobility), which is in the gray area between "fully safe" and "sure to be attacked." For this reason, they are fundamentally unpredictable.

At this stage, we do not have a sound understanding of what triggers self-fulfilling attacks, beyond some evidence that contagion exists.[2] We are just beginning to build up a list of possible weaknesses. Europe 1992 taught us about unemployment, Mexico 1994 about foreign-currency sovereign debt, Asia 1997 about unhedged private debts. Will we ever have an exhaustive list of potentially lethal weaknesses? This is most unlikely because of the familiar argument that if we knew, the crisis would have already occurred.

Capital-Market Liberalization

The importance of multiple equilibria cannot be overstressed. Not only do they make crises unpredictable, but they also profoundly affect both prevention and policy responses. The next section explores these issues. It is useful to start asking why it has taken so long to recognize the existence of self-fulfilling crises and why the IMF is now admitting that the question of capital mobility should be revisited. Is this a new phenomenon, or has it gone unnoticed for a long time? Previous episodes, such as the Latin American crises of the 1980s, may have included elements of speculative attacks. Yet in most cases, macroeconomic imbalances were patently present, so it was natural to focus on interpretations based on first-generation crisis models.

There is another reason why, in the past, self-fulfilling attacks may have played a minor role or no role at all: until the mid-1980s, most countries routinely enforced capital controls. Restrictions to capital movements profoundly affect the pattern of currency crises. As shown in Wyplosz (1986), if controls are effective, an attack does not necessarily lead to the abandonment of a fixed exchange-rate regime. When the volume of speculative capital is bounded over a period of time, the monetary authorities have the possibility of organizing a depreciation without resorting to floating the currency.

This suggests that self-fulfilling attacks have become more visible because capital flows have increased in intensity. Evidence that capital movements have increased is provided by the successive surveys of foreign-exchange markets carried out by the BIS every three years. The average daily transaction volume recorded in 1989 stood at $650 billion; in 1995 it had more than doubled to $1,500 billion. This increase may be deceptive because about 80 percent of these transactions are gross interdealer transactions. They may reflect the increasing use of derivatives instruments that provide insurance through diversification.

Figure 10.1 presents the quarterly volume of net real transborder flows of securities recorded in *International Financial Statistics* for the period 1979 to 1997. For each country, the figure displays the flows and an estimated quadratic trend (or linear when the quadratic term is not statistically significant). The trend does not display any systematic behavior, in sharp contrast with volatility around the trend. The increase in volatility around 1985 to 1987 is striking (and strongly confirmed by formal testing, not reported). Indeed, in the mid-1980s, the OECD countries started to dismantle capital controls, which then remained in widespread use. In addition to evidence of a regime change, the data shown in Figure 10.1 suggest two conclusions. First, more capital mobility does not translate into change into net flows, at least among similar countries. Rather than long-run reallocation of resources, capital mobility leads to more churning. This may correspond to better risk diversification but also to more speculative activity. Second, the volatility of net flows does not increase only in countries that have liberalized their capital accounts but also in countries, such as the United States or Germany, that did not have significant restrictions in place. This indicates the systemic nature of capital-flow liberalization—the "it takes two to tango" effect. When a significant number of countries open up their capital accounts, capital volatility increases on a much wider scale.

Comparable data for emerging markets only allow us to look at Mexico and Korea, two interesting cases. Figure 10.2 confirms the impression gleaned from Figure 10.1: there is a clear break in net flow volatility in the early 1990s. In contrast with OECD countries, there is now a trend of increasing inflows, suggestive of better access and improved international allocation of resources.

The change in the nature of capital movements is compatible with the view that self-fulfilling attacks have become more likely after the mid-1980s. Two possible channels may have been at work. First, multiple equilibria arise only when financial markets are able to overwhelm the monetary authorities, as noted above. Second, for multiple equilibria to exist there must be some weakness that precludes determined reaction by the

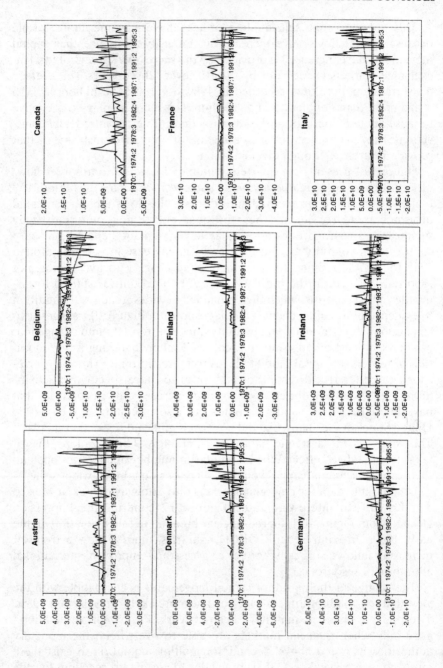

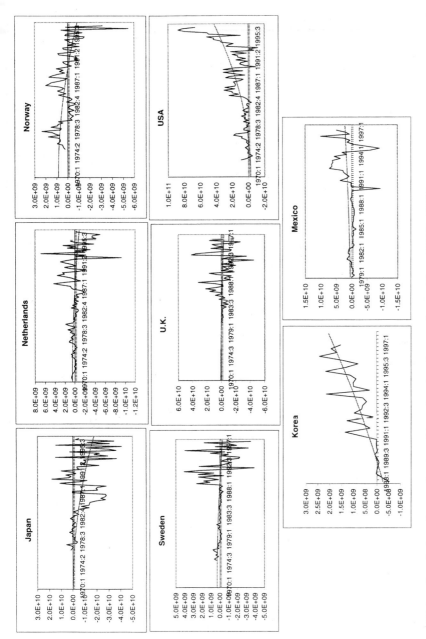

Figure 10.1. Quarterly volume of net real transburden flower of securities, (1979–1997)
Source: *International Financial Statistics* (1979–1997).

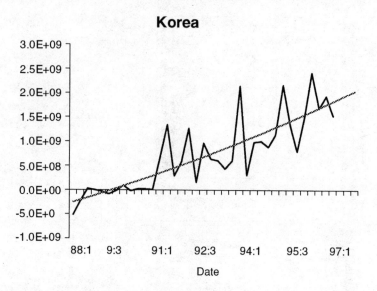

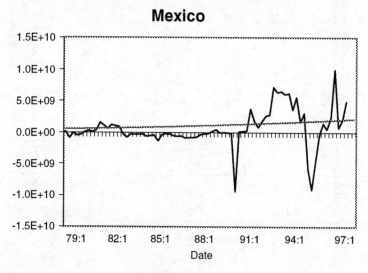

Figure 10.2.
Source: *International Financial Statistics* (1979–1997).

monetary authorities (see Krugman, 1996). One source of weakness is the
time needed for financial markets and institutions, as well as regulation and
supervision, to adjust to the new situation. This second source of weakness
is widely acknowledged to have played a crucial role in Latin America and

Asia, as well as in Europe in the late 1980s and early 1990s (Spain, United Kingdom, Sweden, Finland).

An additional feature worth emphasizing is the global nature of the observed increase in capital mobility, affecting liberalizing countries but also those that had liberalized earlier. This phenomenon is a reminder of the contagious nature of crises. It suggests that liberalization should not be conducted on a case-by-case basis, an issue to which I return below.

The Futility of Early Currency Crises Indicators

Whenever a crisis occurs, a ritual follows. A number of sharp-eyed analysts exhume writings of theirs that had predicted the crisis, probably ignoring other unrealized predictions. The media and governments chastise forecasters and rating agencies for not having issued warning signals. Politicians blame technocrats, borrowers, and investors for not being worth their salt. In response, economists propose new results designed to satisfy this popular thirst for solving the problem once and for all. The Mexican crisis and the Asian debacle have prompted a search for indicators of vulnerability that could be used as leading indicators of crises. Goldstein (1996), Kaminsky, Lizondo, and Reinhart (1997), and Goldstein and Reinhart (1998) are at the forefront of this effort, with several other papers in the making or already available for sale.

In brief, the presumption is that the crisis should have been and needs to be foreseen. The one observation that is ignored is that crises occur by surprise, which is almost a tautology. It is not a tautology since first-generation crises can be rationally anticipated. Second-generation crises, on the contrary, are nearly random. Neither our understanding of what causes crises nor early results provide much hope that the effort at predicting this sort of crises will succeed. There should be no shame in failing to see a self-fulfilling crisis coming and no particular merit in having predicted it: it is all a matter of luck.

Crisis Prediction: The OECD Example

If crises are mostly of the first generation, classic measures of fundamentals should provide a good explanation of crises and can be used for prediction, like with any econometric model used to produce forecasts. If crises are mostly of the second generation, we could also hope to use theory and past experience to identify those weaknesses that make attacks possible and attempt to estimate models to be used for forecasting. However, since these weaknesses are necessary but not sufficient conditions for a crisis to occur, the forecasting properties of such models are likely to be very disappointing.

Using the terminology of statistical tests, leading crisis indicators face Type I errors when they fail to predict attacks that occur and Type II errors when they predict attacks that do not occur. If our understanding of what trigger crises is sketchy, Type I errors are likely to be frequent. If crises are largely self-fulfilling, Type II errors will be widespread. Preliminary testing of such indicators by Kaminsky, Lizondo, and Reinhart (1997) reveal that both types of errors are prevalent.

To further explore this issue, I use the crisis models estimated by Eichengreen, Rose, and Wyplosz (1995) for the OECD countries and by Frankel and Rose (1996) for emerging-market economies. In each case I take the preferred specification, which includes both lagged and leading variables (as these papers were trying to identify both causes and effects of currency crises). I then suppress the leading variables as is proper when building a leading indicator, eliminate the right-hand-side variables that do not enter significantly, and produce within-sample predictions with the resulting regression. This procedure is biased toward making the indicators appear better than they would if they were used, as intended, for out-of-sample predictions. The bad results that follow are therefore better than they would be in a real forecasting context.

Table 10.1 reports the preferred probit regressions for twenty OECD countries over the period 1959 to 1993. It uses the quarterly dataset fully described in Eichengreen, Rose, and Wyplosz (1995). The dependent variable is binary, taking the value of 1 when a crisis occurred and 0 when there was no crisis. Crises are identified using an index of market pressure constructed as the weighted average of exchange and interest-rate changes and foreign-exchange reserves losses, the weights being inversely proportional to the standard deviation of each of the three variables. This index captures either a successful attack (a sharp devaluation) a successful defense (the exchange rate remains unchanged but the monetary authorities deter an attack by a combination of interest-rate increases and foreign-exchange market interventions), or an unsuccessful defense (all three variables move sharply). The index signals a crisis whenever the index departs form its sample mean by more than x standard deviations, x being alternatively set at 2, 1.5, and 1. For $x = 2$, the index identifies forty-one crisis episodes and 1,389 tranquil quarters. With $x = 1$, as many as 238 crises are identified.

Table 10.1. Probit model of currency crises in OECD countries, quarterly observation (1959–1993)

Crisis Criterion	2 Standard Deviations	1.5 Standard Deviations	1 standard Deviation
Crisis in previous period		-0.39	-0.58
		(-1.87)	(-5.43)
		0.06	0.00
Capital controls	-1.42	-1.24	
	(-14.29)	(-14.95)	
	0.00	0.00	
Domestic credit growth	-4.84	-4.70	
	(-1.56)	(-1.79)	
	0.12	0.07	
Inflation	-26.32	-11.15	-34.41
	(-4.39)	(-2.41)	(-14.54)
	0.00	0.02	0.00
GDP growth	-14.39		-14.89
	(-1.60)		(-3.01)
	0.11		0.03
Employment	-8.23	-6.88	
	(-2.55)	(-2.65)	
	0.01	0.01	
Unemployment			0.81
			(1.95)
			0.05
Budget balance			-7.18
			(-3.30)
			0.00
Current account			-9.39
			(-5.53)
			0.00
S.E. of regression	0.273	0.325	0.432
Sum squared resid	106.41	150.13	311.86
Number of observations	1,430	1,430	1,679
Observations with dependent = 0	1,389	1,338	1,441
Observations with dependent = 1	41	92	238

Notes: Dependent is 1 = crisis, 0 = no crisis. Regressors are four quarter equally weighted moving averages. In brackets: z-statistic for no significant effect, below the corresponding p-value.

284 CURRENCY CRISES AND CAPITAL CONTROLS

Each of these regressions is used to generate, for each quarter, a probability of crisis. The estimated probability is next used as a crisis indicator. To do so, we must first determine the threshold above which a crisis signal is issued. Table 10.2 explores this issue for each of the three definitions of a crisis. For example, consider the case when we use the index corresponding to $x = 2$ standard deviations and when a crisis signal is issued whenever the estimated crisis probability exceeds 50 percent. The table shows that the signal would have been issued sixty-six times during the sample's thirty-five years, always wrongly, missing all forty-one crises identified. With 0 percent of crises of crises correctly predicted, this implies a Type I error of 100 percent, while Type II error stands at 5 percent (sixty-six erroneous signals out of 1,389 tranquil quarters).

The table can be used to explore the sensitivity of these two types of error when the threshold is reduced. A lower threshold allows the indicator to signal some actual crises, but at the cost of an even larger number of erroneous warnings. Using the same definition of a crisis ($x = 2$), the table shows the number of warning signals correctly (upper part) and incorrectly (lower part) issued when the threshold is lowered in steps from 50 percent to just 5 percent. At the lower end, the indicator still catches only fourteen of the forty-one crises, while issuing no less than 697 erroneous warning

Table 10.2. Types I and II errors in the OECD countries

	Estimated Proba (crisis)>	2 Standard Deviations	1.5 Standard Deviations	1 Standard Deviation
A crisis actually occurred		41 cases	93 cases	41 cases
	0.5	0	3	34
	0.4	4	14	74
	0.3	5	23	137
	0.2	7	26	176
	0.1	10	35	216
	0.05	14	65	230
No crisis occurred		1,389 cases	1,338 cases	1,441 cases
	0.5	66	74	192
	0.4	212	277	529
	0.3	327	360	887
	0.2	391	394	1,150
	0.1	443	560	1,334
	0.05	697	1,065	1,392

signals. Figure 10.3 summarizes this information. The upper graph shows, for the case $x = 2$, that the proportions of both correct and incorrect signals grow as the trigger is made more sensitive. It seems quite hopeless to try to find the optimal combination of Type I and II errors: both become more

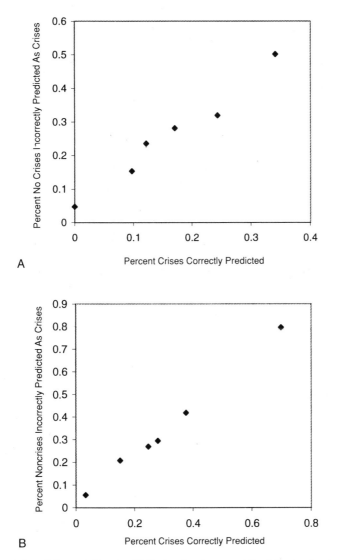

A   Percent Crises Correctly Predicted

B   Percent Crises Correctly Predicted

Figure 10.3.   Crises defined with 2 standard errors (A), 1.5 standard errors (B), and 1 standard error (C)

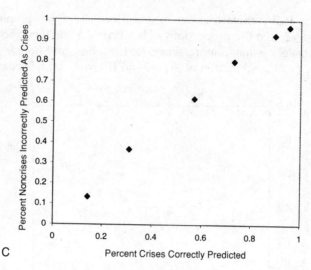

C

Figure 10.3 (*Continued*)

frequent at about the same rate when the signal trigger is made more sensitive.

The table and the figure also illustrate the effect of allowing more foreign-exchange-market tensions to be labeled as crises—that is, by decreasing x, the size of the deviation of the index from its sample mean. Most of the 241 cases identified as crises when $x = 1$ would not make headlines in newspapers. Here too, the tradeoff between a hard and a sensitive trigger for declaring a crisis is quite unfavorable. This comparison has an interesting interpretation. The $x = 1$ crisis indicator misses real crises but detects milder events. Looking at the regressions in Table 10.1, it appears that standard macroeconomic fundamentals (inflation, budget, and current account deficits) are more significant the milder is the definition of a crisis are (the lower is x). Crises appear as knife-hedge events, not as clearly related to traditional fundamentals as periods of moderate exchange-rate pressure. This observation reinforces the view that crises are inherently hard to predict, certainly harder than mild exchange pressure. This is exactly what the theory of self-fulfilling crises would predict.

Crisis Prediction: The Developing Markets Example

This section applies the same methodology to the data collected by Frankel and Rose (1996) for the emerging-market economies. The only difference

concerns the identification of crises. In developing countries interest rates
are rarely market-determined. They cannot be used therefore as a component of the index of market pressure used in the case of OECD countries.
Foreign-exchange reserves are usually imprecisely known, and, in developing countries, they fail to capture a defense that takes the form of emergency borrowing from the IMF, bilateral donors, or private financial
institutions. In addition, defense of the currency frequently includes a tightening of capital controls and increases in reserve requirements. For these
reasons, Frankel and Rose define a currency crisis as a "currency crash"—
that is, a depreciation in excess of 25 percent. For countries where inflation
is endemic and implies an annual rate of depreciation of 25 percent of more,
Frankel and Rose also require that the rate depreciation in any given year
exceeds the previous year's by at least 10 percent. The dataset is annual; it
covers the period 1971 to 1992 and includes 105 countries.

   Table 10.3 presents the regression results. The right-hand-side variables
differ from those used in Table 10.1, in accordance with the models

Table 10.3. Probit model of currency crises in 105
developing countries, annual observations, 1971–
1992

Dependent: Crisis (= 1)	
Concessional debt	−0.77
(percent of total debt)	(−3.28)
	0.00
Foreign direct investment	−2.62
(percent of total debt)	(−2.78)
	= 0.01
Reserves/Imports	−5.36
	(−2.30)
	0.02
Overvaluation	−0.81
	(−3.74)
	0.00
"Northern" growth rate	−9.77
	(−2.85)
	0.00
S.E. of regression	0.225
Sum squared resid	77.79
Number of observations	1,544
Observations with dependent = 0	1,458
Observation with dependent = 1	86

presented in the original papers. They include are more "traditional" fundamentals, as external indebtedness, overvaluation, and the stock of foreign-exchange reserves. The list include also GDP growth in the North, a "push" variable representing economic conditions in the developed countries.

Table 10.4 is patterned after Table 10.2. The upper part shows that the trigger must be lowered to a 20 percent probability of crisis to actually detect one of the eighty-six cases identified by Frankel and Rose. In fact, under this threshold, the signal almost never functions. When the threshold is set at 5 percent, most of the crises (sixty-two out of eighty-six) are detected, but the signal rings wrongly nearly once out of two (630 out of 1,457 tranquil years). Figure 10.4 collects the information from Table 10. There is a slight difference from Figure 10.3: as the trigger is made more sensitive, the ratio of "good" to "bad" signals rises.

This observation corroborates the impression from Table 10.3 that developing countries have been subject to more first-generation crises than developed countries: the more sensitive trigger captures milder exchange-rate movements, which, it is argued above, may be better related to first-generation fundamentals than acute crises. This observation is

Table 10.4. Types I and II errors in the developing countries

	Estimated Proba *(crisis) >*	
A crisis actually occurred		86 cases
	0.5	0
	0.4	0
	0.3	0
	0.2	4
	0.1	34
	0.05	62
No crisis occurred		1,457 cases
	0.5	1
	0.4	1
	0.3	3
	0.2	10
	0.1	165
	0.05	630

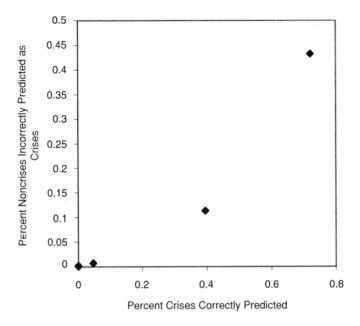

Figure 10.4.

compatible with the view that capital liberalization increases the likelihood of second-generation crises. Simultaneously, it reduces the hope that satisfactory leading indicators of crises can be built.

Policy Implications

Summarizing so far, the chapter argues that there has a been a deep change in the mobility of capital following the wave of liberalization that started in the mid-1980s in the OECD area and in Latin America and then spread to Asia. These changes have had two major effects: making self-fulfilling attacks possible and instilling weaknesses in domestic financial markets. The currency crises that have occurred over the last decade may then increasingly be of the self-fulfilling variety, and there is a serious risk that many more are in the offing. This last conclusion is not very controversial anymore, as is apparent from the latest statements from the IMF in *World Economic Outlook*. What remains to be worked out are the policy responses.

Crisis Prevention

There is little debate on the measures that will help to prevent crises. The list is as long as it is reasonable (see, e.g., *World Economic Outlook*, May 1998). It is based on sustainable macroeconomic policies, sufficient exchange-rate flexibility, adequate regulation and supervision of financial markets and institutions, complete and sincere data reporting, and proper governance in banking, business, and government. Few countries, however, are likely to live up to such standards. In addition, the list reflects the weaknesses revealed by recent experience. It is a fair bet that future crises will reveal other weaknesses.

It is useful, therefore, to look for more modest objectives. In particular, once we recognize that most countries will retain some form or another of weakness for many years to come, we must admit that self-fulfilling crises will remain likely occurrence. We need to think up prevention accordingly. This issue is taken up below. At this stage, it is worth emphasizing that the approach to crisis prevention ought to be both more modest and more prudent than the official line currently suggests.

Crisis Management

Once a crisis is building up, a number of useful steps can be taken. Evidence from past crises shows that rapid action on credit growth may succeed in moderating, if not thwarting, market pressure. Yet it is important to recognize that when a crisis is self-fulfilling, traditional monetary and fiscal policy tightening can be counterproductive. It all depends on the nature of the underlying weakness. This point is best illustrated with two examples.

If the weakness is political, associated with poor growth and rising unemployment, contractionary macroeconomic policy measures will only deepen the problem and further destabilize the government. If the weakness is excessive maturity transformation by shaky banks, an interest-rate defense is likely to precipitate bank failures because it tends to affect more powerfully short-term than long-term rates. In both cases, the usual presumption that higher interest rates strengthen the exchange rate may fail. If higher short-term rates further deepen the weakness that causes the attack, the result may be perverse: the more the authorities raise the interest rate, the more the exchange rate tends to depreciate.

These examples reveal an important feature of self-fulfilling crises: once pressure has built up, traditional macropolicies may be countereffective.

Structural policies (such as strengthening the banking system) are highly desirable but cannot be phased in fast enough. There is a clear need for additional instruments. One such instrument is the imposition of restrictions to capital movements to provide hard-pressed monetary authorities with much needed breathing space, as explained in Eichengreen, Tobin, and Wyplosz (1995) and discussed below. Another instrument is the possibility of suspending debt service, an important issue not explored further here but studied in more detail in Eichengreen and Portes (1995) and Wyplosz (1998).

The New Architecture

The recognition that not all is well in the world of international finance has triggered the search for systemic improvements under the codeword of a "New architecture for the international monetary system." To be useful, this exercise must admit that crisis prevention is a worthy effort, but with limited ability to deter crises, and that crisis management cannot rely on traditional macroeconomic instruments only.

Over the last decade, the official presumption has been that capital liberalization is a worthy goal, one to which developing countries must aspire. The blessing has often turned into a curse, and the recognition that liberalization needs to be careful prepared is a useful step. What remains to be recognized, in light of mounting evidence, is that crises tend to be contagious. Liberalization entails important systemic risks.

One implication of the evidence presented above is that capital mobility increases more when many countries simultaneously liberalize their capital accounts. This externality, if it were confirmed, would imply that the current case-by-case approach needs to be replaced by a systemic one. Not only should a particular country be encouraged to delay financial liberalization until it has eliminated the weaknesses that make multiple equilibria possible, but account should be taken of the effect of such a move on other countries. In particular, due attention should be paid to avoid the bunching of liberalization moves by "similar" countries, unless exchange-rate arrangements are adapted. Bunching occurred in Europe in the late 1980s and led directly to the dismantling of the narrow bands of European Monetary System. It happened again in Asia in the early 1990s.

The natural conclusion is that the new architecture should reverse the presumption that the goal of capital liberalization ought be pursued actively by each country. Free capital movements undoubtedly carry important economic and political benefits, but premature liberalization may result in costs that far outweigh these benefits—in the short-run, at least. Both crisis prevention and crisis management would benefit from adopting the principle that countries should *apply* for capital liberalization and be *authorized* to do so only when they have implemented all the prerequirements and after due account has been taken of the systemic effect.

Market-Friendly Capital Account Restrictions

Most countries have a long history of restrictions to international capital movements, often associated with, and underpinning, domestic financial repression. This combination of administrative measures, which attempt to prevent market forces, has proven ineffective and harmful. For this reason, capital controls of any kind are immediately seen as highly undesirable, a thing of the past. Such a superficial reaction is misguided for two reasons: it overlooks serious financial market failures, and it ignores the possibility of slowing down international financial flows with market-friendly, nonadministrative measures.

Restrictions to capital movements should be approached like any policy intervention: there must be a clearly identified market failure, and the policy measures ought to address the market failure directly. For fundamentals-based crises, the solution lies in the diagnostic: correcting macroeconomic imbalance. Multiple equilibria reflect information asymmetries and the associated inability of participants to coordinate themselves to reach and sustain the better (Pareto-superior) equilibria.

The first-best policy response would be to break the information asymmetry. Since it is extremely unlikely that it will ever be possible to build up sufficient transparency to eliminate information asymmetry, reducing the volume of capital flows while encouraging longer maturity flows can be seen as a second-best response. Market-based measures work by increasing the cost of short-term cross-border flows in the spirit of the Tobin tax. The Tobin tax has never been applied because it requires a worldwide agreement, but it can be adapted. This can be done through an explicit tax or by requiring that a proportion (say, 10 percent or 100 percent) of the target be deposited in a nonremunerated deposit at the central bank. There exists a formal equivalence between a compulsory nonremunerated deposit and an explicit tax. The deposit scheme has two additional features that the tax does not have. First, the implicit tax rate changes with the interest rate. Defense against speculation invariably leads to rising interest rates. Deposit schemes therefore entail lower opportunity costs—therefore low efficiency losses—

in quiet periods, rising just when it is needed in period of turbulence. Second, the deposit can also be seen as a prudential measure that protects counterparts against failure of the agent who initiates the action. It works against the considerable leverage that banks or hedge funds can achieve in as they carry out speculative activities.

Conclusion

The results and the analysis presented here lead to five suggestions to policymakers:

Ignorance. We know very little about financial and currency crises. The usual fundamentals along with the newly identified weaknesses are neither necessary nor sufficient conditions for crises. Those who hold strong view are bound to be wrong, and policy actions based on simple diagnoses were bound to create further havoc.

Modesty. Crisis prevention is good, and much more can be done that has been achieved so far. At the same time we have to admit that there will be crises, no matter what we do to prevent them.

Preparedness. Crises may occur at any time, almost anywhere in the world, and can be violent. We should be surprised by the timing and location but not by the surprise itself. Soothing statements fool those who utter them more often than they fool those to whom they are addressed.

Steadfastness. Financial markets are extraordinary efficient and powerful institutions. They are typically right when policymakers are wrong because they put their money where their analyses tell them to do so. Thus markets deserve respect-but not awe. Markets get it wrong sometimes, they are prone to herd behavior, and they panic. Policymakers also get it wrong and move like a herd, but they should not bow to panicked markets.

Regulation. In particular, the emphasis on liberalization has not been matched by adequate regulation. Financial markets have inherent weaknesses (born out of unavoidable information asymmetries), which call for regulation. Dogmatism tends to associate liberalization with the absence of regulation. The costs of this approach are plain to see.

Notes

1. On the EMS crisis, see Eichengreen and Wyplosz (1993); on the Mexican crisis, see Sachs, Tornell, and Velasc. (1996); on Asia, see Krugman (1998). For a formal test, see Jeanne (1997).
2. Even the causes of contagion are far from clear. Contagion among OECD countries is documented in Eichengreen, Rose, and Wyplosz (1996) and among developing countries in Masson (1998).

References

Artis, Michael, and Mark Taylor. (1990). "Abolishing Exchange Control: The UK Experience." In A.S. Courakis and M.P. Taylor (eds.), *Private Behaviour and Government Policy in Interdependent Economies* (pp. 129–158). Oxford: Oxford University Press, Clarendon Press.

Claassen, Emil, and Charles Wyplosz. (1982). "Capital Controls: Some Principles and the French Experience." *Annales de l'INSEE* (July–December): 237–268.

Eichengreen, Barry, and Richard Portes. (1995). "Crisis? What Crisis? Orderly Workouts for Sovereign Debtors." CEPR, London.

Eichengreen, Barry, Andrew Rose, and Charles Wyplosz. (1995). "Exchange Rate Mayhem: The Antecedents and Aftermath of Speculative Attacks." *Economic Policy* 21: 249–312.

Eichengreen, Barry, Andrew Rose, and Charles Wyplosz. (1996). "Contagious Currency Crises: The First Tests." *Scandinavian Journal of Economics* 98(4): 463–484.

Eichengreen, Barry, James Tobin, and Charles Wyplosz. (1995). "Two Cases for Sand in the Wheels of International Finance." *Economic Journal* 105(1): 162–172.

Eichengreen, Barry, and Charles Wyplosz. (1993). "The Unstable EMS." *Brookings Papers on Economic Activity* (1): 51–144.

Frankel, Jeffrey, and Andrew Rose. (1996). "Currency Crashes in Emerging Markets." *Journal of International Economics* 41(3–4): 351–366.

Goldstein, Morris. (1996). "Presumptive Indicators/Early Warning Signals of Vulnerability to Financial Crises in Emerging Market Economies." Unpublished, Institute for International Economics, Washington, January.

Goldstein, Morris, and Carmen Reinhart. (1998). "Forecasting Financial Crises: Early Warning Signals for Emerging Markets." Institute for International Economics, Washington, DC.

Ito, Takatoshi. (1986). "Capital Controls and Covered Interest Parity Between the Yen and the Dollar." *Economic Studies Quarterly* 37(3) (September): 223–241.

Jeanne, Olivier. (1997). "Are Currency Crises Self-Fulfilling? A Test." *Journal of International Economics* 43: 263–286.

Kaminsky, Graciela, Saul Lizondo, and Carmen Reinhart. (1997). "Leading Indicators of Currency Crises." IMF Working Paper 97-79, Washington, DC.

Krugman, Paul. (1979). "A Model of Balance-of-Payments Crises." *Journal of Money, Credit, and Banking* 11(3): 311–325.

Krugman, Paul. (1996). "Are Currency Crises Self-Fulfilling?" *NBER Macroeconomics Annual*, 345–506.

Krugman, Paul. (1998). "Currency Crises." http://web.mit.edu/krugman/www/crises.html.

Masson, Paul. (1998). "Contagion: Monsoonal Effects, Spillovers, and Jumps Between Multiple Equilibria." Unpublished paper, IMF, Washington, DC.

Obstfeld, Maurice. (1986). "Rational and Self-Fulfilling Balance of Payments Crises." *American Economic Review* 76: 72–81.

Sachs, Jeffrey, Aaron Tornell, and Andrés Velasco. (1996). "The Collapse of the Mexican Peso: What Have We Learned?" *Economic Policy* 22: 13–64.

Wyplosz, Charles. (1986). "Capital Controls and Balance of Payments Crises." *Journal of International Money and Finance*, 167–180.

Wyplosz, Charles. (1998). "International Capital Market Failures: Sources, Costs and Solutions." http://heiwww.unige.ch/∽wyplosz/.

11 NASCENT CAPITAL FLOWS, LEARNING, AND CHILEAN-TYPE CONTROLS

Ricardo Martin

The World Bank

Marcelo Selowsky

The World Bank

Introduction

The recent experience of East Asia has shown the severe impact that sharp interruptions or reversals in the flow of external private capital can have on the economies of the recipient countries. There is still discussion on the relative importance of external factors (such as excessive lending, contagion, and heard behavior) versus domestic factors (such as deficient financial regulation and supervision, politicization of credit allocation, and rigidity in exchange-rate policy).[1] But whether countries were at fault or were innocent victims of *a priori* unjustified panic by foreign investors, the impact of abrupt changes in investors sentiments is likely to be more severe when the country in question has a large stock of short-term debt to start with.[2]

Because of these events, there is now considerable interest in looking at transparent measures that can (differentially) restrict the inflows of short-term capital, such as the Chilean reserve requirement for capital inflows (e.g., Stiglitz, 1998; "Boats, Planer," 1998). This chapter discusses the desirability of that or similar restrictions on the capital account. The first section briefly reviews the pros and cons of capital controls. The second one discusses the Chilean experience, the specific measures taken, and the evidence of their impact on the level and composition of the capital account. The next section proposes a model to analyze the cost of such restrictions. The basic point is that restricting short-term investments may have also a negative impact on investment of longer maturity. The reason is that short-term lending may be part of a natural process by which foreign investors "learn" about the country (or specific domestic banks or corporations), so that after some time they "graduate" to longer-term projects or loans as they become more familiar with the domestic environment. The restriction to short-term flows may interrupt this "learning" process—reducing the steady-state level of long-term investment or debt that otherwise may have been reached. And this can become more important when countries have just opened their capital account and their investment climate is starting to attract external flows—that is, when the process is nascent. In other words, the cost of restricting short-term capital could be particularly high at the beginning of the process—when countries do not yet have a good track record and when capital inflows have recently started. We do not claim this to be the critical factor for all countries, but it may be particularly important for countries just opening their economies to external investors, like the transition countries in Central Europe and the Baltics.

The Economics of Capital Flows

Costs and Benefits of Capital Controls

There is broad consensus among economists (and not just in Washington) about the desirability of an open economy with unrestricted trade of goods and services. The theory and evidence support the view that open trade is good not only on static efficiency grounds[3] but also with regard to growth performance.[4] There is not a similar degree of consensus with respect to the desirability of allowing unrestricted capital movements across countries.

The basic *argument for capital mobility* is a fairly straightforward extension of the argument for free trade: world capital markets expand the set of *intertemporal* consumption possibilities, allowing trade of present and future income on better terms than would be available considering only the domestic market. For example, it allows smoothing out of consumption when there are transitory shocks in income or supplementing of domestic savings to finance higher levels of investment than would be possible in a closed (to capital) economy. A second argument is that the only way that some countries can access some new technologies, quality-control processes, or management methods is when these innovations come bundled with capital inflows, in the form of foreign direct investment.

These arguments make a strong case for allowing capital mobility. They do not, however, imply that fully unrestricted mobility is the optimal policy. If it can be shown that at the margin private decisions do not fully reflect social costs or benefits, some type of restriction could be welfare improving. Of course, since real-world restrictions and regulation are never costless (for example, real resources are used up in their design and administration, and they tend to induce allocative distortions and rent seeking), the benefits should be sizable to justify their imposition.

There are at least three types of *arguments for restricting capital flows*. The first is an extension of the *optimal tariff* argument in international trade. The second highlights the potential role of *government guarantees* in distorting the level of risk-bearing. The third reflects the concern about the *loss of degrees of freedom* on macroeconomic management under open capital account.

- *Optimal tariff* Although individual domestic borrowers normally are too small to affect world interest rates, their combined actions can affect the perception of foreign lenders of the country's overall creditworthiness and, thus, increase the *country premium* charged to all borrowers in the country. This justifies some degree of monitoring of overall borrowing by the government. But clearly it would not justify strong restrictions, particularly at low levels of debt-to-GDP ratios.

- *Implicit guarantee* If foreign lenders perceive an implicit government guarantee, they will not give enough weight to the risk of domestic borrowers and will lend too much and for projects that are too risky (Krugman, 1997; Dooley, 1996a). The obvious first-best response is for the government to be very explicit in denying such a guarantee (with words and actions). The problem is that such denial may not be fully credible, particularly since there have been cases (such as Chile in 1984) where governments did assume external private debt after having repeatedly declared that foreign lenders were assuming the full risk. In more recent crises (such as Korea in 1997) there has been more resistance to nationalizing the external debt, and debtors have borne at least some of the cost of the insolvency of their private domestic borrowers. Hopefully this will reduce the belief in implicit government guarantees.[5]

- *Macroeconomic management* This covers two type of arguments. One is the *loss of autonomy in macro policymaking*, as certain combinations of policy objectives become unfeasible with free capital mobility. As discussed by Mundell (1961), monetary policy is severely restricted when capital can enter and leave the country easily—for example, with perfect capital mobility either domestic interest rates or the exchange rate become out of bounds for the monetary authorities. In Chile in the early 1990s, the tax on capital inflows was introduced to help maintaining a competitive exchange rate in the presence of large capital inflows.[6] Of course, some loss of control may not always be a bad thing, as policy discretionality may be costly— for example, in cases where the "wrong" exchange-rate target is selected and pursued at great cost. It may be better to accept the reduced level of control and learn to live with it. The second argument is *the destabilizing effect of reversal in capital flows*, which makes the economy vulnerable to changes in market sentiment. Reversals in capital flows do not need to result in a crisis, unless they are really massive. If they are, they reflect newly perceived (real or not) vulnerabilities or problems in the country—and it is unlikely that marginal restrictions to flows would have prevented such change in perception. Nevertheless, this remains the best available argument for restrictions, provided they are targeted toward those flows more likely to undergo sudden reversals, like short-term flows.

Restriction to Capital Flows in Chile

There are already several accounts of policies with respect to capital inflows in Chile, including excellent analytical and empirical contributions by economists at the Central Bank of Chile;[7] thus, we present here only a brief summary. The Central Bank first imposed in June 1991 a 20 percent mandatory deposit for up to one year (without interest) of all external credits to the private sector (DFI being exempted). In May 1992 (August for some items), the Central Bank increased this mandatory deposit to 30 percent and set a retention period of one year for direct foreign investment. Since then, several additional small changes have been made to plug loopholes.[8]

It should be noticed that by 1991 the Chilean economy had long since recovered from the deep crisis of 1982 to 1983 (when GDP fell by 16.5 percent and the bailout of the financial system amounted to nearly 30 percent of GDP). From 1983 to 1991 in average GDP grew at 6.4 percent per annum, exports at 11 percent, and there was an overall fiscal surplus. A new banking law, enacted in 1986 (with further amendments in 1989) provided a clear and powerful framework for regulation and supervision of the banking system (see Eyzaguirre and Lefort, 1997). Even more important for foreign investors, the debt to GDP ratio declined from 16 percent in 1986 to 43 percent in 1992, and in 1991 Chile was removed from the list of countries for which U.S. banks were required to make loss provisions on any additional lending. In 1992 Standard & Poor granted Chile a triple-B rating, the highest in Latin America and the only one with investment grade (the rating was improved to BBB+ in December 1993 and to A–in mid-1995) (Larrain, Laban, and Chumacero, 1997).

What effect had these measures on capital flows? Table 11.1 shows that indeed there seems to have been an increase on average maturity, and a sharp decline in financial flows of less than one year. And total flows seem to have fallen, as well. But many others things changed in the early 1990s, so that a more systematic analysis is needed to evaluate the impact of the controls. Several economists at the Central Bank of Chile have done just that.

Herrera and Valdes conclude, from an inventory-type model calibrated to Chilean data, that the controls can explain only a modest covered interest-rate differential, although they do not estimate the impact on that differential or on total flows or their composition. A careful empirical analysis of Eyzaguirre and Schmidt-Hebbel concludes (on the base of regressions with 1991 to 1996 monthly data) that controls had the expected impact on the macroeconomic variables of interest (that is, they reduce inflows,

Table 11.1.   Chile: inflows of external financial loans

	One Year Less		Long-Term		
Year	Mean Maturity (months)[a]	Amounts ($mill)	Mean Maturity (months)[a]	Amounts ($mill)	Total
1989	2.2	$1,452.60	55.0	77.12	$1,529.72
1990	4.2	1,683.15	44.7	181.42	1,864.57
1991	4.1	521.16	88.2	196.12	717.28
1992	8.1	225.20	39.9	554.07	779.27
1993	10.0	140.92	45.8	515.15	656.06
1994	11.6	151.58	61.1	819.70	971.27
1995	11.9	69.68	57.1	1,051.63	1,121.30
1996	12.0	47.25	68.7	2,042.46	2,089.71
1997	10.2	81.13	—	—	—

Source: Banco Central de Chile, Boletin Mensual, several issues.
a. Refers to "Variable LIBOR" inflows, which represents 50 to 90 percent of the total.

depreciate the real exchange rate, and increase domestic interest rates), but these effects have only moderate levels of statistical significance. They also find some ("suggestive") evidence that the measure had an impact on switching the composition of the flows toward the medium and long terms. Soto (1997) also finds empirical support for similar (and small) aggregate impact, using vector autoregression analysis (although VAR models produce detailed dynamic impacts, it is hard to ascertain the statistical significance of the estimates, and the results tend to be quite sensitive to the—essentially arbitrary—choice of included and excluded variables).

Short-Term Investments as a Learning Process

In the last two decades many developing countries (not only transition ones) have liberalized their economies and have allowed their private sectors (through privatization and freer entry) to play a significantly stronger role in infrastructure, banking, and so on. Thus, the incentives for external capital flowing into the domestic private sector of these economies have increased, both on the supply and the demand sides. But these developments are new for potential lenders and domestic intermediaries: policies, institutions, and enterprises need to develop a track record. Not many potential foreign investors are familiar with any particular subset of these recently opened economies, and the process of learning the risk and rewards of working with them is bound to be a slow one. Moreover, although some information is publicly available or can be bought, it may be necessary to actually be (invest) in the country to learn about these risks and rewards—by "learning by doing." This section explores the implications of such gradual learning for the impact of capital controls.

There are many financial instruments available to foreign investors or lenders. For example, they can include in their portfolio domestically issued bonds (from different levels of government, public enterprises, or private firms); they can provide loans to different types of borrowers (such as domestic financial institutions, private firms, and even consumers), with different degrees of collateralization and different maturities; they can purchase stock of domestic firms or directly invest and participate in the management of domestic private enterprises. Investors may be attracted to specific instruments according to their particular knowledge or expertise (for example, FDI in telecommunications usually comes from firms with international experience in that area), their investment objectives, and their risk tolerance.

We develop here a simple model to discuss the tradeoffs of investing in alternative instruments with varying degree of liquidity. From the point of view of the investor, short-term investments have the advantage of allowing investors to recover quickly the funds to use them elsewhere when (1) an alternative use of superior value becomes available (such as an unanticipated investment in the home country or unforeseen consumption needs) or (2) events in the country take a turn for the worse and it becomes a less desirable place for investment.

To illustrate the interaction between learning and short-term risk, we reduce drastically the menu of assets embodying foreign flows to just two: short-term loans with maturity in one period (ST), and long-term loans maturing in three periods (LT),[9] both with returns not fully known in advance. To introduce the link with learning, we postulate that there are two types of countries—let us call them A and B—one of which (A) is more likely to produce high returns than the other (B, for "bad"). The process has noise, so that even in B countries some investments may have good returns in some periods, and not everybody gets good results every period in A countries. But there is a difference between A and B, so that over time, creditors observing actual returns can acquire better information about the actual probability distribution of returns in the country.

There are various possible real-world interpretations of such a model, some of which are discussed below. Our conclusions do not depend on any specific interpretation, although some results are more relevant for some interpretations than for others. One way of interpreting the models is by focusing on the risk of *default*: the investments in question are loans at a given "official" interest rate, but there is a chance that the borrower will not be able to service the loan or repay it at maturity (and there is a larger likelihood of that happening in country B than in country A). Another interpretation would emphasize the cost to the foreign investor of *domestic policy risk*. External returns can be drastically affected by domestic inflation, changes in the exchange rate, domestic interest rates. They also are vulnerable to the imposition of exchange-rate controls, penalties for repatriation, or a discriminatory tax system. A type A country would have a predictable macroeconomic policy and be less propense to big swings on its key relative prices. A third interpretation would look at the *environment for the private sector*, since the actual returns to foreign lenders and investors can differ considerably according to the degree to which the country has a "culture" of compliance with private contracts and enforcing property rights; or the reliability (and timeliness and cost) of the judicial system to resolve business disputes; or the cost of regulations (which may depend strongly on how they are actually enforced at the local level); or

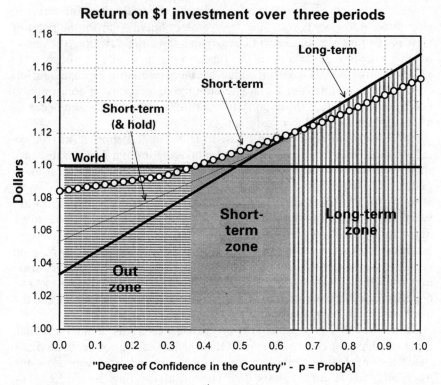

Figure 11.1.   Return on $1 investment over three periods

the prevalence of crime and corruption. Of course, in all these interpretations there is virtually a continuum of possibilities between "good" and "bad." The two cases, A or B, can be taken as polar scenarios, which define the range of likely possibilities for the country in question.[10]

The probability that the country is of type A, which we call p, is a critical variable of the model.[11] Its initial value would be different for different (potential) foreign investors, according to their previous exposure to the country and their specific experience. The larger is p, the more optimistic investors are about the returns from operating in the country. Thus, p can be taken as a measure of the *level of confidence* of foreign investors.

Figure 11.1 shows how the returns of three different types of investments depend on the parameter p. The thick horizontal line (World) indicates the accumulated value of an investment in a safe assets (such as U.S. Treasury bills). It is flat, indicating that the returns do not depend on the degree of confidence in the target country. The upward-sloping thick line (Long-term) shows the expected return of an investment on the country that matures over the same investment period (say, one year). By definition, country A produces higher returns, thus the expected returns increases with the probability p. If those were the only two investment opportunities available, only investors assigning at least a 50 percent probability to the country being good (type A) would invest there.

The other two lines indicate the accumulated value over one year of two different sequences of short-term investments (by assumption, it takes three short-terms to get one long-term investment periods—which equals, for definitiveness, one year). The thin line shows the expected accumulated return when holding (reinvesting) it for the whole long period. The line with markers shows the expected return when and optimal investment sequence is follows: at the end of each period the capital is reinvested only if the expected return, with expectations revised in base of the observed returns, are higher than on the outside safe investment. The difference between the two types of short-term investment sequences indicates the *value of the information* about actual returns.[12]

The figure assumes that LT is more profitable than a sequence of ST investments for countries type A, reflecting the required premium for having funds immobilized for a longer period.[13] Without a yield differential there would not be any reason to ever invest long term. In B countries, on the other hand, ST investments are bad, but LT investments are even worse, as with more time more things can go wrong, and more of the downside events discussed in the real-world interpretations above may come to be.

The result is that we have three different regions for p, marked in the figure by different shadings. The Out zone is relevant for investors with low confidence in the country (they assign it a high probability of being type B): they would maximize returns by staying out and investing elsewhere. The intermediate zone, Short-term, contains those investors who have enough confidence to invest ST but not enough to commit to LT investments. Lastly, the Long-term zone includes investors with the highest degree of confidence, who thus maximize their expected returns by investing long term.

The Revision of Information from Observed Returns

We have argued that the degree of confidence in the country, as indicated by p, the probability of the country being of type A, is a critical parameter determining if an investor would invest or not and, if investing, if it would be short-term or long-term investment. In this section we see how p is revised over time as the actual returns from investment are observed.

The revision of expectations is simple, a consequence of basic principles of probability theory (such as Bayes theorem). When a certain return R_i is observed, the probability of the country being of type A should be increased if R_i is a more likely result in A than in B. Specifically, the probability of A conditional on R_i is

$$Pr[A/R_i] = \frac{p \cdot Pr[R_i/A]}{Pr[R_i]},$$

where $Pr[R_i] = p \cdot Pr[R_i/A] + (1 - p) \cdot Pr[R_i/B]$ is the unconditional probability of the observed return, R_i, a weighted average of its probability in both types of countries.

Figure 11.2 shows how the confidence level is revised from observed returns. To simplify, we present just two potential outcomes: High or Low return, with the former being more likely in A countries, and the latter in B countries. The upper (thicker) line in the first panel shows how different initial values for $p = \text{Prob}(A)$ are revised after observing High returns. For example, if initially $p = 0.50$, after observing one period of high return it would increase to 0.62, as shown by point H1. Successive periods of high return would increase p further along that line (H2 for two consecutive R_H, and so on), as shown also by the upper line in the left panel. A period of Low returns, on the other hand, would reduce p from 0.50 to 0.29, point L1

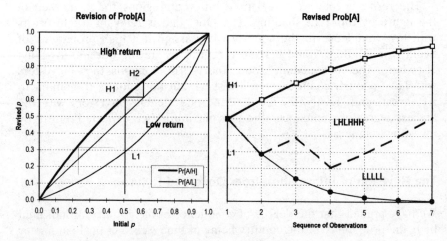

Figure 11.2. How confidence level is revised from observed returns

in the lower line. A sequence of Low returns reduces p further, as shown in the lower line in the left panel, eventually converging to zero. Of course, it is also possible to observe mixed sequences such as Low-High-Low-High-High-High, shown by the broken line in the left panel.

The revision of confidence with investment experience means that investors who are initially in the Short-term investment zone of Figure 11.1 would move over time to the other zones, according to their observed returns. For example, a country that is "good" (type A) but not widely known to investors would likely face at first skeptical investors, who may be willing to invest short run, if at all. Over time, though, as confidence increases, they would start revising p upward and longer-term investments would become more attractive. On the other hand, no learning would occur if the initial level of confidence is too low or if the potential short-run inflows are not allowed in.

The Impact of Chilean-Type Capital Restrictions

The Central Bank of Chile requires 30 percent of foreign capital entering the country to be deposited for one year without interest. This imposes, by design, a disproportionate burden on short-term capital. Figure 11.3 shows how the three zones of Figure 11.1 change with this measure. The Out zone increases as the expected returns from ST and LT investments shift downward. ST shifts further, to the extent that the Short-term zone disappears completely. Figure 11.4 shows a more favorable international environment, as indicated by a lower opportunity cost of capital to foreign investors: under those conditions a small Short-term zone remains even after the tax.

With the same distribution of prior external perceptions than before, more investors would find it unrewarding to enter the country after the restriction (this is its *scale* effect), and a relatively larger fraction of those who decide to enter would come for LT rather than ST investment (*substitution* effect).

These effects may not be of much concern to a country with already ample inflows of foreign capital (or one trying to prevent an appreciation of its currency because of inflation and competitiveness concerns), but they can be significant for countries just starting to open their capital markets to foreigners.

Moreover, our previous analysis implies that those static scale and substitution effects could be just the initial impact of the restrictions and that the final impact could be much larger when the learning effect is significant. The reason is that short-term investment provides information, so that

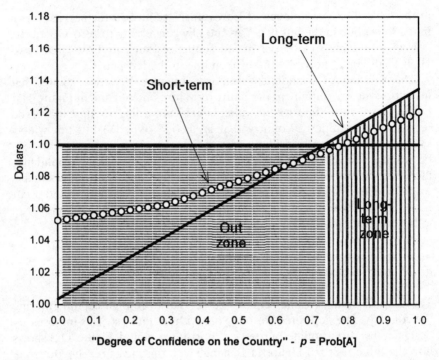

Figure 11.3.   Return on $1 investment over three periods with 30 percent deposit
requirement

those actually investing revise their country assessment over time. Thus,
in Good countries they would move progressively to higher values of p, as
their experience increases their confidence in the country, so that they start
to invest more and at longer terms. When the restrictions reduces or eliminates the Short-term zone, the process of increasing maturities is reduced
(or eliminated), with a larger cumulative impact on total investment.

Extensions

We assumed that actual returns were the only relevant observable variable
generating information about potential returns of project in the country.
Clearly, any other variable observable only to "insiders" and with strong
associations to future returns would work as well.

The model assumes that only investors can learn about the country. To
the extent that there is some free-riding in learning—that is, when even

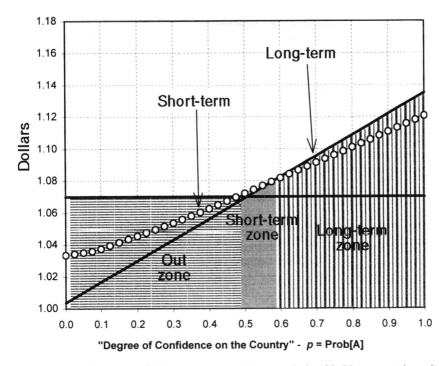

Figure 11.4.   Return on $1 investment over three periods with 30 percent deposit, low world rates

those not investing in the country can progressively change their percep-tions by observing the experience of those operating in the country—the longer-term cost of restrictions to ST inflows are reduced, provided flows are not stopped entirely. But, again, these opportunities for learning from others are more likely to be significant when there is already a certain contingent of foreign operators, but seems more limited in countries at the beginning of their liberalization process—which are the ones that interest us.

Appendix

The Formal Model

The basic model considers two types of countries: A ("good") and B ("bad"), which differ in the distribution of returns to foreign investors (thus, as discussed in the text, the distribution includes exchange-rate risks, risk of delays on payments, expropriation, restrictions to repatriation, and so on.)

First some notation. Let R_i, $i = 1, \ldots, n_R$, be the return (including principal) on the ith "state of the world"; $\pi_i^A = \text{Prob}[R_i/A]$ and $\pi_i^B = \text{Prob}[R_i/B]$ the probabilities of R_i in countries A and B, respectively. Based on information up to now, the representative foreign investors assigns a probability $p = \text{Prob}[A]$ that the country under consideration is indeed of type A (so that $\text{Prob}[B] = 1 - p$).

The expected payoff from a unit invest is

$$E[R] = \Sigma_i R_i \pi_i = p R_A + (1-p) R_B, \tag{11.1}$$

where $\pi_i = p\pi_i^A + (1-p)\pi_i^B = $ unconditional $\text{Prob}(R_i)$; and $R_A = \Sigma_i R_i \pi_i^A$, $R_B = \Sigma_i R_i \pi_i^B$ are expected returns on A and B, respectively. By definition $R_A > R_B$, as A is the "good" country.

Since the probability distribution of returns differs in A and B, observing actual returns provides information about the country, information that can be used to revise the initial likelihood of being an A country, p. Specifically, from Bayes theorem, $\text{Prob}[A/R_i] = \text{Prob}[R_i/A]*\text{Prob}[A]/\text{Prob}[R_i]$—that is,

$$p^i = \text{Prob}[A/R_i] = p\pi_i^A / \pi_i, \quad i = 1, \ldots, n_R. \tag{11.2}$$

Similarly, after observing returns on two periods equal to R_i, R_j, the likelihood of the country being of type A changes to $\text{Prob}[A/R_iR_j] = \text{Prob}[R_i/A] \text{Prob}[R_j/A] \text{Prob}[A]/\text{Prob}[R_i] \text{Prob}[R_j/R_i])$—that is,

$$p^{ij} = \text{Prob}[A/R_iR_j] = p\pi_i^A\pi_j^A/(\pi_i\pi_j^i) = p\pi_i^A\pi_j^A/(p\pi_i^A\pi_j^A + (1-p)\pi_i^B\pi_j^B) \tag{11.3}$$

and $\pi_j^i = \text{Prob}[R_i/R_j] = p^i\pi_i^A + (1-p^i)\pi_i^B. = (p\pi_i^A\pi_j^A + (1-p)\pi_i^B\pi_j^B)/\pi_i.$

Investment Decision

Consider now the expected return from investing in the country. The alternative is a set of international investment, R^*, which include a safe asset such as a United States Treasury bill. A one-period investment of $X in the country would be justified if and only if

$$E[U((W_0 - X)R^* + XR)] > E[U(W_0R^*)], \tag{11.4}$$

where $U(.)$ is the investors' utility function (embodying attitudes toward risk and time discount) and W_0 is the initial level of wealth.

Under *risk neutrality* (that is, when $U(.)$ is linear, which can be taken as a good approximation if the level of investment X is small in relation to W_0), a necessary condition for the investment condition (11.4) is

$$E[R - R^*] > 0. \tag{11.4a}$$

which, from (11.1), and specializing to one risk-free foreign asset, is equivalent to $p > (R^* - R_B)/(R_A - R_B)$, so that only investors sufficiently optimistic about the country would be willing to invest.

In the general case, the condition for a positive level of investment, $X > 0$, is

$$E[(R - R^*)U'] \geq 0. \tag{11.5}$$

There are now two new effects, compared with (11.4a). First, the different alternative returns are now weighted by the marginal utility if income, U', when calculating expected returns. With risk aversion, U' is a decreasing function, so that states where there is low returns (that is, lower wealth) are giving more weight compared for the risk-neutral case. That means that, other things equal, investors will require a bigger *country risk premium* the more risk averse they are.[14]

The second new effect is that foreign investment could be valuable by providing international diversification and, thus, *reducing overall portfolio risk*, when it is recognized that external returns are also likely to be subject to some variability. In terms of the standard mean-variance tradeoff, some level of X could buy a lower variance and, thus, be advisable, even if it reduces the average return (that is, when (11.4a) does not hold). This is more likely to happen if there is a negative covariance between domestic and external returns. This is seen remembering that end of period wealth is $W_1 = W_0 R^* + X(R - R^*)$, so that

$$\mathrm{Var}(W_1) = (W_0 - X)^2 \mathrm{Var}[R^*] + X^2 \mathrm{Var}[R] + 2(W_0 - X)X\mathrm{Cov}[R, R^*],$$

which implies that $\mathrm{Var}[W_1]$ will decrease when some $X > 0$ is added to the portfolio provided that

$$X\mathrm{Var}[R] + (W_0 - 2X)\mathrm{Cov}[R, R^*] < (W_0 - X)\mathrm{Var}[R^*].$$

We will ignore these portfolio diversification issues in what follows, as they would complicate exposition without adding much to the main points we want to discuss. Thus, R^* will be taken as a constant from now on.

Multiperiod Investment

If an amount X_t is invested in period t, this produces at the end of the period the amount $X_t R_i$, for some i in $\{1, \ldots, n_R\}$. In addition, it provides information about the country, as discussed above. Thus, after having invested for one period and obtained a return R_i, the decision about whether to invest for a second period can be made conditionally to the observed return, to maximize the expected utility from second-period wealth:

$$\text{Max} E_{t+1}[U(W_{t+1}^i)] = \Sigma_t U(W_t R^* + X_{t+1}^i (R_j - R^*))\pi_j^i \qquad (11.6)$$

Thus we may have $X_{t+1}^i > 0$ for some i (that is, for those realizations that increase the probability of A), while it could be 0 (the investor would leave the country) for other values of i. The combined two-periods problem is[15]

$$\text{Max} V = \Sigma_i \Sigma_j U((W_{t-1} R^* + X_t (R_i - R^*))R^* + X_{t+1}^i (R_j - R^*))\pi_i \pi_j^i$$
$$\text{for } X_t \geq 0, X_{t+1}^i \geq 0 \text{ and } X_t \leq W_{t-1}, X_{t+1}^i \leq W_t. \qquad (11.7)$$

Clearly, the combined return will generally be larger than if investors were forced to stay two periods (or not enter at all). This means that investors would generally demand a higher return on longer-term (less liquid) investments.

The magnitude of the short-term premium depends on the specifics of the probability distribution and utility functions, which determine how valuable is the information and how much of it is obtained by observing actual returns for one period. (The simulation results using "reasonable" parameter values, shows that it could be very significant).

The generalization of (11.7) to more than two periods is straightforward, if somewhat cumbersome to write. Equation (11.8) is a three-periods version of the portfolio problem introducing, in preparation for next steps, variables for Long-term investment (X^{LT}) and for the amount invested in the safe foreign asset (Z):

$$\text{Max } V = \Sigma_i \Sigma_j \Sigma_k U((X_3^{ij} R_k + Z_3^{ij} R^* + X_1^{LT} R_{ijk}^{LT}))\pi_i \pi_j^i \pi_k^{ij} \qquad (11.8)$$

subject to the constraints

$$X_1 + X^{LT} + Z_1 \leq W_0; \qquad \text{(initial wealth)}$$
$$X_2^i + Z_2^i \leq W_1^i = X_1 R_i + Z_1 R^* \qquad \text{(1st-period wealth)} \quad \text{for } i = 1, \ldots, n_R$$
$$X_3^{ij} + Z_3^{ij} \leq W_2^{ij} = X_2^i R_j + Z_2^i R^* \qquad \text{(2nd-period wealth)} \quad \text{for } i, j = 1, \ldots, n_R,$$
$$(11.9)$$

plus the obvious nonnegativity constraints for all X_s and Z_s.

At the optimal portfolio composition, no further increase in the expected utility of end-of-period wealth can be obtained by allocating an additional small amount to short-term investment in periods 1, 2, or 3 (X_1, X_2^i, and X_3^{ij}), to the safe investment (Z_1, Z_2^i, and Z_3^{ij}), or to long-term investments (X^{LT}). Thus the following inequalities (with standard complementary-slackness conditions) must hold:

$$\lambda_2^{ij} \geq \Sigma_k \pi_i \pi_j^i \pi_k^{ij} R_k U'_{ijk} \quad 0 \leq X_3^{ij} \quad \text{for } i, j = 1, \dots, n_R.$$

$$\lambda_2^{ij} \geq \Sigma_k \pi_i \pi_j^i \pi_k^{ij} R^* U'_{ijk} \quad 0 \leq Z_3^{ij} \quad \text{for } i, j = 1, \dots, n_R.$$

$$\lambda_1^i \geq \Sigma_j \lambda_2^{ij} R_j \quad 0 \leq X_2^i \quad \text{for } i, j = 1, \dots, n_R.$$

$$\lambda_1^i \geq \Sigma_j \lambda_2^{ij} R^* \quad 0 \leq Z_2^i \quad \text{for } i, j = 1, \dots, n_R.$$

$$\lambda_0 \geq \Sigma_j \lambda_1^j R_j \quad 0 \leq X_1$$

$$\lambda_0 \geq \Sigma_j \lambda_1^j R^* \quad 0 \leq Z_1$$

$$\lambda_0 \geq \Sigma_k \pi_i \pi_j^i \pi_k^{ij} R_{ijk}^{LT} U'_{ijk} \quad 0 \leq X^{LT}, \tag{11.10}$$

where the λs are the Lagrange multipliers associated to each of the wealth constraints in (11.8). They can be given the standard interpretion in terms of shadow price of the corresponding constraint at the optimal solution. For example, λ_0 gives the value, in terms of expected utility of third-period wealth, of one additional unit available for investment at the begining of period 1. The last three inequalities in (11.10) state that this marginal value will be the maximum of that provided by the three alternative investments available at that moment: X_1, X^{LT}, and Z_1 (with equality for any alternative with a nonzero level of investment). The three lines in Figure 11.1 are calculated from these equations, for different values of p.

The joint probabilities in (11.8) can be expressed in terms of those for the two types of countries, $\pi^A \pi^B$, and p, the probability of the country being in fact type A:

$$\pi_i \pi_j^i \pi_k^{ij} = p \pi_i^A \pi_j^A \pi_k^A + (1 - p) \pi_i^B \pi_j^B \pi_k^B. \tag{11.11}$$

There is a further refinement needed to (11.8) to (11.10), to make more precise the flow of information over time, and, especially, to accommodate the working of the Chilean-type entry tax into the story. It involves explicitly differentiate between *new investments* and *reinvestments* of proceedings from previous periods. The reason to distinguish these two types of investment is that actual returns are assumed to be *not observable* to those not in the country, so that if $X_1 = 0$, for example, the decisions in the second period cannot in fact be conditional on the actual return on the first period, as implicitly assumed above (since X_2^i is not restricted to take the same value for all i). This can be handled by making *new* investment in the second period unconditional on i, while reinvestment can still depend on previous observations. And similarly for the third period. This way of handing the flow of information obviously ignores the possibility that the new investments are brought by investors already in the country—but that is not a serious problem in our formulation (particularly in the risk-neutral case), as the linearity of the problem implies that only the all funds will go to the alternative with the highest return.

The Chilean Entry Tax

The 30 percent forced deposit for one year required by the Central Bank of Chile since 1992 can be modeled as adding an amount $0.3 \cdot r^*$, where r^* is the annual rate of return in alternative investments.[16] With the tax, the objective function remains the same, but the budget (wealth) constraints must be modified as follows (all Xs and Zs are nonnegative):

$$\beta X_1 + \beta X^{LT} + Z_1 \leq W_0;$$

$$X_2^i + Z_2^i \leq X_1 R_i \qquad \text{(funds in the contry)} \qquad \text{for } i = 1, \ldots, n_R;$$

$$\beta X_2 + Z_2^i \leq Z_1 R^* \qquad \text{(new funds)} \qquad \text{for } i = 1, \ldots, n_R;$$

$$X_3^{ij} + Z_3^{ij} \leq X_2^i R_j \qquad \text{(3rd-period reinvest)} \qquad \text{for } i, j = 1, \ldots, n_R;$$

$$X_3^j + Z_3^j \leq X_2 R_j \qquad \text{(2rd-period reinvest)} \qquad \text{for } j = 1, \ldots, n_R;$$

$$\beta X_3 + Z_3 \leq Z_2 R^* + \Sigma_j Z_2^j R^* \qquad \text{(new funds, 3rd period)},$$

$$(11.12)$$

where $\beta = 1 + 0.3(R^* - 1)$ indicates the entry tax. This is the final formulation used to calculate our simulation results.

Acknowledgments

The views presented here are the authors and do not necessarily reflect those of the World Bank.

Notes

1. We can distinguish two polar models: one (e.g., Radelet and Sachs, 1998) basically sees the crisis as a traditional bank run similar to numerous previous domestic bank panic

episodes, before the existence of depositors insurance and lenders of last resort. The other (e.g., Krugman, 1998a) adds inadequate domestic financial regulation and supervision as biasing domestic bank lending (financed through foreign borrowing) toward excessively risky projects bound to collapse sooner or later.

2. E.g., Radelet and Sachs (1998) present probit regressions on factors affecting the probability of crisis, in which one of the strongest variables is short-term capital, or more precisely, the ratio of short-term debt to reserves (as a policy matter, improving that ratio by increasing the denominator is a losing proposition for the Central Bank, since the cost of short-term debt is normally much higher than the return on reserves. Not everybody agrees that this is a critical factor, though. For example, Kaminsky, Lizondo, and Reinhart (1997) do not include short-term debt among their fifteen "leading indicators of currency crisis."

3. David Ricardo, Samuelson, Bhagwati, Johnson, and many others.

4. Bhagwati, Bela Balassa, Krueger, Papageorgiou-Michaely-Choksi, and others.

5. The reason that lenders (external or domestics) must check the level of risk of projects they finance is that their borrowers, even when betting their money, have their downside exposure limited by the possibility of bankruptcy. Thus, without adequate oversight they may select projects with more than optimal risk. This is, of course, the same reason that banks need to know their clients, tend to specialize by sectors, and so on. An interesting special case is when those borrowing abroad are *domestic banks*. Without proper prudential regulations regarding capital adequacy, portfolio diversification, and they can be even more propense to overexposure to risk, given the small ratio of capital to total assets typical in the financial sector. Thus, if external lenders feel "protected" by the government, the potential for overlending and overexposure to risks can be catastrophically large.

6. Other instruments to limit the appreciation of the peso were severely limited: "sterilization" of the inflows was affecting the balance sheet of the Central Bank (the interest paid on bonds to buy foreign exchange exceeded the return on reserves), and loosening monetary policy was rejected out of inflation concerns.

7. E.g., Eyzaguirre and Schmidt-Hebbel (1997), Soto (1997), Herrera and Valdes (1997), Larrain, Laban, and Chumacero (1997).

8. This is based in Soto (1997).

9. Readers should be warned that the discussion will be kept largely at a heuristic levels; those looking for a more rigorous presentation are referred to the appendix.

10. The model can also be interpreted as an approximation to statistical processes widely used in empirical analysis. Suppose that the returns from investment are generated by a random process with permanent (or durable) shocks or with autocorrelation. Then, observing current returns improves the prediction of future returns, which is the key feature of our model. The two polar cases are not very natural under this interpretation, but most of our results would still follow.

11. The probability that the country is "bad" (of type B) is $1 - p$.

12. The details of the numerical model generating the results presented in the figure can be found in the appendix. The fact that the the two ST lines coincide for type A countries ($p = 1$) is due to the fact that when it is *known with certainty* that the country is type A, there is no revision of expectations whatever the observed results are. Thus, if it is profitable to invest for one period, it is profitable to stay there for the overall investment period (year). At the other extreme, $p = 0$, or countries *known* to be of type B, there is also no revision of expectations, but the optimal strategy is to leave after one period (in fact, it would have been optimal not to enter at all). For that case the difference between the lines does not measure the value of information, but the value of rectifying the mistaken first-period investment. For p in the Out zone of the figure there is a combination of both factors at play.

13. It would not be difficult to generate that differential from a model—for example, by including random income shocks and risk aversion and, thus, a liquidity premium. That would only complicate further the model without adding anything essential to the story.

14. Note, however, that when evaluated at $X = 0$, there is no difference on the level of W across states of the domestic economy, so that abstracting from world risks, the necessary condition for at least some (small) inital investment would still be that $E[R] > R^*$. In equilibrium with $X > 0$, though, W differs for different realizations R_i.

15. Equation (11.7) ignores the possibility of investing the second period without doing so in the first period. But this can never be optimal in our specification where the distribution of returns are stationary. On ther other hand, as discussed in the text, it may be optimal to leave after one period, if the observed return is unfavorable.

16. In fact, investors can pay this amount—with r^* estimated as LIBOR + 4% [400 basic points?]—instead of having the funds frozen for one year (see Soto, 1997, app. 3).

References

"Boats, Planer, and Capital Flows." (1998). *Financial Times*, March 25.

Dewatripont, Mathias, and Jean Tirole. (1994). *The Prudential Regulation of Banks.* Cambridge, MA: MIT Press.

Dooley, Michael. (1996a). "Capital Controls and Emerging Markets." *Intl J. Finance Economics* 1: 197–205.

Dooley, Michael. (1996b). "A Survey of Academic Literature on Controls over International Capital Transactions." *IMF Staff Papers* 43(4) (December).

Eyzaguirre, Nicolas, and Fernando Lefort. (1997). "Capital Markets in Chile 1985–1997: A Case of Successful International Financial Integration."

Eyzaguirre, Nicolas, and Klaus Schmidt-Hebbel. (1997). "Encaje a la entrada de capitales y ajuste macroeconomico."

Herrera, Luis, and Rodrigo Valdes. (1997). "Encaje y autonomia monetaria en Chile."

International Monetary Fund. (1998). *World Economic Outlook.*

Kaminsky, Graciela, Saul Lizondo, and Carmen M. Reinhart. (1997). "Leading Indicators of Currency Crisis." IMF Working Paper, July.

Krugman, Paul. (1998a). "Currency Crisis." P. Krugman home page at MIT, downloaded April 9.

Krugman, Paul. (1998b). "Paradigms of Panic: Asia Goes Back to the Future. *Slate*, posted March 12.

Larrain, Felipe, Raul Laban, and Romulo Chumacero. (1997). "What Determines Capital Inflows? An Empirical Analysis for Chile. Working Paper R97-09, Harvard University, April.

Mundell, Robert A. (1961). "A Theory of Optimum Currency Areas." *American Economic Review* (51): 657.

Sachs, Jeffrey, and Steven Radelet. (1998). "The East Asian Financial Crisis: Diagnosis, Remedies Prospects." Paper prepared for Brookings Panel, March 26–27.

Soto, Claudio. (1997). "Controles a los movimientos de capital: Evaluacion empirica del caso chileno."

12 THE ROLE OF THE CENTRAL BANK IN CAPITAL-ACCOUNT LIBERALIZATION V. THE CASE OF CROATIA

Velimir Šonje
Croatian National Bank

Introduction

In April 1998 the Croatian National Bank imposed restrictions on short-run capital inflows, after four and a half years during which the regime was liberal. In this chapter I analyze the developments that led to this decision. I also discuss the problem of the central bank's responsibility regarding regulation of international financial flows. The analysis is strictly limited to the short run, with a special reference to the nature of the monetary transmission mechanism.

In the first section I discuss the following: (1) should central bankers care about external position and capital mobility, (2) do they (and should they) have the power to regulate international capital flows, and (3) is there a possibility that the central bankers find themselves in a trap among conflicting policy targets if they want to achieve too much. I show that there are two strong arguments in favor of the central banks' ability to influence international capital flows in transition economies in the short run.

Restrictions on international capital flows can help to curtail credit growth, which, if excessive, can lead to banking-sector problems with real sector implications (see, e.g., Pill and McKinnon, 1995). The central bank cannot ignore this danger and should use any possibility to avoid adverse consequences, no matter what the particular monetary and exchange-rate regime look like. Second, restrictions on international capital inflows can presumably influence money, the credit rate, and the exchange rate, which might have some impact on imports and external performance. Of course, the questions are: what is the size of this impact in comparison to some other policy action (fiscal policy), and how does this impact work out through the system?

These questions are dealt with in the second section. I used a Sims-type information variable approach to investigate the monetary transmission mechanism. The focus was on the short-run impact of money, credit, and fiscal variables on imports. The results show that fiscal policy has no impact on imports in the short run. Banks' credits to the private sector also have no short-run impact on imports, but broad money exhibits significant influence.

In the third section I continue the investigation of the transmission mechanism by introducing the interest rate and the exchange rate into the imports equation. The results show that they play no significant role. Hence it remains unclear what the other short-run impacts on imports are beyond the general impact of aggregate demand changes, which are captured by the changes in broad money. Nevertheless, restrictions on capital inflows can be justified on two grounds: raising the quality of financial intermediation and helping to control the broad money, which has significant short-run impact on imports. When using the first argument, one has to keep in mind that banking supervision represents the first-best solution to the problem of quality of financial intermediation. However, when supervision is underdeveloped, restrictions on capital flows can be used as the second-best solution.

Should the Central Bank Care about Capital Mobility and External Performance?

In a small open and advanced transition economy that is trying to find the path toward a dynamically stable external position, by all means the central bank should care about capital mobility and external performance. The main feature of such an economy is shown in Table 12.1. Stable growth, moderate inflation, sound external liquidity, and sound fiscal policy are accompanied by strong capital inflows and widening current-account deficis. From the static perspective the economy looks well, but from the dynamic viewpoint the problem of sustainability of external position has to be solved.

Table 12.1.   Republic of Croatia: Main economic indicators

	1994	1995	1996	1997	1998[a]
Real GDP (%)	5.9	6.8	6.0	6.5	5.5
Inflation (%)[b]	−3.0	3.7	3.4	3.8	5.0
Fiscal balance/GDP (%)	1.7	−0.9	−0.5	−1.4	−0.4
Exports f.o.b.[c]	4,260.4	4,632.7	4,545.8	4,205.9	4,726.5
Imports f.o.b.[c]	5,582.9	7,870.2	8,197.0	9,430.3	9,165.4
Trade deficit	−1,332.5	−3,237.5	−3,651.2	−5,224.4	−4,438.9
Balance of services	1,661.9	1,207.7	1,764.0	2,022.1	2,386.1
Current account balance	785.9	−1,283.2	−880.8	−2,434.9	−1,496.0
Current account/GDP (%)	5.4	−6.8	−4.5	−12.6	−7.0
International reserves of the CNB (millions of U.S. dollars)	1,405.0	1,895.2	2,314.0	2,539.0	2,700.0
Liquid foreign assets of commercial banks	902.4	1,369.5	1,992.1	2,333.2	2,400.0
External debt	2,821.5	3,336.4	4,808.4	6,661.6	7,600.0
External debt/GDP (%)	19.3	17.7	24.3	34.3	35.3
Net external debt/GDP (%)[d]	3.5	0.4	2.5	9.3	11.6
Short-term foreign debt/ total foreign debt (%)[d]	1.8	6.8	8.9	8.1	8.9
Short-term foreign debt/total reserves (%)[e]	2.6	7.3	10.5	15.5	22.3
FDI/GDP (%)	0.7	0.5	2.7	1.8	2.2

a. Author's projections for 1998 (projections done in May 1998).
b. Increase in the rate of inflation is due to the one-time effect of VAT introduction, estimated to be around 1.5 percent. Core inflation remains around 3.5 percent.
c. Commodity exports and imports in millions of U.S. dollars, as recorded in the balance of payments.
d. Foreign debt outstanding minus sum of international reserves of the central bank and liquid short-term foreign assets of commercial banks.
e. Includes only short-term foreign liabilities as recorde in the foreign debt database.
f. Short-term debt is increased for cumulative foreign portfolio investment.

Naturally, the question is whether the central bank is the right place for policymakers to worry about external position and the size of the capital flows. One can argue that central banking should be defined more precisely and narrowly in terms of setting a transparent target such as exchange rate, money, interest rate, or inflation to gain and keep credibility. Any additional goal can lead to conflict among multiple goals and instruments, which can erode credibility.

These considerations are especially relevant for transition countries, where a new institutional infrastructure and market-economy culture are being built from scratch. An important tradeoff arises in such an environment. On one hand, policymakers desperately need an anti-inflationary reputation because, without it, it is impossible to reach inflation levels that do not harm the long-run growth. It is also impossible to build sound public finances in a high inflation environment. On the other hand, transition is a very complex social process, and an economy is exposed to a number of exogenous (nonpolicy) shocks (such as trade reorientation, changes in people's preferences, and so on). In this kind of environment it is preferable for policymakers to have free hands to be able to respond to shocks. However, free hands can imply two types of failures: failure of abuse of freedom (which occurs when policymakers are tempted to execute an unexpected policy shock, which leads to the loss of reputation and negatively affects social welfare in the long run) and coordination failure (which occurs when monetary policymakers want to achieve conflicting targets—that is, overambitious monetary authority).

Croatian authorities followed the "free-hands" policy. Exchange-rate policy was the only exception, and it is discussed later in the chapter. One example of the free-hands policy response occurred in April 1998. From October 1993 until April 1998, capital inflows were on a liberal regime. In April 1998, new restrictions were imposed. Obligatory kuna deposits have to be held by commercial banks with the central bank in the amounts of

- 10 percent of foreign banks' interbank deposits with domestic commercial banks,
- 10 percent of the value of guarantees issued by banks for foreign borrowing of their clients up to three years,
- 30 percent of the value of short-term foreign borrowing up to one year and 5 percent for borrowing up to three years.[1]

Visual inspection of Figures 12.1 to 12.5 will reveal part of the rationale underlying these measures. Consider Figure 12.1, and note that the domestic-currency broad monetary aggregate (M2) increased steadily until the end of the third quarter of 1997, then leveled off, and even declined slightly in the first half of 1998. Mark the difference between M4 and M2, which reflects foreign-exchange deposits held by residents at domestic banks. M4 did not level off and declined as M2 did; M4 just slowed down its growth in the last two quarters on the graph, but residents' foreign-exchange deposits continued to flow in.[2]

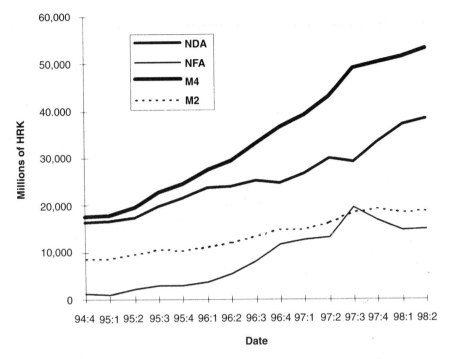

Figure 12.1.   M4, M2, NDA, and NFA in Croatia (end-of-quarter data)

Stagnation of M2 reflects a change in the stance of the monetary policy since September 1997, but it did not have any reflection on credit developments. On the contrary, net domestic assets (NDA) continued to grow in the last quarter of 1997 and in the first quarter of 1998 even more rapidly than before. This rapid increase was slowed down significantly only in the second quarter of 1998, after the new restrictions on capital inflows were imposed.

Domestic credit expansion in the last quarter of 1997 and in the first quarter of 1998 was financed by a rapid decline of the net foreign assets (NFA) of the banking system, mainly by banks' foreign borrowing. This rapid decrease stopped in the second quarter of 1998, after the new capital restrictions were imposed. Figure 12.2 shows how rapidly the net loan inflows from abroad reacted in this period despite of (or because of) restrictive monetary policy.[3] This process also led to a huge current account deficit of 12.6 percent of GDP in 1997.[4] It also inspired the decision to impose new capital restrictions. Data on the same Figure 12.2 also show a sudden

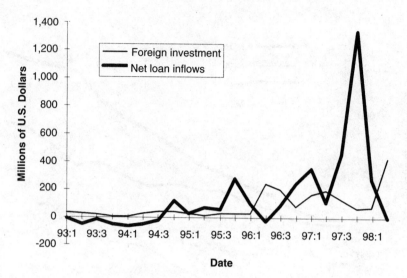

Figure 12.2.   Financing external deficit: net loan inflows and foreign (direct and portfolio) investment

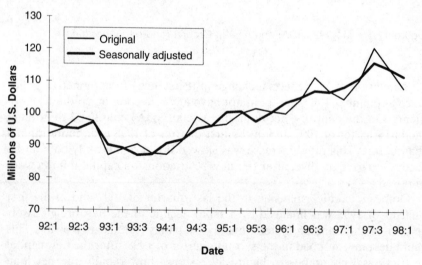

Figure 12.3.   Quarterly index of estimated GDP (1995 = 100)

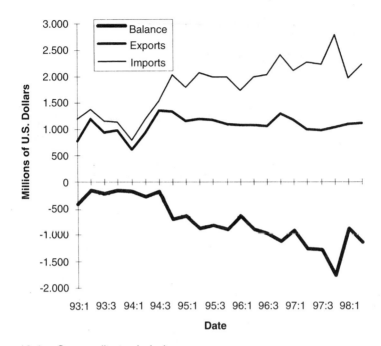

Figure 12.4.   Commodity trade balance

reversal of net loan inflows from abroad after introduction of new capital restrictions in early April 1998.

Figures 12.3 to 12.5 show the results[5] of such monetary developments. Real economic activity increased significantly (Figure 12.3), but in a transitional environment it is mainly driven by structural changes, expectations, and other influences beyond the scope of monetary policy measures. Figure 12.4 depicts international commodity trade deficit. Reader should pay attention to the development of the deficit because (1) it has strong influence on the overall external position of the economy and (2) it is the most sensitive (of all of the current account components) to the excess domestic demand. A widening commodity trade deficit absorbed the effects of expansion of domestic aggregate demand and alleviated the impact on prices (Figure 12.5). So Croatia recorded the lowest inflation among advanced transition countries since 1994.

Note that the 3 percent quarterly inflation rate in the first quarter of 1998 (Figure 12.5) cannot be explained by the demand impact. This inflation is a one-time initial impact that occurred due to the introduction of the value-added tax in January 1998. From February onward inflation was

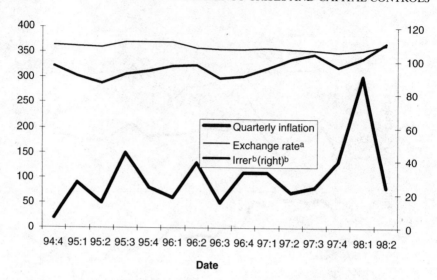

Figure 12.5. Exchange rate (kuna, versus DM, end quarter), CPI inflation (end quarter), and index of the real effective exchange rate (deflated by producers' prices)
[a] Normal exchange rate HRK/DEM
[b] *Index of real effective exchange rate with producers' prices (depreciation = increase).

brought in line with regular developments, comparable to the developments in the last five years.

However, price aggregate may not reflect the implications of policies exactly, so the real effective exchange rate with aggregate prices as deflator perhaps does not reflect the internal real exchange-rate developments exactly. Prices of home goods (nontradable) increased substantially faster than prices of tradable goods, so these price developments (hidden behind the aggregate) might also absorb part of the demand pressure beyond the part of the pressure that spilled over on imports. However, econometric investigation, which is presented in the next section, did not confirm this hypothesis in the short run. So it is more likely that the prices of domestic services (home goods) changed due to autonomous decisions by price makers (public utilities and local governments). These decisions were primarily motivated by the intention to diminish losses in the production of public services, increase wages in public utilities, or increase corporate savings to finance investment plans. So it seems that imports absorbed demand pressures. Restrictions to capital inflows might be needed to control imports, which absorbed part of the demand pressures that necessarily arise when the net capital inflows occurs in a country where the degree of the exchange-rate flexibility is low.

At the same time, neither the nominal or real effective exchange rate changed substantially. The nominal exchange rate versus the German mark has been kept rather stable since late 1993. The band has never been announced, but ex-post inspection of the series reveals that the range of variations since January 1994 was between 3.5 and 3.8 kuna per DM—that is, +/– 4.1 percent. This fact points to the nature of the monetary policy. Although the exchange-rate band has never been announced publicly, nominal exchange-rate stability provided an important anchor. However, the exchange-rate variation was wide enough to open the possibility for different monetary policy reactions to capital inflows.

In addition, central bankers may use the instruments to regulate international capital flows to control domestic credit if they fear that the excessive credit growth can lead to a lower quality of financial intermediation (accumulation of bad loans in the banking system). This factor played an important role in Croatia. The strongest growth of domestic credit occurred just before the new restrictions were imposed in April. This coincided with the problems that suddenly emerged in a few medium-sized banks that grew aggressively in 1996 and 1997.[6]

In conclusion, broadening a set of instruments to cover the management of international financial flows does not imply that monetary authorities will be overburdened with conflicting goals that may lead to policy coordination failure and loss of credibility. On the contrary, availability of instruments needed to manage international financial flows may be needed to restore the effectiveness of the monetary policy in the short run. More generally, they may be needed to keep the policy credible in a complex transitional environment where credibility is not a simple phenomenon because it depends on the whole set of economic developments, including evolution of home goods' prices, quality of financial intermediation, conciliation between fiscal and monetary policy, and structural reforms in general. In such an environment, there are circumstances when instruments are needed to liberalize capital flows, as well as circumstances when they are needed to restrict these flows, like in April 1998. In the case of Croatia, these instruments are in the hands of the central bank, which can activate and use them effectively in the short run.

The central bank, however, has an additional instrument at the disposal: banking supervision. Since capital restrictions can be motivated by the overly fast growth of banks' domestic credit financed from abroad (decrease in net foreign assets), restrictions can be interpreted as the second-best solution if the first-best solution (banking supervision) does not carry out desired outcomes. Of course, this interpretation is relevant if there is market failure in the banking system in times of net capital inflows from abroad (McKinnon and Pill, 1995).

Money, Credit, Fiscal Policy, and Imports

In this section I investigate the nature of the monetary transmission mechanism. I used Sims-type autoregression tests (that is, the information variable approach). The general (unrestricted) form of the model is

$$\Delta M_t = a + \sum_{i=1}^{n} b_i \Delta F_{t-i} + \sum_{i=1}^{n} c_i \Delta G_{t-i} + \sum_{i=1}^{n} c_i \Delta M_{t-i}, \tag{12.1}$$

where M stands for imports, F for monetary variable (credit or some money aggregate; elaborated later in the text), and G for fiscal policy variable. Imports are regressed on n lags of themselves and on the same number of lags of the other two explanatory variables (fiscal and monetary).

This specification enables testing for two types of restrictions. The first restriction that is imposed sets $b_i = 0$, $i = 1, \ldots, n$, so that the F test for validity of zero restrictions on parameters can be performed to see if any explanatory power of the model is lost if the monetary variable is omitted from the regression. The second type of restriction that is imposed is $c_i = 0$, $i = 1, \ldots, n$, so that the F test can be used to see if any explanatory power is lost if the fiscal variable is omitted from the regression. If the null-hypothesis H_0: $b_i = 0$, $i = 1, \ldots, n$, is true, it means that monetary variable carries no incremental information about changes in imports beyond the information carried by the fiscal policy variable and imports itself. By the same token, if the null-hypothesis H_0: $c_i = 0$, $i = 1, \ldots, n$, is true, it means that the fiscal policy variable carries no incremental information about changes in imports beyond the information carried by the monetary variable and imports itself.

It is important to note that this type of analysis goes beyond the problem of causality. As long as movements in fiscal policy variable do not contain information about future changes in imports beyond what is already contained in movements in imports itself and in a financial variable, policymakers can exploit this information in formulation of economic policy regardless of whether information is due to causation, reverse causation based on expectations, or mutual causation by some independent unobserved influence (such as real effective exchange rate). Friedman and

Kuttner (1992) pointed this out in a somewhat different context, and the method has been used extensively in the economic literature (see, e.g., Bernanke and Blinder, 1992, for the United States and Barran and Kegels, 1995, for Hungary).

The dependent variable is monthly merchandise imports on a c.i.f. basis, as reported in international trade statistics. Imports are expressed in DM because most of Croatian trade is denominated in DM. Expressing imports in DM reduces the variability of the time series of imports because of large fluctuations of the DM versus U.S. dollar exchange rate in the period of analysis. the estimation period begins in January 1994 and ends in May 1998.

Imports are used as a dependent variable for two reasons: first, imports can be interpreted as a proxy for real output, as there is no reliable monthly measure of real output.[7] Second, this is a variable that absorbed part of the demand pressures that would otherwise spill over to prices.[8]

Two alternative variables are used to describe the fiscal policy: the monthly series of the central government's expenditures (GS) and monthly series of the central government's deficit (D). Finally, five candidates for monetary variables are used: base money (M0), narrow money (M1), broad domestic money (M2), broad money (M4), and total credits to the private sector (C). The main difference between M4 and M2 are foreign-exchange deposits held by residents (see Figure 12.1 and comments).

All variables except fiscal deficit are expressed in ln form, and the results of stationarity tests as well as description of the series are shown in the appendix. All variables are $I(1)$ when expressed in ln form, and $I(0)$ when expressed in the first difference of the natural logarithm. However, using $I(0)$ variables is not a sufficient condition to be sure that the model is not misspecified. The number of lags had to be chosen in a way that eliminates serial correlation of residuals. In general, usual tests for the optimum number of lags (such as Akaike information criterion, AIC) do not ensure that the optimum number of lags is consistent with the absence of auto-correlation of residuals and presence of their normality properties (see, e.g., Harris, 1995). So, for each estimated equation I performed a test for auto-correlation up to the fifth order to be sure that the conclusions are derived from the equation where the autocorrelation problem was eliminated. Results are shown in Table 12.2.

Each unrestricted form of the imports equation combines one of the two fiscal variables (GS, D) with one of the five monetary variables (M0, M1, M2, M4, C). This gives ten general forms of the imports equation with three explanatory variables: lagged imports, fiscal variable, and monetary variable. Table 12.2 shows three properties of the general forms: R squared,

Table 12.2.   F statistics for fiscal and monetary variables in imports equations

Variable A	Variable B	Number of Lags	R^2	F (autocorrelations)	F (no A)	F (no B)
C	D	3	0.372	1.492	0.135	0.636
C	GS	3	0.355	2.076*	0.060	0.279
M0	D	7	0.565	1.435	1.320	0.480
M0	GS	3	0.382	2.003	0.624	0.343
M1	D	3	0.467	1.828	2.491*	1.058
M1	GS	4	0.501	1.095	2.796**	1.179
M2	D	4	0.490	2.198*	2.604**	0.308
M2	GS	6	0.651	1.617	3.644**	1.534
M4	D	8	0.811	0.571	3.274**	0.644
M4	GS	8	0.823	3.360*	4.793***	1.384

 * 10 percent significance level.
 ** 5 percent significance level.
 *** 1 percent significance level.

number of lags, and F-test for autocorelation up to the fifth order. For each of the general forms two restricted forms were tried: one with zero restriction on parameters with the fiscal variable, and another one with zero restriction on parameters with the mone-tary variable. So there are two additional F tests of the validity of zero restrictions on parameters reported for each of the ten models. The F(no A) label stands for the empirical value of the F test for zero restrictions on parameters with monetary variable (independent variable A), and the F(no B) label stands for the empirical value of the F test for zero restrictions on parameters with fiscal variable (indepen-dent variable B). All estimates are done in the first difference form, and asterisks stand for the level of significance: three asterisks for 1 percent significance level, two for 5 percent significance level, and one for 10 percent level.

Autocorrelation was successfully eliminated for a plausible number of lags in seven cases, so the method gives enough information for making con-clusions. The strongest conclusion is related to the fact that neither the fiscal deficit nor government spending has an impact on imports in the short run. One possible economic interpretation is that fiscal expenditures have a short-run impact on home goods. However, the econometric investigation (results are not shown here) showed that none of the fiscal and monetary variables used in this analysis can explain movements of prices of non-tradable goods. So it is more likely that the prices of domestic services (home goods) changed due to autonomous decisions by price makers—that is public utilities and local governments—to diminish losses in the production of public services, raise wages, or increase corporate savings to finance state-owned corporations' investment plans.

Furthermore, credits and base money have no significant impact on imports. Impact occurs with higher monetary aggregates: M1, M2, and M4. Note that credits and broad money lead to substantially different results regarding the short-run impact on imports, which points to the weak link between money and credit.

Finally, note that monetary and fiscal variables have been used in nominal form. The reason is to be found in the fact that nominal demand spills over to imports in a macroeconomic environment with a stable nominal exchange rate. Regression results with real variables of domestic demand (not shown here) indeed did not point to a different conclusion in comparison to nominal results presented here.

In conclusion, the short-run impact of money on imports justifies capital restrictions as a short-term policy tool for the control of money and domestic demand when there is an explicit or implicit exchange-rate peg. However, there is no evidence about the short-run impact of banks' domestic credit on imports. So, from the credit point of view, the rationale for capital restrictions can be found in controls of the banking market failure when banking supervision is inadequately developed.

The Role of the Exchange Rate and Interest Rate

Further investigation was undertaken to see if the two asset prices (exchange rate and interest rate) have any incremental short-run impact on imports beyond its movements, which are already explained by movements in money and lagged imports. The method applied was the same as in the previous section, but the exchange-rate and the interest-rate changes have been used instead of fiscal variables. Only M2 and M4 have been used as monetary variables for two reasons. First, analysis in the previous section has shown that the two aggregates have short-run impact on imports. Second, since M2 contains only domestic currency subaggregates and M4 includes a substantial part of foreign-exchange deposits (around 60 percent of M4), comparison of results for M2 and M4 can show whether inclusion of foreign-exchange deposits matters. Results for four equations are shown in Table 12.3.[9]

Results in Table 12.3 show that neither the exchange rate nor the interest rate has an impact on imports in the short run. Hence it remains unclear what the other short-run impacts on imports are beyond the

Table 12.3. F statistics for exchange rate (E)[a], interest rate (i)[a], and monetary variables in imports equations

Variable A	Variable B	Number of Lags	R2	F (autocorrelation)	F (no A)	F (no B)
M2	E	4	0.555	1.781	2.530*	2.012
M2	i	6	0.485	1.832	2.094*	0.615
M4	E	8	0.670	1.150	3.863***	1.164
M4	i	8	0.600	1.596	5.092***	1.085

a. For the exact description of the series see the appendix (notes below the table with the results of the unit root tests).
  * 10 percent significance level.
 ** 5 percent significance level.
*** 1 percent significance level.

impact of aggregate demand changes that are captured by the changes in broad money.

Regarding the nominal exchange rate, this result may be due to its low variability. Recall that the exchange rate versus DM fluctuated within the narrow band for more than four years, although the band has never been announced. Variability of +/– 4.1 percent (HRK/DEM) was too small to have any significant impact on imports, and most pressures on the exchange rate have been absorbed by variations in broad money and aggregate demand, as shown in the previous section.[10]

Regarding the nonexisting impact of interest rate on imports,[11] the result may be due to the role played by other factors that influenced the interest-rate variability but that have nothing to do with output and imports. For example, money-market interest rate in Croatia is very sensitive to the events in the banking system, and the variations of the risk premium induce strong variations of the interest rate irrespective of the balance between the total supply and the demand for reserve money. Money-market interest rate tends to move up sharply whenever a bank, which is perceived to be in problems, occurs on the demand side of the money market. Hence interest-rate movements do not have short-run impact on imports because the short-run interest-rate movements reflect banking-sector problems that do not have real implications in the short run, as long as these problems do not have systemic characteristics (such as contagion effects), which they did not have in Croatia under a period of investigation.

This line of reasoning again leads to another justification for the central bank's ability to influence international capital flows in the short run.

Policymakers can use the restrictions on inflows with a prime purpose to control credit growth and prevent banking-sector problems. Further justification for such thoughts is to be found in the fact that, if such channel works, in a system without restrictions on inflows, increase in domestic interest rate can lead to undesired (excessive) capital inflows. This can happen when foreign investors feel that an increase in interest rate is more than high enough to compensate for the systemic risk premium due to banking-sector problems. Since the quality and timeliness of information needed to make judgments about the banking sector is highly imperfect in Croatia (as well as in other transition economies), this is a real danger.

However, it is not possible to give firm econometric support to this argument within the framework of the short-run analysis. For example, it is impossible to prove (using the same method as in the previous section and this section) that credit growth had significant impact on the interest rate.[12] The result may be due to the wrong choice of the interest-rate variable, limitations of the short-run analysis,[13] and the insufficient size of the sample. The later two limitations apply to all the results presented here. Hence they should be interpreted exclusively in the short-run context, keeping in mind the constraints of the short-run analyses.[14]

Conclusions and Policy Implications

There are two strong arguments in favor of the central banks' ability to influence international capital flows in transition economies in the short run. First, restrictions on international capital flows can help to curtail the credit growth, which, if excessive, can lead to the banking-sector problems with real sector implications. Second, restrictions on international capital inflows can presumably influence money, credit, and the exchange rate, which might have some impact on imports and external performance.

Any policymaker who thinks about imposing the capital restrictions has to look for alternative policy measures that might be more efficient than capital restrictions. Fiscal policy is a natural candidate. The econometric analysis has shown that fiscal policy has no impact on imports in the short run. Banks' credits to the private sector also have no short-term impact on imports, but broad money exhibits significant influence. Since the nominal exchange-rate variations have been kept within a narrow range in Croatia, broad money and domestic credit variations partly reflected variations in international capital flows. Hence, management of money and banks' credit can be improved by introducing restrictions on these flows in the short run.

However, introduction of capital restrictions can be interpreted as the second-best solution if the banking supervision is underdeveloped and there are uncertainties regarding the short-run impact of fiscal policy.

Hence broadening a set of instruments to cover the management of international financial flows does not imply that monetary authorities will be overburdened with conflicting goals that may lead to policy coordination failure and loss of credibility. On the contrary, availability of instruments needed to manage international financial flows may be needed to restore effectiveness of the monetary policy in the short run. More generally, they may be needed to keep the policymakers' credibility in a complex transitional environment. In such an environment there are circumstances when instruments are needed to liberalize capital flows, as well as there are circumstances when they are needed to restrict these flows, like in April 1998. In the case of Croatia, these instruments are in the hands of the central bank, which can activate and use them effectively in the short run.

The span of analysis has been limited only to the short run. Hence the underlying belief is that restrictions to international capital flows can be effective only in the short run. There should always be a commitment toward long-run liberalization of international capital flows becauseof superior allocation that occurs in the liberalized environment. However, transitional environment is burdened with market imperfections such as banking-sector failures, which may justify use of restrictions in the short run. By the same token, policymakers should commit theselves to use the first-best solution (strong banking supervision) in the long run. Long-run relationships, however, remained beyond the scope of the analyses presented in this chapter due to the short history of relevant time series.

Appendix: Unit Root Tests

ADF test statistics for all series in levels (logs) and first differences are shown in Table 12.4. Series D (fiscal deficit) and i (money-market interest rate) are not in the form of the natural logarithm (D contains negative values). ADF test statistics are shown for five versions of equations for each series. Versions differ only in respect to the number of lags. Maximum lag length (k) is set to five initially. A constant was included in all regressions, which makes rejection of the null of no stationarity harder than in the case with no deterministic components (see, e.g., Harris, 1995). An asterisk is used to mark significance level: three asterisks for 1 percent significance level, two for 5 percent significance level, and one for 10 percent level.

Table 12.4. ADF test statistics for unit root tests

Series	k = 1	k = 2	k = 3	k = 4	k = 5
M	−2.905*	−2.840*	−2.479	−2.603*	−2.105
ΔM	−7.261***	−7.873***	−4.701***	−4.133***	−4.205***
GS	−2.133	−1.461	−0.930	−0.477	−0.646
ΔGS	−7.318***	−7.168***	−6.729***	−5.721***	−5.181***
D	−4.023***	−2.702*	−2.309	−2.001	−2.089
ΔD	−7.992***	−6.079***	−5.027***	−3.800***	−3.906***
C	−0.462	−0.462	−0.365	−0.439	−0.488
ΔC	−4.796***	−3.229**	−3.045**	−2.756*	−2.851*
M0	−2.963**	−3.195**	−3.244**	−3.546**	−2.621*
ΔM0	−4.915***	−3.888***	−2.830*	−1.988	−3.726***
M1	−2.263	−2.447	−1.890	−1.438	−2.086
ΔM1	5.697***	1.126***	3.292**	−2.389	−4.297***
M2	−3.773***	−3.267**	−1.246	−1.330	−1.027
ΔM2	−3.188**	−4.491***	−2.743*	−4.020***	−5.216***
M4	−1.973	−1.905	−1.967	−1.656	−2.101
ΔM4	−5.170***	−3.851**	−3.203**	−2.402	−2.449
i	−1.958	−2.109	−2.118	−1.779	−1.951
Δi	−2.717*	−2.456	−2.711*	−2.075	−2.113
E	−2.741*	−2.437	−2.153	−1.983	−2.364
ΔE	−3.735***	−2.954**	−2.646*	−2.144	−2.439
P	−1.806	−1.218	−0.983	−0.690	−0.733
ΔP	−5.249***	−3.772***	−3.083**	−2.624*	−2.325

List of variables: M is natural log of monthly goods' imports c.i.f. expressed in german marks; GS is natural log of the monthly central government total spending expressed in million of kuna; D is monthly deficit of the central government in millions of kuna; C is natural log of monthly total banks' credit to the private sector in millions of kuna; M0 is natural log of monthly base money in millions of kuna; M1 is natural log of monthly narrow money in millions of kuna; M2 is M1 + natural log of kuna savings and time deposits; M4 is M2 + other quasi money, mainly forex deposits; i is monthly nominal money market interest rate; E is natural log of kuna versus 100 DM exchange rate, monthly data being averages for intramonth daily data; P is natual log of home goods' price index (1994: 01 = 100), which is equal to index of prices of services used to calculate the cost-of-living index.
    * 10 percent significance level.
   ** 5 percent significance level.
  *** 1 percent significance level.

Critical values for the ADF test are calculated at the basis of MacKinnon's (1991) tables.

The table of results shows that there are two types of series. First, there are series for which the results of the ADF unit root tests strongly support the conclusion that the series in the first difference form is stationary—that is, the original series is I(1). By strong support I mean that the result holds irrespective of the number of lags in the test equation. For example, a null hypothesis of no stationarity cannot be rejected for government spending (GS) in levels but is rejected at 1 percent significance level when a series is transformed in the first difference form. And this result holds for all lags. A similar conclusion holds for credits (C), although at the 1 percent significance level for k = 1, 5 percent for k = 2, 3 and 10 percent for k = 4, 5, as well as for imports. Although null can be rejected in levels for k = 1, 2, 4 at 10 percent level for imports, it can be rejected as well for imports in the first difference form, but at 1 percent significance level regardless of the number of lags. In general, for credit and imports, results in the first difference form are superior over the results in levels irrespective of the number of lags.

For monetary aggregates (M0, M1, M2, and M4), central government budget balance (D), interest rate (i), exchange rate (E), and home goods' prices (P), the evidence is inconclusive. For a deficit, results in the first difference form dominate for k = 2, 3, 4, 5, but for k = 1 both level and first difference form lead to the same conclusion that null can be rejected at 1 percent level. For M0, results in the first difference form dominate for k = 1, 2, 5, but for k = 3,4 reverse conclusion holds. For M1 it is impossible to reach a conclusion at k = 4. For M2, null is rejected both for level and first difference form at k = 1. For M4 the evidence is inconclusive for k = 4, 5, etc.

It is well documented in the literature that unit root tests may lead to dubious results, especially when nonnormality properties of residuals occur in the test equations. The biggest problem is the problem of serial correlation of residuals in equations that are used for computation of ADF test statistic.

Table 12.5 shows results of autocorrelation tests for residuals up to the fifth order in equations that are used to compute the ADF test statistic. F-type test of validity of zero restrictions on lagged residuals in the test equation is shown in Table 12.5. Results from Table 12.4 are interpreted at the basis of results from Table 12.5. Relevant conclusions at the basis of ADF test statistic can be made only for equations for which results in Table 12.5 suggest that the problem of autocorrelation of residuals has been eliminated. This excercise was undertaken for eight series for which the evidence from Table 12.4 was mixed. Again, asterisks represent significance level. Here, a significant test statistic means that null of no autocorrelation is rejected. So results from Table 12.4 can be used to

Table 12.5.   F-statistic for validity of zero restrictions on parameters with lagged residuals up to the fifth order (test of autocorrelation of residuals)

Series	$k = 1$	$k = 5$	$k = 6$	ADF (level)	ADF (Δ)
DEF	1.752	1.650			
M0	3.912***	4.293***	1.295	−1.391	−3.346**
M1	5.110***	4.293***	1.523	−1.500	−5.107***
M2	15.530***	1.508			
M4	4.844***	6.574***	2.718**	−0.986	−3.189**
i	1.966	0.758			
E	1.585	3.803*			
P	1.441	1.337			

  * 10 percent significance level.
 ** 5 percent significance level.
*** 1 percent significance level.

make conclusions only if results from Table 12.5 show no autocorrelation of residuals in particular equation.

During the econometric work it came out that for some series the auto-correlation of residuals tends to be high at a low number of lags and then declines as the number of lags grows. So in Table 12.5 only relevant results are displayed: results for k = 1 and k = 5 for all inconclusive cases, and for k = n, n > 5 (where n is the number of lags in the equation where null of no autocorrelation up to fifth lag of residuals is accepted), for those equations where autocorrelation was still present till the fifth lag. As there are no ADF test statistics reported in Table 12.4 for k > 5, two additional columns are added in Table 12.5, representing ADF test statistics for cases where k > 5 was needed to eliminate autocorrelation of residuals. It came out that with k = 6 null of no autocorrelation could be accepted for M0 and M1, while for M4 test statistics was at minimum with six lags. For higher number of lags, evidence in favor of autocorrelation was even stronger for M4.

Analysis of autocorrelation obviously provides substantial new infor-mation. There is no autocorrelation in the test equation for M2 with five lags. At the basis of the data from Table 12.4, it follows that M2 is I(1) and it is stationary when taken in the first difference form. Furthermore, there is no autocorrelation in tests for M0 and M1 with six lags. Additional ADF test statistics shown in Table 12.5 point to the fact that M0 is I(1) (5 percent significance level) as well as M1 (1 percent significance level).

There is no such straightforward conclusion for broad monetary aggregate M4. A test with six lags minimizes the value of the F statistics, but autocorrelation is still probably present in the model. So there is no new additional information coming out from the extended analysis because the ADF test statistics in Table 12.4 points to the fact that ΔM4 is integrated of the order zero already at the low number of lags, but the null of no autocorrelation has to be rejected.

There are no indications of autocorrelation in different tests for budget deficit. The only strong argument in favor of the mixed evidence is the result with only one lag. As the number of lags grows, evidence in favor of D being I(1) becomes stronger. Since a greater number of lags is generally preferred, I will stick to the conclusion that ΔD is stationary.

The same conclusion holds for the exchange rate. Autocorrelation is eliminated in the equation with one lag, where the test clearly points to the fact that ΔE is stationary. For interest rate and home goods' prices, both equations with k = 1 and k = 5 are relevant, so the evidence is inconclusive. However, the pattern of behavior of the test statistics as the number of lags grows strongly points to the fact that ΔP is stationary, and I stick to the same conclusion, although with less confidence, regarding the series of interest rate.

Acknowledgments

I am thankful to Vanja Jelić and Igeta Drinovac for preparation of the time series used in this chapter. Responsibility for the results is mine only. I am also thankful to the participants at the Fourth Dubrovnik Conference on Transition Economies for their useful comments on the first draft of this essay. I am especially grateful to Robert Feldman (IMF), who was discussant of the draft of the paper. The responsibility for all the views expressed in this essay is mine only.

Notes

1. Note that the first measure is applied on average basis, while the second and third measures are applied on a marginal basis. In addition, a reader should note that obligatory deposit with the central bank is nonremunerated, so that the oportunity cost is equal to $i*D$, where D is the amount of the deposit and i is money-market nominal interest rate. In addition to that, a depost can be withdrawn when the contract expires, so there is no obligation to keep the deposit for, say, one year, regardless of the intrayear duration of the contract. Hence, these measures cannot be interpreted as a tax on speculative inflows. The reason is that these restric-

tions were not imposed because of speculative inflows. It will be shown later in the chapter that the main motive was to restore the impact of monetary policy on the balance of payments.

2. This type of inflow, however, became much weaker than in the last few years when the repatriation of foreign-exchange savings was especially strong.

3. The third important source of financing (repatriation of foreign-exchange deposits) is not shown in Figure 12.2 because there is no comparable quarterly series, but this flow can be approximated by the difference between M4 and M2 in Figure 12.1. Figure 12.2 contains enough information for making conclusions relevant to the subject of this chapter.

4. The deficit was partly influenced by the one-time shock that occured prior to introduction of the value-added tax in January 1998. The importers accumulated large stocks of imported goods in November and December 1997 because of uncertainity created by the introduction of the new tax system. It has been estimated that this effect accounted for U.S. $400 to $500 million higher imports than normal in the two months. However, if this effect is taken into account (subtracted from actual deficit), current account deficit of around U.S. $2 billion would be equal to 10.4 percent of GDP. Note that the same reasoning can be applied to the net loan inflows shown in Figure 12.2. If the net loan inflows of around U.S. $1.4 billion in the last quarter of 1997 would have been lower by U S $400 to $500 million due to lower need for financing the trade deficit, it would be on the strong rise anyway.

5. The word *result* here does not imply simple causal impact of monetary and credit developments on real economic activity, goods and assets prices, and external balances. Some links may be causal, but some can be more complex.

6. Annual rate of growth of total credits to the private sector reached 44 percent in December 1997. In March 1998 problems emerged in the fifth bank by size and in July in the sixth bank by size. Additional problems emerged in one small bank and a small savings bank. All of the problem banks were characterized by aggressive deposit taking in 1996 and 1997, so these banks represent textbook cases of moral hazard and adverse selection. In addition, two of the medium-sized problem banks had access to foreign sources of financing.

7. Seventy percent of Croatian imports are intermediary and capital goods imports, which implies a high correlation with a true measure of real activity.

8. If tariffs were higher and/or the exchange rate lower.

9. The estimation period is shortened in comparison with analysis in the previous section for two monthly observations. January and February 1994 are excluded from the estimation period because the asset prices were still showing high poststabilization (the exchange rate and prices stabilized in November 1993) variability at the very begining of 1994.

10. The same result holds when a measure of the real exchange rate is used instead of nominal exchange rate. The difference between natural logs of nominal HRK/DEM exchange rate and producers' price index was used first, and then the natural log of real effective exchange-rate index (deflated by producers' prices) was used second. The result was practically the same as in the regression shown in the text.

11. Short-run impact of interest rate on imports can be transmitted through two different channels. First, a lower interest rate may induce higher imports via positive impact on real output. Second, a higher domestic interest rate may induce debtors to substitute domestic debt by cheaper foreign debt, which can indirectly influence relative price of domestic versus foreign inputs and lead to substitution of domestic inputs by foreign inputs (higher imports). The same substitution can be transmitted via banks' balance sheets: if the interest rate on domestic currency deposits goes up, banks may substitute marginally more expensive domestic sources of financing by marginally cheaper foreign liabilities, which leads (ceteris paribus) to higher surplus on the financial account of the balance of payments (higher current account deficit). Note that the two transmission channels are not mutually exclusive, and they work in

the opposite direction. Channel via output implies that higher interest rates lead to lower imports, while channel via substitution implies that higher domestic interest rates lead to higher imports. If both channels work with similar size of the impact, econometric investigation cannot reveal these impacts. So the channels have to be tested separately. Since there is no reliable short-run measure of real output, I investigated the impact of domestic deposit interest rates on banks' foreign liabilities as well as the impact of banks' foreign liabilities on imports. The method that was applied was the same as in the main part of the chapter, and the results showed that the short-run impact does not exist. This is broadly in line with the main empirical findings.

12. The rationale is that the money-market interest rate is a proxy for the banking-sector problems.

13. Two-variable cointegration test was performed to see if there is long-run relationship between credit and interest rate. I found no evidenece of any long-run relationship.

14. Estimates of the short-run parameters can be biased if they are not part of the long-run cointegration analyses.

References

Barran, F., and C. Kegels. (1995). "Channels of Monetary Policy in a Transition Country: Hungary." Mimeo, Université catholique of Louvian.

Bernanke, B., and A. Blinder. (1988). "Credit, Money and Aggregate Demand." *American Economic Review* 78(2): 435–439.

Bernanke, B., and A. Blinder. (1992). "The Federal Funds Rate and the Channels of Monetary Transmission." *American Economic Review* 82(4); 901–921.

Cottarelli, C., and A. Kourelis. (1994). "Financial Structure, Bank Lending Rates, and the Transmission Mechanism of Monetary Policy." IMF Working Paper 94-39. Washington, DC: IMF.

Friedman, B., and K. Kuttner. (1992). "Money, Income, Prices and Interest Rates." American Economic Review 82(3): 472–492.

Harris, R.I.D. (1995). *Using Cointegration Analysis in Econometric Modelling.* London: Prentice-Hall/Harvester Wheatshaf.

Koskenkyla, H. (1994). "The Nordic Banking Crises." Bank of Finland Bulletin, August.

Koskenkyla, H., and J. Vesala. (1994). "Finish Deposit Banks 1980–1993: Years of Rapid Growth and Crises." Bank of Finland Discussion Papers 16-94.

McKinnon, R., and H. Pill. (1995). "Credible Liberalizations and International Capital Flows: The Overborrowing Syndrome." Mimeo, Stanford University.

Nyberg, P., and V. Vihriala. (1994). "The Finish Banking Crisis and Its Handling (An Update of Developments Through 1993)." Bank of Finland Discussion Papers 7-94.

VII CURRENCY BOARDS

13 SOME REFLECTIONS ON CURRENCY BOARDS

Steve H. Hanke
The Johns Hopkins University

The dramatic events in Asia and Russia, and the contagion they have spread, have generated a torrent of commentary about exchange rates, hot money, and exchange controls. As someone who was deeply involved in Indonesia (Monetary Mischief, 1998) and who predicted that the ruble would collapse by midyear (Hanke, 1998b), I offer my views as to why most of the commentary has been either half-baked or simply wrong. Indeed, in most instances the international chattering classes have misdiagnosed the patient and, in consequence, prescribed the wrong medicine. A correct diagnosis requires an understanding of alternative exchange-rate regimes.

Exchange-Rate Regimes

There are three types of exchange-rate regimes: floating, fixed, and pegged rates. Each type has different characteristics and generates different results (see Table 13.1). Although floating and fixed rates appear to be dissimilar, they are members of the same family. Both are free-market mechanisms for international payments. With a floating rate, a monetary authority sets a monetary policy but has no exchange-rate policy: the exchange rate is on

Table 13.1. Exchange-rate regimes

Type of Regime	Exchange-Rate Policy	Monetary Policy	Source of Monetary Base Monetary Policy	Conflicts Between Exchange Rate and	Balance-of-Payments Crisis
Floating rate[a]	No	Yes	Domestic	No	No
Fixed rate[b]	Yes	No	Foreign	No	No
Pegged rate[c]	Yes	Yes	Domestic and foreign	Yes	Yes

Source: Hanke (1988a).

a. Floating rates are employed in most developed countries.

b. Fixed rates are employed in several developing countries or regions: Hong Kong (1983), Argentina (1991), Estonia (1992), Lithuania (1994), Bulgaria (1997), and Bosnia 1998.

c. Pegged rates are employed in most developing countries and also among the countries that are members of Europe's Exchange Rate Mechanism.

autopilot. In consequence, the monetary base is determined domestically by a monetary authority. With a fixed rate, a monetary authority sets the exchange rate but has no monetary policy: monetary policy is on autopilot. In consequence, under a fixed-rate regime, the monetary base is determined by the balance of payments. In other words, when a country's official net foreign reserves increase, its monetary base increases and vice versa. With both of these free-market exchange-rate mechanisms, there cannot be conflicts between exchange-rate and monetary policies, and consequently balance-of-payments crises cannot occur. Indeed, under floating and fixed-rate regimes, market forces act to automatically rebalance financial flows and avert balance-of-payments crises.

While both floating and fixed-rate regimes are equally desirable in principle, it must be stressed that floating rates, unlike fixed rates, do not perform well in developing countries because these countries usually have weak monetary authorities and histories of monetary instability. For a recent dramatic example, we have to look no further than Indonesia. It floated the rupiah on August 14, 1997. Unfortunately, but not surprisingly, the rupiah did not float on a sea of tranquillity. Indeed, the rupiah fluctuated wildly and lost over 80 percent of its value against the U.S. dollar in six months.

Another example of the perils of floating is illustrated by the experience of Hong Kong (Culp and Hanke, 1993). It floated the H.K. dollar in November 1974, when the H.K. dollar was trading at about 5H.K.$/U.S.$. Prior to the float, Hong Kong operated with a currency board and a fixed exchange rate, with sterling as the anchor currency.

After the float, the H.K. dollar was volatile and steadily lost value relative to the U.S. dollar. The volatility reached epic proportion in late September 1983, after the end of the fourth round of Sino-British talks on the future of Hong Kong. Indeed, financial markets and the H.K. dollar went into tailspins.

At the end of July 1983, the H.K. dollar was trading 7.3 H.K.$/U.S.$. By Black Saturday, September 24, the H.K. dollar had fallen to 9.55H.K.$/U.S.$, with dealer spreads being reported as large as 10,000 basis points. Hong Kong was in a state of panic, with people hoarding toilet paper, rice, and cooking oil.

The chaos ended abruptly on October 15, when Hong Kong reinstated a currency-board system. The new anchor currency was the U.S. dollar, and the exchange rate has remained fixed at 7.8H.K.$/U.S.$ ever since.

Fixed and pegged rates appear to be the same. However, they are fundamentally different. Pegged rates are not free-market mechanisms for international payments. Pegged rates require a monetary authority to manage both the exchange rate and monetary policy. With a pegged rate, the monetary base contains both domestic and foreign components. Unlike floating and fixed rates, pegged rates invariably result in conflicts between exchange-rate and monetary policies. For example, when capital inflows become "excessive" under a pegged system, a monetary authority often attempts to sterilize the ensuing increase in the foreign component of the monetary base by reducing the domestic component of the monetary base. And when outflows become "excessive," an authority attempts to offset the decrease in the foreign component of the base with an increase in the domestic component of the monetary base. Balance-of-payments crises erupt as a monetary authority begins to offset more and more of the reduction in the foreign component of the monetary base with domestically created base money. When this occurs, it's only a matter of time before currency speculators spot the contradictions between exchange-rate and monetary policies and force a devaluation. This is what happened in Turkey and Mexico in 1994. The same story repeated itself during the summer of 1997 and most recently in Russia. It's time for the international chattering classes to drop their dogma and learn a lesson from history, lest history repeat itself.

The Proof of the Pudding Is in the Eating

Base money is the purview of monetary authorities, either central banks or currency boards. Central banks have broad latitude to create base money. Currency boards do not have that flexibility. A currency-board system requires domestic notes and coins, as well as deposits held at the board, to be fully covered (usually at 100 to 110 percent) by foreign reserves denominated in the board's designated foreign anchor currency. Furthermore, the domestic currency must trade, without restrictions, at an absolutely fixed exchange rate with the anchor currency. An orthodox currency board cannot create credit. Therefore, it cannot extend credit to the fiscal authorities or act as a lender of last resort for the banking system. Currency boards run on automatic pilot, with changes in the monetary base determined solely by changes in the demand for domestic base money—the balance of payments. Table 13.2 presents the characteristics of currency boards and contrasts them with those of central banks.

Currency boards have a rich history. The first currency board was established in 1849, and beginning about 1913 that system spread rapidly throughout most parts of the world. In the 1950s and 1960s, many currency

Table 13.2.

Typical Currency Board	Typical Central Bank
Usually supplies notes and coins only	Supplies notes, coins, and deposits
Fixed exchange rate with reserve currency	Pegged or floating exchange rate
Foreign reserves of 100 percent	Variable foreign reserves
Full convertibility	Limited convertibility
Rule-bound monetary policy	Discretionary monetary policy
Not a lender of last resort	Lender of last resort
Does not regulate commercial banks	Often regulates commercial banks
Transparent	Opaque
Protected from political pressure	Politicized
High credibility	Low credibility
Earns seignorage only from interest	Earns seignorage from interest and inflation
Cannot create inflation	Can create inflation
Cannot finance spending by government	Can finance spending by government
Requires no preconditions for monetary reform	Required preconditions for monetary reform
Rapid monetary reform	Slow monetary reform
Small staff	Large staff

Note: The characteristics listed are those of a typical actual currency board or central bank, especially one in a developing country, and not those of a theoretically ideal or exceptionally good currency board or central bank.

boards were abandoned and replaced by central banks. This was a remarkable development. The performance of currency boards had been excellent. All had maintained full convertibility into their anchor currencies. Furthermore, countries with boards had realized price stability, respectable economic growth, and balanced government budgets.

The demise of currency boards resulted from a confluence of three factors. A choir of influential economists was singing the praises of central banking's flexibility and fine-tuning capacities. In addition to changing intellectual fashions, newly independent states were trying to shake off their ties with their former imperial overlords. And the International Monetary Fund (IMF), anxious to obtain new clients and jobs for the boys, lent its weight and money to the establishment of new central banks. In the end, the Bank of England provided the only institutional voice that favored currency boards. That was obviously not enough. Politics, not the economic record, prevailed.

The picture began to change in 1983. After the currency crises of May to September 1983, Hong Kong stopped floating and reestablished its currency-board system. In the 1990s currency-board systems have gained broader acceptance, with boards being established in Argentina (1991), Estonia (1992), Lithuania (1994), Bulgaria (1997), and Bosnia (1998).

These developments trouble some analysts who fret about the inflexibility of currency boards. *The Economist* summarized these sentiments in a piece titled "The Great Escape," which appeared in the May 3, 1997, issue. That article asserted that currency boards cannot cope with external shocks, that they are vulnerable to surges in inflation triggered by capital inflows, and that with limited lender-of-last-resort capacities they cannot deal effectively with financial emergencies.

The evidence does not support these oft-repeated assertions about the alleged drawbacks of currency boards. Let's look at the data from ninety-eight developing countries during the period 1950 to 1993 (see Table 13.3). The data are separated into one of two categories: countries that have pegged exchange rates and those that have fixed rates. The latter category includes countries that have currency boards, have monetary institutes, and rely solely on foreign currency. Countries with currency boards or board-like systems (fixed exchange rates) have had average growth of rates that were 54 percent times higher than those with pegged exchange rates. Furthermore, the variability of those growth rates (as measured by their standard deviations) was virtually identical, indicating that the lack of discretionary monetary policy with fixed exchange rates did not result in any greater incidence or vulnerability to external economic shocks. As for inflation, fixed rates have proved far superior to pegged rates, with average inflation rates being 4.9 times higher in countries with pegged rates and 4.2 times more variable. In terms of budget deficits, those countries utilizing pegged rates have had deficits that on average were 65 percent larger. Finally, countries with fixed rates have experienced fewer financial emergencies.

Not only has the relative performance of fixed rates (currency boards) been favorable, but so has their performance over time. When currency boards have been introduced, credibility has been established, the demand for local currency has increased along with foreign-exchange reserves. Consequently, through interest-rate arbitrage, interest rates have fallen dramatically.

The superior performance of fixed rates (currency boards) has also been reported in Schuler (1996) and Ghose, Gulde, and Wolf (1998). That said, it is important to acknowledge that currency-board systems are not trouble free. Argentina provides but one case study.

Table 13.3. Performance of fixed versus pegged exchange-rate regimes

Variable	Mean (percent)	Median (percent)	Standard Derivation (percent)	Number of Observations	Minimium (percent)	Maximum (percent)
Annual GDP growth rate						
Complete sample	1.85	1.90	6.57	3,229	−47.40	45.10
Pegged rates	1.69	1.90	6.53	2,694	−47.40	45.10
Fixed rates	2.61	2.60	6.73	535	−32.70	31.80
Annual inflation rate						
Complete sample	29.38	7.71	185.36	3,186	−22.06	4,770.35
Pegged rates	33.79	9.10	201.35	2,663	−22.06	4,770.35
Fixed rates	6.95	3.29	47.86	523	−14.95	1,075.93
Budget deficit as a percent of GDP						
Complete sample	3.43	2.50	4.98	2,107	−22.62	36.65
Pegged rates	3.66	2.70	5.18	1,769	−22.62	36.65
Fixed rates	2.22	1.70	3.53	338	−5.81	20.27

Note: The fixed-rate category also includes countries that were fully dollarized.

Some Thoughts on Argentina's 1995 Crisis

The Convertibility Law (currency board law) was tested in November 1992 and April 1994, when unfounded fears of a devaluation briefly pushed short-term peso interest rates into high double digits. In November 1992, for example, financial markets interpreted a package of new tariffs and export subsidies as a signal that the next step might be a devaluation. The monetary base shrank 300 million pesos, or 3 percent, and interest rates on short-term peso deposits peaked at 85 percent. However, those tests were brief compared to the test Argentina underwent after the Mexican peso was devalued on 20 December 1994. (See Table 13.4 for a summary of the major crisis events in Argentina.) Mexico's currency troubles caused many foreign investors to reappraise investments throughout Latin America in a rather indiscriminate manner. Financial markets slumped not only in Mexico but in Argentina, Brazil, and Chile.

The shock imposed on Argentina by Mexico's financial crisis had four distinct phases (BCRA, 1995). The first phase lasted from December 20, 1994, through February 1995. External drains form the currency board-like system occurred, with the central bank's liquid reserves falling from $15.8 billion before the crisis to $13.3 billion at the end of February. (Note that Argentina's system is not orthodox because only 80 percent of the system's reserves must be held in dollar-denominated assets issued by foreign governments. These are called *liquid reserves*. The remaining reserves must be dollar denominated but can be issued by the Republic of Argentina. Both types of reserves must be valued at current prices.) There were also internal drains of peso deposits from commercial banks. Wholesale banks and small retail banks were most strongly affected. Two small wholesale banks, with a high proportion of their assets in Argentine government bonds, were suspended. (See Table 13.5 for a summary of key financial indicators.)

During the first phase, the broad money supply, M3 (pesos outside banks plus peso and dollar deposits), decreased by 3.6 billion pesos, or 6.5 percent, by the end of February. And bond prices fell sharply, with yields on peso-denominated bonds moving from 22.6 percent before the crisis to 38.9 percent at the end of February. The prime rate on peso-denominated loans also increased during the period, from 12.4 to 22.7 percent. Dollar-denominated bond yields and the dollar prime rate also increased, but not by as much as those on comparable peso-denominated instruments. The peso-dollar bond-yield spreads, for example, increased from 480 basis points to 930 basis points (Pre 1 versus Pre 2 bonds), reflecting an increase in the perceived exchange-rate risk.

Table 13.4. Chronology of Argentina's "tequila-Effect" financial crisis

December 20, 1994	First phase of crisis begins as Mexican peso is devalued 15 percent against U.S. dollar. Pressure on Argentina and other Latin American financial markets results. Depositors begin to withdraw deposits in late December.
December 22	Mexican peso floated.
January 12, 1995	Argentine central bank (BCRA) eliminates spread between buying and selling rates for dollars, reduces reserve requirements for commercial banks, requires commercial banks' required reserves to be held in dollars, and establishes limited safety net.
February 27	Second phase of crisis begins as international banks cut lines of credit to Argentina. Interbank interest rates jump sharply. BCRA law and Law on Financial Institutions amended. Fiduciary Fund for Provincial Development created to help privatize banks owned by provincial governments.
March 10	BCRA allows commercial banks to use up to 50 percent of vault cash to fulfill reserve requirements.
March 14	Height of crisis. Government announces package of measures to contain the crisis, including cuts in government spending, tax increases, and domestic ("patriotic") and foreign bond sales.
March 28	Bank Capitalization Fiduciary Fund created to help privately owned banks with liquidity problems.
Early April	Third phase of crisis begins as situation stabilizes and interest rates begin to fall.
April 12	Deposit Guarantee Fund created to provide deposit insurance.
May 14	Fourth and final phase of crisis begins as President Carlos Menem is reelected. Deposits return to banking system. Interest rates fall further.
July	Definitive end of crisis as interest rates and deposits draw closer to precrisis levels.

The central bank took steps to tighten the link between the peso and the dollar. On January 12, it eliminated the spread between buying and selling rates for dollars, making the rate exactly 1 peso = U.S.$1. It also required banks to hold their current accounts at the central bank in dollars instead of pesos (these accounts are used for clearing and

Table 13.5. Argentine financial indicators

	Phase 1	Phase 2	Phase 3	Phase 4	Crisis Ends	Postcrisis
1. Beginning date of phase	12/15/94	3/1/95	4/1/95	5/15/95	7/31/95	7/31/96
2. Liquid reserves (billions of U.S. dollars)	$15.8	$13.3	$10.2	$11.3	$12.8	$16.1
3. Peso deposits (billions)	$22.3	$19.3	$17.5	$17.7	$19.2	$24.8
4. Dollar deposits (billions)	$22.9	$23.0	$20.8	$19.5	$21.1	$26.7
5. M3 (billions of U.S. dollars)	$55.2	$51.6	$47.2	$47.4	$50.3	$62.6
6. Peso prime rate	12.4%	22.7%	28.1%	24.5%	14.4%	10.5%
7. Dollar prime rate	9.3%	13.5%	20.7%	19.4%	12.2%	9.1%
8. Peso bond yield	22.6%	38.9%	40.8%	28.0%	26.5%	13.6%
9. Dollar bond yield	17.8%	29.6%	27.6%	20.9%	21.5%	10.6%
10. Bond yield spread (b.p.) (peso yield-dollar yield)	480	930	1320	710	500	304

reserve requirements). That reduced the central bank's potential gain from a devaluation.

To increase the liquidity of banks, the central bank temporarily reduced reserve requirements on deposits on December 28 and again January 12. On January 12, it also established a safety net (lender of last resort facility) financed with two percentage points of existing required reserves. These funds could be loaned to solvent banks with liquidity problems. Previously, there had been a private, voluntary safety net to buy loans from banks with temporary liquidity problems.

Subsequently, the government took further action to assure bank liquidity. Decree 286 of February 27 created the Fiduciary Fund for Provincial Development to help privatize banks owned by provincial governments, many of which were notoriously weak. Decree 290 of February 27 amended the Organic Law of the central bank to broaden its power to lend to illiquid banks and amended the Law of Financial Institutions to allow the central bank to play a more active part in reorganizing troubled institutions.

The liquidity squeeze that the financial system had endured became a true crisis in the second, posttequila phase, which started in late February 1995 and lasted through March. On February 27, the international banks with branches in Argentina cut off credit lines to their branch operations, citing "country risk" as the rationale for such drastic action. This shocked branch bank managers and sent them scurrying unprepared into the domestic interbank market. The consequences were predictable. The interbank interest rates rose dramatically, from about 20 percent on peso deposits to over 50 percent within hours after the international credit lines were cut. Also, the massive entry of the international branch banks into the interbank market was interpreted as a vote of no confidence for Argentina's currency board-like system. Consequently, both external drains from the currency board-like system and internal drains from the commercial banks became great floods.

It is important to stress that the withdrawal of the credit lines from the international banks was the event that pushed Argentina from a liquidity squeeze into a liquidity crisis. Viewed from a historical perspective, this event is unusual, if not unique. With absolutely fixed exchange-rate regimes, either currency boards or the classical gold standard (1880–1914), foreign banks have provided liquidity during times of liquidity squeezes (Hanke, Jonung, and Schuler, 1993). Indeed, private foreign banks have traditionally acted as lenders of last resort in absolutely fixed exchange-rate systems. This was not the case in Argentina because its currency-board-like system was relatively immature and untested. Argentina had to pay a price for the sins of its monetary past.

Fuel was added to the crisis, when in the last days of February rumors spread that the government might freeze deposits, as it had done with the "Bonex plan" of early 1990. Many people were also apprehensive that the decrees of February 27 were a prelude to broader powers that would reduce the rule-bound nature of the currency-board-like system. There was also fear that a possible devaluation in Brazil would have effects in Argentina.

In March, the broad money supply fell by 4.4 billion pesos, or 8.5 percent; it reached its low point for the crisis at the end of the month. Peso deposits, dollar deposits, and currency outside banks all fell, reflecting a desire by many Argentines to hold their money outside the local financial system, either in dollar deposits abroad or dollar caches locally. Interest rates jumped; the peso prime rate increased from 22.7 percent at the end of February to a peak of 45 percent in March. Dollar interest rates also increased, with the prime rate peaking at 30 percent. The exchange-rate risk exploded, with the peso-dollar interest rate spread moving from 930 basis points at the end of February to 1,647 basis points at its peak. Since dollar interest rates were many times those prevailing in the United States, market participants evidently perceived that there was a high risk that borrowers of dollars would default or that the Argentine government would interfere with loans and deposits in dollars.

With the crisis worsening the central bank took additional measures to further increase liquidity for banks. On March 10, it temporarily allowed all banks to use up to 50 percent of their peso and dollar vault cash to fulfill reserve requirements and allowed banks that had bought assets from institutions with liquidity problems to use the remaining 50 percent in the same way. The central bank also used its excess reserves to make short-term loans (discounts and repos) exceeding 900 million pesos to solvent banks with liquidity problems. As a result of its loans and the reduction in pesos outside banks, the central bank's liquid reserves fell to a low of 10.2 billion pesos at the end of March, compared with 15.8 billion pesos in late December. However, at no time during the crisis did the ratio of liquid reserves to the monetary base fall below the statutory minimum of 80 percent.

On March 14, the government announced a package of measures, totaling 11.4 billion pesos, to contain the financial crisis. It accelerated privatizations. It reduced its planned government spending by 2 billion pesos, including cutting the wages of senior government employees by 5 to 15 percent. it increased several taxes, most important the value-added tax (a temporary increase of the rate, from 18 to 21 percent). And it announced plans to borrow up to U.S.$7 billion—a three-year $1 billion domestic "patriotic" bond issue from Argentines, a three-year $1 billion bond issue from private foreign lenders, and $5 billion from the IMF, World Bank, and Inter-American Development Bank.

Argentina's success in putting together the (oversubscribed) $1 billion Patriotic Loan turned the corner. The loan was a convincing domestic affirmation of the creditworthiness of the Menem-Cavallo administration, and the IMF et al. tagged along. This soon opened up the system with a fall in interest rates as dramatic as the February-March rise. The crisis was over.

From the beginning of April to the presidential election of May 14, phase three, the crisis leveled off in some respects and eased in others. The broad money supply remained approximately constant: dollar deposits decreased, while peso deposits and pesos outside banks actually increased. Interest rates declined slightly; the peso prime rate eased from about 28.1 percent at the beginning of April to 24.5 percent in mid-May. Perceived exchange-rate risk also declined, with the peso-dollar spread narrowing from 1,320 basis points at the beginning of April to 710 basis points in mid-May. And on April 12, the government announced the creation of a privately financed, voluntary Deposit Guarantee Fund for peso and dollar deposits.

Despite the crisis, the Convertibility Law continued to enjoy support across the political spectrum, including the three leading candidates and parties in the presidential election. Nonetheless, people were apprehensive about what might happen if President Menem were defeated or forced into a runoff election. However, President Menem's reelection in the first round and the strong showing of his Justicialist Party in Congress calmed the fears that a change in the government would undermine the Convertibility Law.

After the presidential election, all monetary indicators improved, marking the last phase the crisis, which ended by the beginning of August. Interest rates fell; the peso prime rate fell from 24.5 percent in mid-May to 14.4 percent by late July, while the dollar prime rate fell from about 19.4 to 12.2 percent in the same period. The broad money supply increased, though by the end of July it was still about 9 percent below the precrisis level. Pesos outside banks, peso deposits, and dollar deposits all registered increases. Bank credit to households and businesses, which had fallen about 4 percent from the beginning of the crisis to the low point at the end of April, began to recover. Further, the central bank reduced its repos by about half between the end of March and the end of July, while its liquid reserves held against the monetary base rose above 90 percent. The perceived exchange-rate risk also eased, with the peso-dollar spread narrowing from 710 basis points at the beginning of phase three to 500 basis points at the end of July.

At the end of July 1996, the Argentine monetary indicators were superior to their the pretequila magnitudes. The peso-dollar exchange rate remained absolutely fixed at 1 to 1. And inflation for 1995 was 1.6 percent, one of the lowest rates in the world and the lowest annual inflation in Argentina since 1944. The central bank's liquid reserves increased to reach $16.1 billion, slightly greater than the pretequila level of $15.8 billion. Peso denominated time deposits in July 1996 were $2.5 billion higher than in December 1994, and M3 exceeded its December 1994 level by $7.4 billion. And the peso and dollar prime interest rates were 10.5 and 9.1 percent, respectively. Both rates were lower than their pretequila levels. The perceived exchange-rate risk was actually lower than the precrisis level, with the peso-dollar spread at 304 basis points, 176 basis points lower than the precrisis spread. Like tempered steel, Argentina's currency-board-like system was toughened by the crisis, as the peso-dollar spread indicates. Although the financial indicators were superior to their pretequila levels (see Table 13.5), the real economy remained restrained. Real GDP declined by 4.4 percent in 1995 and didn't become positive again until the second quarter of 1996 (3 percent). Unemployment increased from 12.2 percent in October 1994 to a peak of 18.6 percent in May 1995. Although the unemployment rate fell to about 17 percent in July 1996, it remains stubbornly high.

Lessons from the Argentine Experience

1. Currency boards, much like the classical gold standard, provide a constraint on monetary authorities. This is not to say that the monetary authorities do not attempt to maneuver around the constraints. Indeed, writing about the gold standard in 1932, Professor F.A. Hayek concluded that "Every effort has been made to obviate [the gold standard's] functioning at any point at which there was dissatisfaction with the tendencies which were being revealed by it" (Hayek, 1984). Argentina's recent experience shows that the authorities also squirmed as much as they could within the confines of Argentina's currency board-like system. However, as much as the monetary authorities tried to maneuver and introduce discretion into Argentina's rule-bound, absolutely fixed-rate system, they failed to shake its irksome constraints.

2. Consequently, currency boards create price stability, even in times of severe crisis.

3. The hard budget constraints imposed by currency boards motivate deeper liberal economic reforms, as well as desired automatic adjustments

in the economy. For example, before the Mexican crisis, Argentina's banking system was notoriously weak. Given that Argentina's Central Bank could not print pesos at will or act liberally as a lender of last resort, many analysts thought that the weak banking system would be Argentina's Achilles' heel. It was not and is not. Argentina's banking system is rapidly being strengthened and consolidated, with a few weak banks going to the wall and many more being bought by strong banks. By the end of 1996, 80 percent of all Argentinean deposits were held in the twenty-five largest banks. In addition, virtually all the weak banks owned by the provinces were on the block in a mass privatization (Fernández, 1996). The discipline imposed by the currency board has put in place a virtuous cycle. Indeed, Argentina's banking system is now rated as the strongest in Latin America.

4. And perhaps most important, the results produced by currency board systems can give politicians a platform from which they can win elections.

Argentina's Devaluation Risk Revisited

From the beginning, many observers have been skeptical that the exchange rate of one peso per dollar would be durable. Peso instruments have carried higher interest rates than dollar instruments with the same country risk; for example, Argentine government peso bonds have carried higher interest rates than the government's dollar bonds of similar maturity.

As late as November 1995, well after the tequila-effect crisis, Bank of America's "Global Financial Markets Forecast" was forecasting that in February 1996 the exchange rate would be 1.50 pesos per dollar. And in 1993, Deutche Bank conducted a risk assessment and concluded that the possibility of the peso being devalued within the next few years was 20 to 40 percent. In early 1995, financial markets agreed: spreads between peso and dollar financial instruments of similar risk and maturity widened from low single digits to as much as 16 percent at the height of the crisis. The country risk spread between Argentina and the United States was widening at the same time by about the same amount, reflecting fears that even dollar assets in Argentina were not safe because the government might repeat the Bonex plan and freeze all deposits, whether in dollars or pesos. The combined effect of country risk and exchange risk led to spreads of 30 to 40 percent over interest rates in the United States at the height of the crisis.

Why were so many people so wrong about the risk of devaluation and of default? A few market participants perceived to devaluation risk and were aggressive investors in Argentine bonds, but they were a small minority (Hanke, 1994, 1995). For the rest, two factors seem to have been at work. One was a misunderstanding of how Argentina's currency-board-like system functions. People thought that the peso had a pegged rate with the dollar rather than a truly fixed rate, so they feared that the Argentine peso would be as susceptible to devaluation as, say, the Mexican peso was. They did not appreciate that, thanks to the Convertibility Law, the Argentine Central Bank held sufficient dollar reserves to withstand a speculative attack. Moreover, with convertibility, the Argentine Central Bank was forced to allow the monetary base to automatically shrink in response to a drain of dollar reserves. This prevented the monetary base from getting far out of line with the demand for pesos. Under a pegged exchange rate, in contrast, central banks frequently keep expanding the monetary base until it is well out of line with demand, and a speculative attack and devaluation serve to bring the real value of the monetary base closer to demand.

It is interesting to note that overnight interest rates remained in mid-double digits even at the height of the crisis. Argentina did not experience the triple-digit interest rates that occur when a devaluation becomes almost a sure thing in the view of market participants. For example, overnight interest rates for the Swedish krona reached 500 percent (annualized) shortly before the krona was devalued against the German mark in 1992. Rates of hundreds of percent have also been common for other pegged exchange-rate systems when they drew near to devaluation. The comparatively low rates in Argentina indicate that, although fear of devaluation was high, expectations of devaluation never became concentrated on a period of a single day or weekend.

Another misunderstanding was former Minister Cavallo's views about speculative attacks and devaluations. He understood that the ultimate weapon against an attack was the full dollarization of the Argentine economy, and he was prepared to use it. By eliminating the peso-dollar exchange rate through dollarization, the possibility of a devaluation would be eliminated. In consequence, even in the worse case scenario, a devaluation in Argentina was not a real possibility.

The other factor that led people to fear devaluation and default was Argentina's long history of botched monetary reforms. Under central banking, Argentina has had frequent devaluations and few periods of monetary stability, especially since World War II. The Menem government had to demonstrate that it was different from previous governments, which were fervently for sound money in their rhetoric but undermined it with their actions. Argentina's currency-board-like system does not yet have the credibility of Hong Kong's currency board system, but its good performance in

1995 earned it new respect, as shown by the narrowing of country risk and devaluation risk. It has become a more mature system.

For a number of reasons, the probability of a devaluation of the peso is close to zero for the next several years. The Convertibility Law worked well through the financial crisis and has support across the political spectrum; there is virtually no sentiment to change it. President Menem has said that the peso will never be devalued while he is in office (his term expires in 1999); given his record, his statement is highly credible. The financial system is now stronger than before because the weakest private banks have been merged into stronger ones and the provincial banks are being privatized. At the same time as the financial system is better able to withstand stress, it is less likely to encounter it. Foreign banks have learned that cutting off credit to their Argentine branches during a financial squeeze costs them profits. Other foreign lenders have also learned that a financial squeeze presents opportunities for interest-rate arbitrage with no risk of devaluation. People have a better understanding of how the system works and are better able to assess accurately the true devaluation risk. In consequence, interest-rate spikes in Argentina will become less frequent, less severe, and of shorter duration.

These conclusions about the peso's devaluation risk and the continuing maturity of the convertibility system have been confirmed by the markets. Specific confirmation comes from the Central Bank's successful establishment of a liquidity fund. Initially, the Central Bank set the fund size at $3 billion. However, it received bids for $6.3 billion from thirteen international banks. The oversubscription represents a major vote of confidence and will ensure that international credit lines are available to meet the type of liquidity crisis that was set off in February 1995, when international banks cut their credit lines to their Argentine branches.

Argentina's Unemployment Problem

Unemployment has been the great cloud over the economic progress Argentina has achieved since 1991. Unemployment averaged 5.5 percent from 1985 to 1989 but has increased since then; it was 12.2 percent in October 1994 and peaked at 18.6 percent in May 1995, before falling to 16.4 percent in October 1995. At present, unemployment remains stubbornly high.

High unemployment in Argentina is a problem caused by laws that make labor markets inflexible and structural changes that have occurred in Argentina's economy. Convertibility and monetary policy have not been the causes of high unemployment. To appreciate this, consider that Argentina's economy grew 35 percent from 1991 to 1994. In that period, almost 1 million new jobs were created in the formal sector of the economy, and employment in the informal economy also boomed. However, unemployment increased from 7.4 percent in 1990 to 11.5 percent in 1994. Convertibility, therefore, generated record levels of aggregate demand in Argentina and many new jobs. However, the demand side boom also increased the labor participation rate, from about 40 percent prior to convertibility to approximately 42.5 percent in May 1995. Even though new jobs were being created during the boom, the number of new jobs was not enough to absorb all the new labor-market participants. In consequence, the unemployment rate continued to climb during the boom period. The economic slump of 1995 has simply added a business cycle component to the worsening long-term unemployment trend.

Until the current government came to power in 1989, economic policy had for many decades been based on "import substitution"—building domestic industry by protecting it from foreign competition with trade barriers. Argentina became a closed economy with many inefficient industries. Workers in protected industries benefited from greater job security and higher wages than they otherwise would have had. To gain the support of labor unions, a very important constituency, successive governments allowed the unions wide-ranging powers. One such power was the principle of "ultra-activity," meaning that if a contract between a union and employers lapsed before a new contract had been agreed to, the provisions of the old contract applied. In practice that meant that the gains unions made were cumulative and that employers had no leverage to introduce more flexible policies. Labor laws made it difficult for employers to fire employees, required sectorwide wage negotiations (convenios colectivos), and required high indemnification for employees. And social security taxes drove a wedge of almost 50 percent between before-tax and after-tax wages.

The economic reforms of the Menem government, including the extensive reduction in trade barriers and the Convertibility Law, introduced deep structural changes. The changes increased the ability of Argentine firms to import foreign capital equipment and to gain access to foreign financing. Labor Laws remained largely unreformed because the government did not think the political timing was right, so labor markets remained rigid. From 1991 to 1995, the cost of capital decreased 25 percent relative to the cost of labor. The federal and provincial governments and privatized former government enterprises, which had been overstaffed, released workers onto a labor market that was not flexible enough to create jobs for all. Additionally, the workforce grew larger as more women and immigrants participated. The informal economy is fairly extensive in Argentina, and some officially unemployed people work in the underground economy.

With convertibility, the Central Bank imposed a hard budget constraint on the fiscal authorities. In consequence, the government could not resort to make-work, public-works projects to soak up the excess labor released by restructuring the economy and increase labor-force participation rates. This, in combination with inflexible labor markets, resulted in increased unemployment rates.

The government moved quite slowly on reforming labor laws until July 1994. In the aftermath of the tequila crisis, the government seems more committed to labor reforms. Several acts have been passed that make the labor market more flexible. It is now easier for employers to hire workers for short periods and on a trial basis. Small firms are exempt from some of the rigid labor laws that apply to larger firms. Social security taxes have been reduced for inexperienced workers up to twenty-five years old and part-time workers. Employers are exempt from paying unemployment compensation to workers dismissed after less than three months. Disability compensation has been reformed to reduce costly litigation (Laws 24.013, 24.465, 24.467, 24.557). Even though the government is committed to the strategy outlined by the "Jobs Study" of the Organization for Economic Co-operation and Development (OECD, 1995), major labor reforms that would reduce the structural ("natural") rate of unemployment in Argentina remain bogged down, however.

Prices, Inflation, and Argentina's Competitiveness

Many analysts claim that the peso is overvalued. Although GDP per person in Argentina is roughly one-third the level of the United States, real estate and the prices of some services are as expensive in Buenos Aires as in New York. Travelers to Argentina notice that the taxi to their hotel is expensive, that the hotel is expensive, and that restaurants in downtown Buenos Aires are expensive, too. From their casual investigation, some foreigners conclude that the peso is overvalued and must eventually be devalued, so that taxi rides, hotels, and restaurants will no longer be so expensive. Incidentally, foreigners often have their views confirmed by Argentine exporters, who frequently assert that the peso is overvalued.

Under conditions of free trade and low transport costs, goods arbitrage ensures the same price level and rate of inflation of traded goods in the currency board country and its anchor currency country. In consequence, wholesale price inflation should tend to be the same in both countries because wholesale price indexes are largely composed of traded goods, such as foodstuffs, minerals, and manufactures.

Unlike wholesale prices, consumer prices can diverge between the two countries on a sustained basis because consumer price indexes contain both traded and nontraded goods. Nontraded goods have local markets that are less closely linked to international markets because transport costs are higher compared to the cost of the goods. This makes arbitrage between markets for nontraded goods more difficult, so their prices can diverge more or less permanently.

This divergence between consumer prices in two countries is motivated when the rate of productivity growth in tradables in one country is higher than nontradables in that country, and when it is also higher than the rate of productivity growth for tradables in the other country. With a currency board and an absolutely fixed exchange rate between the two countries, goods arbitrage ensures that the wholesale prices between the two countries will be the same. And the only way to keep relative prices in line with the relative productivity paths is to have higher inflation in the currency-board country's nontradables and a higher rate of growth in the currency-board country's consumer price index than in the anchor currency country's consumer price index.

Since Hong Kong reestablished its currency board in 1983, these consumer and wholesale price relationships have existed: Hong Kong's consumer prices have risen much more rapidly than wholesale prices, and Hong Kong's consumer prices have risen more rapidly than those in the United States, precisely because productivity in Hong Kong's tradables has exceeded that for tradables in the United States, Hong Kong's anchor currency country.

Has the Hong Kong dollar become overvalued, and have Hong Kong's exporters become uncompetitive? The answer to both these questions is a resounding no (Hawkins and Yiu, 1995). To understand this, one has to realize that to determine whether a country's currency is overvalued or undervalued a purchasing power parity calculation (or a closely related real effective exchange-rate calculation) must be made. These calculations require the use of price indexes in the countries that are being compared. When focusing on competitiveness, it is the wholesale price indexes (tradables), not the consumer prices indexes (tradables and nontradables) that should be used (G.T. Management, 1995).

If the proper calculations are made with Argentina's and the United States' wholesale price indexes, the Argentine peso is not overvalued. Indeed, the real effective exchange rate has remained remarkably stable since the currency-board-like system was installed in 1991. Argentina's strong export growth (exports increased 32.4 percent in 1995, a year of negative GDP growth, compared with 1994), confirms this conclusion.

Many analysts have come to the incorrect conclusion that the Argentine peso is overvalued because they use consumer price indexes when calculating either the peso's purchasing power parity or real effective exchange rate. Indeed, when the consumer prices indexes are used, the peso appears to be approximately 45 percent overvalued, and Argentine exports appear to be uncompetitive.

Some Thoughts on Indonesia

Both theory and evidence soundly support the use of currency boards in developing countries. So why is there such an intense debate about currency boards and fixed exchange rates? Politics, both domestic and international, has provided most of the fuel for the debate and controversy. Economics often has little to do with the choice of an exchange-rate regime. There is no better example of this than Indonesia.

By the first week of February 1998, President Suharto knew that he would be finished if he failed to stabilize the rupiah at a reasonable level.

As Suharto saw it, the IMF, by its own admission, had botched the closing of sixteen banks in November. This aggravated Indonesia's economic troubles by setting off a financial panic and capital flight. In an attempt to stabilize the rupiah, Indonesia signed a second IMF agreement on January 15. That agreement failed to address the rupiah's problems. In consequence, the markets promptly jumped all over the rupiah and put it into a free-fall. Loaded with external debt, Indonesia's private sector was bankrupt. Workers were losing their jobs. And if that wasn't bad enough, prices were rising as a result of the rupiah's devaluation and the Bank of Indonesia's (BI) November–January explosion of credit.

What antidote could counteract this deadly cocktail? As Suharto'sspecial counselor, I proposed a comprehensive rupiah stabilization program.Its linchpin was a currency-board system (CBS), an idea that was endorsed by Nobelists Milton Friedman, Gary Becker, Merton Miller, and Margaret Thatcher's economic guru Sir Alan Walters, among others. My program also included proposals for external debt restructuring, bank restructuring and recapitalization, privatization, a bankruptcy code overhaul, and the breakup of crony capitalism.

The CBS proposal, however, created a firestorm of controversy. Most of the objections to my Indonesian stabilization program amounted to little more than ad hominem attacks on me (for a critique of these attacks, see "Monetary Mischief," 1998) and do not merit comment. The so-called substantive critiques of my comprehensive proposal can be dismissed, too. Indeed, none of the critics had ever read the confidential documents that contained my proposals. This is clear from the fact that the critics made a great deal of general noise about currency boards but never made substantive comments about my detailed CBS proposal and failed to mention one word about other essential parts of my stabilization program.

Some Thoughts on Russia

On his return from the Boar War, Winston Churchill remarked that "Nothing in life is so exhilarating as to be shot at without success." That's how I felt in September of 1998, when Russia, with the blessings of the IMF, gave serious consideration to the CBS idea. This time around, the debate was more civilized than it had been in the case of Indonesia. But the level of substantive discourse was just as low. For example, *The Economist* of September 5, 1998, contained an evaluation of a Russian CBS. This, and other commentary on that topic were meaningless without a CBS law to debate, however. To promote more substantive debate, a Russian CBS law, which I proposed in September, is presented below.

A Currency Board System

To put the ruble on a sound competitive footing, the Russian government should produce a currency-board-system law immediately and announce that it will be implemented as soon as possible. And to work in Russia, a CBS must be ultraorthodox. Indeed, if it is modeled after the currency-board-like systems in Hong Kong, Argentina, Estonia, Lithuania, Bulgaria, and Bosnia, it will probably fail.

To implement a CBS in Russia's truly unique situation, ultraorthodoxy must be embraced, so that the CBS commands the respect and confidence of the justifiably skeptical Russian people. The following orthodox CBS monetary constitution (law) is complete and suited for Russia's truly unique conditions:

1.   The Russian Currency Board System (CBS) is hereby created. The purpose of the CBS is to issue notes and coins in CBS rubles and

to maintain them fully convertible at a fixed exchange rate into a reserve currency as specified in paragraph 6.

2. The CBS shall have its legal seat in Switzerland.

3. a. The CBS shall be governed by a board of five directors. Three directors shall be non-Russian citizens appointed by the Bank for International Settlements in Basel. They shall not be employees of the International Monetary Fund or its member governments. Two directors shall be appointed by the government of Russia with at least one of the directors chosen by the government of Russia.

    b. A quorum shall consist of three member of the boards of directors, including at least one of the directors chosen by the government of Russia. Decisions shall be by majority vote, except as specified in paragraph 15.

    c. The first two directors appointed by the Russian government shall serve terms of one and four years. The first three directors appointed by the Bank for International Settlements shall serve terms of two, three, and five years. Subsequent directors shall serve terms of five years. Directors may be reappointed once. Should a director resign or die, the Bank for International Settlements shall choose a successor to complete the remainder of the term if the former director was a foreigner, or the government should choose the successor if the former director was a Russian.

4. The board of directors shall have the power to hire and fire the CBS's staff and to determine salaries for the staff. The by-laws of the CBS shall determine salaries for the directors.

5. The CBS shall issue notes and coins denominated in CBS rubles. The notes and coins shall be fully convertible into the reserve currency. The notes shall be printed outside Russia. The CBS may accept deposits of the reserve currency.

6. a. The reserve currency is the foreign currency or the commodity to which the CBS ruble has a fixed exchange rate. Initially, the reserve currency shall be the U.S. dollar, and the fixed exchange rate shall be one CBS ruble equals one dollar.

    b. Failure to maintain the fixed exchange rate with the reserve currency shall make the CBS subject to legal action for breach of contract according to the laws of Switzerland. This provision does not apply to embezzled, mutilated, or counterfeited notes, coins, and deposits or to changes of the reserve currency in accord with paragraph 13.

7. The CBS shall charge no commission for exchanging CBS rubles for the reserve currency, or the reverse.

8. The CBS shall begin business with foreign reserves equal to at least 100 percent of its notes and coins in circulation and deposits with it. It shall hold its foreign reserves in securities or other forms payable only in the reserve currency. These reserves shall be held on deposit at the BIS. The CBS shall not hold securities issued by the national or local governments of Russia or by enterprises owned by those governments.

9. The CBS shall pay all net seignorage (profits) into a reserve fund until its unborrowed reserves equal 110 percent of its notes and coins in circulation and deposits. It shall remit to the government of Russia all net seignorage beyond that necessary to maintain 110 percent reserves. The distribution of net seignorage shall occur annually.

10. The head office of the CBS shall be in Moscow. The CBS may establish branches or appoint agents in other cities of Russia. The CBS shall also maintain a branch in Switzerland.

11. The CBS shall publish a financial statement, attested by the directors, monthly or more often. The statement shall appraise the CBS's holdings of securities at their market value.

12. The CBS may issue notes and coins in such denominations as it judges to be appropriate.

13. Should the annual change in the consumer price index in the reserve country fall outside the range—5 percent to 20 percent for more than two years, or 10 percent to 40 percent for more than six months—the CBS must, within sixty days, either
   a. Devalue (if the change in the index is negative) or revalue (if the change in the index is positive) the CBS ruble in terms of the reserve currency by no more than the change in the index during the period just specified, or
   b. Choose a new reserve currency and fix the exchange rate of the CBS ruble to the new currency at the rate then prevailing between the new reserve currency and the former reserve currency.

14. If the CBS chooses a new reserve currency in accord with paragraph 13, it must convert all its foreign reserves into assets payable in the new reserve currency within one year.

15. The CBS may not be dissolved nor may its assets be transferred to a successor organization except by unanimous vote of the board of directors.

16. Beyond an initial loan of reserves from the International Monetary Fund, the CBS may not accept loans or grants of reserves from international agencies or foreign governments.
17. Exchanges of currency by the CBS shall be exempt from taxation by the Russian governments.
18. CBS rubles and the reserve currency shall be legal tender for paying taxes and settling debts in Russia. However, they shall not be forced tender for contracts between private parties.

In addition to legalizing the use of foreign currencies and adopting a currency-board law, the Russians must amend Russian contract law. With a currency board, the ruble-dollar exchange rate would be absolutely fixed. To facilitate relative price adjustments, all other prices in Russia should be allowed to fluctuate freely in relation to the fixed price of the ruble. The indexing of contracts in Russia should, therefore, be strictly prohibited.

The devil always resides in the details, particularly in Russia. Anything less than an ultraorthodox CBS will not command the confidence of the Russian people and doom a Russian CBS.

References

Argentina. Laws (published in *Boletín Oficial de la República Argentina*).

BCRA. Banco Central de la República Argentina. *Boletín Estadístico*, various issues.

BCRA. Banco Central de la República Argentina. *Boletín Monetario y Financiero* (English version: *Bulletin of Monetary and Financial Affairs*), various issues.

BCRA. Banco Central de la República Argentina. *Indicadores Económicos*, various issues.

BCRA. Banco Central de la República Argentina. *Memoria Anual*, various issues.

BCRA. Banco Central de la República Argentina. Communications (to financial institutions).

Culp, C.L., and S.H. Hanke. (1993). "The Hong Kong Linked Exchange Rate Mechanism: Monetary Lessons for Economic Development." Department of Economics, Johns Hopkins University.

Fernández, Roque B. (1996). "Briefing to the Finance Committee of the Chamber of Deputies." *Bulletin of Monetary and Financial Affairs*, Banco Central de la República Argentina (May–March):

Ghosh, A.R., A.M. Gulde, and H. Wolf. (1998). "Currency Boards: The Ultimate Fix?" Working Paper 98-8. Washington, DC: International Monetary Fund.

"The Great Escape." (1997). *The Economist*. May 3.

G.T. Management (Asia) Ltd. (1995). *Emerging Market Trends* (March).

Hanke, Steve H. (1994). "Arbitrage in Argentina." *Forbes* (December 19).

Hanke, Steve H. (1995). "Why Argentina Is Solid." *Forbes* (May. 8).

Hanke, Steve H. (1998a). "How to Establish Monetary Stability in Asia." *Cato Journal* 17(3).

Hanke, Steve H. (1998b). "Is the Ruble Next?" *Forbes* (March 9).

Hanke, Steve H., Lars Jonung, and Kurt Schuler. (1993). *Russian Currency and Finance: A Currency Board Approach to Reform.* London: Routledge.

Hawkins, John, and Matthew Yiu. (1995). "Real and Effective Exchange Rates." In *Money and Banking Hong Kong.* Hong Kong: Hong Kong Monetary Authority.

Hayek, F.A. (1984). *Money, Capital and Fluctuations: Early Essays.* Edited by Roy MacCloughry. Chicago: University of Chicago Press.

"Monetary Mischief." (1998). *Far Eastern Economic Review* (July 2).

OECD. (1995). *The OECD Jobs Study: Implementing the Strategy.* Paris: Organization for Economic Co-operation and Development.

Schuler, K. (1996). *Should Developing Countries Have Central Banks?* Research Monograph No. 52 London: Institute of Economic Affairs.

"Should Russia Try a Currency Board?" *The Economist,* September 5.

14 THE CENTRAL BANK OF BOSNIA AND HERZEGOVINA
Its History and Its Issues
Warren Coats
International Monetary Fund

Introduction

The Dayton peace agreement signed in Paris on December 14, 1995, ended almost four years of devastating war. The treaty provides for the continued existence of Bosnia and Herzegovina within its previous internationally recognized borders and its governance under a central (state) government with very limited powers. The state is responsible for the country's foreign relations. The most important economic responsibilities of the state are monetary and foreign-exchange-rate policy (through a new central bank), external borrowing, and the formulation of countrywide trade and customs tariff policies. Other economic responsibilities are carried out mainly by two entities and their subunits.

The Dayton treaty stipulated that Bosnia and Herzegovina would establish a central bank that operated under currency-board rules for at least its first six years and that its governor would be appointed by the International Monetary Fund (IMF). The Central Bank of Bosnia and Herzegovina (CBBH) started limited operations August 11, 1997, and expanded its operations throughout the country in April and May 1998.

This chapter reviews the background of the currency-board provision of the Dayton agreement, the issues that arose in drafting the central-bank law, and the practical problems that were encountered in operating under currency-board rules in the context of Bosnia and Herzegovina. The version of the central-bank law, and hence of the currency-board arrangement, that was finally adopted and implemented differed in some respects from the version proposed by the IMF. The differences reflect the political c ompromises needed to bring all three ethnic groups to a final agreement with which all were comfortable. None of these compromises has (in my judgment) sacrificed the basic principles of a currency-board arrangement agreed to in Dayton.

The interface between the CBBH and the payment bureaus descended from the Yugoslav Service for Social Bookkeeping (SDK)—the government monopoly provider of domestic payment (and other) services—that operate in the three regions of Bosnia and Herzegovina, posed and continue to pose particular challenges for the operations of the CBBH, and these are discussed in some detail. The chapter sets out a general proposal for the future evolution of the payment-bureau system into a normal bank-based payment system.

Political Background

The Monetary and Exchange Affairs Department's (MAE's) involvement with Bosnia and Herzegovina began in the fall of 1995 when the IMF was asked to prepare a background note for the U.S. negotiating team that was helping to draft a new constitution for Bosnia and Herzegovina as a part of the agreements that ended the tragic war in that country. The IMF's advice was sought on the type of monetary system to establish in light of the strong distrust that existed (and that we could assume would exist after the war ended). The episode exemplifies the quick response to needs for which the IMF staff is proud.

War and Peace

Bosnia and Herzegovina was one of the six republics making up the Socialist Federal Republic of Yugoslavia (SFRY). Following Slovenia and Croatia, which declared independence in the summer of 1991 (and later Macedonia), the Republic of Bosnia and Herzegovina (BH) declared its independence from the SPRY in March 1992.[1] It was quickly recognized by the United Nation and most of its members, but its independence was promptly challenged by the Yugoslav National Army and local Serb militia, who launched a war in April that continued until the last of many cease-fires on October 10, 1995. In the midst of these hostilities, which produced some of the most brutal fighting ever seen in Europe, armed conflict also erupted between forces in the Croat-majority area of BiH and the Republic (Muslim-majority area) army, which lasted from early 1993 until February 25, 1994. The death toll of these combined conflicts in BiH is estimated at about 250,000, and about 3 million of the country's 4.4 million population were displaced from their homes (about 1 million became refugees abroad).

By the end of 1995, Bosnia's three ethnic majority regions had become ethnically more homogeneous as a result of the ethnic cleansing that took place during the recent wars, and each region had its own government, army, and currency arrangements. While German marks (DM) were in use throughout the country, the Croat majority area also used Croatian kuna (HRK), the Serbian majority area used the new Yugoslav dinar (YUD), and the Bosnian majority area used the Bosnia and Herzegovina dinar (BHD) issued by the National Bank of Bosnia and Herzegovina (NBBH), the only domestically issued currency still in use in the country at that time.[2]

Peace between the Croats and Bosnians following their war in 1993 was formalized by the Washington Agreements of August 1994, which resulted in the creation of the Federation of Bosnia and Herzegovina. In reality, however, the Croat majority and Bosniac majority areas remained substantially separate well into 1998. Each, for example, continued to operate separate payment systems and use different currencies (kuna and BHD).

On September 8, 1995, after three and a half years of bloody war, the foreign ministers of BH, Croatia, and the Federal Republic of Yugoslavia (FRY—consisting of the remaining two republics, Serbia and Montenegro) signed the Agreed Basic Principles for a peaceful settlement of the war. This was followed on September 26 by Further Agreed Basic Principles and on October 10 by the final cease-fire. Proximity Talks among the presidents of BH, Croatia, and the FRY on a peace agreement and a new constitution reintegrating the regions of Bosnia and Herzegovina began on November 1, 1995 in Dayton, Ohio. These talks resulted in the initialing on November 21 of a General Framework Agreement for Peace in Bosnia and Herzegovina, which included a Constitution for the continued existence of the country, and were followed by an international peace conference in Paris at which the final agreements were signed on December 14, 1995. Under the constitution Bosnia and Herzegovina continues as one country now consisting of two entities: the Federation and the Republika Srpska (RS).

Dayton's Monetary System

On October 17, 1995, IMF's first deputy managing director, Stanley Fischer, met with the IMF's executive directors from the G7 member countries to discuss issues related to Bosnia and Herzegovina and their possible future membership in the Fund. On behalf of the G7, the directors requested the Fund to prepare a brief note for the upcoming Dayton peace talks outlining the requirements of viable fiscal and monetary structures in confederacies.

In preparing the note the IMF's goal was to find an arrangement for satisfying the monetary and payment needs of Bosnia and Herzegovina that would facilitate the economic recovery of the country and would provide a proper basis for a Fund-supported stabilization program and that would be acceptable to the warring factions.[3] The monetary arrangements should also contribute to the economic reintegration of the divided economy, and should be capable of becoming operational very quickly.

The essential feature of a viable unified monetary system is that the money supply for the confederation as a whole can be properly controlled. This requires, first and foremost, that there be no more than one monetary policy. If there is more than one monetary authority, there must be very clear and binding rules that link their activities together to ensure that the quantity of money is well determined and controlled.

These considerations suggested to us that the most promising options for BiH were for it to choose a foreign currency as its legal tender, to adopt a national currency board, or to adopt two (or three) regional currency boards with the same currency peg and exchange rate. The first option, a foreign currency, had the advantage that no institution had to be put in place. It was an option that was, de facto, already in place and could operate from day one, though it would be desirable to designate one of the currencies in wide use as legal tender to encourage the use of a single foreign currency (though it was not clear that the German Central Bank would agree to the official designation of its currency as legal tender in Bosnia and Herzegovina, if the German mark was chosen). This option came with several costs. The seigniorage from issuing money would be earned by the foreign country whose currency was used (rather than by the domestic central bank, if a domestic currency were issued), and the use of a foreign currency would not contribute to reintegration and nation building in the same way a national currency would.

The case for currency-board arrangements, the second and third options, had seemed obvious to us. Though Bosnia's banking sector was in shambles (as many of its borrowers had been bombed out of existence, and the rest suffered from the general collapse of the economy), the only remaining domestically issued currency. the Bosnia and Herzegovina dinar, was fully convertible into German marks at a fixed rate. The BHD was basically issued by the NBBH following currency-board rules already. Thus, the sort of discipline and stability provided by a currency board was already well understood and accepted. Furthermore, a currency board is easier to set up and to operate than a full-fledged central bank and could thus be put in place more quickly. Perhaps more important, the high level of distrust among the three major ethnic groups and the three warring regions of the country made it very difficult to envisage gaining their support for a central bank with discretionary powers. As a currency board has little or no discretion, surrendering authority to a national currency board should be far more acceptable to the three regions than to any other form of monetary authority.

The second two options, a national or several regional currency boards, would fulfill equally well the criteria of both stable, nondiscretionary monetary policy and administrative simplicity. The option of a national currency board was the marginally more efficient of the two (one institution rather than several) and would contribute more to nation building, if the warring parties were prepared to embark in that direction.

On October 25, the note requested on October 17 containing the above three basic options (with several variants) and supporting arguments, plus a note on Bosnia's external debt and financial workout scenarios, were delivered to the U.S. Treasury for use in Dayton. The note played an important role in the adoption of a currency board arrangement in Bosnia and Herzegovina's new constitution developed in Dayton.

The Constitution of Bosnia and Herzegovina, which was initialed in Dayton November 21, 1995, contains the following section on monetary arrangements:

Article VII. Central Bank

There shall be a Central bank of Bosnia and Herzegovina, which shall be the sole authority for issuing currency and for monetary policy throughout Bosnia and Herzegovina.

1. The Central Bank's responsibilities will be determined by the Parliamentary Assembly. For the first six years after the entry into force of this Constitution, however, it may not extend credit by creating money, operating in this respect as a currency board; thereafter, the Parliamentary Assembly may give it that authority.

2. The first Governing Board of the Central Bank shall consist of a Gover-

nor appointed by the International Monetary Fund, after consultation with the Presidency, and three members appointed by the Presidency, two from the Federation (one Bosniac, one Croat, who shall share one vote), and one from the Republika Srpska, all of whom shall serve a six-year term. The Governor, who shall not be a citizen of Bosnia and Herzegovina or any neighboring state, may cast tie-breaking votes on the Governing Board.

3. Thereafter, the Governing Board of the Central Bank of Bosnia and Herzegovina shall consist of five persons appointed by the Presidency for a term of six years. The Board shall appoint, from among its members, a Governor for a term of six years.

At the end of 1995, only days after the signing of the peace treaty, Bosnia and Herzegovina succeeded to membership in the IMF and became the first member to make use of financing under its policy on emergency postconflict assistance.

The Central-Bank Law

In its purest form, a currency board buys and sells (issues and redeems) its monetary liabilities against a specific foreign currency at a fixed exchange rate and must maintain full backing for its monetary liabilities in the same foreign currency. In fact, the first requirement—passively issuing and redeeming its monetary liabilities against a foreign currency— ensures fulfillment of the second one—full backing, if the resulting reserves are invested so as to preserve their value and to generate net income sufficient to cover the operating cost of the currency board. However, there are no existing currency boards that take this pure form.

In a recent article on currency boards in the Federal Reserve Bank of San Francisco Economic Letter, Mark Spiegel (1998) defined a currency board as "a fixed exchange-rate regime whose currency is fully backed by foreign reserves." There is a subtle but important difference between these two definitions. The fixed-exchange-rate version hints at a more active institution subject to strict rules rather than a purely passive one.

The CBBH is closest to the pure form of currency board of any existing central bank. The issues that took the longest to resolve in the discussions of the draft law for the CBBH concerned just how "pure" the currency-board arrangement should be, how to define the monetary liabilities that needed foreign-exchange backing, and some, more political, issues concerning the makeup and voting strength of members of the board, the location and powers of the central bank's branches, and the differentiation of the design of the banknotes between the two entities.

Currency-Board Issues

General. Conceptually, central banks exist because of the belief that individuals through markets are not able to adjust to monetary and other economic and financial shocks as well as governments.[4] A full-fledged central bank is expected to exercise its judgment over the magnitude and sources of shocks and execute interventions (such as open-market operations, foreign-exchange interventions, reserve-requirement adjustments) that neutralize their disrupting effect at lower social cost than would result from the private sector's adjustments to the same shock. Experience has taught, however, that the nature and magnitude of shocks are not so easily diagnosed at the time they occur and that other objectives and bureaucratic inertia (or conservatism) of government bodies often operate to undercut the potential advantage of government over the private sector in this area (Khatkhate and Coats, 1998). The last half century is rich with examples of monetary shocks delivered by or magnified by central banks or of monetary stability sacrificed for government revenue or other objectives. Hyperinflation was an invention of central banks (which could be, and were often, used to finance government expenditures).

Thus, full-fledged central banks have increasingly been made "independent" of the government by making them accountable to Parliament for the achievement of price stability. The evidence to date indicates that independence has improved central-bank performance, especially in developed countries (Lybek, 1998; IMF, 1996). However, achieving public confidence (credibility) generally requires a long track record. A reputation of virtue is not easily obtained and can be quickly lost.

The primary attraction of a currency board, along with its operational simplicity, is the strong public certainty that can be attached to the policy that it will follow. Currency boards have no, or very limited, discretion and are thus better protected from political interference or their own misjudgments. Unlike a gold or other commodity standard, which puts monetary policy in the impartial hands of mother nature, a currency-board arrangement entrusts monetary policy to the central bank that issues the currency to which the currency board's currency is fixed. To be credible, the commitment of a currency board to its rules must be as strong and as difficult to reverse as possible, and the public must be frequently reassured that the rules are being adhered to.

Under a currency-board arrangement the money supply adjusts to its demand through market mechanisms. The passive issuance or redemption of domestic monetary liabilities at a fixed exchange rate ensures a well-defined quantity of money that adjusts to the public's demand for money (given income, interest rates, price level, and so on) automatically. Rather than an exogenous quantity of money determining the price level, given the public's demand for money, an exogenously determined price level (via the fixed exchange rate and price level in the country of the currency peg) and international interest rates determine the public's demand for money to which the supply adjusts.

The disadvantage of a currency board is the need to give up the potential, but often unrealized, advantages of central banks—the ability to offset shocks. Under a currency-board arrangement the economy must adjust fully to shocks through markets. The speed and ease of such adjustments depend on the efficiency of those markets and the flexibility of prices and the degree of factor mobility. Consider in turn a shock to reserve money and a shock to the money multiplier:

Consider the case of a capital outflow. As domestic money is exchanged for foreign currency and transferred abroad, the monetary liabilities of the currency board and its foreign assets will fall by the same amount, thus preserving the full backing of its diminished monetary liabilities. The resulting monetary contraction will increase domestic interest rates until the capital outflow is stopped. The monetary contraction will also put downward pressure on domestic prices, which should eventually improve the country's current account balance. Thus, automatic market adjustments in interest rates and prices will offset and eventually neutralize the initial capital outflow. The immediate liquidity squeeze, which would normally be offset or softened by a central bank, must be dealt with by an increase in short-term borrowing abroad by banks or by the liquidation of some of their foreign assets. If short-term borrowing abroad cannot be easily obtained, or if price level and current account adjustments are slow, domestic interest-rate increases are likely to overshoot with adverse consequences for investment and output. On the other hand, if a central bank prevents a sufficient adjustment in interest rates or attempts to maintain rates at an inappropriate level, adjustment will be delayed resulting in a larger capital outflow than otherwise.

In the case of an increase in the public's preference for cash relative to bank deposits (for example, as a result of a loss of confidence in banks in general), the monetary liabilities (and foreign-exchange assets) of the currency board don't change, but banks lose balances in their reserve accounts with the central bank. Again a monetary contraction (from a reduction in the money multiplier) results in an increase in interest rates and downward pressure on prices. The contraction will generally be moderated by a capital inflow in response to the higher interest rates and a current account improvement as a result of improved export competitiveness. And again, the short-term liquidity squeeze must be dealt with by an inflow of foreign exchange because the liquidity shortfall is systemwide. An adjustment to a change in the money multiplier with no change in aggregate money demand, will surely be more costly when made through market interest rate and price-level adjustments, than when made by a central-bank adjustment in the monetary base. The neutralization of shifts in the money multiplier probably represents one of the clearest cases for the potentially positive role of a central bank.

The purest currency board would only issue banknotes against foreign exchange. However, all existing currency boards are also central banks, they accept deposits from banks with which banks may settle interbank payments and thus play a role in the noncash-payment system.

The IMF recommended that in addition to issuing banknotes, the CBBH should also accept deposits from banks and from the government. The use of bank deposits with the CBBH for the settlement of interbank payments was seen as facilitating the unification of the financial system in the war torn and fragmented country and contributing to a more efficient system of payments. However, involving the CBBH in the settlement of noncash payments, by allowing it to accept deposits from banks, opened it to the risk that it might be drawn indirectly into extending credit as a part of the settlement process. Such credit would increase the Central Bank's monetary liabilities without increasing its foreign-exchange assets and would thus violate currency-board rules.

The implications of the strict rules of a currency board for liquidity management by banks is best appreciated by examining the daily settlements of domestic noncash payments processed through the payment bureaus in Bosnia and Herzegovina (Bosnia and Herzegovina's payment-bureau operations are discussed below). This is the context in which the problems of dealing with liquidity shocks in the real world of daily payment operations in Bosnia and Herzegovina can be seen most clearly. To settle the day's net clearing-house payments (or to preserve required reserves), an individual bank that experiences a net loss of reserves during the day as a result of its and its customers' payments (as in the above examples of capital outflows or a decline in the money multiplier) can borrow from other banks, sell liquid domestic assets, sell foreign exchange (if it can anticipate the problem two days in advance), or borrow from the central bank. If the banking system in aggregate needs liquidity, then the only options are for banks to sell foreign exchange or borrow from the central bank. The CBBH is not permitted to extend credit to banks or anyone else. The lack of a lender of last resort has led banks to hold liquid foreign-exchange assets and excess reserves with the CBBH at higher levels than they would under a full-fledged central bank. This adds to the cost of banking. This implication of no lender of last resort would be true whether banks were able to settle their payments with the central bank or not.

Deciding just how strict the currency board should be was one of the most important issues that the authorities faced. The IMF took the position that the public's confidence in the Central Bank's adherence to the currency-board arrangement required by the Dayton agreement would be strengthened by giving the Central Bank limited tools of liquidity management, while rigidly binding it to the requirement that it freely convert its monetary liabilities for foreign exchange. We also felt that its credibility required a total prohibition against extending credit of any kind for any purpose. We reasoned that the credibility of the Central Bank's commitment to currency-board rules would be strengthened by giving it the tools to deal with one of the greatest weaknesses of the currency board within the limitations of no credit to anyone and full foreign-exchange backing.[5] Specifically, the draft law that was developed and recommended by the IMF team that I headed in December 1996 provided for the CBBH to issue bills (which would be part of its monetary liabilities that must be backed by foreign exchange), to conduct open-market operations in those bills, to impose a reserve requirement uniformly on all bank deposits, and to borrow abroad up to 50 percent of its capital, while forbidding it to extend credit.

CBBH Bills. As noted above, with no lender of last resort a banking system that needs liquidity in the aggregate (needs additional balances in its reserve/settlement accounts with the Central Bank) can sell foreign-exchange or domestic assets to the Central Bank. But the sale of foreign-currency assets held abroad (a Central Bank operating under currency-board rules can sell reserve account balances only for the foreign currency it is required to hold as backing) can only be settled with two-day value (one day at best when attempting to correct a reserve shortfall late in the day). Thus, the sale of foreign exchange is not an option for a bank that discovers it needs additional liquidity late in the day. If, however, the Central Bank could buy domestic assets as long as it did not violate its 100 percent foreign-exchange cover requirement, the settlement of such a transaction could be confirmed immediately, giving rise to an immediate credit to the selling bank's reserve account.

The IMF considered several options for providing banks with this kind of liquidity management instrument. One approach would be to permit the CBBH to purchase government securities to the extent that it held foreign-exchange assets in excess of its backing requirement. Another, which has been adopted by Bulgaria's currency board, would be to allow the CBBH to extend settlement credit (by a separate department of the Bank) to the extent that it held foreign-exchange assets in excess of its backing requirement. We chose to permit the CBBH to issue and to buy back its own bills and to require it to include its bills held by the public in its monetary liabilities that required foreign-exchange backing. This was a very conservative approach to giving the market a liquidity management asset that could be highly useful for very short-term liquidity adjustments (in either direction). The CBBH could not be expansionary via this instrument because it could only buy back bills that it had previously issued and the issuance (sale) of its bills was itself contractionary. The public could purchase CBBH bills with foreign exchange, in which case both monetary liabilities and assets of the CBBH would increase by the same amount or with domestic cash or bank deposits (both monetary liabilities of the CBBH), in which case the mix of the CBBH's monetary liabilities would change but not the total.

Reserve Requirement. A second instrument recommended by the IMF was a reserve requirement uniformly applied to all bank deposits. The instrument had two purposes. By increasing or decreasing the requirement ratio, the CBBH could affect the money multiplier and thus wholly or in part neutralize monetary shocks: it would provide an instrument of limited monetary control. Once the required ratio had been reduced to zero, however, its expansionary potential would have been spent. The IMF's advice was that the required ratio of reserves to deposits should be set and held at a moderate level (say, 10 percent) and adjusted downward only in the event of a sudden and temporary contraction of liquidity. Required reserves were to be remunerated at market interest rates.

The more important purpose of the requirement, which was to be met on an average basis over each month, was to provide an additional instrument to banks for liquidity management. Required reserves could be used on any day for the settlement of that day's payments (perhaps while waiting for the delivery two days later of the proceeds of a sale of foreign exchange) as long as appropriately higher levels were held on other days.

Gross Assets and Liabilities and Borrowing. The IMF proposed a gross monetary assets and liabilities approach to the foreign-exchange backing requirement because it was easier to define and because it opened the possibility for the Central Bank to borrow foreign exchange abroad to maintain the required backing.

The IMF preferred a comprehensive definition of monetary liabilities to provide no exceptions to the backing requirement. The draft law we prepared defined *gross monetary liabilities* of the CBBH as the sum of

all outstanding banknotes, coins, and debt securities issued by the Central Bank; and

the credit balances of all accounts maintained on the books of the Central Bank by account holders.

IMF Deposits. Other modern currency boards exclude deposits due to the IMF from the central-bank's liabilities that must be backed with foreign exchange. These deposits reflect the local-currency counterpart of any purchases of foreign exchange by the country from the IMF.[6] Normally, the government sells the foreign exchange it purchases from the IMF (or anyone else, for that matter) to its central bank in exchange for a deposit of an equivalent amount of domestic currency. The domestic-currency deposit of the government can then be used to provide the IMF with the funds it must hold in its deposit with the central bank. The operation enlarges the foreign-exchange reserves of the central bank and its monetary liabilities to the same extent. Thus, such an operation has little point for a currency board.

Often, however, purchases from the IMF are used to supplement the government's budget resources, in which case the government borrows the domestic currency from the central bank that it must transfer to the IMF as the counterpart of its purchase. In such cases the central bank then acquires a claim on the government matched by its liability to the IMF (the IMF's deposit). The argument in favor of this exception to the rule of no central-bank credit is that the credit, while expansionary, is embedded in and controlled by the conditionality of the economic policy arrangement supported by the IMF. Those of us working on Bosnia and Herzegovina argued within the IMF that no exceptions to the currency-board rules against central-bank credit should be introduced, not even for the IMF. This view was accepted.[7]

Government Deposits. The above definition also includes government deposits. An increase in government deposits at the central bank normally results from the payment of taxes or of other obligations of the public to the government. Thus, bank reserves (and reserve money) drop by the amount of the increase in government balances with the central bank. Most "smoothing" operations of central banks are directed at neutralizing this effect so that the normal fluctuations of government balances do not translate into fluctuations in banking-sector liquidity and the money supply.

We debated for a while whether to exclude government deposits (thus adopting a definition that would coincide with reserve money—that is, the monetary base). The case for excluding them (reducing the banking-sector liquidity consequences of fluctuations in government deposits) also underlies the definition of reserve money as the aggregate that results in a more stable money multiplier (central government deposits are generally not included in the definition of reserve money or broad money). If we excluded government deposits from the backing requirement, an increase in such deposits would reduce the CBBH's monetary liabilities with no change in its foreign-exchange assets. This would automatically open a surplus of foreign-exchange assets over liabilities that might be used to offset the drop in reserve money. The resulting excess foreign exchange would allow a limited range for stabilizing activism by the Central Bank that might strengthen the functioning of the currency-board arrangement.

Government deposits can also increase from the proceeds of foreign borrowing, in which case there is no decline in reserve money to neutralize. In addition, excluding government deposits from the backing requirement would allow offsetting temporary fluctuations in reserve money only if it were accompanied by limited open-market operations or lending in domestic currency. This seemed to us to open too many doors that might result in abuse thus undermining the currency-board arrangement. While in some settings such an instrument might be defended, we concluded that in Bosnia and Herzegovina, with the high degree of distrust by each side toward the others, we should stay closer to the pure form of currency board. Thus in the end the IMF rejected the idea and included government deposits in the definition of monetary liabilities, while recognizing that dealing with the liquidity consequences of changes in reserve money of induced government deposits would be an important challenge for the system.[8]

Foreign Borrowing. As already noted, the use of gross rather than net assets and liabilities opens the door to the central bank to borrow abroad to cover any foreign-exchange backing shortfall (as might occur if the central bank's operations incurred a loss or from investment losses in the value of the bank's foreign-exchange assets). This possibility might also be abused (if, for example, the central bank can extend credit as long as it has foreign-exchange backing). Thus, the IMF proposed two safeguards. The primary one was the absolute prohibition against the Central Bank extending credit of any kind. A secondary one was a limit on the amount of foreign borrowing by the Central Bank of 50 percent of its capital and reserves.

Political Issues

The above economic issues consumed most of the time we spent on drafting the law in Washington and almost none of our time discussing and refining it with our counterparts in Bosnia and Herzegovina. What might be called the more political issues of power and symbols, which took up almost none of our time in Washington, dominated it in Sarajevo and Pale (the seat, at that time of the Republic of Serbia government). The IMF's goal was to implement the Dayton agreement, which was meant to keep the country together while respecting its ethnic diversity. A single monetary system was one of the important elements holding the country together. The officials in the Federation and the RS, on the other hand, were very concerned to ensure that the structure being put in place would not prevent them from functioning in the event of separation (with or without another war).

Initially the IMF's discussions of the law, which started on June 26, 1996,[9] were with representatives of all three ethnic majority areas of Bosnia and Herzegovina under the umbrella of an interentity working group. At that time the Bosnian Serb position was to have multiple central banks in the two entities, issuing separate currencies. In September 1996, the National Bank of Republika Srpska (NBRS) proposed a single central bank that would share most of its responsibilities with the NBRS and a proposed National Bank of the Federation. But on October 29, 1996, reflecting a shift in sentiment that allowed discussions to become more serious, the three members of Bosnia and Herzegovina's joint presidency approved the IMF's appointment of Serge Robert, a French banker and at that moment an IMF-appointed advisor to the governor of the Central Bank of Haiti, as governor of the future CBBH and appointed the three members of the Board called for in the Dayton agreement.[10] The IMF's discussions of the draft law were then taken up with this group—the Board of the future central bank. In November 1996 we spent a full week of *intense* meetings (the most diplomatic word I can find to describe them) with the Board in Sarajevo and Pale, after which the IMF issued its recommended draft of the law. Agreement on all issues was not achieved among Board members, however, until May 1997 (see below).[11]

Glasses. Obviously, the national currency would need a name and a design, and we knew that agreement on these would be difficult. However, these issues could be saved for the end as they had no implications for the central-bank law itself. In the discussions of the draft law with our counterparts we used the name *glasses* (imaginations were running thin at that time) for the unnamed new currency to facilitate our discussions of the law.

Intense discussions ensued over the meaning of a single currency and of legal tender. The Bosnian Serbs wanted their own version of glasses, which would be issued by their branch of the CBBH but would be legal tender throughout the country and fully interchangeable with the Federation version. There was even a discussion of whether the foreign-exchange backing would be owned by and invested by each branch. The Bosnian Serb member of the Board presented us with a number of lessons in the great diversity of currency arrangements in the world to fortify his argument that a single currency could have two versions. He liked the example of the Scottish pound in the United Kingdom. We pointed out that the twelve different versions of Federal Reserve notes in the United State resulted from the fact that the twelve Reserve Banks were legally separate entities and that the branches of the CBBH would not be legally separate. Furthermore, the differences between the twelve versions of Federal Reserve notes are barely noticeable. We argued that the Belgian (and Canadian) banknotes provided a good model of reflecting their countries' ethnic diversity by emphasizing one group and language on one denomination and the other on another denomination, but with only one version of each denomination. There is indeed more diversity in the world's monetary arrangements than I had realized.

To test whether a single currency with two designs was really a single currency in the minds of the Board, I pointed out that noncash glasses (deposit balances) had no design at all, only amounts that could not be distinguished in terms of which branch had issued them. This was understood and accepted.

It was particularly important for the Bosnian Serbs that the new monetary arrangements would not interfere with their close financial ties with Yugoslavia (Belgrade). The Yugoslav dinar was legal tender in the RS, and domestic payments were made in Yugoslav dinar and settled through the Yugoslav-wide payment-bureau system. Furthermore, the Yugoslav dinar was not a freely convertible currency. Thus, the introduction of a new national currency, which would be the sole legal tender in both the Federation and the RS, was an important and sensitive issue. It was fully accepted by everyone that people would remain free to transact in the currencies of their mutual choice. Nonetheless only glasses would be legal tender. We had lengthy discussions with our counterparts of what *legal tender* meant, leading to a long and unique article in the law setting out the implications of legal tender.

Branches. The role of branches was a hotly debated issue. Having relaxed somewhat the initial position that there should be separate central banks in the two entities, the Bosnian Serb representative sought to preserve as much autonomy as possible for the entities by assigning important powers to the branches of the central bank that would be established in each entity. The Bosnian Serb position was a mix of symbolism and substance. Indeed, the issues on which all three representatives took strong positions were often a mix of symbolism and substance. The Serbs had long insisted that the branches be named "Central Banks" even if they were subordinate to the Headquarters of the Central Bank in Sarajevo. Of greater substance, they fought for the law to explicitly delegate significant authority to the branches.

The board. The Constitution adopted in Dayton had several unusual provisions that became the sources of considerable discussion when drafting the central-bank law. The first of these was the sharing of one (Federation) vote by the Bosniac and Croat members of the Board. Did this mean that if they disagreed no Federation vote would be cast or that opposing half votes would be cast? In fact, there is no circumstance under which it would matter which interpretation was given. However, considerable discussion arose over the difference of treatment of the RS member and the Federation members. The two Federation members where ethnically specified, but the RS member was not. Could, for example, a Bosniac (Moslem) from Banja Luka hold the RS seat?[12] The central-bank law that was finally adopted, with the agreement of the Office of the High Representative (OHR), ignored this peculiarity and provided for a Croat and a Bosniac from the Federation and a Serb from the RS.

The Dayton agreement states that the governor may break tie votes of the Board. The other controversy, and it was one of the last issues resolved before the central-bank law was approved, was whether the governor was a regular member of the Board. If so, he could create a tie and then break it. As a member of the Board, the governor would also be entitled to vote. Thus, if the Federation members disagreed (and either split their vote or cast no vote) and the governor and the RS member disagreed, the Board would be tied, and the governor could then cast another vote to break the tie, and the governor's views would prevail. Under the other interpretation, the governor would vote only when there was a tie, and the same configuration of votes in the preceding example would result in the Serb's views prevailing. The interpretation that won out in the central-bank law, which was the interpretation that the IMF staff gave to the Dayton agreement, was that the governor was a regular voting member of the Board.

There was also a difference of views among the members of the Board over whether they should have executive powers. Though practice varies among central banks, our view was that the Board should approve policy and monitor its implementation. A conflict of interest could arise if Board members also executed policy. The difference of views among the Board members had mainly to do with their personal desires to be devoted full time (or not) to the work of the CBBH and the related salary implications of whether the position was executive or not. The central-bank law finally adopted does not give executive powers to the Board.

The Final Agreement

The Board of the CBBH continued to discuss and amend the draft law that the IMF had provided in December 1996 until May 1997. Following intensive discussions between U.S. Treasury officials and the Bosnian Serb authorities in May that were undertaken to break the apparent deadlock over the law, a number of important changes were made that are now a part of the Central Bank Law that was presented to the Joint Presidency on May 29, 1997, and adopted by the State (National) Parliament on June 20, 1997. While preserving the basic provisions of the draft we had proposed, the law finally adopted introduced some important changes.

Currency Name and Note Design.   Many interesting and worthy suggestions for a name for the new currency were made between November 1996 and May 1997, but before there was a political will and commitment to move forward, no name would be acceptable to all three groups. When that point was reached in May, all of the really good names had already been rejected. At that point David Lipton of the U.S. Treasury suggested the pedestrian but descriptive name *convertible marka* (KM), which was immediately accepted.

The law makes KM legal tender, while explicitly protecting the right of private persons and companies to transact in any mutually acceptable currency. The law requires public officials to

> undertake all efforts to promote the use of the Convertible Marka in the payments of all revenues and expenditures of the budgets, public agencies, and public enterprises at all levels of government. During that process, other currencies in

use prior to the entry into force of this Law will continue to be used. Following the introduction of the Convertible Marka by the Central Bank, the Presidency of Bosnia and Herzegovina will review these efforts every three months on the basis of an analysis submitted by the International Monetary Fund of the efforts made by the authorities to promote the use of the Convertible Marka. (Article 38.5)

The law also provided that "as an interim measure until a permanent solution for the design of the notes has been agreed upon," the CBBH would issue "Coupons":

The Coupons will have common design elements as well as distinct design elements for the Federation of Bosnia and Herzegovina and the Republika Srpska. . . . Both versions of the coupon will have equal status as legal tender throughout the territory of Bosnia and Herzegovina. (Article 42.3)

The design for each entity had to be acceptable to the other and no agreement was reached until the Office of the High Representative took a decision on the design and presented it to the Joint Presidency in February 1998.[13] Before the notes were printed, the OHR ruled that they were banknotes rather than coupons and the word *coupon* was removed from the design. This permits the CBBH to introduce coins, which was forbidden by the law "as long as the Coupons are in circulation."

The new banknotes were first issued on June 15, and the Bosnia and Herzegovina dinar will be demonetized June 30.

Liquidity Management Instruments. The law that was adopted removed all of the limited discretionary elements of liquidity management that were in the IMF draft except for the reserve requirement, and it severely limited the Central Bank's scope for adjusting the reserve requirement. The CBBH may not issue its own bills (other than banknotes) and may not engage in open-market operations in these (or any other) bills. And, as had also been provided in the IMF draft of the law, the CBBH "shall not under any circumstances, grant any credit" (Article 67.1.a).

While the very limited authority to borrow abroad remains in the law, it cannot serve the purpose we had seen for it (to cover shortfalls in the foreign-exchange backing of monetary liabilities). The law changed the backing requirement from the gross foreign-exchange assets that we had recommended, to a net concept—that is, the monetary liabilities of the CBBH must be covered by *net* foreign-exchange assets of equivalent value. Thus, any increase in gross foreign-exchange assets as a result of borrowing would leave net foreign-exchange assets unchanged, and thus such borrowing could not remove a shortfall in the required backing of the CBBH's monetary liabilities.[14]

As a practical matter, the law leaves three ways in which the banking system can deal with a potential liquidity shortfall at the time of the end-of-day net settlement of domestic noncash payments.[15] The first two are for banks to hold reserves in excess of the required level (excess reserves) and to sell German mark banknotes on hand in their vaults to the Central Bank, both of which are costly in terms of forgone interest earnings. The third is to utilize required reserves, if the requirement permits averaging. To maximize the value of the reserve requirement for this liquidity management purpose, the IMF draft law had granted the CBBH the power to establish by regulation a uniform requirement on all deposits that would be met on an average basis and that would be substantially remunerated. The first three of five provisions in our draft law (Article 38) were:

1.   In the conduct of its monetary policy, the Central Bank may require by regulation that banks shall maintain deposits with the Central Bank at prescribed minimum levels that relate to the size of their deposits, borrowed funds and such other liabilities as the Central Bank may determine by regulation (required reserves). Reserve requirements shall be applied uniformly to all banks.

2.   Required reserves shall be maintained by way of such cash holdings or by way of such money deposits with the Central Bank and shall be calculated as average daily reserves over such time periods as the Central Bank may from time to time prescribe by regulation.

3.   The banks shall be paid interest at market-related rates by the Central Bank on the amounts by which their required reserves exceed the equivalent of three percent of the aggregate amounts of their respective liabilities.

We had in mind a one-month settlement period for a required ratio of 10 percent of all deposits to give considerable scope to liquidity management by banks.

During the debates over the draft law, there appeared to be some danger that the reserve requirement would be lost along with the other liquidity management tools (though the source of this danger was never clear to me). In the end, the reserve requirement was saved but in a greatly restricted form spelled out quite fully and rigidly in the law. The law provided for a short ten-day settlement period and a limited range for the requirement ratio and was made applicable only to KM deposits, which for some time were bound to be rather small. This also potentially disadvantaged KM deposits as other deposits were not subject to such a requirement and remuneration of required reserves was more limited than we had proposed. The Law provides in the first three of five sections in Article 36:

1. The Governing Board of the Central Bank will require by regulation that banks shall maintain deposits with the Central Bank, through its head office or main units, at prescribed minimum levels of between ten and fifteen percent of their deposits and borrowed funds denominated in Convertible Marka. Reserve requirements shall be applied uniformly to all banks.

2. Required reserves shall be maintained by way of cash holdings or by way of deposits with the Central Bank, through its head office and main units, and shall be calculated as average daily reserves over ten-day periods.

3. The banks shall be paid interest at market related rates by the Central Bank on the amounts by which their required reserves exceed the equivalent of five percent of the aggregate amounts of their respective liabilities.

Exchange-Rate Spread. The central function of a currency board is its obligation to convert domestic currency for a foreign one at a fixed exchange rate. The law establishes this obligation in two Articles:

The official exchange rate for the currency of Bosnia and Herzegovina shall be one Convertible Marka per Deutsche mark. (Article 32)

1. The Central Bank shall without restriction purchase and sell Convertible Marka on demand for Deutsche marks within the territories of Bosnia and Herzegovina at the exchange rate indicated in Article 32 of this Law. (Article 33)

To provide a financial incentive to conduct normal foreign-exchange business outside the CBBH, the IMF's draft law had permitted the Central Bank to transact at rates within one-quarter of 1 percent of the official rate and to limit its transactions to banks or other financial institutions. It would also have been permitted to limit the fees and commissions charged by banks for buying and selling KM against DM with the public.

To maximize public acceptance of KM, the Law adopted removed these spreads for the CBBH and for banks all together and required the participation of banks:

2. Commercial banks and other financial institutions in Bosnia and Herzegovina shall purchase and sell without restriction, fees, commissions, or other charges Convertible Marka for Deutsche marks on demand, at the exchange rate indicated in Article 32 of this Law. (Article 33)

After a transition period, we intend to recommend the amendment of these provisions along the lines of our original proposal, to encourage the development of the foreign-exchange market outside of the CBBH. In the meantime, we have recommended that the CBBH remunerate banks for the subsidy to the public implicit in the absences of spreads or fees in their dealings with the public.

Branches. The Law preserved the essence of the IMF draft law's treatment of branches of the CBBH. However, the sensitivity of and struggle over this issue can be clearly seen in the language on this subject in the Law as finally adopted. The IMF draft stated that

> The Central Bank shall have its head office in Sarajevo. The Central Bank shall establish and maintain branch offices in the Federation of Bosnia and Herzegovina and the Republika Srpska; these branch offices shall have no legal status or authority ••

The Law as adopted states that

> The Central Bank shall have its head office in Sarajevo. However, it will decentralize its activities in other locations of the common institutions of Bosnia and Herzegovina. The Central Bank shall establish and maintain a head office and main units in the Federation of Bosnia and Herzegovina and the Republika Srpska; these main units shall be established in the Federation, and one in the Republika Srpska. They will perform their duties as decided by the Governing Board and the Governor, and under this law they may operate through accounts opened with the appropriate authorities in the payment system. (Article 1.3)

> The main unit in the Republika Srpska shall be called:
> Main Bank of the Republika Srpska
> Of the Central Bank of BiH. (Article 74.I)

When I first read the above name of the branch in RS, I assumed that it was a typo. But it was not, and I was not present for what must have been a fascinating discussion leading to that language, so that I cannot shed any light on what exactly motivated it. In fact, however, when the Main Bank of the Republika Srpska opened in Pale (it has since been moved to Banja Luka), *Central Bank of Bosnia and Herzegovina* was spelled out in full on the front of the building housing the branch office.

Throughout the Law there are references to "tasks of the head office of the Central Bank and of the main units." One of many examples can be seen in the reserve-requirement provisions quoted above.

One argument put forth by all sides, but more strongly by the Bosnian Serbs, with which we had considerable sympathy was that to gain public acceptance of the new Central Bank and its currency, each group would need to see them as (to some extent) their own.

The Payment Bureaus

The operations of a currency board are, of course, straightforward with regard to its core functions. It needs to have an efficient procedure for banks to buy and sell cash and noncash forms of its currency and for investing the foreign-exchange counterpart in a safe, liquid manner that will generate enough income to finance its operations.[16] The most challenging aspect of establishing the operations of the CBBH was to ensure that a very unusual system of domestic noncash payments would not inadvertently result in the extension of credit by the CBBH to banks as part of the daily payment settlement process and to link the three separate payment-bureau operations in the country into one national system of payment.

The Present System

The present system of domestic noncash payments in BiH grew out of the Yugoslav Service for Social Bookkeeping (SDK). SDK was a system designed to maximize state control over economic activities in a centrally planned economy.[17] The payment system in each of the three ethnic majority regions in Bosnia and Herzegovina is still dominated by its own unique payment bureau (the ZPP in the Bosniac majority area, the ZAP in the Croat majority area, and the SPP in the Serbian majority area). These payment bureaus, though all once part of the Yugoslav SDK, have developed differently in each region, and they continue to use different currencies (plus DM) so that there is currently no homogenous technical and operational base for the installation of a countrywide noncash system of payment.

Each successor payment bureau in BiH has (in practice) a monopoly over domestic noncash payments in the area it serves. To make a domestic noncash payment a (natural or legal) person must have positive balances in a Giro account with the regional payment bureau. Deposits are transferred on the basis of "payment orders" submitted by bank customers directly to the payment bureau office at which that person has its Giro account.

Credit balances in customer Giro accounts are obtained by the customer depositing currency or receiving a deposit transfer from another depositor in the system. When depositing currency, the payment bureau credits the customer's Giro account and debits the Currency in Circulation account of the CBBH.[18] Customer Giro accounts are "allocated" to the bank with which the customer has a deposit contract.[19] Thus, such a "deposit" results in an increase in the customer's Giro account balance and its bank's reserve account with the CBBH. The increased reserve account balance is matched by a reduction in cash in circulation so that the CBBH's monetary liabilities are unchanged by such deposits.

Though banks are not involved in providing domestic payment services, the payment bureaus have no deposit liabilities of their own and no assets against the Giro account balances they maintain. All payment orders submitted to the system are accepted only when the customer's Giro account has sufficient funds and are cleared every afternoon. The resulting net payment or receipt by each bank (on its own account or on account of its customers) increases or decreases each bank's Giro account balance. Since the opening of the CBBH on August 11, 1997, these daily net amounts due to or from each bank with Giro accounts in the ZPP have been settled by debiting and crediting reserve-account balances with the CBBH. Since May 1998 this operation has expanded to the other two payment bureaus, the ZAP and the SPP (now known as the State Bank of Republika Srpska, SBRS).

This system does not permit banks to know the impact of domestic payments on their reserve accounts until the net clearing at the end of the day, which creates a problem for banks' liquidity management.[20] As a result and because the CBBH cannot extend any credit to banks that might end the day with insufficient reserve account balances to settle their net payments, the finality of payments cannot be confirmed until the end of the day or the next day. Thus, settlement of time-sensitive payments (interbank securities or foreign-exchange transactions) are delayed. Nor does the system permit any direct relationship between banks and their depositors with regard to payments, which is generally considered important for the overall relationship between a bank and its customers and for the development of new and/or improved payment instruments and services. In addition, depositors often incorrectly assume that their deposits are with the payment bureau rather than with their bank, so that the possible loss of deposits in the event of a bank failure would be difficult for depositors to understand.

The Future System

The IMF has recommended that Bosnia and Herzegovina develop the general payment-system structure found in developed market economies in which banks provide domestic payment services by dealing directly with their depositors and by transferring their customers' deposits as their own (1) directly to the banks of payees with immediate settlement (using their reserve account balances), when immediate finality of settlement is important or (2) by clearing payment instructions through a clearing house with delayed net settlement. This would require developing a large value transfer system between banks and the CBBH and converting the payment bureaus into clearing houses. The development of new retail (or wholesale) payment instruments would be at the initiative of banks and other service providers (that is, the private sector).

This very general blueprint could be achieved in a variety of ways. The IMF has recommended the creation of a national payments council that would discuss the strategy for transforming and modernizing the payment system. The BiH Payments Council is to be established July 1998.

The Transformation Strategy

Any transformation of existing payment arrangements must be undertaken in a way that does not disrupt the ongoing payment activity, without which the economy cannot function. The IMF's advice in the payment area to data has been consistent with the gradual evolution toward the above types of systems, while continuing to rely on existing structures. In addition to the steps already taken—settlement of interbank payments on the books of the Central Bank under the control of the CBBH, establishing direct use of reserve accounts between banks and the Central Bank without the use of the payment bureaus—a transformation strategy might proceed by modernizing the payments law, improving the efficiency and risk management of the clearing functions of each payment bureau, while building up the technical efficiency of bank's direct access to their reserve accounts (LVTS). The adoption of the amendments to the domestic payment laws recommended by the IMF will enable customers to submit payment orders directly to their banks without having a Giro account with the payment bureau. Such an approach will allow a modern system of payment to develop alongside the continued use of the existing system and permits the continued use of payment-bureau clearing services for as long as they remain competitive. In the medium term (the next two to three years), the following additional steps would contribute to the further modernization of payments in BiH:

- Development and adoption of comprehensive modern clearing-house rules and procedures for each clearing house (payment bureau),
- Installation of modern large value transfer technology,
- Privatization of the ownership of each clearing house (banks should be the main or sole owners), and
- Adoption of a new, modern, domestic payment law.

We have cautioned the payment bureaus against following the example of Slovenia, which has recently technically modernized the old Yugoslav system. While the centralized, Yugoslav system has certain advantages and can be made technically very efficient, it suffers from the lack of innovation and growth more typical of competitive, decentralized, market-based systems.

Central-Bank Startup

The CBBH may not extend credit of any kind to anyone, must buy and sell KM for DM with banks at the exchange rate of one to one, and must execute payment orders from banks to transfer money from their reserve accounts when those accounts contain sufficient resources. It must invest and disinvest the foreign-exchange counterpart of its monetary liabilities as needed and monitor banks' compliance with its reserve requirement.

When the CBBH opened for business on Monday, August 11, 1997, it meant that a new system of settling KM payments commenced. All banks that had maintained Bosnia and Herzegovina dinar deposits (which were redenominated over that weekend to KM) had established reserve accounts with the CBBH during the preceding week.[21] These reserve accounts were initially funded on opening day by the transfer of the deposits these banks had with the NBBH at the close of business Friday, August 8. An equivalent value of foreign exchange was transferred from the NBBH to the CBBH on the same day.[22] In addition, the liability represented by the BHD banknotes that had been printed were transferred to the CBBH along with the banknotes in the vaults of the NBBH (including in the vaults of the ZPP as its agent) as was an equivalent value of foreign exchange for the difference—that is, for BHD notes in circulation (held by the public or in the vaults of banks).

Considerable work at the ZPP had preceded the opening on that Monday so as to produce a Friday closing balance for the NBBH by Monday morning and to settle payments each evening using banks' reserve accounts with the CBBH. Prior to that day, the entire operation had been conducted by the ZPP. The ZPP had not only cleared all payment orders but had settled them as well by posting the net payments of each bank to its account with the NBBH. If it was revealed at the end of the day that a bank did not have sufficient funds in its settlement account, the shortfall was transferred by the ZPP from the bank's required reserve holdings (which were, at that time, in a separate, block account). If the bank's required reserve balances were not sufficient, the ZPP created a credit from the NBBH (which rarely happened). The ZPP came to think of itself as actually holding the resources of the banks and the NBBH that stood behind its operations. It took many discussions to convince the ZPP that under the new Central Bank, which was not allowed to give credit of any kind, the payments that it cleared every day would not be settled and final until the CBBH verified that every bank participating in the net settlement had sufficient reserve-account balances.

The procedure that was introduced on August 11 works as follows:

- Each morning every bank informs its payment bureau and the CBBH of the amount of its reserve-account balance that it wishes to set aside for settling that day's net payment-bureau payments.
- The CBBH verifies and records these amounts and confirms them to the payment bureau as the banks' opening (giro account) balance with the payment bureau.
- The payment bureau accepts payment orders from customers (of banks) that have sufficient balances in their giro accounts recorded at their payment-bureau office. The ZPP is not technically able to know on a real-time basis the impact of these payments on individual banks' giro-account (and hence ultimately their reserve-account) balances.
- At the end of the payment day the payment bureau nets all payment orders against the opening giro account balance for each bank and submits the result to the CBBH for settlement. If a bank does not have sufficient funds in its giro account for this purpose, it is notified (by the payment bureau) and given time to borrow from another bank or to deliver cash. If all else fails, the payment bureau must withdraw (unwind) sufficient payments by the defaulting bank to permit it, and all other banks, to settle.
- Settlement is confirmed (to each bank and the payment bureau) by the CBBH when it posts the result to banks' reserve accounts.
- Starting in June 1998, with the addition of banks clearing through the ZPP and SPP, the daily settlement now incorporates interregional (interpayment bureau) payments, which are settled the same day as part of the evening settlement of intrabureau payment orders. This replaces the interregional settlements by physically transporting DM banknotes between payment bureaus several times a week, which has been in operation since late 1996.

The NBBH Problem

The startup of this new operation on August 11, and subsequent operations went relatively smoothly with one major exception. The tipoff of problems to come came in the form of a request from a branch office of the ZPP on behalf of some customer to buy cash for wage payments. For some reason the procedures we had put in place didn't seem to work for this customer. Within a few days we came to understand that the customer was a municipality that, like all entity organs or their subunits, had its deposits with the NBBH. The accounting system of the ZPP had been designed around the treatment of the NBBH as the central bank, a function that has bee transferred to the CBBH, but because not all of the NBBH's deposits had been transferred to the CBBH (or to other banks), this left the NBBH's treatment by the ZPP in an awkward limbo. The ZPP was not sure how to handle a payment order from a depositor with the NBBH.

We had expected entity government deposits at the NBBH to be transferred to the CBBH, and the NBBH to be liquidated. Because of last-minute changes to the draft of the Central Bank Law, the CBBH was not allowed to accept entity government deposits unless both entities agreed, which they did not. Thus, in the Federation these deposits were still with the NBBH[23] and, of course, still being actively used for the needs of government.

Within a few days after the CBBH's opening on August 11, the CBBH's monetary liabilities had increased without an increase in its foreign-exchange assets, thus violating the currency-board rules (and the Central Bank Law). What was happening was that deposits with the NBBH were being debited for cash (which now belonged to the CBBH) and to make net payments to other banks. At the end of the day the CBBH posted the increase in reserve-account balances of the other banks but not the reduction in balances in the reserve account that the NBBH did not have. As a result the CBBH's net monetary liabilities increased.[24]

Because the NBBH did not have a reserve account with the CBBH for settling payments between itself and other banks, there were two circuits of payments, and payment orders could transfer funds between the two creating a hole (that is, a gap between monetary liabilities and foreign-exchange backing) in the one operated by the CBBH. Every time the deposits held with the NBBH dropped, the CBBH's monetary liabilities increased because it reflected the increase in currency in circulation or reserve deposits of other banks without reflecting the decrease for the NBBH.

Before the end of that first week of operation in August, I obtained the agreement of the governor of the NBBH and the governor of the CBBH to open a reserve account for the NBBH with the CBBH and for the ZPP to treat the NBBH like any other bank. This would close the hole. Unfortunately, the agreed approach was not implemented. The ZPP was not prepared to accept the instructions that they treat the NBBH like any other bank (in part, I assume, because it would have resulted in a negative balance of an NBBH reserve account, which was not permitted). Instead, the NBBH transferred an additional DM 10 million to a special deposit with the CBBH to cover the potential the net use of its deposit liabilities on the assumption that, as the government maintains a balanced budget, over time inflows should match outflows.

In practice, the alternative scheme was not properly monitored. The above shortcomings in the procedures for settling payments involving deposits with the NBBH resulted in the end of December 1997 monetary liabilities of the CBBH exceeding its monetary assets by KM 16.6 million. An additional DM 10 million was transferred from the NBBH to the CBBH in March 1998, but it also proved to be inadequate to cover the net outflow of deposits from the NBBH.[25] The situation was beginning to create a public scandal that was undermining confidence in the new Central Bank. Banks in RS and Mostar areas were not being asked (by the regional political authorities) to open reserve accounts, nor was the Mostar main branch opened (until April 6, 1998), in part because the authorities in those areas were concerned about the integrity of the currency board operation as a result of payments by depositors of the NBBH.[26]

Proper implementation of the use of the NBBH's reserve account requires the cooperation of the ZPP and the NBBH. The ZPP must provide daily information on the NBBH's giro account balance in the same way it does for other banks and must provide the CBBH with daily information on changes in its holdings of KM (BHD) banknotes (held as agent of the CBBH), that result from deposits and withdrawals of cash from the CBBH (that is, from the payment bureaus as agent of the CBBH). When I returned to Sarajevo in February 1998, I obtained a new agreement to implement the original proposal while waiting for the liquidation of the NBBH to begin. The NBBH opened a reserve account with the CBBH on March 20, 1998, but the related settlement procedure was suspended several days later when the CBBH's accounts suggested that the NBBH was overdrawn, while those of the NBBH showed a positive balance.

As a result of these delays, the monthly balance sheets of the CBBH continued to show currency board violations in February and March. The local press was becoming more loudly critical. I returned to Sarajevo April 16 and 17 to try again to resolve the problem, which seemed then to turn on resolving the differences between the ZPP's and the CBBH's data on reserve-account balances. It turned out that the ZPP was not able to process some payment orders completely within the same day giving rise to payment-system float (some debits where made to the giro accounts of paying banks a day or two before the credits were made to the receiving banks). Thus, the category of "items in transit" was added to the CBBH's accounts to reconcile the difference in the CBBH's and the ZPP's versions of bank reserve-account balances, and the ZPP accepted to treat the NBBH like any other bank. At the same time the NBBH was formally put into liquidation, though for the following six weeks depositors at the NBBH continued to enjoy the full use of their funds (as long as the NBBH reserve account was not overdrawn). The NBBH's reserve account was finally put into full operation on April 21, 1998, and the NBBH issued instructions to transfer an addition DM 20 million to its new reserve account with the CBBH.

Aside from most of the additional foreign exchange not arriving at the CBBH,[27] the new arrangement worked properly, and the funds in the NBBH's reserve account at the CBBH proved sufficient to settle all net payments by its depositors until May 5 when another modest overdraft occurred. On that occasion, both the ZPP failed to adhere to the settlement instructions requiring it to unwind the excess payments, and the CBBH failed to hold up the settlement of payments for the day. On the following day the overdraft was reversed on its own. As a result of these combined failures, which again caused the currency-board rules to be violated, the IMF postponed the meeting of its Executive Board to consider approval of the financial package that had been negotiated with the authorities by the IMF staff. Following the acceptance of a liquidation plan, which included the principles for loss sharing by creditors, and the freezing of all deposits with the NBBH for which there was not sufficient foreign-exchange backing, the IMF approved the financing package on May 29, 1998, and hopefully this chapter in the history of the CBBH is closed.

With the full resolution of the NBBH problem, and the opening of the CBBH's branches in Mostar and Banja Luka, all banks had opened their reserve accounts with the CBBH by May 20, 1998, and nationwide payments in noncash KM became possible. The final element for the full operation of the CBBH was the introduction of KM banknotes.

KM Banknotes

The KM banknotes introduced in Bosnia and Herzegovina starting June 22, 1998, have two versions for each denomination. One version features literary figures and symbols chosen by the authorities in RS, and the other version features such figures and symbols chosen by the authorities in the Federation. Both versions, however, look very much alike and will clearly be seen as the same currency. The Serbian design is being introduced initially in the RS and Federation design in the Federation. No attempt will be made over time, however, to keep the two separated, and they are used in making payments throughout the country.

KM banknotes could be acquired from the CBBH (through banks and payment bureaus as its agents) in exchange for BiH dinar banknotes at the rate of 100 dinar per KM between June 15 and July 3 (after which BiH dinar's will be demonetized) or at any time for German marks at the rate of one for one. Needless, to say they may be returned to the CBBH at any time for German marks at the same rate. They may trade freely in the market for any currency at market rates.

Thus, all of the elements of a national monetary system now seem to be in place.

Conclusion

The currency-board arrangement now in place in Bosnia and Herzegovina has greatly facilitated public acceptance of the new Central Bank and its currency. It also simplified the already sufficiently complex task of setting up a new central bank. The major challenge to the establishment of the CBBH came from the payment-bureau system inherited from Yugoslavia. The further modernization of domestic payments in Bosnia and Herzegovina depends heavily on success in transforming this system of payments.

The ultimate test of the currency board arrangement in Bosnia and Herzegovina will consist of the extent to which the public shifts over time from the German mark (soon to be the Euro) and other foreign currencies to the KM, which will shift the seigniorage now earned abroad to the CBBH and lower the cost of transacting throughout the country. The viability of the arrangement will depend on banks' and the payment bureaus' success in managing their liquidity without a lender of last resort.[28] We will all be monitoring these two developments closely over the next two to three years.

Acknowledgments

This chapter presents a very personal account of the history of the CBBH. Thus, those aspects in which I (and hence MAE) was personally involved are treated in much more detail. This is not to suggest, of course, that those events and aspects on which I am not able to report in such detail were less important or less interesting.

Notes

1. Slovenia won a brief war against the FRY army in the summer of 1991, and in August Croatia declared war on the FRY in response to ethnic cleansing in the Serb-majority area of Croatia's Krajina region (which had declared its independence from Croatia in March 1991). Bosnia's parliament voted for independence in October 1991, but the majority of Bosnia's Serbs voted to remain in the FRY. In November 1991, the European Union's Badinter Commission found that the Republic of Bosnia and Herzegovina satisfied the necessary conditions for recognition by the EU, if the desire for independence was confirmed by popular referendum. Such a referendum was held March 1, 1992. The two-thirds of the adult population that voted almost unanimously favored independence. The other, nonvoting third consisted largely of Bosnian Serbs, many of whom had decided to boycott the referendum.

2. The (old) BH dinar was introduced by the NBBH as legal tender on August 18, 1992. Following a period of wartime hyperinflaton, the currency was stabilized in mid-1994 and was replaced by a new BH dinar on August 14, 1994. Somewhat later that fall, new (redenominated) banknotes replaced the old ones. The exchange rate of the new BH dinar was fixed at 100 per German mark and issued (generally) in accordance with currency board rules. The Serb majority area established its own central bank in early 1992, the National Bank of Republika Srpska (NBRS), and issued the Republika Srpska dinar, which also suffered wartime hyperinflation and was abandoned for the new Yugoslav dinar (YUD), which was stabilized at par with the German mark in mid-1994.

3. This over all effort in the IMF was coordinated by Scott Brown, who has lead the IMF's negotiations with the authorities in Bosnia and Herzegovina from the cease-fire in October 1995 until its first stand-by arrangement with the IMF in May 1998.

4. I say "conceptually" because I am not purporting to provide a historical analysis of the origins of central banks.

5. It should be noted that historically currency boards, which were plentiful and extremely successful during the colonial period, did not have to deal with the day-to-day liquidity problems being discussed here because the banks that operated under currency boards were generally branches of banks with headquarters abroad—generally the country of the colonial reler—and as such had almost unlimited access to liquidity from their head offices.

6. IMF "loans" are technically swaps of monetary assets. A member country with a weak currency buys a strong currency from the IMF in exchange for its own currency. The IMF holds the members' currency in a deposit with the country's central bank. The process is reversed when the loan is repaid (repurchased).

7. If a purchase by Bosnia and Herzegovina from the IMF is to be used to finance budgetary expenditures, the domestic currency counterpart of the purchase will need to be arranged off the books of the CBBH. The IMF will also accept a security from the government, in lieu of a deposit with the CBBH. The security can be held for the IMF by the CBBH but cannot be a liability of the CBBH. This arrangement allows the CBBH to oversee the administration of the arrangement between the IMF and the government and to provide the IMF with one source of monetary data for the country.

8. Another solution for the liquidity consequences of fluctuations in government deposits in the central bank is to move them to commercial banks. This would introduce a new set of problems in Bosnia and Herzegovina. The banking system was in a very weakened condition after the war, and most of the transition from a command to a market economy had not yet been made. In addition, banking supervision is only beginning to develop. Furthermore, placing government deposits with banks is open to favoritism, or the claim of favoritism, just as withdrawals can lead to a bank's collapse.

9. The IMF had prepared model central-bank and -banking laws as the basis of discussion in December 1995. As appropriate counterparts were difficult to identify or contact at that time, it is not clear who actually saw these initial models.

10. Most of the Dayton Agreement's one-page discussion of monetary arrangements dealt with the composition of the central bank's Board. The Agreement explicitly called for the managing director of the IMF to nominate a governor from a nonbordering foreign country.

11. Between the initial discussion of the draft central bank law on June 26, 1996, which was attended by Scott Brown, Alessandro Zanello (the IMF resident representative), and myself, and the final adoption of the law, Mr. Zanello chaired many meetings of the Inter-Entity Working Group and of the future members of the Board that discussed the draft law with the authorities.

12. It would be interesting to know what was said during the discussions in Dayton that resulted in that language.

13. The first IMF nominated governor, Serge Robert, served for almost one year. The second IMF nominated governor, Peter Nicholl, a former deputy governor of the Reserve Bank of New Zealand, became governor in December 1997 and played an active role in settling the currency design issue.

14. As the result of an oversight, this last-minute switch from gross to net foreign-exchange reserves created an inconsistency in the definitions until the definition of monetary liabilities was adjusted to refer only to liabilities to residence. This oversight was corrected by inserting the word *resident* in

Article 31.2.a.(B) after the draft law had been accepted by the Joint Presidency but before it was adopted by the Parliament.

15. For an individual bank, interbank transfers of the proceeds of an asset sale or a loan should become the most flexible instrument of liquidity management. But such interbank transfers will not alleviate a systemwide shortage of reserves.

16. This is not to suggest that organizing the printing, safe keeping, distribution, and maintenance of the stock of banknotes, or the organization and opperation of administrative and accounting systems, and statistical and analytical functions are trivial undertakings.

17. The SDK executed all domestic noncash payments, provided all bank and government accounting services, functioned as the government's treasury, and conducted audits of banks and enterprises. Its operations ensured a very high level of tax compliance.

18. The payment bureaus provide the central bank's cash storage and distribution operation as its fiscal agent.

19. In the ZPP there remain a few accounts of customers who do not have a contract with a bank. These were allocated to the NBBH but have been moved to banks since April 1998.

20. The more technically modern system in the RS will soon provide multiple clearings during the day, thus giving banks better information on their reserve account positions.

21. These were the banks that cleared domestic payments through the ZPP—that is, the Bosniac majority area.

22. About DM 5 million was transferred by the physical delivery (turning over of the vault) or German mark banknotes in Sarajevo. The rest was on deposit with foreign banks abroad and was transferred by payment order to new foreign accounts established by the CBBH.

23. The Republika Srpska had turned its payment bureau into a state bank and transferred its government deposits from the National Bank of Republika Srpska to the new state bank/payment bureau.

24. There is a simple truth about net (clearing-house) settlements. If any one of the participants does not have sufficient funds in its settlement account to cover its net payments, the

only way the others who do have sufficient balances can settle is if someone extends credit to the one in deficit. In the case of settlement on the books of the Central Bank, if the CBBH posts the clearing results at the payment bureau to the reserve accounts of those banks with sufficient funds and leaves out ("refuses to settle") the one with insufficient funds, the CBBH will have extended credit to the bank in deficit.

25. Lurking in the background was the fact, well known to the public, that the NBBH did not have sufficient foreign-exchange assets to cover its deposit liabilities, without which it would be difficult for depositors to withdraw (use) their funds from the NBBH. Only foreign exchange could be accepted by the CBBH when transfers were made across reserve accounts, and only foreign exchange was likely to be acceptable to banks as the basis for establishing deposit balances. The NBBH's shortage of foreign-exchange backing, the exact amount of which was not known at the time, amounted to about DM 35 million (assuming that an additional DM 10 million deposited with a "foreign" bank can be recovered).

26. The CBBH Main Branch in Republika Srpska (RS) was opened in Pale on September 22, 1997, with a staff of nine and a Headquarters Research and Development Department staff of seven. However, none of the banks in that area opened their KM reserve accounts until May 1998. The Main Branch in RS is expected to be relocated to Banja Luka, where a branch was opened June 11, 1998.

27. The Croatian bank holding the funds claimed to be having temporary liquidity problems (which have lasted until this moment).

28. The restoration of health to the banking sector will naturally be important as well.

References

Baliño, Tomás, Charles Enoch, Alain Ize, Veerathai Santiprabhob, and Peter Stella. (1997). *Currency Board Arrangements: Issues, Experiences, and Implications for Fund-Supported Programs*. IMF Occasional Paper 151. Washington, DC: International Monetary Fund.

Coats, Warren. (1994). "In Search of a Monetary Anchor: A New Monetary Standard." Occasional Papers Number 48. International Center for Economic Growth, San Francisco.

International Monetary Fund. (1996). *World Economic Outlook, October 1996*. Washington, DC: IMF.

Khatkhate, Deena, and Warren Coats. (1998). "Money and Monetary Policy in Less Developed Countries." In (ed.), *Money and Finance, Issues, Institutions, Policies*. Orient Longman.

Lybek, Tonny. (1998). *Elements of Central Bank Autonomy and Accountability*. IMF-MAE Operational Paper 98-1. Washington, DC: International Monetary Fund.

Spiegel, Mark. (1998). *FRBSF Economic Letter Number 98-09*. San Francisco: Federal Reserve Bank of San Francisco, March 20.

Wolf, Thomas, Warren Coats, Daniel Citrin, and Adrienne Cheasty. (1994). *Financial Relations Among Countries of the Former Soviet Union*. IMF Economic Review No. 1. Washington, DC: International Monetary Fund.

VIII EMU AND TRANSITION ECONOMIES

15 THE INTERNATIONAL IMPACT OF THE EURO AND ITS IMPLICATIONS FOR TRANSITION COUNTRIES

Robert A. Mundell

Columbia University

Features of Great International Currencies

The introduction of the euro promises to be one of the great events in modern history. It will certainly be an event comparable to the breakdown of the Bretton Woods arrangements in the early 1970s when the anchored dollar standard broke down and drifted into a dollar standard and then flexible exchange rates. But its significance lies even deeper. The collapse of the Bretton Woods arrangements did not change the power configuration of the system. Both before and after the breakdown, the dollar was far and away the dominant currency. By contrast, the introduction of the euro will challenge the status of the dollar and alter the power configuration of the system. For this reason the introduction of the euro is the most important development in the international monetary system since the dollar replaced the pound sterling as the dominant international currency after the outbreak of World War I.[1]

Great Currencies and Great Powers

A decade from now the international monetary system will look very different. Exactly how different will depend on how well the euro stacks up against the dollar and the new configuration of important currency areas. To investigate this phenomenon, it is necessary to investigate the properties of great international currencies in the past.

The international monetary system is at any time composed of a multiplicity of currencies. The history of money would be hopelessly complicated if it were necessary to consider each and every currency that has ever existed. Theory, however, earns its keep by forging simplifications and generalizations that economize on unnecessary thought and information. The simplification in the field of money arises from the fact that important currencies are typically identified with important powers. In the last century it was sterling, and in this century it has ben the dollar largely because the British empire in its heyday and the United States today have been or are top powers.

It was not different in earlier centuries. The history of important international currencies parallels the history of top powers. It is not my intention to enter into this subject at any length here. Instead, I have sketched a crude summary of dominant currencies that have held the position of the "dollars" of their respective times (see Table 15.1). Let us now consider most important features associated with these currencies.

Transactions Domain

What makes a currency important internationally? Obviously, confidence in its stability is the key characteristic. But stability is a vector that depends on several factors: size of transactions domain, stability of monetary policy, freedom from controls, security of the issuing state, and fall-back value. Together, these characteristics must generate a sense of permanence and consequently low interest rates. I shall comment on each of these elements before making a general assessment of the prospects of the euro.

Size in the sense of depth and breadth of the market is a measure of the degree to which a currency can exploit the economies of scale and scope inherent in money as a public good. Size feeds on itself. The larger is the transactions domain, the more liquid the currency. The simplest surrogate for transactions domain is gross domestic product (GDP); an alternative measure is the size of the capital market. The size of a single-currency area determines its liquidity. Obviously, a currency that is money for 100 million people is much more liquid than a currency that is money for 1 million. Size is also important for a different reason. The larger the single-currency area, the better it can act as a cushion against shocks. If you consider a shock

Table 15.1. Great powers and great international currencies

Era	Power	Currency		
		Silver	Gold	Paper
Pre-7th century B.C.	Babylonia	Shekel		
6th–7th centuries B.C.	Persia		Daric	
5th–4th centuries B.C.	Greece	Drachma	Stater	
4th–3rd centuries B.C.	Macedonia		Stater	
3rd century B.C.–4th century A.D.	Rome	Denarius, sesterce	Solidus, aureus	
4th–13th centuries	Byzantium	Siliqua	Solidus, besant	
7th–13th centuries	Islam	Dirham	Dinar	
8th–12th centuries	Carolingian	Denier		
9th–13th centuries	China	Tael		Chuen
13th–16th centuries	Italy	Grosso	Florin, sequin, ducat	
16th–17th centuries	Spain	Real	Escudos	
17th–18th centuries	France	Denier, sol	Louis d'or	
18th century	India	Rupee	Mohur	
19th century	France	Franc	10, 20, 40, 100 franc	
19th–20th centuries	Britain	Shilling	Pound	Pound
19th–20th centuries	United States	Dollar	Eagle, dbl eagle	
20th century	United States			Dollar

such as German unification in 1990, manifested in a debt-financed increase in annual government spending and transfers east of more than 150 billion German marks (DM), close to destabilizing the German economy, then think of the effect of the same shock on a smaller economy. Alternatively, think how much more easily the shock would have been handled had there been in 1992 a stable European currency.

Size is relative. How the euro will survive depends on the competition. Its two rivals are obviously the dollar and the yen. How such a tricurrency world would work out depends importantly on relative market sizes.

From the standpoint of size, the outlook for the euro is very favorable. The EU-15 has a population of 375 million, and the EU-11, which includes those countries slated to enter European Monetary Union (EMU) in the first round, contains 292 million, somewhat larger than the United States; by comparison, Japan has 125 million. At current exchange rates, the GDP of the EU-15 is running at the rate of $8.4 trillion, that of the EU-11, at $6.6

trillion. These compare to U.S. GDP running at $8.5 trillion and Japanese GDP at $4.1 trillion. All of a sudden, with or without the four countries that will not proceed to the first round, the European Union (EU) becomes a player on the same scale as the United States and Japan. Over time, as the other countries join, as the per capita incomes of the poorer members of EU catch up, and as the EU expands into the rest of Central Europe, the EU will have a substantially larger GDP than the United States.

Openness also plays a role because it affects dependence. The less open, the more self-sufficient. As measured by the ratios of exports or imports to GDP, the G-3 economies are about equally open. The percentage of current exports to GDP in Europe is now around 30 percent, but when intra-European exports and imports are netted out, the openness figures are remarkably similar. It makes a difference whether openness is measured by exports or imports; economies with trade deficits will have higher import than export ratios. The U.S. ratio of imports to GDP is the highest, at nearly 11 percent; the EU-15 and Japan's import ratios are substantially lower, at around 8 percent. With openness measured by exports, on the other hand, Japan's and the EU-15's ratios are around 9 percent, while the United States' is a little over 8 percent. What emerges from these numbers is the significant fact that the three giant economies are all relatively closed, creating the risk that the monetary authorities may tend to underestimate the importance of the exchange rate and lead to more volatility of exchange rates.

Monetary Policy

The importance of monetary policy can hardly be underestimated. No currency has ever survived as an international currency with a high rate of inflation or with a recurring risk of debasement or devaluation. The lower the rate of inflation, the lower the cost of holding money balances, and the more of them will be held. In addition to a low rate of inflation, a *stable* rate is also desirable; because inflation and variance go hand in hand, however, much of the problem is avoided if inflation is kept low.

Additional considerations are predictability and consistency in monetary policy. In a democracy, both are abetted by *transparency*. If the monetary authorities openly state their targets and their strategies for achieving them, the market and the critical public will be able to make its own judgment about inflation outcomes.

From the standpoint of sound monetary policy, the outlook for the euro is also very favorable. The Maastricht Treaty is unambiguous in making price stability the target of monetary policy; while the European System of Central Banks (ESCB) can and should assist the monetary union in carrying out its other objectives, it is forbidden to do so if such assistance would conflict with price stability. Monetary policy will not be used to reduce unemployment by "surprise inflation" or to inflate away embarrassing public debts.

There remains considerable discretion for the independent European Central Bank (ECB), which is part of the ESCB. They will have to determine how price stability can best be achieved. The problem is complicated by lags in the effect of monetary policy. The best approach for a large economy like the EU is to target the inflation rate, formulating monetary policy actions on forecasts of inflationary pressures. Leading indicators that should always be taken into account include gold prices, other commodity prices, rates of change in the different monetary aggregates, the growth rate, and bond prices. The most successful central bankers have been pragmatists. But there is no reason that an independent ECB, modeled partly after the Bundesbank, cannot be as effective a body as the Federal Reserve System in the United States or the Bank of Japan. As Otto Pohl once said, "Credibility is the capital stock of any central bank," and you can be sure that the management of the ECB will do its best to establish credibility at the outset.

Controls

Exchange controls are frequently a symptom of a currency's weakness, anathema to the prospects of a currency being successful internationally. But controls are often imposed for political reasons, to enforce sanctions or carry out other objectives of foreign policy. Gone are the days when George Washington in the midst of revolution could draw on his account at the Bank of England.

The Security Factor

Monetary stability depends on monetary policy. But monetary policy is in turn affected by its sine qua non, political stability. Strong international currencies have always been linked to strong central states in their ascendancy. The reason is not far to seek. When a state collapses, the currency goes up in smoke. Examples include the hyperinflation of Germany and a few other countries after World War I, the collapse of the ruble after the October 1917 revolution, the hyperinflation of Kuomintang China after the Communist forces of Mao-Tse-Tung crossed the Yang-Tse, and the hyperinflations in the former Yugoslavia in the 1990s. It does not bode well for its currency if a state is not powerful enough to defend itself against enemies from outside and within.

What about the euro and the EU? Is the EU a strong central state? It is here that one can see a *potential* weakness in the euro. Of course, we could simply assume universal peace and go on to the next syllogism. If our assumption proved to be correct, the EU would not have to worry about enemies from without. It would be sufficient to hold itself together. Yet even here nothing can be completely taken for granted. Monetary union is supposed to be irrevocable. But it might not be in the face of a violent economic crisis. A real test would be its ability to hold itself together in the face of a drastic terms-of-trade shock such as that experienced in the 1970s when oil prices quadrupled.

The problems arising from the weakness of the central state cannot be swept under the rug. However, there are strong mitigating factors. The cold war ended, putting aside what was in the postwar years the most dangerous threat to European security. A closely connected factor is NATO, probably the most successful alliance in history. As long as the EU is tied to NATO and the military alliance with the United States, the EU will be able to fend off enemies from without even if it is not a strong central state. At the same time the process of monetary union will itself be a catalyst for closer political union, quickly bringing to common attention the most fissiparous issues. These factors greatly mitigate what would otherwise be a fatal defect.

Fall-Back Value Factor

Historical analogies can be treacherous. Modern currencies differ from the great currencies of the past, which were all either gold or silver or convertible into one or both of those metals. Unlike paper currencies, they had a fall-back value if the state collapsed. If any of the Italian city-states coining the sequins, florins, or ducats of the Middle Ages collapsed, the 3.5 gram gold content would always have a fallback value in metal. Metallic currencies frequently outlive the state issuing them, as the flourishing of Macedonian staters in the centuries after Alexander's death clearly attest. A more recent example is the Maria Theresa thaler, which continued to circulate in Eastern Africa long after that lady and the Austro-Hungarian

Empire were no more. That does not hold for a paper currency. After the Battle of Gettysburg in the United States, Confederate notes became worthless. Until the advent of the dollar, there is no historical record of any fiat currency achieving great international significance. Before the twentieth century all the great international currencies were metallic. The predecessor of the dollar, the pound sterling, achieved its great distinction as a metallic currency and came to be phased out when it ceased to be freely convertible into gold and even into its successor as top currency, the dollar. The inconvertible pound of the 1940s and 1950s was a far cry from its predecessor of the nineteenth century when the pound was as good as gold and an account at the Bank of England would never be blocked. The threat of inconvertibility and exchange controls toward the end of the viable life of a currency's international status is a factor further undermining the fall-back value of a currency.

The dollar achieved its international importance as a gold currency. When it was selected as the unofficial anchor at Bretton Woods, it had ceased to be internally redeemable but was still externally convertible into gold, the only such currency apart from the Swiss franc. If the dollar is now a fiat currency, as a "ghost of gold" it is the exception that makes the rule.

The introduction of the SDR provides an illustration of the importance of the fall-back factor. When first distributed in 1970, it had a gold weight guarantee confirmed in the Second Amendment to the Articles of A greement of the IMF. The gold guarantee made it a substitute for gold rather than the dollar and, at a time when gold was underpriced, a coveted asset that was in great demand. After the dollar was taken off gold, however, the international monetary authorities reneged on the gold guarantee, and the SDR went through a series of transformations, ultimately turning into a five-currency basket. When the euro comes into existence and the mark and franc and perhaps also the pound are scrapped, the SDR will have to be changed again. Had its gold guarantee been maintained, however, the SDR would have been much more important in the international monetary system and perhaps qualified as a useful supranational unit of account. Lacking both a commodity fallback value and the backing of a strong state, the SDR fell by the wayside on the scrap heap of forgotten dreams.

There is in this a lesson for the euro. In any great political emergency, and especially one that threatened the durability of the EU, there would be a run on the euro that would not be mitigated by any fall-back value. A run or even the risk of a run would make it difficult to float long-term securities in euros. The same strictures hold for the risks of exchange control.

It might be argued against this, that economies like Germany's thrived even when it was on the front line of the Cold War. Yet two factors need to be understood. The first was the existence of NATO, which kept Germany under the security umbrella of the United States. The second was that Germany, like most of the other countries on the European continent, did not—or only rarely—issued debt exceeding ten to fifteen years. The substantial quantities of really long-term securities issued in Europe have been phenomena of the post–Cold War world.

Such an emergency might also weaken the dollar. Total political and military security can never be assumed. Nevertheless, the U.S. situation differs in that the dollar has an established reputation; the United States, though a federation, has a strong central government; and it is military superpower. The lesson in this for the euro is that the ESCB will need larger holdings of external reserves than otherwise or than the United States. Fortunately, the EU countries have dollars and gold in abundance and will therefore be able to meet any foreseeable contingency.

Can the Euro Stack Up to the Dollar?

All things considered, the euro should stand up very well. It has two great strengths: a large and expanding transactions size and a culture of stability surrounding the ECB in Frankfurt. Initially, the EU-11 will be smaller than the dollar area, but as other members enter, as the EU expands, and as the poorer countries catch up, the euro area will eventually be larger than the dollar area. From the standpoint of monetary policies, there is also not much to choose between the two areas. Information is globally mobile, and there is no reason why the ECB should not become as efficient as the Federal Reserve System in the United States.

The euro also has also two weaknesses: it is not backed by a central state, and it has no fall-back value. In an unstable world, these weaknesses would be fatal. But the present environment is far from unstable. The Pax Americana has been just as efficient in preventing major conflicts as the Pax Britannica and the Pax Romana of earlier eras. If, as one should expect, NATO survives in a posteuro world, the stability of the next decades should be as assured as the past four decades. Coupled with very substantial EU gold and currency reserves, which could be centralized or earmarked for the ECB if the need arises, membership in NATO suffices to mitigate the weakness of the EU central government. Provided political coordination proceeds in the direction of integration, and important conflicts of conceit and nationalism are resolved, the euro should be able to maintain itself on an even keel with the dollar.

National and International Liquidity Effects

The ECB will be at the outset faced with tests of its credibility. There has been very little discussion of the impact of the euro on liquidity. My own view has been that it will be substantial.

The Change in the Liquidity of Money

When the currencies of the EU-11 or EU-15 are phased out and replaced by the euro, there will be a once-for-all liquidity effect that will be the same as a sudden, once-for-all increase in the European money supply, with proportionate inflationary effects. This is because the liquidity of the euro is greater than the liquidity of the sum of its parts. When, say, 500 billion euros worth of national currencies are replaced by 500 billion euros, European liquidity will be increased just as if there had been a sudden increase in the European money supply. After the euro is introduced, nine (say) euros or fewer euros will do the work that ten euros worth of the former national currencies. It is not known how large this effect will be, but it can hardly be less than 10 to 15 percent. As a consequence, the act of replacement will create an excess of liquidity and, other things equal, the need for additional monetary restraint to prevent an outbreak of inflation.

Liquidity Effect in the Bond Market

A similar effect will be experienced in the bond market. Like all assets, bonds have a liquidity dimension. Liquidity is measured by the ease with which an asset can be turned into cash and back without loss; it is inversely related to the cost of turning a bond into cash and then reacquiring it. Bonds with a large market are more liquid than bonds with a small market. The redenomination of national debts and corporate bonds from local currencies to euros will all of a sudden create a vast single market in euro-denominated bonds, a bond market of the same massive scale as that of the United States. The liquidity of this debt will be much larger than the liquidity of the combined public and corporate debts now denominated in national currencies. At the same time, the new ability of corporations to issue debt in euros will cheapen the access to capital and be a factor in fomenting an investment boom. The redenomination of these national debts is bound to create a revolution in the European and in world capital markets.

How important is this liquidity effect likely to be? Some indication can be got by comparing the degree of securitization in Europe with that of the United States and Japan, the two countries in the world with the largest bond markets. Outstanding government and corporate bonds in the Big Three markets—taking the EU-15 as a single entity—amounted to just short of $40 trillion in 1995. Of this total, $12.5 trillion was accounted for by the EU-15, and the remainder of $27 trillion by the United States and Japan together. The liquidity of the EU-15 debt will be greatly enhanced by the adoption of the single currency.

Reduction in the Cost of Capital

There is a related issue. The superiority of the new facility—the ability to issue euro-denominated debt—will make it attractive to increase the aggregate outstanding. But by how much? One heroic (or crude) way to estimating the potential increase is to compare ratios of outstanding bonds to GDP—securitization ratios—in different countries. Using the outstanding-debt figures cited above for 1995, and taking the 1995 GDPs of the EU-15, the United States, and Japan as $8,422 trillion, $7,265 trillion, and $5,135 trillion, respectively (remember these are translated into dollars at 1995 exchange rates), the securitization ratios in the EU and the United States + Japan come to, respectively, 1.5 and 2.18. This is a remarkable difference, and at least part of it can be attributed to the disadvantage the EU countries have up until now faced in their national-currency bond markets. No doubt there will be some shift from the other markets to the European markets and also an increase in total outstanding issues in Europe. Outstanding bonds in the EU-15 in 1995 would have had to have been an additional $6 trillion to equal the ratio in the United States and Japan. The euro will create magnificent new openings until the market reaches maturity.

The Money Multiplier

Another liquidity effect concerns the money multiplier. The new money multiplier will be the EU-15 money supply divided by the total supply of euro currency outstanding. One coordination problem is likely to arise because of different legal or conventional reserve ratios in the different member countries. Unwarranted or unintended inflationary of deflationary effects could arise as a result of balance of payments disequilibrium. Inflationary effects would be produced if a low-reserve-ratio country had a surplus and a high-reserve-ratio country had a deficit; similarly, deflationary effects would arise from the opposite case. In the long run the best way to eliminate these unwarranted effects is to harmonize reserve ratios among the EMU members.

Another more serious problem arises because of the possibility of euro substitutes. Because the replacement of a national currency by the euro transfers seigniorage to the ECB, each country has an incentive to minimize the use of euros; even though nations now use the euro as their own currency, from the standpoint of seigniorage it has effects like a foreign currency. To be sure, this effect is partly weakened by the redistribution of ECB profits to the national central banks (NCBs).[2] Yet it remains important. The experience of the United States is relevant here. From the beginning of the currency union in 1792, a conflict existed over the right of the states to create banks. Only after several decades was this problem sorted out in the courts and the states denied the right. Even today, however, several local communities in the United States create their own means of payment, economizing on federal dollars and gaining seigniorage.

What if one or more of the National Central Banks created a lender-of-last resort facility that enabled the banks to get by on a far smaller ratio of euros to deposit liabilities? The incentive for NCBs to do so may be eliminated for the most part by the provision by which their money incomes are earmarked for the general account and then "allocated to the national central banks in proportion to their paid-up shares in the capital of the ECB."[3] There nevertheless remain opportunities for the private sector or another branch of the government to perform functions previously performed by the NCBs. The EU's money multiplier will have to be watched closely.

The Centralization of Reserves

Much more well-known liquidity effects will arise from the centralization of international reserves. It is convenient to divide these reserves into three types: (1) foreign exchange held in European currencies, ECUs, IMF reserve positions, and SDRs, (2) foreign exchange held in non-European currencies, and (3) gold. Category 1 assets "may" be held and managed by the ECB. The ECB will also receive "up to an amount equivalent to" ECU 50 billion. The contributions of each member state will be fixed in proportion to its share in the subscribed capital of the ECB.[4]

Reserve needs in Europe will be lower on two counts. First, once EMU is formed, intraunion deficits and surpluses will be netted out and reserve needs for the union as a whole will be considerably smaller than the sum of the reserve needs of individual members. If external (mainly dollar) reserves were at an appropriate level before the union, they will be excessive after it. The same holds for gold reserves, of which the EU countries hold almost half the world's monetary reserves—although here gold reserves could partially compensate for the absence of the strong central state. Any immediate action to dispose of the part of these reserves that are considered excessive would be damaging to exchange-rate stability

The "Exorbitant Privilege" Effect

A factor that in the long run will be much more important is that the ESCB's need for foreign-exchange reserves will decline drastically once the euro is successfully launched. The euro will then become a reserve currency of choice for many countries around the world. Reserve-currency countries have less need for reserves—especially if there is confidence in its monetary policy—because its own currency is liquid internationally; reserve-currency status is a widow's cruse that keeps the owner in perpetual liquidity.

Apart from IMF positions and SDRs, EU-15 reserves at the end of 1996 amounted to 350.6 million ounces of gold (to which could be added 92.0 million held by the EMI). The other big holders were the United States with 261.7 million ounces, Switzerland with 83.3 million ounces, and the IMF with 103.4 million. These countries and institutions thus hold 891 million ounces or 80 percent of the world total of 1,108.1 million ounces. Pooling all foreign exchange would give the ECB $387 billion, or 25.9 percent of the world total of $1,498 billion at the end of 1996. This compared with the holdings of $209 billion in foreign exchange in Japan or about $300 billion in Greater China (China, Taiwan, and Hong Kong).

The foreign-exchange reserves would not seem so excessive (at least compared to the Asian holdings) were it not for the fact that the euro, as already mentioned, will itself become a widely used international currency, conferring on the EU the "exorbitant privilege" to run a "deficit without tears"—to use the phrases of Charles De Gaulle and Jacques Rueff in their prickly attacks on the dollar in the 1960s. China, for one, has already said it will hold part of its reserves in euros.

International Reactions to the Euro

It should not be thought that a change as momentous as the introduction of the euro promises to be will leave "other things constant." The only constants are the laws of change, which includes competition and expansion. Let us assume that the euro-11 is on its way to being launched successfully. Let us consider the impact on the non-EMU members of the EU—Britain, Denmark, Sweden, and Greece—and then consider the future demand for euros as an international reserve asset.

EU Countries with a Derogation

Let us consider first the stake of Britain. As the largest of the EU members with a "derogation," Britain's position is especially important. The issue is intensely political in Britain. The damage done by Britain's short-lived experience in the ERM in the early 1990s was great. Britain opted out in November 1997 with the argument that the pound was near the peak of its cycle and that entering at a high rate would only repeat the bad experience it had with the ERM between October 1990 and September 1992. The Conservative Party opposition is split on the issue, but its leader has taken a dogmatic stand against joining. The Labor Party government has taken a cautious approach and will test the issue with a referendum. The U.K. Treasury has set down five tests (see, for example, Plenderleith, 1998) that it considers define whether a clear and unambiguous case can be made for joining EMU:

- Sustainable convergence between Britain and the economies of a single currency,
- Sufficient flexibility to cope with economic change,
- Favorable impact on investment,
- Favorable impact on the United Kingdom's financial-services industry, and
- Favorable impact on employment.

There is a good chance that most if not all of these conditions will or can be satisfied. But even if one or more of them are not satisfied, it might still be in Britain's interest to join. In the first place, the addition of Britain would add great weight to the euro area and would therefore enhance its stability and chances of success. Second, Britain would give Euroland a better political balance, taking the edge off the twin evils of Franco-German rivalry and Franco-German domination; in this connection also, Europe with Britain would be more likely to lean toward a path of cooperation rather than rivalry with the United States. Third, London is the natural capital market for Europe, with as many employees in the financial industry as the entire population of, say, Frankfurt. Fourth, the costs for Britain of staying out are high—including political marginalization within the EU, economic disadvantages for its banking system in the consolidation movement in European finance, and loss of investment to the Continent. Even if it could be argued (and I would not make the argument) that Britain might be better off had the concept of euro never came up, the existence of the euro stacks the case in favor of Britain's entry.

For these reasons, as the euro is launched successfully, I would expect Britain's objections to be overcome and that the referendum for entry has a better than 60 percent chance of success. If Britain elects to join, the chances are high that Sweden will not be far behind, and, given that Denmark and Greece have already indicated their intention to join the new ERM, the chances are high that all four countries will be on board when the transition period ends on June 30, 2002.

The Use of the Euro as an International Reserve

Once the euro has been launched, central banks will want to rethink their portfolio decisions. Of about $1.5 billion in currency reserves in 1998 about two-thirds are in dollars and the rest are in marks, francs, yen, and a few other currencies. It can be assumed that most countries that hold EU currencies will want to exchange them for euros. For example, the CFA franc area will convert its francs into euros at the locked entry rate and adopt a euro instead of a franc anchor. Currency boards, like Estonia, that use the mark as an anchor will do the same as will central banks, like Poland and Hungary, that use marks in their currency basket. Taking into account conversion of existing holdings of EU currencies in reserves, perhaps as much as $300 billion will be held in euros at the end of the transition period in the middle of the year 2002.

To estimate the demand for euros, it is necessary to examine first the demand for reserves as a whole. From IMF tables, it can be seen that reserves have been rising secularly as a proportion of imports. World reserves represented 8.6 weeks of annual world imports in 1967, 11.6 weeks in 1976, 12.6 weeks in 1986, and 15.2 weeks in 1996 (IMF, 1997). Over the past two decades, imports have been rising at the rate of about 8 percent a year (7.4 percent in 1977 to 1986, 8.8 percent in 1987 to 1996). With imports more than doubling every nine years, and the ratio of reserves to imports rising, an extrapolation of past trends would suggest a doubling of reserves every eight years or so. If that relationship held, world reserves, taken at $1.5 trillion in 1998, would be $3.0 trillion in 2006. How would this increase of $1.5 trillion in currency reserves by 2006 be distributed between dollars and euros?

By 2006, with the other four members of EU in Euroland, with a GDP considerably higher than the United States, it seems reasonable to assume that the demand for currency reserves would be equally divided between dollars and euros. That, however, would represent a tremendous adjustment in international financial arrangements, as Table 15.2 shows.

On the assumptions made, demand for dollars would increase by only $100 billion over the eight-year period, while demand for euros would increase by $800 billion. In other words, euro demand would amount to $100 billion a year. In the absence of capital flows, this demand would impose on the euroland a current account deficit of the same amount, reversing the surplus that has characterized EU accounts in recent years. Alternatively, to resist the change in the current account balance, capital exports from the EU of $100 billion a year would be required.

For the United States, the situation will be more difficult. Over the past fifteen years, between 1982 and 1988, the U.S. current account deficit has been close to $1.7 trillion (IMF, 1997). Over this period, the U.S. net investment position deteriorated from $265 billion to −$774 billion, a turnaround of over $1 trillion. In other words the $1.7 trillion of accumulated current account deficits has been financed by $1 trillion of capital inflows and $0.7 trillion of increased dollar holdings. Over the next eight years, only a tiny amount of the U.S. current accounts can be financed by increased dollar holdings, thrusting the burden of financing the deficits almost entirely

Table 15.2.   Projections of global demand for reserves (trillions of U.S. dollars)

	U.S. Dollars	Euros + Eurocurrencies	Other	Total
1998	1.0	0.3	0.2	1.5
2002	0.9?	0.9?	0.45?	2.25
2006	1.2	1.2	0.6	3.0

on capital flows. It is much more likely that the United States will have to reduce drastically its current account deficit.

So much for the "long" period of eight years. For the intermediate future, the situation looks much worse. As Table 15.2 shows, growth in demand for dollar reserves in the early years will not just slow down but turn negative, as attempts are made to diversify out of dollars. It would be easy to envisage an excess supply of dollars appearing in the years between 2000 and 2004, which would put downward pressure on the dollar and upward pressure on the euro. The diversification phenomena could create a monetary crisis of the first magnitude if these portfolio shifts were allowed to create expectations for a substantial appreciation of the euro against the dollar.

The Euro as an Anchor for the Transition Countries

The main change in the international monetary situation facing the transition countries, and especially those with geographical or political propinquity to euroland, is that there will in future be a huge and tight currency area that opens new opportunities and threats. The opportunities stem from the fact that the euro will represented a currency on the same scale as the dollar. The threat arises from the increasing bilateral character of relations between the EU and its neighbors.

The most important decision countries will have to make concerns their exchange-rate policy. There is, of course, in the abstract, a complete spectrum of possible arrangements, ranging from complete freedom of floating rates to the completely fixed rates of a currency board or monetary union.[5] The pursuit of monetary stability requires that a country stabilize monetary aggregates, the price level, the exchange rate, a quasi-monetary commodity such as gold, or a combination of several or all variables. But before one or more of the stabilization policies can be introduced, certain preconditions must be met. The monetary authorities, for example, cannot pursue an independent stabilization policy if, for example, the central bank is required to finance budget deficits. Fiscal balance is a prerequisite for stabilization policy.

Given fiscal balance, the choice of targets to stabilize depends on a number of factors, including the initial conditions from which stabilization begins. I have argued elsewhere (Mundell, 1997a) that high-inflation countries—inflation rates higher than 20 percent a year (or 2 percent a month)—should engage in monetary targeting, whereas countries with low inflation rates—5 to 20 percent a year—should engage in inflation targeting. One the other hand, countries with very low inflation—less than 5 percent a year—

should consider fixing their exchange rates, provided certain conditions are met.

Using the Euro in the CEEC-5

Fixing the exchange rate is a very attractive option for some countries for which the necessary conditions are met. What are these conditions? One is obviously that a country—call it the home country—can anchor its currency at a given rate to an anchor currency only if a suitable anchor currency exists for that country. An anchor currency must (1) encompass a large transactions area relative to the home country, (2) have a stable and low inflation rate, and (3) be issued by a country that is politically compatible to it. A fixed exchange-rate policy, for example, is not an option for the United States because, while the dollar is suitable as an anchor for many other currencies, there is no other currency that is a suitable anchor for the dollar.

The advent of the euro means that there will exist in Europe an anchor currency that is suitable for all the neighboring countries to which the European Union is politically compatible. That necessarily includes the five Central and East European Countries that have applied for EU membership, the so-called CEEC-5—Poland, Hungary, Czech Republic, Slovenia, and Estonia. Although membership before 2002 is unlikely, the convergence process will have to begin considerably before membership is achieved.

The prospective entrants will be full members of the EU with a derogation from EMU; they will, however, be eligible to join. A formal legal requirement imposed by the Maastricht Treaty requires that before being admitted, they are in the ERM—effectively it will be a new ERM-II—for two years without a devaluation. (The same requirement will be applied to the "pre-ins" of Britain, Sweden, Denmark, and Greece). Upon accession to the EU, the national banks will become members of the ESCB, required to fulfill all the institutional and legal provisions in the field of central-bank independence. These require legislation for central-bank independence and also convertibility requirements. In the CEEC-5 countries the independence requirements have already been passed, and the five countries have also declared convertibility consistent with the provisions of Article VIII of the IMF Articles of Agreement (see Backe and Linder, 1996).

Because monetary union imposes the same discipline on monetary policy as a currency-board arrangement or fixed-exchange-rate system in which the central bank eschews changes in its domestic assets (allowing its monetary policy to be completely determined by central-bank purchases and

Table 15.3. Growth (G), inflation (I), and exchange rates (E) in the CEEC-5 countries (E = national currency units per U.S. dollar)

		1994	1995	1996	1997	1998[a]
Slovenia	G	5.3	4.9	3.1	3.3	3.5
	I	19.8	12.6	8.8	8.9	9.5
	E	127	130	141	168	175
Czech R.	G	2.6	4.8	4.1	1.4	2.7
	I	10.2	7.9	8.6	10.0	11.6
	E	29	27	27	31	36
Poland	G	5.2	7.0	6.1	6.9	5.6
	I	29.5	21.6	18.5	13.0	10.0
	E	2.3	2.5	2.7	3.2	3.6
Hungary	G	2.9	1.5	1.3	3.9	4.5
	I	21.2	28.3	19.8	18.0	15
	E	105	126	153	186	210
Estonia	G	−3.2	2.9	3.0	9.0	6
	I	41.7	28.9	14.8	10.0	8
	E	12.5	11.5	12.4	12.5	

Sources: IMF (1997 and monthly issues); WEFA (1998).
a. WEFA forecasts.

sales of foreign exchange), the best program for convergence for the CEEC-5 involves a tight fixed exchange rates arrangement or currency board. Let us consider these countries in turn, drawing on the recent growth, inflation, and exchange-rate information about these countries depicted in Table 15.3.

There is a curious incompatibility between the Maastricht requirements for central, bank independence and the convergence requirements in ERM-II. Independence was imposed in imitation of the Bundesbank's policy. But after EMU, only the European Central Bank will be "independent." The NCBs will have no power whatsoever. Yet exchange-rate decisions must inevitably be political decisions, as they are in nearly every country. The Bundesbank, for example, would not be legally entitled to fix the DM to another currency, including the ecu or euro, without the sanction of the government. The CEEC-5 parliaments have each established legislation providing for central-bank independence along the lines of the Maastricht requirement, yet government still retain the legal authority to fix exchange rates to the euro in currency-board fashion despite the fact that this would strip all discretion from the "independent" central bank.

It could be argued that true central-bank independence must imply authority to control exchange rates. If so, that would grant them more power than the Bundesbank or the Federal Reserve System. It would also imply that the central banks have the power to veto any government decision to establish fixed exchange rates or a currency board with the euro. Although it seems unlikely that any central-bank council would go so far as to reject a major government initiative in the field of exchange-rate policy, it is easy to see that it could exercise its power to prevent such an initiative from coming into being.

Why Inflation May Differ in the Euro Zone

Use of the euro as an anchor generally means that countries will share the same inflation rate as the countries in euroland. There are, however, three qualifications that need to be taken into account.

Incorrect Initial Rates.   The first qualification is needed to allow exchange rates that are out of equilibrium. If, when the country enters a fixed-exchange-rate arrangement, a currency is overvalued relative to its anchor partners, it will experience excess supply, unemployment, and a lower rate of inflation until equilibrium has been restored. If, on the other hand, it is undervalued, it will experience excess demand and inflationary pressure until equilibrium has been restored. One of the most difficult problems in joining a currency area is to choose the right exchange rate at which to enter.

Britain's entry into the ERM in October 1990 presents a possible example of an overvaluation. Many people in the United Kingdom believe that it entered the ERM at a rate (DM 2.95 = IUK 1) that overvalued the pound against the mark, setting in motion tendencies that led Britain to abandon its peg during the ERM crisis of September 1992. The "overvaluation" however, had the salutary effect of reducing Britain's inflation rate from 9.5 percent in 1990 to 5.9 percent in 1991 and to 3.6 percent in 1992; despite the depreciation of the pound after Britain left the ERM, inflation continued to drop to 1.6 percent in 1993 and averaged less than 3 percent in subsequent years. British policy was therefore highly successful even if it could not be considered a ringing endorsement of the ERM.

An example of an undervaluation was the case of the kroon. When Estonia reintroduced[6] the kroon in June 1992, pegged to the German mark at a rate of 8 kroons = 1 DM, the purchasing power of 8 kroons was about four times higher than the purchasing power of one DM. As a result inflation continued to soar in the last half of 1992, and was 90 percent in 1993, 48 percent in 1994, 29 percent in 1995, 23 percent in 1996, 15 percent in 1997 and is expected to be 10 percent in 1998. With the nominal exchange rate fixed this represented a tremendous real appreciation. The story is somewhat further complicated by productivity increases in traded goods that were greater than those in nontraded goods, so that initial undervaluation may not have been the sole cause of the inflation subsequent to the establishment of the currency board. But it can hardly be gainsaid that the exchange rate of 8 kroons per mark undervalued the kroon.[7]

Differential Productivity Growth. The second qualification is needed to allow for changes in productivity that necessitate changes in the real exchange rate. In the absence of changes in the terms of trade, the real exchange rate can be identified with changes in the relative prices of traded (international) and nontraded (domestic) goods. Suppose that productivity in the international goods industries increases, lowering real production costs. At a constant *nominal* exchange rate, international goods can only fall relative to domestic goods if the latter rises, increasing the inflation index.

As already noted, the high inflation in Estonia after the establishment of the currency board could have been due partly to a more rapid increase in productivity in international goods than in domestic goods. But a more spectacular example occurs in the case of Hong Kong. Hong Kong established its currency board in 1983, partly to cope with rapid inflation and a depreciating currency. The rate of $H.K. 7.8 = $ U.S. 1.00 may have somewhat undervalued the HK dollar because inflation continued at 8.5 percent in 1984 before falling to an average of 3.3 percent in the next two years. After 1986, however, inflation persisted at a continually higher level than the United States, averaging 8.7 percent over the 1987 to 1996 decade. How could this be at a time that inflation averaged only 3.6 percent in the same decade? The answer is that trade was expanding at a decade-average rate of 18 percent and productivity in the traded-goods industries was soaring as Hong Kong's comparative advantage was shifting from a manufacturing center to a service center with specialization in finance, shipping, and commerce. With the U.S. dollar fixed to the Hong Kong dollar, the only way the real exchange rate could appreciate was by an increase in the prices of domestic goods and factors.

Different Weights in Price Indexes. The third qualification is necessary because of the use of price indexes with different weights. National price indexes differ from country to country and when relative prices change the price indexes diverge even in a common currency area. Thus when the euro becomes established—and relative prices change—the national price indexes and therefore "inflation rates" in the eleven countries will differ. Economic policy will have to target an inflation rate that is derived from a price index with common weights.

The three causes of the divergence of inflation rates between a country anchoring its currency to a foreign currency do not constitute arguments against the use of a currency board to achieve convergence before entering a monetary union. Except for the first cause, the entry problem, members of a monetary union will also experience divergences arising from differential productivity growth rates or different weights in inflation indexes. As far as the entry problem is concerned, it must be faced at some point, and the earlier it is faced, the earlier the home country will become part of the purchasing-power parity area of the monetary union.

We may conclude that there are strong arguments for generating convergence in each of the CEEC-5 group by adopting an exchange rate fixed to the euro using the mechanism of adjustment required by a currency board. That is the mechanism of adjustment that will prevail under the monetary union, and the sooner they introduce it, the earlier convergence and admittance to the monetary union will come about.

Policies in Related Countries

Several other transition countries have not been accepted for the next round of admittance to the EU but nevertheless have to be considered potential candidates once they take steps to increase convergence in political, social, and economic policies. These countries include six countries: Slovakia, Croatia, Latvia, Lithuania, Romania, and Bulgaria. Table 15.4 shows the basic data for these countries. Of these six countries, Romania is furthest from inflation control. The inflation rate in Bulgaria is still high, but the establishment of a currency board in 1997, with the help (indeed insistence) of the IMF, will, if it is maintained, bring to an end the high inflation that has racked that country since the transition began.

Slovakia, Croatia, and Latvia are all in a position to gain from the assumed stability of the euro and to stabilize their own currencies to it. Lithuania (which like Latvia and unlike Estonia was not invited to EU membership) has taken a step away from convergence. It introduced a currency board on April 1, 1994, at the rate of 4 lita = $US 1 but, astonishingly, scrapped it three years later. The real reasons are not entirely clear. The

Table 15.4. Growth (G), inflation (I), and exchange rates (E) (E = national currency units per U.S. dollar)

		1994	1995	1996	1997	1998[a]
Slovakia	G	5.0	7.0	6.9	5.9	5.6
	I	13.4	9.9	5.8	6.4	8.0
	E	32	30	31	33	37
Croatia	G					
	I	107	4	4	5	6
	E	6.0	5.2	5.4	6.1	6.4
Latvia	G	0.6	−1.6	2.8	5	5
	I	36	25	18	8	6
	E	0.55	0.54	0.56	0.59	0.57
Lithuania	G	6.0	3.0	3.0	6	5
	I	72	40	25	9	7.0
	E	4	4	4	4	4.4
Romania	G	3.4	7.1	4.1	−6.5	−3.0
	I	61.7	27.8	56.9	152.0	60.0
	E	1,655	2,033	3,084	7,168	10,411
Bulgaria	G	1.8	2.1	−10.9	−7.4	2.5
	E	121.9	32.9	310.8	579.0	25.0
	I	49	68	173	1,750	1,845

Sources: IMF (1997 and monthly issues); WEFA (1998).
a. WEFA forecasts.

Bank of Lithuania (1997) asserted that "it will only be possible to take a more active position in the process of harmonization towards the EU monetary policy after getting back to the modern central bank model." This seems to represent a colossal confusion, that the route to the EU would be faster by adopting the central-bank model, which will in fact apply only to the European Central Bank, in Lithuania. What in fact would be needed was not a change from the currency board to a central bank, but a shift from an anchor to the dollar to an anchor to the euro.

Conclusions

1. The introduction of the euro is one of the most important monetary events in the twentieth century.
2. Despite misgivings in several quarters, it will be a success, and the purchasing power of the euro will be relatively stable.

3. Britain, Sweden, Denmark, and Greece will eventually join the EU-11 in the monetary union.

4. The euro will revolutionize Europe's money and banking industries and inaugurate an unprecedented wave of consolidations and mergers.

5. International demand for the euro will be large and growing, equal to an average of nearly $100 billion a year over the next few years, rising to a $1 trillion over the next decade.

6. Diversification from the dollar will take place, putting upward pressure on the dollar-euro exchange rate.

7. Some form of international monetary coordination between the United States, euroland, and Japan will be required to smooth potentially damaging swings in exchange rates.

8. If these reversible swings are successfully combated, the stability of the international monetary system will be improved by the addition of a euro alternative to the dollar as a reserve and key currency.

9. Nearly every country in the world will want to hold some euros in its reserves.

10. A smaller group of countries in Central and Eastern Europe will find it useful to use the euro as an anchor for their own currencies, as will the CFA franc area and several other Mediterranean and African countries.

11. Joining the euro area is likely to best meet the needs of the countries intending to join the EU when economic convergence conditions permit.

12. The CEEC-5 countries—Slovenia, Poland, Hungary, Czech Republic, and Estonia—which have been invited to join the EU in the next round, should seek fiscal balance and, if they have not already done so, then adopt currency-board-like arrangements, with national currencies rigidly fixed to the euro, and the elimination of all credit operations not matched by changes in foreign-exchange reserves. Estonia's currency board with the mark can stay in place, making the conversion to the euro when the latter comes into being.

13. Other countries intent on establishing conditions for entry into the EU should also consider fixed exchange rates and automatic adjustment with the euro. Latvia could establish convergence most quickly by a currency board arrangement with the euro. Lithuania, however, has been moving in the wrong direction; it should reverse course and establish a new currency board with the mark and then the euro.

14. Slovakia and Croatia are in a position now to establish a currency board with the euro as soon as political conditions permit.
15. Romania is still a long way from stabilization. Bulgaria, with a new IMF-sponsored currency board, fixed to the mark at 1,000 lev, has taken a step in the right direction.

Notes

1. One could even go further and argue that the shift from the pound to the dollar as the main unit of account in the international monetary system was not that important insofar as it had become inevitable. Already by the 1870s and U.S. economy had overtaken the British economy and by 1914 was thrice as large as the economies of either Britain or Germany. Because of the inertia that prevails in international monetary systems, the pound continued as the main benchmark currency as long as its convertibility into gold was assured. By 1915, however, convertibility was in doubt, and, for several years after the war ended, the pound was an inconvertible paper currency. Bearing this in mind, one could argue that the introduction of the euro is the most important event since the downfall of bimetallism and the rise of the gold standard in the 1870s.

2. Article 33(1.b) of the Protocols and Declarations annexed to the Treaty provides for the transfer of ECB's net profits (except for a maximum of 20 percent transferred to the general reserve fund) to the shareholders of the ECB (that is, the NCBs) in proportion to their paid-up shares.

3. Article 32.5 of Protocols and Declarations [http://europa.eu.int/euro/en/pap7/pap716.asp?nav=en].

4. See *Complication of Community Legislation* [http://europa.eu.int/euro/en/pag716.asp?nav=en].

5. I have discussed the alternatives at some length in Mundell (1997a, 1997b).

6. The kroon had been Estonia's currency before that country lost its independence to the Soviet Union in 1939.

7. To say that the kroon was substantially undervalued is not quite the same as saying that a mistake was made in fixing the kroon at that rate. In theory it might have been better to restrict the money supply and let the real exchange rate appreciate by an increase in the exchange value of the kroon. But in the middle of 1992, it was considered necessary to make a political statement that would sharply differentiate Estonia's currency from the other inflationary currencies of the former Soviet Union. That political objective was achieved by the policy in fact pursued.

References

Backe, Peer, and Isabella Lindner. (1996). "European Monetary Union: Prospects for EU Member States and Selected Candidate Countries from Central and Eastern Europe." *Focus on Transition* 2.

Bank of Lithuania. (1997). *Monetary Policy Programme of the Bank of Lithuania for 1997–99*. Vilnius: Bank of Lithuania.

Corden, W. Max. (1997). "The Dilemmas of Currency Boards." In Guillermo E. Perry (ed.), *Currency Boards and External Shocks: How Much Pain, How Much Gain?*: World Bank, Latin American and Caribbean Studies (February).

Hanke, Steve H., Lars Joning, and Kurt Schuler. (1993). *Russian Currency and Finance: A Currency Board Approach to Reform.* London: Routledge.

International Monetary Fund. (1997). *International Financial Statistics Yearbook.*: IMF.

Mundell, R.A. (1997a). "Exchange Rate Arrangements in the Transition Countries." Paper presented at the Third Dubrovnik Conference, June 23–25.

Mundell, R.A. (1997b). "Updating the Agenda for Monetary Union." In M.I. Blejer, J.A. Frenkel, L. Leiderman, and A. Razin (eds.), *Optimum Currency Areas: New Analytical and Policy Developments* (pp. 29–48). Washington, DC: International Monetary Fund.

Mundell, R.A. (1998a). "Great Expectations for the Euro: Parts I & II." *Wall Street Journal*, March 24, March 25.

Mundell, R.A. (1998b). "Making the Euro Work." *Wall Street Journal*, April 30.

Plenderleith, Ian. (1998). ICMB (Genera) Occasional Pagers No. 12, May.

Schuler, Kurt. (1996). *Should Developing Countries Have Central Banks? Currency Quality and Monetary Systems in 155 Countries.* London: Institute for International Affairs.

Williamson, John. (1995). *What Role for Currency Boards?* Washington, DC: Institute for International Economics.

World Economic Financial Association. WEFA. (1998). *World Economic Outlook: Developing Countries and Economic.* WEFA.

16 MONETARY AND EXCHANGE-RATE POLICIES OF TRANSITION ECONOMIES OF CENTRAL AND EASTERN EUROPE AFTER THE LAUNCH OF EMU

Paul R. Masson

Introduction

For several years now, the more advanced transition economies of Central and Eastern Europe (CEECs)[1] have reached a new stage in their adaptation to market forces and convergence toward the structures and economic outcomes exhibited in Western Europe. Growth has strengthened, inflation has been reduced markedly, and public and private institutions have been developed to provide the infrastructure for liberal, competitive, and efficient economies. Moreover, European Union (EU) accession negotiations began in March 1998 for five of these economies—Czech Republic, Estonia, Hungary, Poland, and Slovenia—presaging membership in the next few years and further progress toward convergence with the West.

It therefore makes sense to begin to evaluate economic policy options and regimes on the same basis as for advanced market economies. In the early years of transition, exchange-rate and monetary policies were constrained by thin financial markets, the absence of indirect monetary policy instruments, weak and dependent central banks, large budget deficits, and the special needs of these economies for rapid adjustment of relative prices. Pegged exchange rates served a special, and in several economies, a temporary, role in anchoring price levels and relative prices to those in market economies and in disciplining monetary and fiscal policies. As the transition process progressed, several CEEC economies moved to greater exchange-rate flexibility, though a number of them continued to operate de facto or de jure fixed pegs and currency boards.

As the prospects for accession to the EU increase and with the launching of the euro on January 1, 1999, monetary and exchange-rate policies are likely to face new pressures for further mutation. New members of the EU will be expected to adopt the *acquis communautaire*, and this will include the European Monetary Union (EMU). While no country from the current members of the EU can be forced to join EMU (and countries can deliberately avoid a formal obligation by not meeting all the criteria), it may well be expected that countries negotiating to join would make some commitment to try to become part of the euro-bloc on some mutually agreed timetable. Furthermore, they may be expected in the meantime, between joining the EU and adopting the euro, to participate in the so-called ERM2 arrangement, which will limit fluctuations of non-EMU EU countries' currencies relative to the euro.[2] Even before joining the EU, countries negotiating accession may feel that they can improve their chances of a successful outcome through showing that they are good Europeans by pegging to the euro, or in any case orienting their monetary policies around a euro-based exchange-rate target.

This chapter explores the implications of that choice and discusses whether alternative monetary policy strategies—and, in particular, inflation targeting—may be more appropriate for some CEECs at this stage in their transition process. Two hazards are identified with a premature euro peg: first, that capital flows to CEECs, like those to many emerging markets, may be strong and volatile, making the defense of pegged rates difficult; and second, that faster productivity growth may produce a trend real exchange-rate appreciation, which would be inconsistent with a combination of nominal exchange-rate stability and low inflation. It is recognized, however, that EU membership seems a likely and desirable goal for most CEECs, and hence integration with Western Europe and adoption of the euro are likely long-run objectives. The relevant questions are not whether but when such a policy should be adopted and also how to ensure a smooth convergence to EMU membership.

After a brief review of the macroeconomic performance of CEECs, the chapter considers the implications of EMU for them. Data for a very simple "optimum currency area" criterion are presented to assess the advisability of pegging to, or adopting, the euro in the current situation. In addition, the prospects for capital flows are considered.

Then, the requirements for an effective inflation-targeting framework are discussed as well as the potential benefits of such a strategy. The chapter concludes that inflation targeting is unlikely to be the simple answer to the dilemma and that in practice a hybrid strategy giving a weight to both the exchange rate and inflation is likely to emerge in the transition to EMU membership. This is not necessarily incompatible with the ERM2, at least in principle; however, it is important for the latter not to take on the excessive rigidity that characterized the ERM in the early 1990s.

Exchange-rate Arrangements and Macroeconomic Performance to Date

Table 16.1 shows the dramatic progress made by CEECs in the last few years. After an initial period of sharp output declines (though the data are subject to measurement problems), by 1994 most countries had begun to see positive growth. There have also been substantial inflation reductions though, for some countries (especially Albania, Bulgaria, and Romania), inflation rose sharply after an initial decline (Table 16.7).[3] By 1997, all countries except the above three were seeing robust growth, and inflation rates were in the single digits or low double digits. Thus, convergence toward EU

Table 16.1. CEECs: real GDP growth, 1991–1997 (in percent)

	1991	1992	1993	1994	1995	1996	1997
Albania	−28.0	−7.2	9.6	9.4	8.9	9.1	−7.0
Bulgaria	−11.7	−7.3	−1.5	1.8	2.1	−10.9	−7.4
Croatia	−17.0	−11.7	−0.9	0.6	1.7	4.3	6.3
Czech Republic	−11.5	−3.3	0.6	2.7	5.9	4.1	1.2
Estonia	−7.9	−21.6	−8.2	−1.8	4.3	4.0	5.0
Hungary	−11.9	−3.1	−0.6	2.9	1.5	1.3	4.0
Latvia	−11.1	−35.2	−16.1	2.1	0.3	2.8	6.0
Lithuania	−6.0	−19.6	−17.1	−11.2	2.3	5.1	6.0
Macedonia, FYR	−17.0	−21.1	−9.4	−2.7	−1.6	0.9	1.5
Poland	−7.0	2.6	3.8	5.2	7.0	6.1	6.9
Romania	−12.9	−8.8	1.5	3.9	6.9	3.9	−6.6
Slovak Republic	−15.9	−6.7	−3.7	4.6	6.8	7.0	5.7
Slovenia	−8.9	−5.5	2.8	5.3	4.1	3.2	3.7

Source: IPIF (1998).

levels was being achieved both on the real side, through higher per capita growth than in the EU, and on the nominal side, with declines of inflation toward EU levels.

This common pattern was associated with a variety of exchange-rate arrangements. Though exchange-rate fixity was an initial choice for Poland and Czechoslovakia, by 1998 each of them had moved to greater flexibility.[4] In Poland's case the move to a crawling peg was a deliberate policy to avoid losses of competitiveness associated with inflation that remained persistently above those in industrial countries, while in the Czech Republic, the move to greater flexibility was forced on the authorities by an exchange-rate crisis triggered by strong capital outflows. Estonia has had a long period of successful growth performance while operating a currency board, while Bulgaria has more recently introduced one after failed attempts to stabilize. Hungary has since the beginning of the transition process maintained some degree of exchange-rate flexibility, either a managed float or (more recently) a crawling band, though the exchange rate has typically been at one edge of the crawling band so that de facto flexibility has been less than appears. Romania, though nominally allowing the exchange rate to fluctuate, in fact limited fluctuations during various periods of time. Table 16.2 summarizes current exchange-rate arrangements. Depending on those exchange arrangements and the consequent commitments to intervene to limit fluctuations in some cases, foreign-exchange reserves have on occasion exhibited large movements, but on average there has been a strong trend increase in holdings of reserves, even as a proportion of imports, which themselves have grown strongly (Table 16.3).

Despite differences in exchange regime, a common feature of these economies has been a trend real appreciation, measured on the basis of relative consumer price indexes—at least after an initial short period of sharp and erratic price movements (Figure 16.1). Such a trend appreciation would be consistent with real-wage increases associated with rapid productivity growth, but the experience of CEECs is not necessarily the result of faster productivity growth in traded than nontraded sectors, as in the standard Balassa-Samuelson story. Grafe and Wyplosz (1997) argue that in transition economies, appreciating real exchange rates (increases in nontraded versus traded goods prices) are needed to raise wages and output in the underdeveloped nontraded goods sector (including services).[5]

A further important feature of the transition process has been a reorientation of trade toward the West, associated with liberalization of trade restrictions and the exploitation of comparative advantage. Access to EU markets has been favored by Association Agreements of these

Table 16.2. CEECS: exchange-rate regimes

	Exchange-Rate Regime	*Basket/Target*	*Fluctuation Band*
Albania	Independent floating		
Bulgaria	Currency board	DM	0%
Croatia	Managed floating	De facto narrow target band vis-a-vis DM	
Czech Republic	Managed floating		
Estonia	Currency board	DM	0%
Hungary	Crawling peg[a]	Basket: DM (70%) US$ (30%)	±2.25%
Latvia	Fixed peg	SDR	±2%
Lithuania	Currency board	US$	0%
Macedonia, FYR	Managed floating	De facto peg to DM	
Poland	Crawling peg[b]	Basket: US$ (45%) DM (35%), Lstg. (10%) FF (5%), SWF (5%)	±7%
Romania	Independent floating		
Slovak Republic	Fixed peg	Basket: DM (60%), US$ (40%)	±7%
Slovenia	Managed floating	De facto shadowing of DM, combined with real exchange-rate rule	

Source: Temprano-Arroyo and Feldman (1998).
a. Midpoint of band is devalued monthly by 0.9 percent.
b. Midpoint of band is devalued monthly by 1 percent.

countries with the European Union, which have eliminated EU tariffs and import restrictions, except on agricultural products. As a result, by 1997 the EU was the destination of some 58 percent of exports of CEECs, though the percentages varied widely, constituting only 38 percent of Lithuania's[6] exports but 65 percent of Poland's (Table 16.4). "Other Europe," which serves as a reasonably good proxy for the countries of the former CMEA, was the destination for a declining percentage of exports of four of the five countries for which a comparison of 1997 with 1990 could be made—all except Bulgaria. However, the average proportion for all CEECs was higher in 1997 than in 1993, with Bulgaria showing substantial increases, and Croatia, Poland, and Slovenia showing more moderate ones.

Table 16.3. Central and Eastern Europe: nongold reserves, 1990–1997

	1990	1991	1992	1993	1994	1995	1996	1997
	(In millions of U.S. dollars)							
Albania	...	...	...	147	205	241	281	309
Bulgaria	...	311	902	655	1,002	1,236	484	2,249
Croatia	...	...	167	617	1,410	2,036	2,440	2,686
Czech Republic	...	...	...	3,789	6,145	13,843	12,352	9,734
Estonia	...	...	170	386	443	580	637	758
Hungary	1,070	3,936	4,428	6,771	6,810	12,052	9,795	8,476
Latvia	...	...	...	432	545	506	654	704
Lithuania	...	...	45	350	525	757	772	1,010
Macedonia, FYR	...	...	...	105	149	257	240	257
Poland	4,492	3,633	4,099	4,092	5,842	14,774	17,844	20,407
Romania	524	695	826	995	2,086	1,579	2,103	3,803
Slovak Republic	...	...	...	416	1,691	3,364	3,419	3,230
Slovenia	...	112	716	788	1,499	1,821	2,297	3,315
	(In months of imports)							
Albania	...	...	...	3.2	4.1	4.1	4.0	3.8
Bulgaria	...	1.5	2.4	1.6	2.9	2.6	1.2	5.5
Croatia	...	...	0.4	1.6	3.2	3.3	3.8	3.5
Czech Republic	...	...	...	3.4	4.7	6.3	5.0	4.2
Estonia	...	...	...	5.2	3.2	2.7	2.4	2.1
Hungary	1.5	4.1	4.8	6.5	5.7	9.6	7.4	5.2
Latvia	...	...	...	5.9	5.2	3.4	3.4	3.1
Lithuania	...	...	...	1.8	2.7	2.5	2.1	2.1
Macedonia, FYR	...	...	...	1.0	1.2	1.8	1.8	1.8
Poland	6.4	2.8	3.1	2.6	3.3	6.1	5.8	5.8
Romania	0.6	1.4	1.6	1.8	3.5	1.8	2.2	4.0
Slovak Republic	...	...	...	0.7	3.0	4.4	3.6	3.5
Slovenia	...	...	1.4	1.5	2.5	2.3	2.9	4.3

Source: IMF, *International Financial Statistics*, *World Economic Outlook* database, and staff estimates.

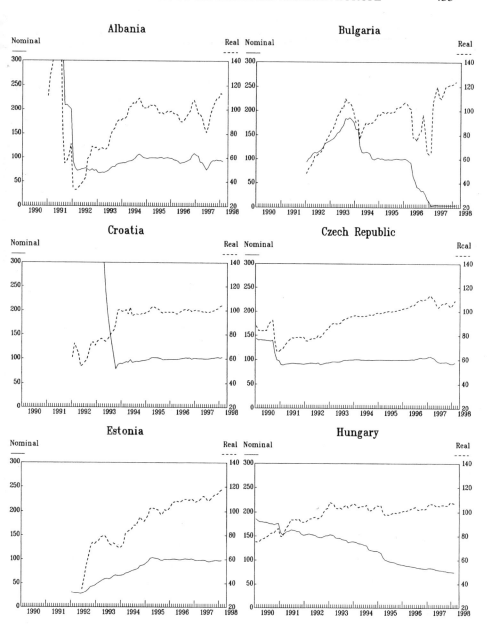

Figure 16.1. Central and Eastern Europe: nominal and real effective exchange rates (*indices, 1995* = 100)
Source: IMF, Information Notices System (INS) database.

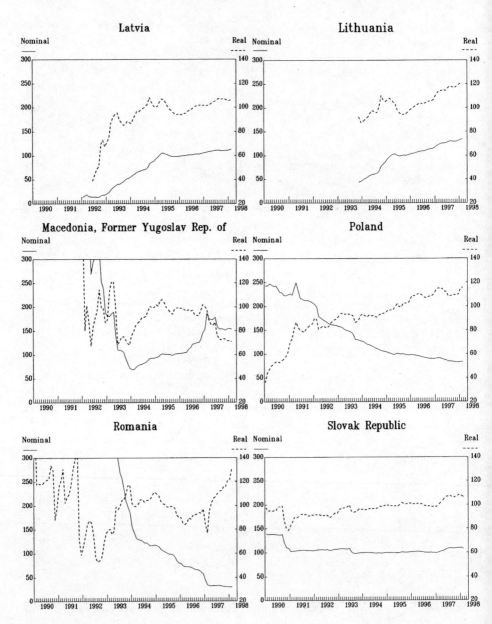

Figure 16.1. (*continued*)

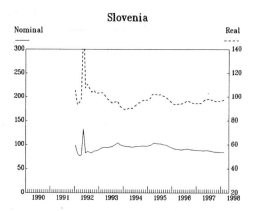

Figure 16.1. (*continued*)

Implications of EMU for Monetary and Exchange-rate Policies of CEECs

The creation of the euro as of January 1, 1999, when eleven of fifteen EU countries proceed to stage 3 of EMU, is a major event for Europe and the international monetary system.[7] The euro will overnight become the world's second-most-important currency, and it can be expected over time to rival the U.S. dollar in importance. For non-EU countries, the euro should be a more attractive currency peg than existing European currencies such as the German mark because it will underlie a much larger proportion of trade and capital flows and be based on a deep and liquid capital market. For those reasons also, the euro should eventually gain attractiveness as a reserve currency, though in proportions that are hard to gauge.[8]

For countries negotiating accession or contemplating doing so, the euro will have a more direct impact on their monetary policy options. As described in Temprano-Arroyo and Feldman (1998), EMU will have become part of the *acquis communautaire* that new members of the EU will be expected to adopt. Moreover, the EU has decided that no more opt-out clauses from EMU, such as those accorded to Denmark and the United Kingdom in the Maastricht Treaty, will be granted. Temprano-Arroyo and Feldman (1998) note that though transitional periods for joining EMU might be given to new entrants, they are unlikely. Many of the new entrants are not likely to satisfy the Maastricht convergence criteria immediately in any case, so that adoption of the euro will probably not occur until a number of years after EU membership.[9] Though general government fiscal balances are in several cases below 3 percent of GDP, these are not necessarily

Table 16.4. CEECs: trade with European Union and other European countries[a]
(*in percent of total exports and imports*)

	1990		1993		1997	
	Exports	*Imports*	*Exports*	*Imports*	*Exports*	*Imports*
Albania						
EU	47.9	46.3	70.6	87.3	87.5	83.8
Other Europe	30.8	26.4	2.3	2.8	10.3	14.1
Bulgaria						
EU	38.5	51.7	48.0	43.3	45.0	41.9
Other Europe	32.2	17.1	16.1	40.7	39.0	41.2
Croatia						
EU	...	...	56.2	54.7	51.3	59.4
Other Europe	...	...	34.8	29.4	39.0	23.1
Czech Republic						
EU	...	...	55.5	51.1	56.1	61.9
Other Europe	...	...	34.9	37.9	33.0	27.9
Estonia						
EU	...	...	48.3	60.4	56.9	65.9
Other Europe	...	...	45.5	28.7	32.2	22.9
Hungary						
EU	45.4	48.9	57.9	54.6	68.7	64.2
Other Europe	34.2	30.4	27.1	29.8	20.1	19.6
Latvia						
EU	...	...	32.1	27.0	42.9	53.2
Other Europe	...	...	56.7	67.9	43.8	38.4
Lithuania						
EU	...	...	20.5	23.5	33.5	46.5
Other Europe	...	...	57.4	67.2	46.4	29.3
Macedonia, FYR						
EU	...	...	34.5	33.5	41.7	42.2
Other Europe	...	...	50.2	55.2	38.4	46.0
Poland						
EU	54.8	51.4	69.3	64.8	65.1	68.9
Other Europe	25.1	28.0	13.0	13.6	22.5	15.5
Romania						
EU	33.4	21.5	41.4	45.3	56.7	52.5
Other Europe	39.9	39.1	21.9	23.6	18.5	24.0
Slovak Republic						
EU	...	...	29.6	27.9	42.9	43.8
Other Europe	...	...	61.4	63.2	50.3	49.1
Slovenia						
EU	...	...	63.2	65.6	63.6	67.4
Other Europe	...	...	26.5	20.1	28.4	17.6
Averages of above countries						
EU	...	...	55.5	53.0	58.1	60.3
Other Europe	...	...	29.1	30.6	29.9	25.9

Source: IMF, *Direction of Trade Statistics.*
a. Central and Eastern Europe, plus other countries of the former Soviet Union.

defined in a way consistent with Maastricht definitions. Quasi-fiscal deficits, if incorporated into the budget, could substantially inflate the figures. Inflation is well above 1.5 percentage points over the three best-performing EU countries, where inflation is currently under 2 percent (see Table 16.7 below). In addition, interest rates are considerably above those in the EU, though as recent experience of the former "high-yielding" EU countries has shown, good prospects of EMU membership bring about a virtuous circle of narrowing of spreads.

For current EU members, one of the conditions for qualification for EMU has been absence of a devaluation of their currencies for two years in the context of the exchange-rate mechanism (ERM) of the European Monetary System, which stipulates that currencies need to be kept within 15 percent of central parities (the normal margins of fluctuation having been widened from 2.25 percent in mid-1993, after a generalized exchange-rate crisis in the ERM). With the creation of the euro, the provisions of the ERM, which de jure if not de facto treat participating currencies symmetrically, will become inappropriate to a system where the euro (and the European Central Bank) have dominant roles. Hence, an asymmetric system where non-EMU central banks have the primary responsibility for maintaining the stability of their currencies relative to the euro was designed for EU countries which do not yet participate in EMU but are preparing to do so. Acceding CEECs would at some stage be expected to join the ERM2 (which will not be open to non-EU members).

In the meantime, there may also be pressures for limiting exchange fluctuations relative to the euro as countries negotiating accession want to prepare for membership in ERM2 and eventual EMU membership, and perhaps improve their chances of joining the EU by proving their willingness to take necessary measures. For instance, Bulgaria has announced that it intends to translate its currency board from a DM peg to the equivalent exchange rate against the euro, while Lithuania has expressed its intention to change gradually from a dollar to a euro exchange-rate peg in the context of moving away from its currency-board arrangement.

Is an Early Peg to the Euro Desirable for CEECs?

There are three basic alternatives facing CEECs in their choice of exchange-rate policies: (1) a currency board, (2) a band around an adjustable central parity (the ERM2), and (3) a more flexible exchange rate (such as a crawling band or managed float), perhaps augmented by another nominal anchor for monetary policy (an inflation targeting

440

CURRENCY BOARDS

framework is discussed below). Each has its advantages and disadvantages. A complicating factor is that these must be thought of as *transitional strategies*, since the ultimate objective for most of these countries is EU (and EMU) membership.

In considering the desirability of establishing a currency board, the crucial factors are the gains to credibility of tying the hands of the monetary authorities and the possible costs if the country concerned is likely to face different shocks from those hitting the currency area to which it is linked. This latter question, emphasized by the literature on "optimum currency areas,"[10] has been considered in great detail for Western Europe in the run up to EMU but much less so for CEECs. In large part, the scarcity of econometric work for CEECs reflects the lack of adequate data, both because long-time series do not exist and even the shorter ones are affected by structural changes associated with the transition process.

A simple measure of exposure to different real shocks would involve comparing the production structures of CEECs and the EU. Similarity would make it less likely that countries would experience very different terms of trade shocks or different world demand conditions for their exports. Table 16.5 gives a rough division into industry, agriculture, and "other," mainly services. Not surprisingly, many CEECs have a smaller proportion of their GDP in services, though this share is growing fast, and in 1995 over 60 percent of production was in the "other" category for Croatia, Estonia, Hungary, Latvia, Slovak Republic, and Slovenia. Agriculture constitutes a larger proportion of production than in the average EU country, but those countries negotiating accession have lower ratios than some of the EMU members like Greece. Thus the structure of production, at least for those five economies, does not identify obvious problems of potential asymmetric shocks, though one needs to be cautious in interpreting such aggregated data. Moreover, these structures can be expected to evolve further in the direction of those in Western Europe.[11]

Because currency boards constrain monetary policy in a transparent way, they are generally little subject to speculative pressures. In contrast, an adjustable peg may be especially vulnerable to them, as has been the case in a number of emerging-market countries. While this chapter is not the place to consider the causes of the crises that originated in Mexico in 1994 to 1995 and in Thailand in 1997, both countries had initially faced strong capital inflows that were suddenly and violently reversed. Moreover, neighboring countries seem to have been subject to contagion effects, which were only partly explainable by their own economic fundamentals.[12] The tremendous expansion of capital flows from industrial to developing and transition economies, though bringing benefits, also tends to make exchange-rate

Table 16.5.   Central and Eastern Europe and selected European Union countries: structure of production (*in percent of GDP*)

	Industry			Agriculture			Other		
	1990	*1993*	*1995*	*1990*	*1993*	*1995*	*1990*	*1993*	*1995*
Central and Eastern Europe									
Albania	46.4	23.0	21.3	37.0	54.6	55.8	16.6	22.4	22.9
Bulgaria	51.3	36.5	33.9	17.8	12.4	12.9	31.0	51.0	53.2
Croatia	30.3	25.9	20.1	9.5	11.1	9.8	60.3	63.0	70.1
Czech Republic	48.3	39.8	...	7.3	6.2	...	44.4	54.0	...
Estonia	41.0	27.9	24.8	15.6	9.9	7.1	43.4	62.2	68.1
Hungary	32.7	28.0	28.3	12.5	5.8	6.4	54.8	66.2	65.3
Latvia	44.5	31.8	27.1	21.1	10.7	8.1	34.4	57.5	64.8
Lithuania	43.3	43.3	30.8	27.8	14.0	9.5	28.9	42.7	59.7
Poland	50.1	40.0	39.4	8.3	6.6	6.5	41.6	53.4	54.1
Romania	45.9	37.5	39.3	21.8	21.0	20.4	32.3	41.5	40.3
Slovak Republic	59.1	40.4	33.2	7.4	6.1	5.6	33.5	53.5	61.1
Slovenia	...	35.1	34.4	...	4.3	4.3	...	60.6	61.3
	1990	*1993*	*1994*	*1990*	*1993*	*1994*	*1990*	*1993*	*1994*
European Union									
Austria	35.7	34.4	34.4	3.2	2.2	2.2	61.2	63.4	63.5
Belgium	30.1	27.7	28.0	1.9	1.6	1.6	68.0	70.7	70.4
Denmark	23.8	23.7	23.9	3.8	3.2	3.3	72.4	73.2	72.8
Finland	31.1	28.2	29.5	5.6	4.6	4.8	63.3	67.3	65.8
France	29.2	27.2	26.6	3.4	2.3	2.4	67.4	70.5	71.1
Greece	24.5	22.2	21.2	12.7	11.8	12.7	62.9	66.0	66.2
Netherlands	28.9	27.1	26.9	4.0	3.2	3.4	67.1	69.7	69.7
Sweden	29.6	26.7	27.5	2.6	1.9	2.0	67.9	71.4	70.5
United Kingdom	30.5	27.0	27.2	1.6	1.7	1.7	67.8	71.3	71.1

Source: World Bank, World Development Indicators (WDIEUR) database.

commitments more fragile. This has led to a trend away from adjustable pegs and toward greater flexibility in exchange-rate arrangements (see Eichengreen, Masson, and others, 1998).

Table 16.6 and Figure 16.2 summarize net capital flows to the CEECs, both in per capita terms (in dollars) and as a percent of GDP for the thirteen countries included. It can be seen that there has been a strong upward trend in these flows. After a slow start, since 1993 net inflows have exceeded 3 percent of GDP for the whole of the region. Thus, the possibility of a

Table 16.6. Current and capital account flows to CEECs, 1991–1997

	1991	1992	1993	1994	1995	1996	1997
U.S. dollar per capita							
Current account	−32.1	13.2	−45.3	−20.4	−32.2	−125.7	−124.1
Foreign direct investment	19.0	22.2	36.9	32.6	83.9	67.1	77.9
Short-term flows[a]	−28.6	−30.7	−4.2	13.1	110.9	44.9	38.2
Long-term flows	−77.5	−13.1	40.8	36.9	64.0	27.1	46.5
Change in net reserves[b]	−7.0	−25.7	−56.3	−56.3	−230.1	−12.3	−36.5
Other[c]	126.3	34.1	28.1	−5.9	3.4	−1.0	−2.0
As percent of GDP							
Current account	−0.7	0.7	−2.1	−0.9	−1.1	−4.0	−3.9
Foreign direct investment	0.4	1.2	1.7	1.4	2.9	2.2	2.4
Short-term flows	−0.7	−1.7	−0.2	0.6	3.8	1.4	1.2
Long-term flows	−1.8	−0.7	1.9	1.6	2.2	0.9	1.5
Net reserves	−0.2	−1.4	−2.7	−2.4	−7.8	−0.4	−1.1
Other	2.9	1.9	1.3	−0.2	0.1	0.0	−0.1

Source: Garibaldi, Mora, Sahay, and Zettelmeyer (1998).
a. Portfolio investment, trade-related credit, change in net foreign assets of commercial banks, other short-term capital, and errors and omissions.
b. Negative sign indicates an increase.
c. Exceptional financing such as change in arrears, rescheduling, and deferrals.

withdrawal, if not reversal, of those flows cannot be ignored. It is true that a substantial proportion of these flows is constituted by foreign direct investment, which tends to be more stable. However, increasing integration and eventual EU membership will lead to a dismantling of capital controls, making it easy for investors to take large positions against a currency if it is viewed as being vulnerable to attack.

The vulnerability of adjustable pegs suggests a clear preference for currency boards (or fixed pegs in general). However, the lack of flexibility of the latter may be a problem because of different trend behavior of CEECs and advanced economies. As discussed above, transition has tended to produce real appreciation of the exchange rates of CEECs. Such trend appreciation, it is argued, is justified by rapid productivity growth and hence is not a bad thing in itself: properly measured, competitiveness would not register a deterioration. This suggests both that monetary policy should not try to resist the appreciation and that if it does, it will in any case not be

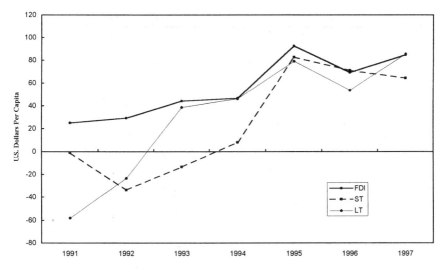

Figure 16.2.   Average foreign direct investment, short-term and long-term flows to CEE and Baltic countries, per capita
Source: Garibaldi, Mora, Sahay, and Zettelmeyer (1998).

successful. Nevertheless, the monetary-policy choice can be significant because it implies different things for domestic inflation and possibly also for the behavior of real interest rates and real exchange rates over the business cycle. Even if inflation is the result of equilibrium relative price movements, it will be important for policy not to ignore it because one of the qualifying criteria for EMU membership is convergence to EU inflation.

The possible inconsistency between exchange-rate stability and low inflation can be illustrated in the simplest of models, in which both non-traded and traded goods are produced, but the latter sector exhibits pro-ductivity growth but the former does not. Thus we adopt the standard Balassa-Samuelson model for real appreciation, contrary to Grafe and Wyplosz (1997). The implications of the latter model are in principle the same for inflation, though in practice the size of the real appreciation may be considerably larger if it is due to a generalized change in the structure of production, as occurred in the early stages of transition. As Székely (1997) points out, the latter story becomes increasingly less relevant, and, since we are considering the period leading up to the still distant EMU membership, we choose to treat CEECs as being similar to other (fast-growing) developing countries.

The price level p includes both nontraded and traded goods, with weights and $(1 - \alpha)$, respectively. Traded goods prices are assumed given in foreign-currency terms (normalized to unity, corresponding to zero foreign inflation), so that consumer prices can be written

$$p = (p^N)^\alpha e^{1-\alpha},$$

where e is the exchange rate (an increase indicates depreciation) and p^N is the price of nontraded goods. It is assumed that preferences are Cobb-Douglas, so that demands are fixed proportions of nominal income Y, which is equal to the sum of the income from producing the two goods:

$$Y = p^N Q^N + p^T Q^T.$$

So domestic demands for nontraded and traded goods are given by

$$p^N D^N = \alpha Y$$

$$p^T D^T = (1-\alpha)Y.$$

Supplies of traded goods are affected by growing productivity, while nontraded goods are not. Supplies are assumed to be linear in the labor resources allocated to each of the two sectors, which are constrained to sum to the total labor force ($L = L^N + L^T$):

$$Q^N = AL^N$$

$$Q^T = A exp(\beta t)L^T.$$

For simplicity, we assume that there is a single wage rate that is equalized across the two sectors. In these circumstances, macroeconomic equilibrium requires that the supply of nontradables equal the domestic demand for them:

$$Q^N = D^N,$$

and this implies that the rate of change of the real exchange rate—that is, the ratio of the prices of nontradables to tradables—be given by

$$\Delta \ln q = \Delta \ln(p^N / p^T) = \Delta \ln p^N - \Delta \ln e = \beta.$$

Moreover, the rate of CPI inflation will equal

$$\Delta \ln p = \alpha \ln p^N + (1-\alpha)\Delta \ln p^T = \alpha \Delta \ln p^N + (1-\alpha)\Delta \ln e$$
$$= \alpha \Delta \ln q + \Delta \ln e = \alpha\beta + \Delta \ln e.$$

So stability of the overall price level is possible only if the exchange rate appreciates (that is, negative $\Delta \ln e$) at rate $\alpha\beta$. On the contrary, exchange-rate stability $\ln e = 0$ will produce inflation at a higher rate than in foreign (that is, EU) countries at a rate $\alpha\beta$. A rough quantification would suggest that the share of nontraded goods times the rate of technical progress in the tradable goods sector could produce extra inflation of several percentage points a year. Though in this example, such inflation is the result of equilibrium relative price movements, it may be a cause for concern because one of the Maastricht convergence criteria requires that inflation be no more than 1.5 percentage points above that of the best-performing EU members. More generally, the inflation process may also involve inertia that leads to overshooting and loss of competitiveness if left to proceed unchecked.

All three factors—concerns about asymmetric shocks, vulnerability to speculation, and the possibility of trend real appreciation—need to be taken into account in considering the desirable extent of fixity against the euro. Strong capital flows and productivity increases may make nominal exchange-rate changes desirable at times, and this is difficult to achieve in the context of a currency board. The ERM crises of 1992 to 1993 underline the dangers of a premature move to an adjustable peg system with insufficient flexibility, so that it provides easy targets for speculation. The ERM2 mechanism, which will link the euro to noneuro EU currencies, is intended to be more flexible than the ERM of the early 1990s, since bands are considerably wider. However, it needs to be recognized that in March 1995 strong pressures within the wider bands also developed, leading to the devaluation of the peseta and escudo. In practice, well before exchange rates reach the 15 percent limit of fluctuations, strong expectations of a realignment develop, forcing changes in a crisis atmosphere.

An Alternative Monetary Policy: Inflation Targeting

It may therefore be useful to consider, at least in a transition period, adopting greater exchange-rate flexibility supplemented by other guides or anchors for monetary policy. One obvious alternative is inflation targeting, which has been adopted by half a dozen industrial countries since the late 1980s. Such a monetary policy framework has the advantage that it does not involve trying to defend against speculative attacks, and its transparency can provide a boost to the credibility of macro policy. Moreover, it targets an important convergence criterion, whose value needs to be close to EU levels for a country to qualify for EMU membership. Indeed, inflation targeting was at one time proposed as a better way to achieve convergence to monetary union than the ERM.[13] However, to generate benefits from a firm anchor for monetary policy in the context of a transparent and credible operating framework, inflation targeting (IT) needs to involve more than vague commitments to bring inflation down to EU levels.

As argued in Masson, Savastano, and Sharma (1997), an effective and credible IT framework needs to satisfy certain prerequisites. They include the freedom to carry out an independent monetary policy and a quantitative framework linking policy instruments to inflation. In particular, monetary policies in many developing countries have, at least until recently, been subject to fiscal dominance, in that budgetary deficits have dictated monetary growth. In the absence of developed domestic financial markets, treasuries are not able to finance deficit spending except by resort to the central bank. In these circumstances, central banks cannot effectively pursue any other objective, whether an exchange-rate peg, a target for the inflation rate, or one for a monetary aggregate. On the second point, inflation is not controllable in the short run by monetary policy, and therefore hitting a target requires forecasting the effects of policy instruments at a one or two year horizon. Indeed, some (e.g., Svensson, 1997) have characterized IT, as carried out by those advanced countries that practice it, as inflation *forecast* targeting. It is therefore essential to have a reliable and generally accepted way of making those forecasts, so as to justify raising interest rates when necessary to preempt potential inflationary pressures that may not be visible in actual inflation data.

We argued in Masson, Savastano, and Sharma (1997) that in fact most developing countries do not satisfy those prerequisites. In practice, seigniorage is significantly higher in the typical developing country than in industrial countries. Central banks are typically not independent of the fiscal authorities, and even countries announcing inflation targets (such as Israel) have other announced targets that sometimes get in the way of the inflation target. The industrial countries successfully practicing IT do not have other targets assigned to the central bank, though of course maintaining real activity is always an implicit, though deliberately downplayed, objective.

The question then arises whether CEECs satisfy the above prerequisites for successful targeting of inflation. Table 16.7 gives some illustrative data. It can be seen that estimated seigniorage,[14] like inflation, has declined dramatically, but for all but a few countries (Czech Republic, Macedonia, and Slovenia, where it was below 1 percent) the average for 1996 to 1997 is still significantly higher than for industrial countries. Budget deficits are now reasonably well contained for all but a few countries, suggesting that fiscal dominance is not necessarily a problem. As for measures of central-bank independence, the data compiled for instance by Cukierman (1992) already suggested that Hungary ranked with some of the successful inflation targeters, while recent changes to central-bank legislation have made some CEECs more legally independent than many advanced economies (Cukierman, Miller, and Neyapti, 1998), though one can question whether this also applies to de facto independence. Székely (1997) points out that independence of the central bank removes

Table 16.7. Central and Eastern Europe: seigniorage, inflation, and government balance, 1993–1997 (*in percent*)

	1993	1994	1995	1996	1997	Average 1996–1997
Seigniorage[a]						
Albania	...	...	5.3	2.7	8.7	5.7
Bulgaria	3.4	6.4	7.4	11.3	10.3	10.8
Croatia	4.9	2.9	2.1	2.0	1.4	1.7
Czech Republic	...	5.7	16.1	−3.9	5.3	0.7
Estonia	9.0	1.4	2.0	2.1	3.6	2.9
Hungary	3.7	3.4	6.2	2.1	2.8	2.5
Latvia	...	2.1	0.2	2.3	3.3	2.8
Lithuania	...	3.3	2.8	0.1	2.1	1.1
Macedonia, FYR	...	2.1	1.4	−0.2	1.2	0.5
Poland	0.7	1.7	3.1	1.6	1.8	1.7
Romania	5.8	3.6	3.0	2.8	4.5	3.7
Slovak Republic	...	2.1	5.4	1.1	2.0	1.6
Slovenia	1.0	1.6	0.9	0.6	0.9	0.8
Memo: Advanced economies	0.4	0.3	0.2	0.4	0.3	0.4
CPI Inflation (End period)[b]						
Albania	30.9	15.8	6.0	17.4	42.1	29.8
Bulgaria	63.9	121.9	32.9	310.8	578.5	444.7
Croatia	1120.5	2.4	4.6	3.7	5.0	4.4
Czech Republic	...	9.7	7.9	8.6	10.0	9.3
Estonia	37.9	41.6	26.5	14.8	12.5	13.7
Hungary	21.1	21.2	28.3	19.8	18.5	19.2
Latvia	34.9	26.3	23.1	13.2	7.0	10.1
Lithuania	188.6	45.1	35.7	13.1	8.4	10.8
Macedonia, FYR	256.0	58.1	10.0	0.8	5.4	3.1
Poland	37.7	29.4	21.9	18.7	13.2	16.0
Romania	295.5	61.8	27.7	56.9	151.4	104.2
Slovak Republic	...	11.7	7.2	5.4	6.5	6.0
Slovenia	22.9	18.3	8.6	8.8	9.4	9.1
Memo: Advanced economies	2.9	2.5	2.4	2.5	1.9	2.2
General Government Balance as a Ratio to GDP						
Albania	−9.1	−7.0	−6.7	−10.7	−11.7	−11.2
Bulgaria	−10.9	−5.8	−5.7	−11.0	−6.2	−8.6
Croatia	−0.8	1.5	−0.9	−0.5	−1.4	−1.0
Czech Republic	0.5	−1.2	−1.8	−1.2	−2.1	−1.7
Estonia	−0.7	1.3	−1.2	−1.5	2.4	0.5
Hungary	−8.5	−8.3	−7.1	−3.1	−4.6	−3.9
Latvia	0.6	−4.0	−3.3	−1.3	1.4	0.0
Lithuania	−5.4	−4.8	−4.5	−4.6	−1.9	−3.3
Macedonia, FYR	−13.6	−3.2	−1.3	−0.4	−0.3	−0.4
Poland	−4.0	−2.0	−2.7	−2.5	−1.7	−2.1
Romania	−0.4	−1.9	−2.6	−3.9	−4.5	−4.2
Slovak Republic	−7.0	−1.3	0.2	−1.3	−4.9	−3.1
Slovenia	0.3	−0.2	0.0	0.3	−1.2	−0.5
Memo: Advanced economies	−4.2	−3.4	−3.3	−2.5	−1.3	−1.9

Sources: IMF, International Financial Statistics, World Economic Outlook database and staff estimates.
a. The change in reserve money divided by GDP.
b. From December of previous year.

much of its incentive to use surprise inflation to improve the government's fiscal position.

More problematical are two other requirements of IT identified in Masson, Savastano, and Sharma (1997)—namely, a political consensus in favor of low inflation and the existence of a stable and predictable relationship linking monetary policy instruments to future inflation. On the first point, it may be felt in some countries that other objectives, especially structural transformations of the economy, should take priority over reducing inflation. To some extent, the crawling peg arrangements of Hungary and Poland reflect that fact. "Price stability" may also mean different things in transition economies; Škreb (1998) argues that the biases identified by the Boskin Report for the United States are undoubtedly larger in CEECs. A target of 5 percent inflation might therefore not be considered excessive. Even that target is not attained in many transition economies, he argues, because of lack of political support.

On the second point, structural changes are bound to affect the stability of relationships for forecasting inflation. Transition economies are likely to face large relative price movements, increasing inflation variability, and, in the presence of nominal rigidities, also increasing average inflation. Reliable inflation forecasting tools are essential if an IT framework is to deliver inflation close to its targeted value with a reasonable degree of confidence. If not, then instead of aiding to consolidate central-bank credibility (and that of macroeconomic policy generally), IT will have the opposite effect.

In sum, inflation targeting, though it has some desirable features for transition economies, also presupposes some features of those economies that are not yet present. In practice, it seems likely that some weight will be given to attaining low inflation without, however, making it the centerpiece of monetary policy. Over time, as inflation declines and experience with IT develops, it could be that IT would receive increasing weight, as has been the case in Israel. However, this possibility depends very much on what weight the EU wants to give, in considering EMU membership, to exchange-rate and price-level stability, which we have argued above may be incompatible in the case of CEECs.[15]

One can envision two sorts of transitions to EMU, one in which achieving low inflation is emphasized (and currencies are not too constrained in their fluctuations against the euro), and another in which a close currency link to the euro (such as a currency board) is sufficient to prove the fitness of a country to enter into monetary union (even if inflation is significantly higher than in the euro region). It will be important to choose between them in order not to set impossible tasks for acceding CEECs. Not to do so may inadvertently lengthen the transitional period, forcing CEECs to have settled down to the same productivity growth as industrial countries before they can formally enter the euro zone.

Conclusions

We have attempted to present a broad overview of the monetary and exchange-rate policy choices facing the transition economies of central and eastern Europe at a crucial juncture—the launch by the European Union of the euro and preparations for EU accession by several of them. At present, the CEECs are pursuing a number of different monetary-policy and exchange-rate strategies, but in the future they may face tacit pressures to orient those policies toward a fixed relationship with the euro. This chapter, while not disputing that membership in the EU and EMU no doubt holds out long-run benefits, has raised two considerations—the likelihood of continuing equilibrium real appreciation and the vulnerability to reversals in capital flows—that suggest caution in attempting to peg to or shadow the euro in the short run. An alternative, inflation targeting, has some advantages over pegged rates but is also unlikely to provide in the short run the single answer to optimal monetary policy choice, given that prerequisites for successfully implementing such a framework are not yet present. In practice, a hybrid system with some weight given to both inflation and the exchange rate may emerge. Furthermore, it will be important for the EU to specify clearly that it is not necessary for CEECs to achieve *both* exchange-rate and price-level stability, and which objective should be given priority, as a fixed peg to the euro will imply higher inflation than in the EU if the currencies of the CEECs continue to appreciate in real terms.

A hybrid system would not necessarily be inconsistent with the ERM2, when the latter is put in place. In principle, the ERM2 in its current nebulous form will admit of a variety of possible exchange-rate arrangements. It will be important, however, not to limit excessively the degree of flexibility, as occurred in the (narrow-band) ERM of the early 1990s. Even with the wider (15 percent) bands of the present ERM, structural differences between CEECs (should they join such an exchange-rate mechanism) and western Europe may make adjustable pegs especially vulnerable to speculative attack.

Notes

1. In this chapter, CEECs are taken to include Albania, Bulgaria, Croatia, Czech Republic, Estonia, Hungary, Latvia, Lithuania, FYR Macedonia, Poland, Romania, Slovak Republic, and Slovenia.

2. To my knowledge, there has been no clear statement of EU policy on this issue, and views differ both on its desirability and on whether acceding CEECs would be expected to participate early in the ERM2.

3. The experience of disinflation has been discussed in a number of articles, some them collected in Cottarelli and Szapáry (1998).

4. See Borensztein and Masson (1993) for a discussion of the early experience.

5. Other papers discussing the reasons for a trend appreciation of the real exchange rate include Halpern and Wyplosz (1997) and Krajnyák and Zettelmeyer (1997).

6. Lithuania's limited trade reorientation toward the EU may have been a result in part of the creation of a Baltic Free Trade Area in 1994, as well as due to the composition of its exports. Lithuania continues to export a substantial amount of refined petroleum products and agricultural goods to its neighbors (including Russia) (see Sorsa, 1997).

7. For a discussion of some of the international implications of EMU, see Masson, Krueger, and Turtelboom (1997).

8. An attempt is made in Masson and Turtelboom (1997) to evaluate the risk-return characteristics of the euro and implications for demands for reserves.

9. Temprano-Arroyo and Feldman (1998) assess how close CEECs were to satisfying the criteria in 1996 to 1997.

10. This work has built on the seminal article by Mundell (1961). See Masson and Taylor (1993) for a survey of the extensive literature on this topic.

11. Fischer, Sahay, and Végh (1998) estimate that the average per capita income of CEECs will take a generation to converge to that of the low-income EU countries (Greece, Portugal, and Spain). However, per capita income does not seem directly relevant to the choice of exchange-rate regime.

12. For a discussion of contagion, see Masson (1998).

13. Costs and benefits of the two approaches for EU countries are discussed by Canzoneri, Nolan, and Yates (1996).

14. This measure is an imperfect one, in particular for countries that remunerate bank reserves. However, this measurement problem does not seriously distort the comparison of CEECs with advanced economies presented in Table 16.7.

15. We have ignored the possible use of fiscal policy to make the two compatible, since typically it is aimed at other objectives and its effects on prices and exchange rates are not easily fine-tuned.

References

Borensztein, E., and P.R. Masson. (1993). "Part II. Exchange Arrangements of Previously Centrally Planned Economies." *Financial Sector Reforms and Exchange Arrangements in Eastern Europe.* Occasional Paper No. 102. Washington, DC: International Monetary Fund, February.

Canzoneri, M.B., C. Nolan, and A. Yates. (1996). "Mechanisms for Achieving

Monetary Stability: Inflation Targeting Versus the ERM." CEPR Discussion Paper Series No. 1418, London, June.

Cottarelli, C., and G. Szapáry (eds.). (1998). *Moderate Inflation: The Experience of Transition Economies.* Washington, DC: International Monetary Fund and National Bank of Hungary.

Cukierman, A. (1992). *Central Bank Strategy, Credibility, and Independence: Theory and Evidence.* Cambridge, MA: MIT Press.

Cukierman, A., G.P. Miller, and B. Neyapti. (1998). "Central Bank Reform, Liberalization and Inflation in Transition Economies: An International Perspective." Paper presented at the conference.

Eichengreen, B., P. Masson, and others. (1998). *Exit Strategies: Policy Options for Countries Seeking Greater Exchange-Rate Flexibility.* Occasional Paper No. 168. Washington, DC: International Monetary Fund.

Fischer, S., R. Sahay, and C.A. Végh. (1998). "How Far Is Eastern Europe from Brussels?" IMF Working Paper 98-53. Washington DC: International Monetary Fund, March.

Garibaldi, P., N. Mora, R. Sahay, and J. Zettelmeyer. (1998). "What Moves Capital to Transition Economies?" IMF Working Paper. Washington, DC: International Monetary Fund.

Grafe, C., and C. Wyplosz. (1997). "The Real Exchange Rate in Transition Economies." Paper presented at the Third Dubrovnik Conference on Transition Economies, Dubrovnik, Croatia, June 25–28.

Halpern, L., and C. Wyplosz. (1997). "Equilibrium Exchange Rates in Transition Economies." *Staff Papers* (international Monetary Fund) 44(4) (December).

International Monetary Fund. (1998). *World Economic Outlook* (Spring).

Krajnyák, K., and J. Zettelmeyer. (1997). "Competitiveness in Transition Economies: What Scope for Real Appreciation?" IMF Working Paper 97-149. Washington, DC: International Monetary Fund, November.

Masson, P.R., T.H. Krueger, and B.G. Turtelboom (eds.). (1997). *EMU and the International Monetary System.* Washington, DC: International Monetary Fund.

Masson, P.R., and B.G. Turtelboom. (1997). "Characteristics of the Euro, the Demand for Reserves, and Policy Coordination Under EMU." In Paul R. Masson, Thomas H. Krueger, and Bart G. Turtelboom (eds.), *EMU and the International Monetary System.* Washington, DC: International Monetary Fund.

Masson, P.R., and M.P. Taylor. (1993). "Currency Unions: A Survey of the Literature." In Paul R. Masson and Mark P. Taylor (eds.), *Policy Issues in the Operation of Currency Unions.* Cambridge: Cambridge University Press.

Masson, P. (1998). "Contagion: Monsoonal Effects, Spillovers, and Jumps Between Multiple Equilibria." Mimeo. Washington, DC: International Monetary Fund.

Masson, P.R., M.A. Savastano, and S. Sharma. (1997). "The Scope for Inflation Targeting in Developing Countries." IMF Working Paper 97-130. Washington, DC: International Monetary Fund, October.

Mundell, R.A (1961). "A Theory of Optimum Currency Areas." *American Economic Review* 51 (September): 657–665.

Škreb, M. (1998). "A Note on Inflation." In Cottarelli and Szapáry (1998, pp. 179–184).

Sorsa, P. (1997). "Regional Integration and Baltic Trade and Investment Performance." IMF Working Paper 97-167. Washington, DC: International Monetary Fund, December.

Svensson, L. (1997). "Inflation Forecast Targeting: Implementing and Monitoring Inflation Targets." *European Economic Review* 41:1111–46.

Székely, I. (1997). "The Relationship Between Monetary Policy and Exchange-Rate Policy in Associated Countries: Is There Room for Independent Monetary Policy on the Way to EU Membership?" Paper presented at the CEPR conference on lessons from the Czech Exchange-Rate Crisis, Prague. November 10–11.

Temprano-Arroyo. H., and R. Feldman. (1998). "Selected Transition and Mediterranean Countries: An Institutional Primer on EMU and EU Relations." IMF Working Paper 98-82. Washington, DC: International Monetary Fund, June.

Index